Praise for
The Intent to Live

"*The Intent to Live* does what any great acting book must do. It refuses to choose between craft and spontaneity. It introduces and thoroughly explores the *craft* of acting the nuts and bolts, the roll-up-your-sleeves, practical, tactical, doable how-tos—while never losing sight of the fact that great actors learn those things to create—emotion, intimacy, chaos, mayhem, revolution, in themselves and in the audience. Buy this book!"—**Helen Hunt, actor**

"Working with Larry is thrilling, challenging, inspiring, occasionally frustrating, endlessly interesting, and always exhilarating. When it comes to acting he approaches his work with the enthusiasm of a child and the wisdom of a sage. I'm delighted that so many people can share the same experience I had in this wonderful new book."—**Tobey Maguire, actor**

"I felt compelled to open up the door of my private life in the first few moments of meeting Larry. Perhaps it was the feeling that he was another soldier who had been through more suffering than me, or perhaps it was that look in his eye that said, 'Nothing but the truth will do.' Larry is joyful. Larry is sad. Larry is angry, but Larry is Larry. He's not something made up. He can spot a counterfeit right away. In any case, within the first couple of sessions my habitual obstacles were exposed, my barriers broken, and my raw emotional tools had been salvaged. He was brilliant and it was only the beginning."—**Jim Carrey, actor**

"This book belongs in every actor's hands. But even if you're not an actor but just love actors and are fascinated by how they do their jobs, this book is a gem."
—*Hollywood Behind-the-Scenes*

"Larry's unwavering commitment to his craft, his encyclopedic knowledge of the arts, and his sincere enthusiasm for the art of acting itself make his process exciting, inspiring, and truly transformational as an actor. I would recommend his technique and process not only to first timers, but also seasoned veterans of the craft."—**Leonardo DiCaprio, actor**

"I studied with Larry Moss for fourteen years. I have been his friend even longer. I thought I knew everything he had to offer. I was wrong. I have dog-eared and highlighted page after page and line after line of his brilliant book. *The Intent to Live* is a textbook, an exercise book, and a holy bible. Epiphanies are on every page."—**Jason Alexander, actor**

"It has been my great luck to direct several actors who had just finished working out with Larry Moss. I can pay him therefore the highest Hollywood compliment. He can Botox your talent. He can make your face shine and your spirit vibrate with youth. He somehow manages to combine passion and certitude with the humility which comes from, yes, total respect for the work at hand." —**James L. Brooks, director**

"Moss has become the Hollywood go-to guy when there's a performance mountain to conquer." —*Los Angeles Daily News*

"Larry continues to inspire me to search fearlessly for the truth in the character I am playing and in myself as a human being. I am in awe of this profoundly gifted, articulate teacher. He is a godsend, as is evident in his book, *The Intent to Live*." —**Hilary Swank, actor**

"A revelation. A superlative treatise on the art of acting from one whose knowledge of the subject is matched only by his love for it. A master class in acting from the master himself." —**Swoosie Kurtz, actor**

"*The Intent to Live* is insightful, funny, and very informative. It's an important book for actors and anyone who is interested not only in the craft of acting but also in that elusive and magical contact with their creative self. Larry Moss is not only a great teacher but a wonderful writer with an immensely generous spirit." —**Sally Field, actor**

"I am eternally grateful to Larry. He helped me to clearly see what a gift it is to get to be a performer; and he opened my eyes and showed me that less is not always more!" —**Christian Slater, actor**

"Larry Moss has been an invaluable acting coach and source of inspiration to me. He is a *touchstone* of integrity and honor in the profession of acting. The combination of influences in his own training and experiences has resulted in his becoming an incomparable teacher, who knows how to teach a student not only the techniques but the practical applications in their work and in their life. By the end of the first chapter of this book, I wanted to give it to *every* actor I know. It is essential reading because it is about how to be truly alive in your work and in the life you *choose* to live. It is quite simply the best book about the craft of acting that I have *ever* read." —**Donna Murphy, actor**

"Unlike most 'teaching' books, this one succeeds in giving readers the feeling that we are in class with its author. . . . Actors of all levels can benefit from his accessible and challenging book." —*Back Stage West*

"Larry Moss picks up the mantle from Stella Adler, Sandy Meisner, and a handful of others, breathing life and love into the craft of acting for a whole new generation of artists. In these pages you see the wonder, the scope, the struggle (yes, the method), and the majesty that acting can be. It's a tremendous piece of work and we're all lucky that he's written it." —**Gary Ross, writer and director**

"Moss has profound insights as to the tickings of drama and players, and an intimacy to his writing that puts you in his room. This very original, very useful book will surely become one of the primary handbooks of the art form." —**Twyla Tharp, choreographer and director**

"Larry Moss manages to capture the inspirational, challenging, wise, and unsettling voice of his teaching style on the printed page. No small feat. He is a magician of sorts, with the ability to see the unique instrument in every actor. He makes alchemy commonplace. He leads with respect and ferocity. He wants you to love acting and actors as much as he does. Like all great teachers, he engenders awe and fierce loyalty. And the book is a lot cheaper than a private audience." —**David Duchovny, actor**

"Larry Moss's illuminating book opens up all the questions that need to be addressed when we tackle the art and craft of acting—the possibilities, the mysteries, and the dreams. Larry speaks from his heart as a teacher and from his vast experience directing. His book is an essential key to opening up the secrets of performing in both theater and movies." —**Patricia Bosworth, writer**

"Larry Moss was my secret weapon on *The Green Mile*, for it was his uncanny abilities as a teacher that unlocked the door to Michael Clarke Duncan's deep well of talent and allowed that talent to shine. Under Larry's guidance, Michael blossomed as an actor before my eyes in ways that still surprise and inspire me, resulting in an indelible performance that earned Michael a Best Supporting Actor nomination that year. If you want to act, anything Larry Moss has to say on the subject are things you need to hear, making this book not only indispensable but a rare privilege." —**Frank Darabont, director**

"Larry taught me and I was nominated for an Academy Award for my role of John Coffey in *The Green Mile*. I had it in me but Larry was the key that unlocked it." —**Michael Clarke Duncan, actor**

"Larry Moss is perhaps the greatest acting coach of our times. Having had the privilege of being coached by him, I can tell you that this book is a *must* for any actor passionate about taking his craft to the next level." —**Brad Garrett, actor**

ABOUT THE AUTHOR

LARRY MOSS studied his craft with such luminaries as Stella Adler, Sanford Meisner, and Warren Robertson. Her began his career at New York's famed cabaret Upstairs at the Downstairs and went on to appear on Broadway in numerous productions. After teaching at Juilliard and Circle in the Square, Moss returned to Los Angeles and founded the Larry Moss Studio in 1990. His directing credits include the off-Broadway hit *The Syringa Tree*, which won the 2001 Obie for Best Play of the Year, and the 2005 New York premiere of the award-winning play *Beast on the Moon*.

The Intent to Live

ACHIEVING YOUR TRUE POTENTIAL

AS AN ACTOR

LARRY MOSS

Bantam Books

New York   Toronto   London   Sydney   Auckland

THE INTENT TO LIVE

ACHIEVING YOUR TRUE POTENTIAL AS AN ACTOR

A Bantam Book

PUBLISHING HISTORY

Bantam hardcover edition published January 2005

Bantam trade paperback edition / January 2006

Published by
Bantam Dell
A Division of Random House, Inc.
New York, New York

Excerpt from Act One, Scene 2 from "Lobby Hero" by Kenneth Lonergan.
Copyright © 2002 by Kenneth Lonergan. Reprinted by permission of the author.
Cover photograph by Raul Vega

Book design by Patrice Sheridan

Library of Congress Catalog Card Number: 2004057358

Bantam Books and the rooster colophon are registered trademarks of Random House, Inc.

ISBN 978-0-553-38120-7

Printed in the United States of America
Published simultaneously in Canada

randomhousebooks.com

BVG 20 19

DEDICATION

I would like to dedicate this book to the great teachers I studied with: Stella Adler, who taught me the absolute necessity for script analysis; Sanford Meisner, who forced me to understand what it was to be in the moment; Warren Robertson, who opened emotional doors and gave me my first chance to teach; Charles Nelson Reilly, who taught me the pure joy of facing an audience with no apology; David Craig, who heightened singing in the theater to a true art form; Tim Phillips, who opened my eyes to being more specific than I thought I could be; Sam Schacht, who brought me to the center of sensory work; Kenneth MacMillan, who taught me what intelligent support from a teacher can do to give an actor confidence; Jim Tuttle, who ignited my passion for acting when I was young and inexperienced; Patsy Rodenburg, who made Shakespeare leap off the page by teaching me how urgent his ideas become when performed with clarity and the right kind of focused physical energy; and my present voice teacher, Bruce Eckstut, who taught me the right technique and allowed me to sing freely and fully for the first time.

CONTENTS

INTRODUCTION:
DISCOVERING THE DREAM

The summer I was eleven years old, I rode my bike every Saturday in the blazing heat to the El Portal Theatre in North Hollywood for the first matinee. I couldn't wait to get inside the theater, where I knew I would be cool and buy my popcorn and sit, as I always did, on the aisle halfway down. I was always alone. I don't mean that as sad; I liked it; it was an adventure. I never knew what I was going to see and it didn't matter. I was in my world: the movies.

One Saturday, after the newsreel and coming attractions, an explosion hit the screen—Elia Kazan's *East of Eden,* the story of a lonely outcast who desperately needed his father's love, whose brother was the special one, whose mother had vanished. As the film continued, I saw this kid's life, searching, desperate, heartbroken, mean, haunted, confused. I wasn't in a movie, I was in my life. *I was this kid*. He cried, raged, was romantic, weak, uncertain, vengeful, and ultimately, brave. When the movie ended I was shaking all over. It was freezing from the air conditioning, but that wasn't the reason I was shaking.

As I walked out of the theater in shock, I was hit with hundred-degree heat, and I almost passed out. I had just seen my life on the screen, but it wasn't my life, it was John Steinbeck's, and Elia Kazan's, and James Dean's, and Julie Harris's, and Jo Van Fleet's—great artists. I cried for days. I woke up in the middle of the night, every night. My heart was so full, I was so alive with ideas, and with hope. After that blistering day in North Hollywood, my life was never the same. I was connected to a dream—the dream of becoming an actor.

When I was fifteen the explosion happened again, only this time it was in live theater. I read a review in the paper that said there was a searing performance by a brilliant New York actress that should not be missed. The reviewer seemed to be so excited by what he had seen that I felt propelled to get on a bus and take the long trek downtown to see *The Far Country,* starring Kim Stanley. The play is about the father of psychoanalysis, Sigmund Freud, and his discovery of the cause of hysterical paralysis. At the end of the second act, Freud tells a young woman that the reason she can't walk is that the night her father died, she did not go upstairs to give him the medication he needed because she was tired, and that somewhere within her she wanted him to die so that she could be free. Sitting in the front row of the theater, I watched Kim Stanley's cheeks turn bright red; then suddenly tears shot out of her eyes so fast and in such torrents that I clutched the edge of my chair. At that moment, the curtain started coming down as Ms. Stanley screamed with everything in her, "No, it's a lie!" And when the curtain hit the stage floor, she continued screaming in the darkness.

Thirty seconds later they brought the house lights up, and the theater went mad. People started talking to each other, grabbing at each other, for they had just witnessed a great actress give a performance that didn't seem to be a performance at all but a trauma in a real person's life that we shouldn't be allowed to watch. And yet we were. Once again, I walked out of the theater in a complete daze. I was deeply moved by the character's journey and by Ms. Stanley's amazing performance, and I was overwhelmed with curiosity as to how a human being at a given moment could demand such intense emotions as Ms. Stanley did night after night.

The need to know how she did it kept haunting me and made me see every live theater production that Los Angeles had to offer during those years. And there were many, because, luckily, at that time the great theater actors, after making enormous hits on Broadway, traveled the country with their plays for at least a year. My experiences of watching great actors continued to excite me but they also confounded me, because it seemed incomprehensible to me that these actors could bring such powerful feeling, beautiful voices, fascinating physical behavior, and spontaneity to their performances on demand.

When I was nineteen years old, embarking on my life as an acting student, I went to an art museum in Washington, D.C. It was the first time I'd gone to a museum on my own to observe paintings, and as I looked at the collection of Impressionists, I suddenly stopped in front of a Van Gogh, the first I'd ever seen in person, and became transfixed. The painting was of a farmhouse with a rickety fence surrounding it. What amazed me, and seemed to awaken me, was that every slat of the fence was a slightly different shade of brown, from the lightest beige close to white to light brown to medium brown and on to the darkest brown close to black. I could not walk away. The fence seemed to be alive with energy and with what I realized later were the artist's *choices:* Van Gogh's impression of light and shadow, Van Gogh's interpretation in color, texture, and form. Van Gogh's "simple" fence spoke to me of transition and subtlety and boldness. I knew intuitively that what I was seeing was deeply connected to acting, but it took me years to understand exactly how.

At that point in my life, music, dance, film, theater, and literature had become my salvation, my life's blood, my reason to live. I was all feeling, all desire, but with no concrete way to express all this drama within me. I had just begun to study voice, dance, acting, script analysis, and my own inner world. I became obsessed with learning; if there was a way to answer the questions I had about acting, I had to know it. After much tumult in my life, many mistakes, and much avoidance of responsibility, I finally learned that there were answers to my burning questions about acting as well as about life.

I want this book to help you in your journey as an actor. In it I have distilled the important techniques and tools that I learned and have taught in my thirty-two years as an acting teacher and coach, and that I've seen work for many of my students who have gone on to have significant careers. Whether you are a beginner or a more advanced actor, I want to give you specific meat-and-potatoes ideas that you can bring to your work today—right now—as if you were sitting in my class and I was working with you directly. Some of the ideas are simple and some are more complicated. Read the book slowly and demand of yourself that you do all the tasks and the homework that I give you. Read the plays and watch the videos of the films I use as examples. Do the exercises—and do them as fully as you can. I promise you, it will pay off.

One of the most important things I've learned about acting is that you can't separate how you live your life and how you practice your art. For that reason, I'm also going to share with you what my life experience has taught me about aiming high and believing in yourself and not allowing anything or anyone—not even yourself—to stand in the way of your dream, which in Chapter Two you'll find is your superobjective.

I call this book *The Intent to Live* rather than *The Intent to Act* because great actors like James Dean and Kim Stanley don't seem to be acting, they seem to be actually living. You know you're in the presence of the best actors when you forget that you're sitting in an audience watching make-believe and instead you are catapulted onto the screen or stage and blasted into the lives of the characters. I want to pass along to you what I've learned about *living* in a role. A huge part of this has to do with interpretation, which, I now understand, is what Van Gogh's fence was speaking to me about. A picket fence isn't just a picket fence—not to an artist. Because an artist says "I'm going to use these specific colors to bring this fence to life as *I* see it, fully, with emotion and character." That's what we do as actors as *we bring a script to life*.

I want to tell you another, more personal reason for the title of this book. When I was a young actor, I had many negative feelings about myself and about my life. I made a decision not to destroy myself but to understand and heal the pain that at times seemed so overwhelming. In other words, I made a decision to live. And one of the things that helped me was learning the craft of acting.

I was not at first encouraged to be an actor. The first musical theater teacher I had informed me in front of the entire class that I had "the worst singing voice" he had ever heard. Needless to say, that felt horrible and humiliating. And, as you will read later, my first acting teacher, Sanford Meisner, told me that I had no ability to act or react with any truth whatsoever. But my desire was greater than my humiliation, and I kept studying and exercised my voice two to four hours every day. By the time I was twenty years old a raw talent that had been lurking beneath the surface, unable to reveal itself because of fear and lack of technique, emerged. I actually began having a career as an actor and I achieved a dream—working on Broadway. I was still in many ways unformed, but I had acquired enough technique to be considered a professional actor for hire while I continued to learn.

Sometimes we feel we have a gift to give that no one can see because we don't have the tools or the confidence to reveal it. Sometimes we have a raw talent that comes out every now and then, maybe even brilliantly, but because we lack technique we don't know *how* to consistently give the gift to its greatest effect. That is simply a lack of education about how to do the job technically—whether we feel like it or not, whether we are terrified, intimidated, or emotionally blocked. I have experienced all of this so I understand the journey, a journey I am still taking. I hope that this book will inspire you to apply and dedicate yourself to learning the craft of acting and to have faith that if you persevere and you love the craft, you can become the kind of actor who lives on stage and screen.

When you do this, you can affect people in ways you may not ever imagine or know about. One night at a midnight screening of Steven Spielberg's film *ET,* I watched a very angry, lonely teenager sit down in front of me, sink way down into his seat, and look at the screen with complete contempt. His vibrations were so powerfully violent that I wanted to move, but by that time the theater was full. At the start of the film, the teenager shifted noisily in his seat, but soon he stopped moving completely. I saw him go from disdain to amusement to surprise to awe and, finally, to unashamed weeping. Just as the movie was ending, he ran out of the theater, embarrassed to be so moved. He didn't want anybody to see how vulnerable he really was. As vulnerable as I was at eleven when I watched James Dean. That's what our work can do: we remind people that things can change, that wounds can heal, that people can be forgiven, and that closed hearts can open again.

1

GIVEN CIRCUMSTANCES:
BUILDING FROM THE GROUND UP

Eighteen years ago I was invited to a dinner that was given expressly to introduce me to the legendary acting teacher Stella Adler. It was a small, elegant gathering of eight at which everyone was dressed up, no one more than Stella, who appeared in a floor-length red gown with jewels adorning the famous Stella Adler cleavage. I'd already studied script analysis with Ms. Adler for three years. But since her lecture classes included seventy-five or more people and Ms. Adler did all the talking, I knew she probably wouldn't remember me.

Except for size, the dinner party was not dissimilar to the lecture course, and I once again said nothing. As Stella discoursed on George Bernard Shaw and Henrik Ibsen, everyone at the party, many of whom were as famous as she, hung on her every word. I was seated at Ms. Adler's right. When we finished our entrée, she suddenly turned to me and asked imperiously, "What do you do, young man?" "Well," I said, "I'm an acting teacher, Stella." Her eyes blazed for a moment and then she said, challengingly, "And what do you teach?" And I said, almost shyly, "I was in your script analysis class for three years and I'm hoping to carry on some of the traditions and techniques that I learned from you." Stella impulsively and startlingly grabbed my hand, stared me straight in the eye, and passionately blurted out, "Don't let it die! I beg of you, please pass these ideas on." Then she put her head down and began to weep. At which point everyone else at the table, including me, also began to weep. So there we were, eight theater people with our heads in what remained of our chicken dinners, gurgling and gasping at how much our love for the art of acting meant to each of us and what we wanted it to mean for the next generation. This book is part of my keeping this promise to her.

I'm going to teach you acting from the beginning, and the beginning is script analysis.

In a way, the technique of script analysis is comparable to the process a detective uses to solve a mystery. Just as the detective learns to examine and understand the lives of the people involved in his case (their backgrounds, their relationships, their behaviors, their motives), you will use the technique I'm teaching you to examine and understand the lives of your character and the other characters in a script and see them as real people with real lives, and in so doing you will begin to discover the overall dynamic of that play or film. You'll be able to define precisely what drives your character, the other characters, and the story.

If this sounds like an intellectual exercise, I want to assure you that *nothing* in this book is simply an intellectual exercise. Everything I'm teaching you about acting has one aim only: to fire you up emotionally and behaviorally so that you can give a vivid, involving, and memorable performance. So when I talk to you about using your mind, ultimately it's to use your mind to *carbonate* your emotions and imagination. You know how soda is carbonated? It's not just flat in the glass; it's filled with bubbles rising, bumping into each other, bursting, alive. That's the point of everything I'm teaching you—to make you not act but live.

Given circumstances is the term used in acting for everything the writer tells you in the script about your character and the situation they find themselves in. Given circumstances are the *facts;* they are the information that is not subject to debate. In other words, given circumstances are irrefutable. They are the ground on which you build your creative choices, the *only* place you can begin. Later, we'll talk about your interpretation of a role, but the facts are the facts and you cannot afford to overlook them.

I know this sounds obvious, but I've seen actors forget that the character they are playing has been written to have a cold, or is entering from a snowstorm, or has just found out that his mother has a fatal disease—the kind of given circumstance that should color how you play a scene from the moment of your entrance.

To the extent that a character's actions toward and reactions to other characters are specified in the script, they are also part of the given circumstances. *Anything the script tells you about who your character is or about what the character has done before the story starts is part of the character's given circumstances.*

That's why it's so important to read the text. And read it again, until nothing in the script is vague to you. I've heard some actors say, "Well, I didn't even read the whole screenplay, I just read the scenes I'm in." I think that's irresponsible and arrogant, because the given circumstances are so integral to the work that you can't give a full performance without including them.

I'm going to give you several examples of given circumstances to make the idea clear to you and I'm going to begin with the given circumstances of one of history's greatest plays, *Hamlet*. At the beginning of the play, Shakespeare tells you that Hamlet's father is dead and that Hamlet has come home to Denmark to mourn and to be with his mother, Gertrude, who has quickly, and shockingly, married his dead father's brother, Claudius. In the last scene of Act I, Hamlet is told by his father's ghost that Claudius has murdered him and the ghost asks Hamlet to avenge his death. Through the ghost, Hamlet learns that his mother is complicit with his evil uncle, but whether she knew about the murder or simply lusted indecently for Claudius seems open to interpretation, and this ambiguity creates more torment for Hamlet. The ghost also tells Hamlet that while Hamlet must take revenge on Claudius, he should leave Gertrude to heaven and her own inner turmoil. If you're playing Hamlet, the fact of your father's death, why you have returned, and the ghost's visit, as well as the information the ghost imparts, are not subject to debate. Hamlet's father is not just *possibly* dead, nor did Hamlet return to Denmark because he wants to marry his girlfriend, Ophelia, or celebrate the hasty wedding of his mother and uncle. His father's death, Hamlet's grief, the ghost's appearance and demand for revenge against Claudius, and Gertrude's unseemly lack of mourning are the absolutes; they are the given circumstances.

Taken all together, the given circumstances—the facts that the writer gives you—are the *foundation* of the performance; what you add to that foundation is your specific *interpretation*. Will you choose to make Hamlet

an angry, aggressive character, a muted, tormented, self-hating character—or both? The text Shakespeare gives you allows for these and other
interpretations. That is the actor's job: *to interpret*. But you cannot change
the basic facts of the script, and if you ignore these facts your performance will begin to fall apart and the play or film will not make any
sense.

A couple of years ago in my class, two young actors were presenting
one of the final scenes from Anton Chekhov's play *The Seagull*. In the
scene, the young writer, Treplyev, begs Nina, an actress whom he's long
loved unrequitedly, to make him part of her life. She rejects him cruelly
by expressing her passionate love for another man, Trigorin, a more successful writer whom Treplyev envies. At this point, the actor playing the
tormented Treplyev started to beat the actress playing Nina and throw
her about the room. The startled young actress began to speed through
her final monologue so that she could escape with her life, after which
Treplyev, as the script demands, burned every piece of his writing, put a
gun to his head, and ended his life.

In my critique, I asked the actor where he found the evidence in the
text to support his choice to be physically aggressive toward Nina right
before he blows his brains out. The actor's intriguing answer: "I'm so tired
of seeing Treplyev played like a victim. I wanted to give the play new life."

I suggested to the actor that, in fact, he had killed the play by refusing
to accept the character's given circumstances. At that point in the play,
Chekhov never gives Treplyev any lines to express his rage over his great
loss of love. The tidal wave of feelings within Treplyev remains choked
back. In addition, Nina is written in such a way that she is insensitive to
the intensity of Treplyev's pain. If Treplyev were to express his rage physically toward her, she would have to comment on it, and there are no
lines that allow her to do that. All Treplyev reveals in this scene is vulnerable love, need, and helplessness. If he could so easily lash out physically
at Nina and be so direct with his anger, maybe he wouldn't have to tear up
everything he's written and put that gun to his temple.

As Chekhov wrote the part, Treplyev *is* a victim. He is a victim of his
mother's narcissistic indifference, which has left him with a feeling of
worthlessness. This is a given circumstance. It is why he chooses Nina,
who is a duplicate of his mother in that she, too, cannot truly see or value
him. It is the intolerable feeling of being invisible to those whom he
needs to love him that causes Treplyev to self-destruct. The young actor

in my class was making an effort to be creative in his choices and, perhaps, something in him needed to communicate this anger, but it was totally inappropriate and harmful to the scene. His desire to be creative and to express himself blinded him to the needs of the play.

Let me add that Chekhov does give Treplyev a chance to be aggressive toward Nina when she first rejects him at the play's beginning, but as Treplyev grows older, he grows more internal and more repressed and depressed. In order to play Treplyev successfully, you must understand the given circumstances, which come out of the depth of Chekhov's understanding of human psychology. Chekhov understood that Treplyev's suicidal depression is his anger turned inward. As an actor playing Treplyev, you need to understand Treplyev's behavior, his interactions with Nina, and his *point of view* on life as it is expressed very specifically in the text.

Chekhov makes it clear from the start of the play that Treplyev sees the world as a frustrating, cheating, unloving place, and that his only hope for happiness is to be respected as a playwright and loved as a man by Nina, dreams that are painfully eluding him. Look at how many facts about Treplyev's given circumstances are given in his dialogue in the first scene in which he appears. He tells his uncle, Sorin, "My mother doesn't love me. Why should she? She wants excitement, romance, and pretty clothes. I'm twenty-five now. That reminds her she's no longer young. When I'm not around she's thirty-two, when I am she's forty-three. She hates me for that." In that line alone, Chekhov establishes the context from which Treplyev views life: he is an unloved son who feels that his mother wishes him out of existence.

And Treplyev goes on to detail his humiliations and defeats: "Maybe I'm selfish, but I wish she weren't a famous actress. Can you imagine what life is like with her, Uncle—the house always full of famous actors and writers? Can you imagine how I feel? The only nobody there is me." His mother, who is clearly comfortably off, has refused to support him. "I left university my third year," Treplyev says, "due to circumstances, as they say, beyond my control. I haven't a kopeck." He feels socially inferior: "According to my passport, I'm a 'bourgeois of Kiev.' That's my social position. My father was a 'bourgeois of Kiev,' too, but he was a famous actor." Treplyev's father—whom we learn is dead—overcame his middle-class position through his talent for acting, but Treplyev says he has "no talent." Later Treplyev says, "When my mother's famous actor, writer and musician friends deign to notice me, I feel them measuring my insignificance. I imagine their thoughts. It's humiliating." In just a few short lines, Chekhov tells us almost everything we need to know about Treplyev's point of view.

I've heard that John Malkovich has said if he understands his character's point of view of the world, it gives him a great clue about how to play all the scenes. Sometimes, as with Treplyev, a character's point of view is given to you clearly in the script, other times you have to glean it from the facts that the script gives you. You have to study the text very diligently until you can say, based on what the script tells you about the character's history, how the character is treated by others, the character's reactions to that treatment, and what the character actually does—not just what they *say* but what they *do*—that the character sees the world in a certain way. In this way, your character's point of view is part of, and inextricably tied to, their given circumstances.

In James Brooks's film *As Good as It Gets*, it is a given circumstance that Melvin Udall (Jack Nicholson) has obsessive-compulsive disorder and sees his life exclusively through that lens. This is not my psychoanalysis of Melvin, it is a fact that is spelled out vividly, and often hilariously, in the script. The first time we see Melvin, he is anxiously walking on the street toward his favorite restaurant, desperately trying not to touch or be touched by anyone he passes (saying to people who walk by, "Don't touch! Don't touch!"). He is also trying to avoid stepping on cracks in the sidewalk. At the restaurant he impatiently waits for the exact table and the exact waitress—Carol Connelly (Helen Hunt)—that he always has. He accosts the people sitting at the table he wants and talks *at* them about their having big noses and being Jewish until they are so affronted that they flee. So the given circumstances of the scene are that he is an obsessive-compulsive middle-aged man who comes to the restaurant where he wants *his* particular table and *his* particular waitress, someone else is at *his* table and he needs to have everything in harmony with his compulsions in order to feel safe and not become hysterical with terror. Part of his behavior, because of his disorder, is that he will insult anyone about anything if he's frustrated or frightened.

The given circumstances for Carol are that she's a single mother working as a waitress, whose entire life is devoted to taking care of her dangerously asthmatic son. She has no other priority, no other life. She has waited on Melvin many times before, and she knows him. In that opening scene, Carol warns Melvin to behave and at the same time protects him from the glowering restaurant manager, who wants to throw him out.

Carol's point of view is not spelled out in the script as explicitly as Melvin's is, but you can still get it from the text. Despite having a severely ill son and meager financial resources to take care of him, it's clear from the script in the way Carol interacts with the other waiters and waitresses and with Melvin that she is warm, has great humor, and a kind of bemused patience. So part of the given circumstance of her character is that she's a positive person; she doesn't wear her problems on her sleeve; she's a survivor and makes the best of the situation she's in.

When I worked with Helen Hunt as she prepared for the role, she came up with some brilliant interpretative choices for Carol, which I will talk about in the chapter titled "The Actor's Choice." But, again, all good interpretive choices build on the given circumstances—the facts the writer gives you in the script.

Here's an exercise I often give to actors when they prepare for a role. After they have digested the material in the script, I ask them to express the character's point of view of the world in the following way: "My name is [character's name], and the world is [six descriptive words or phrases]." For example, if you were playing Melvin in *As Good as It Gets,* you could say, "My name is Melvin Udall and the world is a terrifying, vicious, unfair, desperate mine field in which I must get them before they get me, and I must keep control of everything in my life so the world doesn't explode into chaos where all the germs will get me." This is how Melvin walks into the story. You must walk into every script with this kind of specificity about who you are, why you're there, and your whole unique life experience.

During Roxie Hart's first major scene in the movie musical *Chicago,* Roxie (Renée Zellweger) is making love with her lover in the bedroom she usually shares with her husband. Why? Because she wants to be a famous singer and she has been led to believe her lover can get her a job in show business. She's not going to bed with him just because she's attracted to him: the given circumstance is that she wants him to do something for her hoped-for career in show business.

She hopes she's trading sex for a career, and when her lover brushes her off, she shoots him. If you're playing Roxie and you think you're going to bed with him just because you think he's hot, the scene is not going to work—because it won't make any sense for you to kill him. You kill him because you find out he lied: he's not going to do anything for your career because he doesn't have the connections he said he did; furthermore, he hurts you physically and humiliates you when you confront him with his lie. This makes you as Roxie feel your worst fear: that you are invisible and that you have sold yourself cheap for no good outcome. That's why you take your husband's gun and shoot your lover.

So the given circumstances at the beginning of the scene are that your lover is still alive; at the end of the scene the given circumstances are that you've shot your lover, you've been arrested because your husband makes a stupid mistake and incriminates you, you are going directly to prison, and will probably be hanged for the murder. As you can see, the given circumstances for your character are constantly changing and you must be diligent in recognizing the changing facts.

Roxie doesn't know she's going to kill her lover until he says he just wanted to lay her, that he has no intention of helping her because he has no show business connections. When she pushes the issue of his helping her in her so-called aspiring career, he hits her and pushes her to the floor. What makes Renée Zellweger's performance live is that she didn't *anticipate* her disappointment or her humiliation or that she even has murderous impulses—at the beginning of the scene, as far as she's concerned, her life is hunky-dory; she's going straight to the top. She discovers these other facts moment to moment as the scene goes on.

As you study a script, write the given circumstances on a list, scene by scene. Ask yourself:

Where does the scene take place?
Who is in the scene?
What do I as a character know about the other characters in the
    scene?
What are my relationships with them emotionally?
What do the other characters say about me?
Given what the script tells me, is it true?
What do I as a character know about myself that is relevant to
    the scene (my background, my attitudes) as I enter?
What does my character literally *do* during the scene?
What do other characters *do* to me? How do they treat me?

When you've gone through the whole script and written down every piece of information it tells you about your character, you will have a list of your character's given circumstances and you will see the way they change as the story develops.

This is all *homework,* a word you're going to hear me use many times in this book. When you are actually performing the scene, you forget everything you know except for the specific need and point of view of your character at the beginning of each scene. We do all this homework to give our performance inner structure and specificity, but when we actually act, we have to forget what we know—and by that I mean we need to be innocent—until our character is confronted with new events. *Don't bring into the scene something your character doesn't know yet.* If you're working moment to moment, these new events should surprise you and give you a chance to react spontaneously in performance. This is what makes your character live.

I want to say here that I use the word *character,* as in *a character* in a play, but I mean a human being, a person. Don't distance yourself from the role you're playing by thinking of it as a character if that word doesn't convey to you a flesh-and-blood human being.

When you're doing script analysis, you'll find that what your character says is not always the same thing as what they do, and you have to note this as part of the given circumstances. For example, in one scene, a character—think *person*—may say, "I don't love you, and I never will," and in the next scene, she may passionately kiss the man she just said she didn't love. Remember Norman Jewison's film *Moonstruck* with a wonderful script by John Patrick Shanley? When Ronny Cammareri (Nicolas Cage) tells Loretta Castorini (Cher) that he's in love with her, she slaps him and tells him to snap out of it. Yet a very short time later, she falls into his arms. If you're playing Loretta and you take your character at her word, you're not seeing how she *really* feels. How she really feels is revealed by what she does: she kisses him. Characters, like people in your own life, say a lot of things, but we understand them primarily through their behavior, which is why I said earlier that you have to define a character's point of view primarily by what they *do,* not necessarily by what they *say*.

Again, the specific ways that you bring your character to life—your physical choices, vocal choices, the range and depth of your emotions, your rhythms and tempos, the choices you make about how you're going to deliver the writer's lines, the colors and hues of your performance—are all part of your interpretation, but *the given circumstances are always the same, no matter who acts the part.*

When I was nineteen years old, I was in the audience for the very first preview performance of Edward Albee's play *Who's Afraid of Virginia Woolf?* starring the gifted actress and acting teacher Uta Hagen and Arthur Hill. The play opens with George and Martha, a couple married twenty years, coming home late at night—2:00 A.M.—from a party given by Martha's father, who is president of the college where George teaches. George thinks they're coming home to sleep, but Martha knows that she's invited guests, a young couple, Nick and Honey, whom she met at the party. Those are given circumstances of the first scene. But they're not the only given circumstances.

Martha is disappointed in and angry at George because George didn't mix well at the party (she says, "I watched you at Daddy's party and you weren't there"). That's her point of view toward her husband: she's disappointed, and therefore aggressive ("Jesus H. Christ!" she says when they walk into their house. "What a dump!"). George's point of view is that he wants to go to sleep since they're both inebriated, and he had a lousy time at the party (another given circumstance). When he finds out what Martha has done, George is irritated and resentful. He begins to whine, complain, and jab at her with sarcasm, and finally rejects Martha's sexual overture. That's the beginning of the war between them that night.

George likes irritating Martha, because he's as angry at her as she is at him. This does not mean that they're not strongly bound to each other out of need and out of their own version of love. One of the great problems in their marriage, as this scene reveals to us, is that Martha is daddy's girl, and somewhere within her she wants George to separate her from the emotional incest with her father which has kept her a crippled child. She is angry that George hasn't been strong enough to succeed in her father's college and thereby rescue her. She wanted George to be a man who was going to go places, and for years she has punished him for his failures and weakness. These are part of the given circumstances of the play, too, and they are the foundation for the characters' points of view and interactions in the first scene.

And Martha has a loud voice. How do I know? The script tells me. At one point early in the play, George tells Martha, "At least I don't go around braying at everybody." Obviously Martha has to be loud enough vocally at times that George could call her "braying." The play also tells me there are reasons why Martha is so loud; it's to protect her from the razor-sharp comments that George makes to try to wound her and beat her at their savage game.

If you're playing George or Martha, you need to know that from the moment you walk in the door, you have to be convincing as a bickering couple that's been together for twenty years—and you have to understand, through analyzing the given circumstances not just of the first scene but of the entire play, the issues that underlie the bickering. Included in these circumstances is the history of their imaginary son, "the kid."

I learned an interesting lesson when, forty years after I saw the first preview of the Broadway production, I saw an excellent staged reading of the play with Uta Hagen reprising her role as Martha and the excellent Jonathan Pryce as George. During the opening scene in this production, Martha and George took each other so much for granted that they barely looked at each other but they also had a humorous, odd affection. Their George and Martha were certainly angry, but for much of this scene they seemed to be entertaining each other, until George's sexual rejection of Martha, at which point she became lacerating. They brought to life the conflict of that couple of twenty years—the given circumstances—but they did it *their* way. With the same given circumstances, Uta Hagen interpreted the role very differently in the original Broadway production I saw. She was far more vitriolic and predatory as Martha from the start. In the same production, Arthur Hill played the first scene withdrawn, passive, and tired, whereas Jonathan Pryce was playing the game of provoking Martha almost from the beginning. Both interpretations were absolutely valid for the given circumstances.

In the beginning of the 1940 classic film *The Letter,* a woman, Leslie Crosbie (Bette Davis), is brutally shooting a man to death as only a rejected leading lady in a 1940s Warner Brothers movie melodrama could. These are the given circumstances that start the whole story in motion. The audience is presented with these circumstances right away, and a few moments later we see Leslie lie to her husband and tell him that the man she killed was an intruder who had tried to rape her. These are similar to the given circumstances in *Chicago,* but *Chicago* is comedic and satiric, and *The Letter* is emotional and deeply dramatic.

Based on W. Somerset Maugham's short story, *The Letter* truly stands the test of time, as does Bette Davis's performance. When you see the look on her face as she shoots her lover dead, you know she's a rejected woman. What's great about Ms. Davis's performance is that you can see in her eyes as she lies first to her husband and then to everyone around her, including a jury, that the real given circumstance of the shooting— her rejection—is boiling underneath her skin as she tries to save her life. And in her eyes is another given circumstance as well: the full knowledge that she's killed the only man she'll ever love. She makes you feel her love for the man she killed, even though you never see one scene of their actual affair. It's the actress's deep commitment to bringing out all these given circumstances that makes the performance alive over sixty years after it was filmed.

Stella Adler famously said, "It's not enough to have talent. You have to have a talent for your talent." One of the talents you need is to be able to break down a script and to identify all the facts that the writer gives you that help you understand your character, what each scene is about, and what the whole script is about. These given circumstances may make you emotional when you read them, and that's important, because that shows you that you're connecting to the material. But just as critical as your emotional response is being completely clear about the actual facts of the story. Because only by identifying and investing in these facts can you bring your truth—your interpretation—to your performance. Root your performance to the earth (the given circumstances), and you can begin to fly.

2

SUPEROBJECTIVE AND OBJECTIVE:
WHAT DO YOU WANT?

After a scene has been done in my class, I always ask how each actor feels about their work on the scene they just completed. Then I often ask, what did you as the character want to accomplish in the scene? What did your character try to get from the other person? Affection, understanding, money, power, sex, information, forgiveness? In other words, what did you *want*? What did you identify as your character's *objective* in the scene as specified by the writer?

I use the word *objective* because I like it; it sings to me. Other synonyms you can use and that are used in the business of acting are my *want*, my *action*, my *desire*, my *goal*. Say it however you like, it's all about human needs. The objective is what your character wants in a certain scene in order to try to fulfill their needs.

Of course, your character's wants don't begin with that scene. As a character you walk into a play or a film from a prior life, and something has happened in that prior life—something deeply emotional—that has created for your character a wish or dream that is called the *superobjective*.

The objective of each individual scene is connected to your overall super-objective, your driving passion. The superobjective is the engine that propels you through the journey of the play or film; it is the dream that moves you through the story, for in plays and films as in life, without dreams we don't take action.

The Russian actor, teacher, and director Konstantin Stanislavski, who is thought of as the father of the so-called Method, said that the super-objective—the dream, which comes from a deep yearning within the character—is the spine of the actor's performance, and that the objectives in each individual scene are the ribs connected to that spine. One of the exciting things about reading a script is beginning to find what Stanislavski called "the system of wants." This system of wants for each character means that character's desires—objectives—in each scene. It is vital to every play or film you will act in, because without objectives, and without obstacles in the way of those objectives, you have nothing to act.

If I'm playing Richard Nixon and Nixon's dream is *to become the most revered president in the history of the world,* then each scene in the story of my life is a rib on the spine of that superobjective: my success at gaining visibility in the HUAC (House Un-American Activities Committee) hearings; my becoming vice president under Dwight Eisenhower; my victory over Hubert Humphrey; my successful space program when the first astronauts land on the moon; my meeting with the Russian leader Brezhnev; my successful trip to China; my resounding victory over George McGovern for my second term; the Watergate scandal; the threat of impeachment. Each scene, even those that dramatize my downfall, is connected to the spine of being the most revered president in the history of the world, because that dream—the superobjective—is what drives me emotionally whether I am trying to rise or to survive a downward spiral. Each scene will have a particular, specific objective that I pursue in order to attempt to fulfill my dream, my superobjective.

When Nixon lost the California gubernatorial race, he famously said to the media, "You won't have Dick Nixon to kick around anymore." This was a man who was deeply wounded in his childhood, a man scarred by humiliation and repression. Nixon's way of coping with these unbearable feelings was to create the dream of becoming the most revered president in the history of the world. His defeats—the presidential election of 1960, in the California gubernatorial race of 1962—made him cling to this dream with even more intensity.

Every superobjective has a *justification,* an emotional reason for its birth. Mr. Nixon's dream was birthed in childhood humiliation, and humiliation followed and drove him for much of his life. For years he seemed to be perpetually in a flop sweat due to the elusiveness of his desperate dream.

To make the connection between superobjective and emotional justification clearer, I'd like you to watch the 1950s movie *The Goddess,* written by Paddy Chayevsky and starring the great Kim Stanley. It is Chayevsky's imaginative telling of Marilyn Monroe's life. Early in the movie, Emily Ann Faulkner (Kim Stanley) allows young men in her high school to have sex with her because her mother screams, "I don't want her. I never wanted her," which makes Emily desperate for any kind of love. Emily's well of pain is deepened when she discovers that the one boy she believes likes her for herself, the one who made her feel that he cared, has been lying. As he begins to hungrily undress her and use her, she begins to softly cry, and says, "I'm going to Hollywood and become a movie star."

The superobjective is so emotionally powerful to your character that it will make you try to obliterate any obstacle in your path. Emily first tries to obliterate the obstacles to becoming a star. Then she tries to obliterate the deep depression that haunts her even after she attains stardom. The reason I'm using the word *obliterate,* which means to destroy, is that the superobjective is intensely passionate; it always comes from deep pain, deep joy, or deep fear. Emily's superobjective is not to become a movie star, it is to *have a feeling of being deeply cared about and loved,* which she never truly attains.

Where do you find the superobjective that drives your character? You find it in the script—the same place you find the objectives of each scene. It's the road that the writer provides for you. This superobjective, this dream, and these wants *drive* the story forward, and as an actor your job is to tell that particular story. If you misunderstand your character's driving needs, wants, objectives—all these words mean the same thing—the play or film will fail to truly reach the audience and live powerfully.

In Arthur Miller's brilliant tragedy *Death of a Salesman,* although there are many scenes in which Biff, the older son of Willy Loman, the salesman of the play's title, attacks his father, it is a great mistake to play Biff as attacking his father only with anger. A vital given circumstance of the play is that Willy is preparing his suicide so that his family can obtain his life insurance and he can feel he left the world with power and dignity. His death will leave the family with the only thing that has true significance in his mind: money. Of course it's madness, but there is a kind of love in it. Willy wants Biff to be successful, which to Willy means money and power—the American dream—the very things that have eluded him. Because Willy realizes that Biff is lost and has no road toward success and prosperity, he criticizes him, he baits him, and he humiliates him. Biff retaliates in kind, but they do these things out of a distorted need for love.

Biff attacks with anger, yes, but he also begs, pleads, confesses his own failures, warns his father, creates ultimatums, hugs, pushes his father, demands him to face the truth about Willy's own failures and false dreams of attaining greatness, all out of a need for love, all because Biff wants *to save his family and find himself.* This is the superobjective that drives Biff through the play. Everything he does, he does because he needs his father's love, not because he hates him. The opposite of love is indifference, not hate. Biff may have moments of hatred toward Willy because he despises his actions and is enraged by his choices, but *Biff wants to save Willy so he can mend the family and himself.* If you are an angry son yourself, you may miss the intense need for love—don't!

Remember, you use yourself to act, but the character is not you; the character comes through you. Actors, don't get all huffy and close the book now, saying, "But my teacher says there's no character, there's only me adjusted." If you don't separate the character as written from your own life you will miss qualities that are imperative to capturing this person's personality. Yes, you use yourself deeply—*your* emotions, *your* imagination, *your* interpretation, *your* physical behavior, all subjects I will discuss later in the book—but I say again, the character stands on his own and your job is to bring him to life.

There are flashbacks in *Death of a Salesman* where Biff and his brother, Happy, idolize their father. When you are young and have that feeling toward a parent, and then the parent reveals his weakness and is abusive, you may forget that you once idolized him because your pain turns to depression and vindictiveness. The desire for love drives you for the rest of your life unless you resolve it. Notice that I'm talking here about Biff's need for love from Willy as opposed to his love for Willy, for I believe that between father and sons in the Loman family, no one has truly felt love, just the aching desire for it.

If a really powerful superobjective is never obtained, you never arrive at your destination. That keeps you in a state of wanting and aliveness until the curtain comes down or the screen flashes "The End." In the last moments of *Death of a Salesman,* Biff realizes that he has to discover a way of living for himself that separates him from his father's inflated, empty dreams of power and glory. But by that time Willy is dead and the family is destroyed. So even though Biff starts to find himself, he has not, and never could have, saved his family and gotten his father's love. Willy didn't know how to love Biff. How could he when he didn't know how to value himself?

On the television series *Inside the Actors Studio,* Sydney Pollack talked about how he tries to sum up each film he directs in one sentence. In Pollack's film *Out of Africa,* the one sentence is the superobjective of Meryl Streep's character, Karen Blixen-Finecke (I'm going to phrase this in terms you would use if you were acting the role): *to tame Africa and to tame the man I love.* When you watch the film you'll notice that Pollack uses sweeping aerial views of the immense land that is Africa. No human being can ever own that land or change its essential nature, any more than Karen can tame the wild heart of the man she loves. At the end of the film, Karen says at the funeral of her lover, Denys Finch Hatton (Robert Redford), "He was never mine, he was never ours," and the camera cuts to the grave of Finch Hatton with lions guarding it. They are wild, he is still wild, even in death, and Africa pulsates as the film ends. Karen Blixen-Finecke's desire to own the land and the man drives her through the film, but she never achieves her dream.

What we *want,* what we *desire,* what we *must have:* each scene has at least two opposing objectives—one coming from your character, the other coming from another character. These create conflict and raise the scene to heightened reality. This is what Alfred Hitchcock called "life with all the boring bits cut out." These conflicting wants are among the obstacles to characters' obtaining their objectives, a subject we'll explore in the next chapter.

One of my goals in this book is to clarify technical tools; another is to excite your imagination and creative instincts by making the technical tools immediately useful. I use well-known, classic plays for many of my examples because they formed my love for the theater. If you haven't already read them, then you must—not only for personal growth, but also to get the most out of this book. My creative life was born from the depth and power of these plays; they are great, and they always will be great, for they speak about the difficulty of being human in extraordinary ways. That's why these plays are still being performed all over the world.

I like to talk about Tennessee Williams's play *A Streetcar Named Desire,* because it is one of the few great modern masterpieces. *Streetcar* is about the visit of Blanche DuBois, a fading Southern beauty with a genteel background and many secrets, to the home of her younger sister, Stella, and Stella's new working-class husband, Stanley, in a seedy section of the French Quarter in New Orleans. The fourth major character is Stanley's friend Mitch, who becomes a potential suitor to Blanche. Each character's superobjective moves them through the entire play.

Blanche DuBois—*to find a safe place*. In every scene that Blanche is in, she is trying, through gentility of manners, through humor, seduction, blame, and revealing past pain, to find a safe place;

Stanley Kowalski—*to stay king of my castle*. In order to stay king, Stanley dominates Stella (and any other woman) through his sexuality, his bullying, and his little-boy helplessness. He dominates his buddies through brute physical force. Everything Stanley does to bully, to entertain, to seduce, to create a ruckus, to destroy, and to beg—those active verbs that are his *active intentions* in each scene—is in the service of his superobjective;

Stella Kowalski—*to bring my sister and my husband together to form a new family*. In almost every scene, Stella tries to inspire affection, understanding, and patience in Stanley toward Blanche and in Blanche toward Stanley;

Mitch—*to end my loneliness*. Mitch is ultrapolite, gentle, accommodating, almost reverential toward Blanche because she appears to be fragile, like a woman he had loved who died. He sees Blanche as a potential life partner—which he desperately needs because his mother, with whom he lives, is dying.

In one searing moment, after Blanche reveals her complicity in the death of her homosexual husband years ago, Mitch says, "You need somebody and I need somebody too. Could it be—you and me, Blanche?" Then Williams writes the stage directions, "*She stares at him vacantly for a moment, then with a soft cry, cuddles in his embrace. She makes a sobbing effort to speak, but the words won't come. He kisses her forehead and her eyes and finally her lips. The polka tune fades out. Her breath is drawn and released, graceful sobs.*" And Blanche says: "Sometimes—there's God—so quickly!" For Blanche, "the safe place" *is* God. But this is the only moment in *Streetcar* where two of the characters' superobjectives meet—and from then on they are torn apart.

As I've said, you identify your superobjective by finding it in the script. In scene after scene, Blanche says, in essence—and this is supported by her actions, as well as her behavior—"I'm tapped out, my youth is fading now, I don't have those options anymore, I can't turn the trick anymore." That's why she must find a safe place; she has nowhere else to go; the streetcar has reached the end of the line. And Stanley declares—and demonstrates through his actions—"I'm the king in this house, and don't you ever forget it"—an instruction that Blanche ignores. And Stella tries to smooth the waters in scene after scene. She coddles and waits on Blanche; she begs Stanley, "Try to be kind to her, Stanley. Tell her how pretty she looks." Stella behaves toward Stanley as if he's a sexual narcotic she can't get enough of. "When he's away for one night," she tells Blanche, "I nearly go insane." She implores them to value each other because she can't bear the thought of hurting either one of them.

It's not enough just to identify the superobjective intellectually, you have to *justify* it, to find the emotional drive behind it. You need your own *specific interpretation* of the superobjective of your character so that every time you think of it, it makes you emotional and drives you into action. The words you use to describe your superobjective might be different from the words used by another actor. For one actress playing Blanche, the phrase "to find a safe place" might be emotionally compelling; for another actress, the phrase "to find protection" or "to find a beautiful corner for myself" might be the language that carbonates her. I believe that when you're playing a part, the justification for your superobjective should be so emotional, so passionate and alive to *you,* that when you think about it, it makes you weep, rage, or burst into joy and fall on your knees in gratitude. In performance, just reminding yourself of your justified superobjective may be all you need to keep you emotionally galvanized for the whole play.

One way to discover your emotional justification is to ask yourself, "What if I don't get my dream?" and imagine what would become of your life if you didn't. The given circumstances of *Streetcar* are that Blanche has lost everything that had meaning for her before she arrives at Stella and Stanley's. She's lost her husband, most of her family, the plantation called Belle Rêve (which, ironically, means beautiful dream), and her income—having been fired from her teaching job. She is left with the desperation of one wish: to find that safe place. You can see that the emotion of her justification is all-consuming. At the end of the play, Blanche cannot find a safe place in reality and she leaves reality behind altogether. As she is being led away to an asylum for the insane, she moves into the past of the genteel Old South, proclaiming the famous line, "Whoever you are—I've always depended on the kindness of strangers."

The emotional justification for the superobjective cannot be general;

it must be specific. If you are playing Richard Nixon, it's too general to say that you want to be the most revered president in the world in order to make up for former humiliation in your life. The passion behind the dream needs to be created by your imagination as a *specific,* unbearable humiliating moment or series of moments.

Nixon's life, because it's been well documented, is known to contain many such moments. One of these occurred at the HUAC hearings, when Nixon was prosecuting Alger Hiss for Communist activities. During an exchange between the two, Hiss snapped at Nixon, "I am familiar with the law. I attended Harvard Law School. I believe yours was Whittier." HUAC staff member Robert Stripling says that Nixon's face became "red, then blue, and red again. You could see the hackles on his back practically pushing his coat up." This moment is the kind of specific humiliation that you could use to justify your superobjective emotionally. But if it doesn't incite you, you would need to find another moment, or to create one, that made you turn red, blue, and red again.

Sometimes the emotional justification is in the given circumstances of the script, and sometimes it's only hinted at. Let's look at another Williams play, *Cat on a Hot Tin Roof.* The play is about a marriage in the South, in which the husband, Brick, is ignoring his wife, Maggie, while he mourns the death of his best friend, Skipper, who may have been his lover. The script also tells you that there's a huge economic difference between Brick and Maggie: he grew up with money, a tortured prince, while Maggie, despite family social connections, is low-rent, low-class, and a social climber, haunted by her former poverty. Maggie's superobjective is *to have so much money that I never have the fear of being poor for the rest of my life.* Why does she feel this way?

Again, the script tells you that Maggie's family was poor. Maggie also declares to Brick: "You can be young without money but you can't be old without it. You've got to be old *with* money, because to be old without it is just too awful." But finding the specific emotional justification that propels Maggie's dream is up to you; you've got to know *exactly* what your "too awful" is. Perhaps Maggie remembers how her mother clutched her hand as she lay dying in a public institution, unable to get proper medical attention because they couldn't afford it. Maggie doesn't describe this in the play, but it's something that you as an actress might come up with from your *imagination* that fits the character of Maggie. To watch your mother die in agony in a public ward is an intense and painful justification to make sure you don't end up that way.

If you don't understand that Maggie's superobjective is economic security, you might think her dream is for her husband, Brick, to love her—which would be a mistake, because if she wants to be loved by him, why would she irritate him and enrage him, which she does quite purposely? If, however, you understand that Maggie wants economic security, and you've found the personal justification for that need, then you understand that she'd want to put a fire under Brick in whatever way she can. Maggie needs Brick to make amends with his dying father so that they will get a share of the inheritance. Of course Maggie feels, and rightfully so, that they're more apt to get the money if she can get pregnant and give Brick's father a male heir. This is particularly important because Brick's brother and sister-in-law, May, "that monster of fertility," are way ahead of them in the baby-producing department. She irritates and enrages Brick because she wants to get through his armor and make him *feel something* before he gets too drunk, so that perhaps he will impregnate her and go downstairs and celebrate his father's birthday—and *get the money*. Whether he loves her or not is beside the point to Maggie; it would be nice, but it's not what drives her. She may truly love Brick, and I believe it's better for the play if she does, but it's not love that drives her; it's terror. How do I know? I found it in the play! I found it by reading the script and observing what Maggie does scene by scene.

How badly does Maggie want her superobjective? She wants it *at any cost*. I know this because Maggie brings up to Brick the most dangerous and vulnerable injury in his psyche, his possible sexual relationship with his best friend, Skipper. "I just can't keep my hands off a sore," she says. Brick, a former athlete who has broken his ankle and is now on crutches, later says, "Don't you know that I could kill you with this crutch?" And Maggie answers, "Good Lord, man, do you think I'd care if you did?" It's an all-or-nothing game for Maggie. Because Brick is ignoring her, and because he's turning into a drunk, and time is running out for the family's money machine—Brick's father, Big Daddy, who's dying of cancer—she's desperate. She doesn't want to die, but she can't go on the way she's living. Maggie tells Brick that if she thought he would "never, never, never" make love to her again, she would go downstairs into the kitchen and get "the longest and sharpest knife I could find and stick it straight into my heart. I swear I would." That's how much Maggie wants what she wants. Maggie is written with great humor, and that delicious sense of humor must be played, but don't let that blind you to her primary goal in life—*money*.

The superobjective, the dream, tells you how you feel about everything in the play or film, including the other characters, and in every scene it drives you to actions that you believe will help you to get what you want.

Sometimes a character has a *conscious* and an *unconscious* superobjective. Take, for example, Eddie Carbone, the leading character in Arthur Miller's play *A View from the Bridge,* which is about an Italian-American family in a working-class neighborhood in Brooklyn. Eddie's unconscious superobjective—and remember, *unconscious* means exactly that: as a character you are not aware of it—is that he wants to have a sexual relationship with his niece, Catherine, whom he and his wife, Beatrice, raised after Beatrice's sister died. Although Eddie is not conscious of this, as an actor playing the character you must be aware of it, or you will not have the TNT to play the part. Watching this young girl flower into womanhood excites Eddie's desire, but this is so unbearable for him to face that he channels this sexual energy into becoming overprotective and suspicious of any man who would court her. He believes her suitors want only one thing—exactly what he wants but can't admit to himself. Eddie becomes obsessively controlling and tries to destroy an innocent young man who falls in love with Catherine and wants to marry her. So Eddie's conscious superobjective is *to keep my niece with me forever to protect her from the dirty hands that will soil her purity*.

How does Eddie justify this? He tells himself that he and Beatrice vowed to her sister that they would care for Catherine and never let anything bad happen to her. At the same time he's impotent with his wife, who is pushing him to have sex. When Beatrice brings up their lack of sexual intimacy, he explodes, saying, in effect, "Don't tell me what to do because I'm the head of this family and the man is law and I have to protect all of you and how dare you question my virility! I am the head of this family!" He tries to justify his unconscious desire with his conscious superobjective. The play ends in tragedy because he can't.

Whenever you get confused about what you're doing in a part—whether you're working on it at home, auditioning, rehearsing, or in performance—say to yourself, "Wait a minute, what's driving me? Oh, right! My dream, my superobjective. Now what is happening in this scene, or with this relationship that I'm involved in, and how is it connected to my superobjective?" You have to keep asking and answering these questions for yourself to keep your performance on track and alive. If you stay clear about your superobjective and objectives, and are emotionally connected to them through your justification as you relate to the other characters, you will always feel the emotional carbonation that gives you a reason to be in the story.

Sometimes a character has a double-pronged superobjective. This was true of Carol Connelly in *As Good as It Gets*. At the start of the film, Carol, single mother of a son with life-threatening asthma, has the dream *to save my son's life at any cost*. When Melvin tells her that he'll take care of her and her son so that she'll no longer have to worry about paying for the treatment her son needs, Carol's life moves into a new stage. What Helen and I found in analyzing the script was that in some ways up to that point Carol was still an adolescent; she never grew up to be a fulfilled woman in relationships with men because she didn't have the time. So this is a comparatively rare instance when the character does get their superobjective and, because they do, a new superobjective is born, which, in Carol's case, is *to find a romantic life and create a new family*.

Remember that the objectives of your character in each scene are ribs on the spine of the superobjective. Start observing your own life and see that this is true not just of plays and films but of all of us.

As a young actor in New York, I wanted desperately to star in a Broadway musical; I thought there was nothing more exciting, thrilling, or challenging than singing, dancing, and acting in front of a live audience. When I was growing up in L.A., my parents would bring home the programs from musicals they had seen in New York, and they would talk about Broadway in excited and glamorous terms. In my child's mind I thought if I became one of those people on the stage that my parents had talked about as important, then I, too, would be considered important and lovable. So you could say that my superobjective was *to gain my parents' love through becoming a Broadway musical star*.

My obstacle: I was nineteen years old, I had no money, no technique, and I knew no one in the theater. This was during the 1960s, when New York was elegant, down and dirty, chic, and discotheque mad. I applied for a job as the second dishwasher at a discotheque called Steve Paul's The Scene. So I was trying to get my parents' love and attention by becoming a Broadway star, but in order to achieve my dream, I had to get money to study my craft. If there was a scene about my job interview in this play entitled *I Will Be Loved and Adored by My Family If I Am a Broadway Star*, the scene would be about how my character sweet-talked, joked, and pleaded with the boss of this disco to let me be a dishwasher in a greasy, smelly, overheated, hysterical kitchen in order to make money to take classes to achieve my dream. My objective in this particular scene, then, is *to get the job as a dishwasher so I can study and become a Broadway star.*

You can begin to see in a very practical, very human way that every day of your life you have a system of wants, desires, objectives from the moment you get up in the morning till the time you go to sleep at night. Understanding this about yourself will make it much easier for you to break down a script and identify the wants of characters in different scenes. I'll end with an exercise I assign to my students: My System of Wants.

My System of Wants Exercise

Go through a day in your life and write down every single thing you *want*—and I mean the subtle things like, "I want to get the sleep out of my eyes," "I want a cup of a particular kind of coffee," "I want to call a particular friend for a particular reason," "I want to mend an argument with my sister and therefore I will make the call I do not want to make because I will have to hide my anger and try to get her to understand my point of view."

Throughout the day, also be aware of how your body feels: when you are hungry, when you are tired, when you are sad, joyful, lustful. Then observe what you do about it. Sometimes we want things and we know that they are bad for us so we do something else instead. It doesn't mean that we didn't want the thing that was bad for us, but that for some very specific reason we choose to do what is better for us. The system of wants may start with, "I *want* to eat that pint of Häagen-Dazs," but it will switch to "I will eat an apple instead so I can fit into my clothes."

I *want*, I *want*, I *want*—objective, objective, objective—all day long, every day, every second. That's why superobjectives and objectives are so fundamental to your work as an actor; they, along with given circumstances, are the bedrock of life—and of every part you will ever play.

3

Obstacle and Intention:
How Will You Get It?

Drama is created by wants—objectives—but it can't really be drama unless there's an *obstacle* standing in the way of achieving the want. In every play or film, there's someone who can't or won't give you what you want, or you're in a place where you can't get it, or there's something else you have to overcome to get it. Having obstacles is basic to dramatic structure. It's also basic to life.

I said that as a young man my superobjective was *to gain my parents' love through becoming a Broadway star*. Then I listed my obstacles: I was nineteen years old, I had no money, no technique, and I knew no one in the theater. One of my objectives on my way to becoming a success was that I wanted to get a job so I could support myself and take classes. That objective brought me to apply for the dishwashing job in the discotheque. In order to get the job—my objective—I had to face new obstacles: I had to compete with other guys wanting the job and to impress the owner, Steve Paul. To overcome these obstacles, I did specific *active* things. I ingratiated myself, I joked, and I pleaded with him to work in his greasy kitchen. *To ingratiate, to joke, to plead*—these are all verbs, and in acting they are called *intentions* or *active intentions*.

Intentions are *active doings* aimed at overcoming obstacles and achieving your objectives. They are *how* you go about getting what you want. The degree to which you overcome an obstacle with your intention is the degree to which you're successful in achieving your want. Once your character achieves what they want, a new want is immediately born with a new obstacle, because that's what makes the story develop. *Objective, obstacle, and intention are the triad of all acting*. They are in every scene you will ever play. Once you discern the wants and the obstacles in the scene, you then begin to discover and define the active intentions your character uses to try to remove the obstacles and gain your objective.

I want to spend a moment on the word *intention. Webster's Ninth New Collegiate Dictionary* defines *intention* both as "a determination to act in a certain way" and as "what one intends to do or bring about." Let's look at a line of Martha's from the first scene of *Who's Afraid of Virginia Woolf?* As she and George argue about the guests she has invited and George expresses his displeasure, Martha says to him, "Poor Georgie-Porgie, put-upon pie (*as he sulks*). Awwwwww . . . What are you doing? Are you sulking? Hunh? Let me see . . . Are you sulking? Is that what you're doing?" What is Martha's design in saying this? What is she aiming at? What is she *intending* to do or to bring about?

Martha is not simply asking George a question; she's *making fun of him* in order to get him to respond to her in a feeling way (her objective) because he withdraws and she feels unloved. She tries to provoke his anger (the same objective), because that would be preferable to nothing. To this end she *infantilizes him and herself* when she calls him Georgie-Porgie, just as she does earlier in the scene when she talks about her father's party as "Daddy's party." So what are her intentions with this line? They could be defined as *to treat George like a baby, to infantilize him, to mock him, to bait him*. As an actress playing Martha, do you play all of these intentions with this one line? No, you pick the intention that most excites *you* to bring this portion of the scene to life and to affect George (your objective), and then you *watch for George's reaction* to see if your intention affected him. *Active intentions are aimed to get reactions from the other characters in the scene.* It's by getting them to react in specific ways that you gain your objectives. When one intention doesn't achieve your objective, you may find that the writer transitions into another intention or gives you the opportunity to choose another intention, and you have to be sensitive to the writing in order to see where a new intention is called for or may be appropriate and exciting.

That's why Stella Adler said, "It's not the lines, it's the life." The life has to do with *what you want* (your objective), *why you want it* (your emotional justification), and *how you go about getting it* (your intention) to overcome the obstacles. Take a simple line: "Good morning." Depending on the given circumstances of your character, your character's objective and the obstacles they face, the line might be played with the intention *to guilt-trip the other character* (you expected a call the night before that never came); or *to express warmth and gratitude for sexual fulfillment* (if the night before went very well); or even *to dismiss* or *to annihilate the other character* (for having hurt or disappointed you). The circumstances of the scene might clearly give you a way of saying good morning, but if they don't, if the choice just seems open to your interpretation, you must make a choice that adds interesting color to your character's life and that fits with the circumstances.

Picking a specific intention is the same thing as a painter picking a specific shade or hue of a color to create a certain drama on the canvas. Some roses may be red, but what shade of red? One of Stella Adler's first exercises was to make her young students in New York go to Central Park and bring back twenty different shades of green. Just as Van Gogh used many shades of brown from the lightest beige to the darkest shade of brown before black to interpret a specific fence and bring it to life, and just as the green in Central Park is actually many shades of green, the diversity of human behavior offers you many specific choices of intention to make your characters live.

Now here is a controversial point. Some actors, directors, and teachers don't like the term or the idea of *intention*. They fear that if you pick an intention to overcome your obstacle, it will put you in your head. In other words, they fear that you'll start to be mental instead of connecting emotionally to the scene. But that's a misconception. Clearly, as an actor playing a character, you must try to accomplish getting what you want in some specific way. That's what moves the story forward and makes it interesting to the audience: the *ways* you try to get what you want. Call the ways you do that *intentions,* call them *actions,* or call them *"spinach,"* as the excellent director and teacher Bobby Lewis did to show that what you call it doesn't matter. It all comes down to active doings, behaviors toward other characters to remove obstacles and get what you want. Believe me, you do it in life every day.

If you read scripts carefully, you will see that most of them lay out a map of what characters say and do to get their objectives. By breaking down a script into given circumstances, a superobjective, objectives, obstacles, and intentions, you make your own personal map of the text, and that is the basis for your interpretation of a role. It will tell you your point of view toward your lines and it will help you to discover behaviors for your character. Those who reject the idea of intention fear that it will keep you from having spontaneous reactions in the moment. Being spontaneous in the moment is vital to good acting. I don't see a conflict between having an intention and being spontaneous, because *within the exploration of the intention,* you are living and responding moment to moment. As an actor, I want to see *in performance* if what I'm doing is working on the other character to get me what I want. *This means observing moment to moment to see how they're reacting to the active intentions I'm playing.* That's what I mean by exploration. You make your choice of active intentions in rehearsal and then you are alive in the moment during performance to see how they are working on the other characters.

In rehearsal you are exploring the most interesting and provocative ways to reveal your character *by the way they try to achieve their objectives.* How does your character manipulate the world to get what they want? I'm not using the word *manipulate* in a pejorative way; consciously or unconsciously, we all try to manipulate the world from the moment we're born. We have to find ways to get our needs met, and from childhood on we're learning what works best for us. These are the choices you're looking for as active intentions in a scene; they make it not only clear but involving and entertaining to the audience watching.

A warning: a lot of you reading this book, I believe, will be excited by these techniques, but you could make an error and *show* your active intention in an overstated way. That's when a director or a casting director says, "That's too theatrical. You're acting too much." When they say that, they don't mean to stop your intention, they mean that you should stop *leaning* on it, stop *showing* everyone your point of view. For example, let's say in a realistic play or film you're *complimenting somebody* and to do so you jut your head forward, smile maniacally, and bat your eyes; you're leaning on your intention instead of simply letting it live within you. This kind of broad exhibition of your point of view, if done truthfully—meaning that you're doing it for an emotionally justified reason and not just trying to be funny—can work in farce or broad comedy. We certainly see it in sitcoms every night. But much film, theater, and television is realistic, and if you advertise or wear your point of view more theatrically than you would in life, it pushes the audience away. Uta Hagen said it brilliantly in a class: "Don't show me your point of view. Have one."

When you *commit* to a character's given circumstances and objectives and to your choice of intentions, that commitment will stir your emotions and make your character live. But all characters live differently, depending on who they are. Some characters are emotionally explosive and express themselves in very overt ways. Others hold their emotions in. You have to know what kind of person your character is so that you can know the amount of emotional intensity you need to bring your character alive. If you're too intense for the way the character is written, the director, particularly in film, might say, "Give me less" or "Make it subtler"; they don't mean "Invest less"; once again they mean "Show me less." If you're not intense enough, they'll say, "It needs more edge" or "more energy" or "more anger"; in other words they will talk in *results*—which is to say they will give you a specific emotion or quality they want you to play but they won't tell you the internal work you must do to get there. You may not like directors talking in result terms, but they will, and your job is to translate what they mean and know how to do the internal work so that it will feel real to you.

You will be grateful when a director talks to you in terms of intention instead of results, when they tell you *to pick a fight with the character, to annoy them, to romance them,* or *to soothe them*. These directions are much more actable than "Be angry," "Be sour," "Be sexy," or "Be relaxed." You have to pick an intention because of its emotional heat; that's what makes intentions so actable. Sometimes in a play you won't find the most provocative intention until you're in rehearsal examining the material. In a film, because often you don't have rehearsal time, you'll have to do this on your own as homework and then the director may give you an adjustment between takes. And yes, sometimes you'll do a great take in a movie and seemingly throw all of your previous ideas out the window and go with an impulse that feels right at the moment. But later as you watch yourself in the scene on the screen, you will see that you're playing intentions, listening to the other characters, and that the scene has emotional heat as you seek your objective. What brought you to that moment of freedom during filming was the exploration you did before you got to the set as well as things you discovered while you were there—the other actors' energy and choices, the set and costumes, the director's input—and an intense, intuitive understanding of the character and their circumstances.

Sometimes you'll find that your intuitive understanding of your character is so strong that you make effective choices instinctively. That's your raw talent and your affinity for *certain* roles—but not *all* roles. The techniques and tools I'm giving you are to help you be better when you're already good and good when your intuition alone isn't enough to tell you what to do.

Hunt for interesting choices of intention, choices that are specific to your character and to the text and that stir you toward interesting, provocative human behavior. But make sure you don't cement a choice too soon. A more specific and active choice may occur to you as you work on a scene. Explore the full range of possible intentions: *treating the other person like a servant; inspiring them; flattering them; treating them like royalty; tickling their funny bone; hitting them with the knife of truth; confronting their lie; persecuting them; threatening them as though they were a little puppy.* I'm using these examples because they are active verbs and phrases that should excite you to behavior toward other characters that will help you eradicate obstacles and achieve what you want in a scene while revealing your character in an interesting way. When you commit to these intentions fully, you will feel creatively alive, because your body will join you with physical impulses and behavior as you use them to pursue your objectives. As you explore an intention, commit to it fully, because it's only by committing fully that you'll find what works best. You'll feel when you've found the choice that sizzles when the scene becomes so active and involving for you that you've stopped trying to act and are just living.

Remember: an intention is never an end in itself; it is a means to overcome an obstacle and get what you want.

Be aware that your acting partners are doing specific things to *you* to get what *they* want, and when they do, it's going to create an absolute need in you to treat them in a new way based on how you're being treated. This is one of the ways in which you discover intentions in rehearsal. Some actors try never to do things the same way twice. They pride themselves on finding different ways to achieve their wants in every performance. That can be very exciting, and that's one way of doing it. Other actors will stay with the choices—and discover them anew every night or in every take. Neither way is better than the other. What remains a constant is that some choices are more powerful for a text than others. Remember: the play or film script is what's important to deliver.

Phrasing your intentions in the vernacular of the particular character you're playing—using their words and speech pattern, based on their social and economic background—will make similar intentions quite different. Here's an example: George in *Who's Afraid of Virginia Woolf?* might try *to dryly critique Martha,* while Stanley in *Streetcar* tries *to shove Blanche's face in her own shit.* Both men are trying to dominate women but the tonality of their intentions is unique to each man. Describing your character's intentions in words that *they would use* will help to excite your emotion and imagination. It will also connect you deeply to the specific script and character you're working on.

Another way of looking at intentions is that they are created to help you send ideas to another character. *Now hear this: acting is about sending ideas to other people—not just* emotions *but* ideas. It was a revelation to me in Stella Adler's class when she informed us that ideas are alive and that good writers are filled with ideas that they are sending to the audience through their characters. So you want to be clear about and fascinated by the ideas you're sending. Often the other characters' ideas are obstacles to your getting what you want, and ideas you are sending to them are your attempts to overcome these obstacles. *How* you send the idea is your active intention. You might *try to seduce another character with an idea,* you might *try to intimidate them with it,* you might *try to shame their idea out of existence,* or *to humiliate* or *denigrate their idea with your idea.* It's the active intention you choose to send your idea with that makes your idea live instead of being just a bunch of words.

For a real education in sending ideas about human beings, class, politics, and the desire to find the God in man, read George Bernard Shaw. His play *Mrs. Warren's Profession* is about a woman who runs a brothel and the daughter she raises. The mother believes there's nothing wrong with being the madam of a brothel if it gives her independence and enough money to educate her daughter; her daughter believes that her mother should have spent more time with her during her childhood and not made money off the flesh of innocent girls. There's a great scene at the end of the play in which mother and daughter fight out their differing points of view. It is deeply emotional and wrenching, and the ideas are electrified by Shaw's compassion for both characters' perspectives and his showing how they can never truly love each other because they can never change the ideas they see as integral to their identities.

I've found that the best way to work with intentions is to make notes on the side of your script. Intentions will change during a scene and writing them in the margin lets you see at a glance how you've scored the scene for your character, just as a conductor may make notes in a musical score. As you analyze your character's dialogue, you may discover, "Oh, they're beginning *to criticize the other character;* they're beginning *to make fun of them;* they're beginning *to court them.*" One intention may last as briefly as a line or two or as long as an entire scene.

A classic scene in Martin Scorsese's mob picture *Goodfellas* offers an incredible use of delicate, incisively, surgically picked intentions that in one part of the scene change from line to line. In this scene, Joe Pesci as Tommy DeVito says to Ray Liotta as Henry Hill, "How am I funny? What the fuck is so funny about me?" At first, DeVito's kind of *joking with Hill;* then, as he keeps demanding an answer, the intention changes to *softly confronting him,* then to *toying with him like a cat with a mouse.* Then it veers toward *threatening him.* The fact that he doesn't go to an all-out attack is what makes it so scary, because we sense the violence of Tommy's internal life, and we've seen him be psychopathic in the past, so we're waiting for him to go out of control. But he won't, because his objective is to terrify and humiliate Hill in front of his friends, which he does effectively by *torturing him with implied violence,* as if he's not even worth the energy of a real fight. Pesci didn't have the biggest role in the film, but the way he terrorized the young mobster is indelible.

You have to be sure to examine the *subtext*—the emotions that are taking place beneath the surface—to know which intentions are appropriate for a line. You can't always take a line literally. The character may say "I respect you," but it may really be a threat or a put-down or a way of making a sexual conquest. *The intention is picked in order to make the other character feel or do something that you want.* You can only determine if your choice of intention will work by testing to see if the script supports it and trying it in rehearsal.

The better the writing, the more interesting the obstacles and the more interesting your choices of intentions can be. In Tennessee Williams's plays, he gives you tremendous obstacles and juicy possibilities for picking creative active intentions. As Maggie walks into *Cat on a Hot Tin Roof,* she's already walking in with one obstacle, which is her soiled dress. Her dress has been hit by a hot buttered biscuit and she says to her husband, Brick, "Brick! Brick— One of those no-neck monsters hits me with a hot buttered biscuit, so I have t' change!" "Wha'd you say, Maggie? Water was on s'loud I couldn't hear ya," Brick responds. "Well, I—I just remarked that— One of th' no-neck monsters messed up m'lovely lace dress so I got t' change. . . ." Williams has given her a physical problem to overcome the minute she enters the play. Then there's the obstacle of Brick's not hearing her, which makes her repeat herself. Soon she reveals, "I tell you I got so nervous at that table tonight I thought I would throw back my head and utter a scream you could hear across the Arkansas border an' parts of Louisiana and Tennessee," so she's filled with rage and frustration at the obstacles she's gone through even before she got to the bedroom where Brick is.

What are her intentions with these lines? She is *tattling on and ridiculing* the no-neck monsters that belong to Brick's brother and sister-in-law, whom she resents because their having so many children means that Brick's father will probably leave them his considerable money since the old man wants heirs. She's also *announcing her aloneness and vulnerability without Brick* since she had to be at his father's birthday dinner by herself while Brick was in their bedroom getting drunk. She's *pleading for help* by telling him what she had to put up with, and underneath it all is the scream, "I *need* you to help me!" Maggie desperately needs Brick to help her accomplish her superobjective *to have so much money that I never have to fear being poor for the rest of my life.*

As the scene develops, Maggie wants to get Brick to sign a birthday card for his father and join the party; she wants him to make love to her so she can have a child; she wants to get him to stop drinking; so how does she do that? Through active intentions. As she speaks, she *tries to seduce him* by showing her body (she takes off her soiled dress and parades around in her slip); she tries to make him jealous *by preening while revealing that other men, including his father, find her sexually attractive* ("I sometimes suspect that Big Daddy sometimes harbors a little unconscious 'letch' fo' me"); and by literally *telling Brick that she's deeply lonely and wants him to make love to her* and *by revealing to him that the depth of her desperation would drive her to suicide if he doesn't fulfill her* ("You know, if I thought that you would never, never, *never* make love to me again—I would go downstairs to the kitchen and pick out the longest and sharpest knife I could find, and stick it straight into my heart, I swear that I would!").

Brick is her major obstacle; he is the brick wall to her getting what she wants. And therefore in this scene she uses a lot of intentions to break through this brick wall—she *attacks,* she *warns,* she *complains,* she *reminisces,* she *educates him about what's going on in the family that will keep them from financial security,* she *insults him,* she *damns him,* she *begs him,* she *taunts him.* Again, the script is *not* about Maggie's desire for sex; it's about her desperate hunger for financial security. Sex is one of the intentions that Maggie uses to remove the brick wall so that she won't be poor. She may want sex because it will make her feel less lonely—in fact, as I've said, she may even love Brick—but that is secondary to her needing sex from Brick in order to produce an heir. Sex is, above all, a means to her super-objective. The clue that Maggie's objective in this scene is to break through Brick's wall is that when she finally produces rage in Brick, she says to him, "That's the first time I've heard you raise your voice in a long time, Brick. A crack in the wall?—Of composure?"

The way Williams wrote the scene, the physical obstacle of the soiled dress isn't just stage *business* (physical activity for the character), it is related to Maggie's superobjective and the obstacles that Brick creates. She tells him she has to change and that she wants to look pretty and fresh because she wants Brick to see her as other men, including Big Daddy, Brick's father, see her. While in her slip and *flirting with and taunting* Brick (intentions), Maggie remarks, "I think it's mighty fine that that ole fellow, on the doorstep of death, still takes in my shape with what I think is deserved appreciation!" Maggie is full of humor and she is her own entertainment center; she has to be, because she's so alone in this family.

One of the intentions I think is very usable for an actress playing Maggie is *wanting to irritate Brick, trying get under his skin, picking at him, nagging him*—because that's what she's really doing: *trying to get under his skin in order to make him itch*. If she can irritate him and make him fight, they can begin to live before life passes them both by. She knows if he drinks himself to death, she's lost. In order to personalize Maggie's intentions, you have to find the words that move you to compelling behavior. For example, you might not choose the intention *to irritate;* the words *to get under his skin* might carbonate you more. Now go further. What are you going to do *to irritate him* or *to get under his skin?* Are you going *to allure him? To pick at his scab? To challenge him? To bait him? To unfold your flower before him? To battle for Brick even though he hates me for it?* Brick's possible bisexuality and his obsession with Skipper's death are part of the wall he presents to Maggie, and it takes courage and pluckiness for Maggie to serve herself up sexually to Brick when he shows no sign of wanting the meal. That's what makes choosing intentions for Maggie so creative.

While Maggie's obstacle is Brick's wall, sometimes characters face their own *inner obstacles* to getting what they want. Inner obstacles include, among others, shyness, fear, stubbornness, being thin-skinned, and lack of self-worth.

At the start of *As Good as It Gets,* as we've seen, Carol's whole reason for living is to keep her son alive. She is terrified he will die because of his severe asthma. Besides the external obstacles of her son's illness and her need for money, Carol has an inner obstacle: to overcome her terror of her son's possible death. She does this by staying constantly busy as a waitress and as her son's live-in nurse. When I worked with Helen, we talked about a critical point in the script when Melvin comments to Carol, "We are all going to die soon—I will—you will—and it sure sounds like your son will." This is the worst thing Melvin could ever say, because he touches the terror inside of her and threatens her superobjective, which is *to save my son's life at any cost.* When Carol hears Melvin's unbelievably insensitive remark, the look on Helen's face as Carol is heartbreaking, icy fury. This actress knew what her son meant to her; it was in her heart. Carol says to Melvin, "If you ever mention my son again, you will never be able to eat here again. Do you understand? Give me some sign that you understand or leave now. Do you understand me, you crazy fuck? Do you?" It's a terrific line, but the life that Helen brought to it is almost shocking to watch. What Melvin says ignites the terror that she keeps trying to stave off by working hard, by taking care of her son, by making sure he's eating and taking his medication, by doting on him as if doting on him will keep him alive. In answering Melvin as she does, Carol's intention seems to be *to viciously threaten him like a mother lion protecting her cub.* It is primitive and dangerous.

Remember, an intention is chosen to create a specific emotion in the other character, and in this case it is to fill Melvin with the terror of complete and total abandonment. Carol knows Melvin is an obsessive-compulsive, and she is threatening him in his most vulnerable area. She is the one waitress he feels comfortable with in the frenzied, chaotic world he is trying to control, so her saying she'd never wait on him again is psychologically big stuff. The intention that Helen brings to the delivery of the line communicates the threat so powerfully that it arouses terror in Melvin's heart, which was Carol's desire.

I learned about inner obstacles alone in my apartment in Manhattan at 2:00 A.M. on a freezing winter's night. As fate would have it, I happened to have been working on the part of Treplyev in *The Seagull.* In the scene I was doing, Treplyev has just heard that Nina, whom he loves, is back in town. It's a cold and windy night and as Treplyev tries to work on his writing, he keeps on criticizing himself and comparing himself to the man Nina prefers to him, the more successful writer Trigorin. When I sat down to prepare for the next day's acting class, I had just come home from my night job. I was exhausted after hours on my feet slinging tacos and margaritas (I'd been promoted from dishwashing). I didn't want to work on anything, I wanted to go to sleep, but it was *The Seagull* and I loved it, so I had to. There I was at my kitchen table trying to figure out a way to do the scene where Treplyev is trying to figure out a way to be a good writer but is battling his inner obstacles of feeling inadequate and envious. I thought to myself, "I can't do this scene. Tom [an actor my teacher thought was particularly gifted] would be great in it. It would be easy for him. But I don't know how to play this soliloquy, and I'm not a writer, how do I hold the pen? What do I do with the notebook? How do I show my frustration?"

Suddenly I froze and said out loud, "Oh, my God, *you are him, RIGHT NOW!* Treplyev is trying to overcome his inner obstacles of self-criticism and jealousy so he can write and you are doing the same thing in trying to understand how to play him!" It was such an epiphany for me! I was struggling with the very thing I needed to play the part! Suddenly I knew how to hold the pen with tense fingers, to cross words out that I didn't like, rip the page out of the notebook and throw it on the floor and bury my face in my hands with helplessness. I didn't have to *act* Treplyev, I *was* Treplyev. I even had the exact weather outside my apartment that Chekhov describes, bitterly cold and windy, and as I worked on the scene I could hear the windows rattling.

I want to talk about another film I worked on, *Boys Don't Cry,* because to play the role of Teena Brandon, the outsider protagonist at the center of the movie, Hilary Swank had to find creative choices of intentions to try to overcome both external and inner obstacles. Teena, a young woman, wants to have a sex change operation. Before she undergoes the surgery and hormone replacement, she begins to pass herself off as a young man, using the name Brandon Teena. Her superobjective is *to live my life as a man and find a woman to love;* the great obstacle is that she's not a man, that she has a vagina instead of a penis. Although Brandon dresses as a boy, she faces the obstacle of trying to get people to believe that she *is* a boy. Since she has no beard and has to tape down her breasts, she's always afraid that someone will find out. So she has the external obstacle of her physical body and the inner obstacle of her fear of being discovered. She tries to assuage her fear by checking out the reactions of the men around her to her masculinity. Her intentions are *to appear masculine and athletic, to joke as one of the guys, to treat the women gallantly*, and *to protect herself from prying eyes.* As it turns out, the character's fear is well founded; when the men around her discover that she is, in fact, a young woman, they savagely murder her. The story of *Boys Don't Cry* is relatively simple, but the given circumstances are so powerful that committing to them fully, and finding her superobjective, objectives, obstacles, and intentions made Hilary's performance memorable and deeply moving.

An intention is *always* active. Even a character who is passive is active in their intentions. One mistake I've seen actors make with Brick in *Cat on a Hot Tin Roof* is identifying him as passive and playing the first act in a somnambulistic, introverted way because Brick is drinking heavily. But Brick's obstacle in that act is that he's not drunk enough to feel what he calls "the click"—the signal that he is finally totally turned off. In other words, Brick is sober enough to feel things he doesn't want to; he is, in every sense of the word, both externally and internally, uncomfortable. His effort to drink enough is accompanied by several active intentions. These include *trying to keep Maggie at a distance by patronizing her while half-heartedly engaging her; trying to deal with the irritation caused by the cast on his broken foot; trying to ignore the sexual bait that Maggie keeps throwing at him by shaming her for being open and forward in her enjoyment of sex.*

An interesting sidelight is that as Brick talks about waiting for "the click" of deep inebriation, he may be experiencing another inner obstacle as well. Later in the play, Brick reveals that he feels guilty because he hung up on his friend Skipper, and soon after, Skipper drank and drugged himself to death. As an actor playing Brick, when you talk about waiting for "the click," you might also play the inner obstacle of hearing the click as you hung up the phone after your best friend has sobbed his guts out to you, proclaiming his love, right before he goes on a fast slide to death.

Jules Feiffer's play *Little Murders,* written in the 1960s, which was so prescient about urban violence in regard to guns, was made into a film starring Elliott Gould as Alfred Chamberlain, an acutely passive photographer, who interestingly enough is fascinated by taking photos of shit (literally). Patsy, the woman who loves him, can never get him to feel anything emotional or to be expressive toward her. Finally, out of frustration, she yells at him, "You're a wall! You won't fight! You don't even blink! Will somebody tell me why I love you so much?" His character *passionately* doesn't want to feel. So what is his superobjective? *To stay happy and quiet and gentle and loving, with no ripples in the water,* which enrages his fiancée, Patsy. His intention, therefore, is not to be passive but rather the active intentions *to maintain my well-being and calm* and *to soothe others and give them understanding and patience.*

The film *The Hours* presents illuminating examples of the relationships between objectives, obstacles, and intentions and of how important it is to pick intentions you can play. The film is about three women— Clarissa Vaughan (Meryl Streep), Laura Brown (Julianne Moore), and Virginia Woolf (Nicole Kidman)—who are all trying to deal with depression, and who are all connected by Virginia Woolf's novel *Mrs. Dalloway*, which focuses on a day in the life of a woman who is planning a party while trying to come to terms with the pain in her life.

Julianne Moore's character, Laura, is another one of the rare cases where there's a double superobjective. Laura is a housewife in a California suburb in 1949. In the first part of the movie, her superobjective is *to try to find a reason to continue living the life I have chosen.* She has different objectives connected to this spine. One of them is to bake a cake for her husband's birthday, which she does with difficulty. Another objective is to be a good mother to her young son, Richard. When Laura says to her son with anger, "What do you want from me?" you know she's incapable of mothering. Her obstacles to all of these things are her depression and her deep guilt about her misery with being a wife and mother.

Being a wife and mother is clearly an act that Laura is working hard to perform. She starts distracted; we can see through Moore's performance that Laura is being torn apart by what she is attempting because she is in such deep conflict. She's trying to make her husband and child believe that she's there with them, while something else is pulling at her. She's fighting to find a way to live because she wants to die. But you can't act *to hide a death wish,* and you can't act "misery." Misery is an emotional mood, and mood spelled backward is *doom!* You *can't* and should *never* try to act a mood. Again, you have to find active behavior.

As Laura, you can hide a death wish by *trying to mother my child sweetly and kindly,* by *trying to encourage my husband,* and by *trying to experience a mother-and-child bond by making a cake together.* But underlying all of this is her emotional condition, which is despair. As an actress, you prepare emotionally for despair and try to overcome it with active intentions. So the steps are preparing yourself emotionally for a deep sadness (which is your inner obstacle) and then actively playing intentions to try to overcome it. Remember, you can't *play* an emotional condition; you *have* an emotional condition, and because you have that condition, you *try to overcome it with active doings* (intentions).

If you were playing Laura, one way of giving yourself a sense of being distracted by despair and suicidal thoughts would be a preoccupation with morbidity, which could be the image of seeing yourself in a coffin. You would have to create a specific image of the particular coffin you're in, the dress you're wearing, and the look of peaceful resignation on your dead face that is attractive to you and keeps pulling you back to the thought of death, which is your escape. You work on this image as homework. Then you feed yourself this image in your mind's eye while you engage in your active intentions with your son and husband. It will be a distraction and it will add a color of darkness and depression and a sense that you're not quite present in the scene—which in most other characters and circumstances as an actor would be a disaster. The stronger your image of despair, the more you must commit to your active intentions, and the more you fail at them—which is correct for the character of Laura Brown—the more you will make her three-dimensional, emotionally rich, and disturbing, as Moore did. (I'll talk more about techniques for preparing emotional conditions in the three chapters "Inner Imagery," "Battling Acting Teachers," and "Emotion on Demand.")

The Hours contains an extraordinary scene with a clear example of playing an active intention over an emotional condition that the character doesn't want anyone else to see. Laura is sitting in the bathroom at night, weeping, holding her hand over her mouth, and when her husband calls her to come to bed, she makes her voice sound happy so that her husband will believe she's ready to make love and be in a normal marriage. Over her despair, her active intentions are *to convince him with her voice that she's happy, loving, and involved with him.* The fact that she kissed a woman in a romantic way that very day makes this even more poignant, since she's on her way to making love with a husband that she has no true connection to.

Once Laura drops her son off with a neighbor and goes to a hotel by herself, she is resolute about ending her life. We see her in the hotel room with multitudes of sleeping pills and as she falls asleep, she dreams of being enveloped in water, which is her release from the emotional pain. Laura doesn't take the pills that day, but we assume that she will eventually. When she reappears at the end of the film, as a much older woman, we realize that she abandoned her son and husband and found a way to go on living. Laura's superobjective changed. She did not meet her original superobjective *to try to find a reason to continue living the life I have chosen.* Her new superobjective became *to go on living and try to forgive myself for my failures to my son and husband.* She has gone on living, but as the film makes clear, she hasn't forgiven herself.

I'd like to share with you an interpretive technique for finding active intentions that Helen Hunt and I developed while she was working on an audition for the role of Isabella in Shakespeare's *Measure for Measure.* This technique will help you discover unique active intentions and different nuances and tones for a scene rather than settling for choices that are mundane. Start by choosing one active verb that you think is right for a specific moment in a scene, then find all the synonyms in the thesaurus for that verb and try out the dialogue as one by one you play the different possibilities. Each word will create different emotions within you and different physical impulses that will translate into behavior. You'll find that this is a gold mine of inspiration!

When Helen and I analyzed *Measure for Measure,* we started considering different intentions for Isabella. Isabella has many obstacles in the play. Primary among them is that her brother has been imprisoned. The only way to stop his execution is for Isabella to sacrifice her virginity to an amoral and manipulative official. To make her dilemma worse, poor Isabella is a nun (Shakespeare doesn't kid around with obstacles). Helen and I became excited about the possible active intentions for Isabella to overcome the obstacle of the official's demanding her sexual favors and the further obstacle of her brother wanting her to give in so that he won't die. At one point we were struggling to find the right active verbs to describe the choices for Isabella's intentions. We found two verbs—*to demand, to beg*—but Helen said that although they were accurate, they didn't incite her creatively. They weren't the right words to ignite her. That's when we thought of using the thesaurus, and we were thrilled to find synonym after synonym to choose from.

For *to demand,* the thesaurus lists, among other choices, *to claim as a right, to order, to extort, to seek, to ask, to call for, to insist on, to importune, to clamor [for], to cry, to supplicate, to entreat, to invoke, to press, to urge, to exact, to impose, to require, to stand in need of, to call for, to ache for.* Among the synonyms for *to beg* are *to appeal to, to implore, to beseech, to entreat, to plead, to pray, to crave, to petition.* Helen found the right verb for her, and you have to find the right verb or verb phrase for you.

This is what the Van Gogh fence is about: all the different tones of color you can choose from to bring something to life. Don't resist using the thesaurus because you think it's an intellectual exercise; words were invented to express feelings, that's why we have language. But you have to find the words that are emotional for you.

If you get caught in your acting feeling redundant, feeling that you're playing the same notes too often—which occurs especially with long, intricate scenes or monologues—if you feel that a scene is not going into full ignition and rising to the height that you think the writing should and can, choosing and exploring new active intentions can offer you new vistas for a stirring performance. Remember, the thesaurus is always there in your back pocket for your creative use.

4

Stakes: What Is It Worth to You?

How important is it for your character to get what they want? What lengths will your character go to to get it? What will happen if they don't get it? These are your character's *stakes*. In the chapter on superobjective and objectives, I mentioned several characters who want to achieve their dreams "at any cost." These words describe what the stakes are for them: *at any cost*.

Remember when you wanted a certain pair of roller skates, or when you demanded that your parents let you go to an R-rated movie or to a certain party? It almost seemed like life or death. It caused you to cry, to scream in rage, to slam a door, to curse your parents, to say that you would die if you didn't get it. What about being invited to that party or being accepted into the right crowd in school? The intensity of your feelings about these desires was an expression of what the stakes were for you. It expressed your passionate wanting, what you felt you had to gain by getting what you wanted, or lose if you didn't get it.

As you move into your adult life, your desires may change but the stakes only get higher: that wife or husband; that important job; that house; that car; mending your relationships, if they're in conflict, with your parents and siblings. If you're unlucky enough to get into debt, how painful your life is as the debts threaten to sink you. Much more importantly and sadly, you may want to save a parent's life or save a marriage that's dying, but be helpless to do so.

Look to your life and the lives of those around you and you will see what having high stakes means in a play or film. As you explore a script, ask yourself, how far would my character go to achieve their goals? Would they sacrifice their pride and self-respect? Would they kill? Would they die? Would they rob, cheat, ruin other people's lives? What do they *do*—again, not *say* but *do*—in the script? This tells you what the stakes are for them.

The reason I object to teachers, writers, or critics saying that a character or a performance is bigger than life is that *nothing* is bigger than life. Look at the Kennedys. If someone wrote the story of the Kennedys, starting with Joseph and ending with John Jr.'s and his wife's deaths, and all the tragedies in between—JFK's assassination, Bobby's assassination, Chappaquiddick, the alcoholism, drug addiction, infidelities—you'd say it had to be fiction, it could never happen in life. But it did. And in front of the world's eyes. Talk about drama, talk about high stakes.

The film *Lady Sings the Blues* is the story of jazz legend Billie Holiday. There is a scene where Billie Holiday (Diana Ross) is sitting on a toilet, trying to give herself a shot of heroin. When the man she loves (Billy Dee Williams) tries to stop her, she grabs a straight razor. That's how badly a heroin addict wants that shot, badly enough to threaten to kill the man she loves. These are the stakes.

But high stakes aren't just important in dramas; the intensity of high stakes also gives comedy its charge. In Neil Simon's *Plaza Suite,* George C. Scott played Roy Hubley, the father of the bride, as though he were King Lear. The reason that it worked so brilliantly and was so terribly funny was George C. Scott's and Neil Simon's decision to raise the stakes of Hubley and his wife's desire for a proper wedding for their daughter. To the Hubleys, it's not some casual desire, something they would just *like* to have; it's something that they desperately *must* achieve to hold their heads up in the society they live in. And, as Roy never lets us forget, they also stand to lose a huge amount of money if the wedding doesn't come off.

I want to talk for a moment about the phrase *life or death*. It's too easy to say the stakes are life or death without asking yourself, what do you really mean? When Stella Adler taught *Hamlet* at the Yale School of Drama, the students kept asking, "Why doesn't he just kill Claudius? Why does he just talk and talk and talk?" Stella brought in half a cow carcass, gave each of the students a butcher knife and said to them, "Now stab into that." They got to experience firsthand how difficult it was to cut through the muscle, the bone, and the flesh of that raw carcass. After they'd struggled for a while, she said to them, "It's not so easy to pick up a knife and kill someone, is it?" She made them take responsibility for the terror of committing an act of violence. After that experience, they saw Hamlet's anguish and indecision in a completely different way.

What are the stakes for Hamlet? Again, life and death; he cannot go on unless he solves and avenges the murder of his father. It's the life-or-death stakes for Hamlet that put him in the position of feeling he must kill Claudius once he's sure Claudius is his father's murderer. Yes, Hamlet puts his dilemma (whether he has the right to kill Claudius) in philosophical terms, but he feels the life-or-death importance of his problem in his gut; it takes over his brain and his heart and leaves room for nothing else. He literally perceives his situation as, "If I don't solve this problem, I will die."

Sometimes when we're young, our lack of experience of ourselves and others, and sometimes, too, our lack of true empathy and compassion, make us arrogant simply because we don't realize the difficulty of other people's lives. Don't ever judge or underestimate or dismiss a character you play because at first reading the character's concerns seem unworthy to you or you can't immediately relate to them; respect the character's life experience and find a way to identify with their plight. Every character deserves as much respect as you do. Don't cheat them by judging them. This is one of the ways that stakes can help you. If you analyze the script and come to understand your character's emotional stakes, you'll play them with depth and insight, whether the story takes place in the sixteenth century or the twenty-first. For the actor, every play or film takes place *now. Compassion* and *empathy,* actors, these are the keys for getting to the soul of your character.

When you're playing royalty, you may say, "But I'm a middle-class Jew from Encino." (Well, that's what I would say.) But you can look at the life of Prince William of England and imagine living with the pressure and the pomp and circumstance surrounding him. See how fate dealt this boy the heartbreaking blow of his parents' divorce followed by his mother's death. Imagine yourself going through that and then being watched by the world to see if you measure up. You'll have more compassion for Hamlet.

In Noël Coward's classic comedy *Private Lives,* Amanda and Elyot, an immensely rich and glamorous upper-class English couple, were married and got a divorce. When the play opens, each of them has just remarried and, although they don't know it, they and their new spouses have just checked into adjoining rooms at the same hotel. They both step out onto their balconies and see each other—an amazing moment and the start of a wonderful comedy. As soon becomes apparent, Amanda and Elyot can't live with each other but they can't live without each other. How high are the stakes? So high that on the first night of their marriages to other people, they're willing to run away with each other because they suddenly realize that they're still madly in love. Their need for each other is *huge*! It's so great that they're willing to break the hearts of their new spouses, risk facing the problems they have with each other, and break every rule of social decency. Amanda and Elyot are *obsessed* with each other—meaning, literally, that they cannot live without the other. And remember, they can't live with each other, either. The truth is, they are in love with conflict: the clue to the comedy in this timelessly witty play is that the moment they have one minute of happiness, they ruin it.

If you are playing Amanda and Elyot and you don't understand the psychology of their relationship and the high stakes in *Private Lives,* you will make it a boring play—because you'll think it's all about being witty. The play is, of course, witty, but it is not *about* being witty; the play is about passion. If you don't understand that passion shakes these people to the very core, then you can't play the play—because if you don't understand your stakes, then the character can't live with full blood!

In the film *Affliction,* starring the extraordinary Nick Nolte, Wade Whitehouse (Nolte), a sheriff, has an intensely destructive, abusive father, Glen (James Coburn). The stakes for Wade are life or death: one of them has to die in order for the other to live. Ultimately Glen is so cruel and emasculating to his son that Wade finally kills him and sets him on fire. It's like a Greek tragedy; the stakes are huge. To play Wade, you have to understand why those are the stakes; you have to understand that Wade feels that he will die unless he kills his father. Nolte expresses the terrible grief and rage of an abused child who is completely enmeshed with his abuser. He makes us feel this pain and makes us understand why that pain makes the stakes so high that it leads to murder.

Let's look again at Blanche DuBois in *A Streetcar Named Desire*. I've said that the superobjective for Blanche is *to find a safe place*. She's destitute; this is her last chance. As an actress playing Blanche, once you've understood the facts of Blanche's life that make her need for a safe place so intense, your job is to find something within yourself that carbonates these high stakes for you, something that will make Blanche's stakes *live within you*. You must find within yourself the terror of abandonment. There are many ways to do this, which I will begin to explore in the next two chapters, but I'll tell you this much now: think of a little girl being abandoned by her mother, think of how she would scream and cry and beg her not to leave her as she sees her disappearing forever. Then you will understand the depth of Blanche's fear and helplessness. If you don't find that terror within yourself, playing the part will be like playing a piano with the lid over the keys: there will be no music; nothing will resonate.

The difference between a really great performance or even a good performance and a mediocre one is how much the actor makes us feel and care. We in the audience have to feel that we're watching a life being lived in front of us. The actor has to not just *know* the stakes but make us *feel emotionally* how important they are. We may be able to see through Blanche's deceptions, but we still have to want her *to find a safe place;* we have to want to protect her.

Stephen Frears's film *The Grifters* centers on a con artist mother and son, Lilly (Anjelica Huston) and Doug Dillon (John Cusack). How much does Lilly need her son Doug's money so that she can run away and keep herself from being killed? She needs it to the point that she tries to seduce him. She needs it enough to grapple with him for his attaché case full of money, inadvertently smashing a glass that he's holding, and cutting his jugular vein. Lilly doesn't mean to kill her son, but she's willing to accept that she has in order to save her own life. I have rarely seen a braver artistic choice than Huston on all fours as Lilly, making sounds that you associate with a wounded animal, moaning over the death of her child, grabbing the bloody money around his quivering, dying body, and fleeing to her own safety.

The protagonist in the great American comedy *Tootsie* begins the film with one superobjective and then develops a second. At the start of the film, Michael's (Dustin Hoffman's) superobjective is *to be acknowledged as the greatest actor in the world*. His stakes are to do this at almost any cost— the cost being that he becomes an actress, Dorothy, in pursuit of his dream. After he meets Julie (Jessica Lange), his superobjective grows to include *to have a committed love relationship with the love of my life,* and, again, because she is the love of his life, the stakes are truly high.

Early in the film, the desperate Michael is auditioning for a play. When Michael is done with his audition, he waits in anxious anticipation for their response. They say thank you and dismiss him, but Michael, unable to tolerate rejection, will not take no for an answer. He says, "I can do it another way." They say to him, "No, actually we've seen enough. We need someone a little taller." Michael says, "I can be taller." They tell him, "We need someone funnier." He says, "I can be funnier." Finally, out of exasperation, they bluntly say, "You don't understand. We want someone else." Michael's intense resistance to hearing this terrible news shows how high the stakes are for him.

Clearly, in his feelings, his career is at stake. And what is career to him? At the beginning of the film, Michael's career gives him his only sense of whether he's a valuable human being. Do I have value as a person? Do I have a right to be on this earth? At first he answers these questions only in terms of his career because he *isn't* a person, he's an actor. When his agent tells him, "Nobody wants to hire you," he feels his validity is canceled. The stakes are so high that Michael feels the only option that is available so that his acting talent can be appreciated is to pass himself off as a woman, Dorothy, so that he can get a woman's part in a soap opera. And of course the great comic obstacle to his being a woman is that he's a man. And because the subtext is rooted in real pain and humiliation, the farce has all the more energy.

When he becomes Dorothy, and Dorothy becomes a soap opera star, Michael starts to satisfy his desire for a career, which starts to give him a sense of self-worth. But his obstacles in pretending to be a woman increase when he falls in love with Julie and has to pretend to be her girlfriend while at the same time being so hot for her that he can hardly stand it (an inner obstacle). His obstacles further increase when her father, Les (Charles Durning), meeting Dorothy off-camera, gets a crush on her. Michael's performance is not only good as Dorothy, it's great—so much so that it creates new obstacles for him while he's achieving the goal of having his acting talent appreciated now that he's an actress. As Dorothy, some of the intentions he plays are *to demand respect as a woman; to bloom as a delicate but strong Southern flower; to stand up for other women with dignity;* and *to torment the producer* (Dabney Colman) *who has a letch for Julie.* His dual superobjectives—*to be acknowledged as the greatest actor in the world* and *to have a committed love relationship with the love of my life* are at odds with each other, and increase the stakes twice as high, adding to the comedy and to the emotion.

Hoffman, the writers, and the director found that the theme of the movie was: *how a man becomes a better man by becoming a woman*. So in becoming Dorothy, the self-absorbed Michael ultimately starts being aware of others for the first time in his life. This leads him to feel protective toward Julie and toward women in general, because as Dorothy he discovers (and is shocked by) how women are treated. He begins to see Julie as a real person, not just as a sexual object. This is his maturation into being a grown-up, and his sensitive behavior with Julie is in stark contrast to how misogynistically he treated Sandy (Teri Garr) at the opening of the film. Again, when the second superobjective is born and is at war with the first, the stakes raise. Michael has to choose, and he gives up his career success as Dorothy in order to have a chance for love with Julie.

In analyzing the plays and movies in this chapter, I'm sure you noticed that I reviewed the concepts of superobjective, obstacle, and intention. In my thirty-two years of teaching, I've discovered that repetition is absolutely essential to breaking through actors' defense mechanisms. You can hear something a hundred times without ever understanding it if you don't want to—and you may not even be consciously aware that you don't want to. Why wouldn't you want to? Because once you understand how to apply these lessons, you are no longer in the dark and you are responsible for committing fully to any role.

Many people fail because they don't set their sights high enough and raise their own artistic stakes. So I'd like to break through any fear that you may have and help you really learn the craft. When you do, you will give something to the audience rather than waiting for somebody to give you your dream of fame and fortune. If repetition insults your intelligence, I can't help it, since it took me a solid year in an acting class to understand that an objective is what you want and an intention is how you get it. But when I finally understood this, my income skyrocketed by $50,000—that alone should make you feel thrilled by my repetitiveness!

And now that we've discussed the basic tools for script analysis and the first techniques for making interpretive choices, I'm going to show you how to use these tools and techniques to help you audition. I've stressed that it's vital to read the entire script until you understand it thoroughly, but what if the people you're auditioning for give you just one scene? And say you have just ten minutes to look at the scene before you have to read for a part. You can still identify your character's given circumstances, objectives, and obstacles, and choose active intentions, and at least get a sense of your character's stakes. Even in one scene you will find facts about your character. The scene may not tell you much, but it will tell you something, and you have to build your performance on the foundation of the information you have.

Ask yourself:

What does the scene tell me about who my character is: their age, physical condition, or any other defining details, including socioeconomic class, that is vital for the scene to work?

What literally happens to my character in the scene?

Why is my character in this particular scene? What would be missing if I weren't in it?

What does my character actually do in the scene?

Who is my character with?

What is my character's emotional relationship to each person?

What are the other characters' relationships to my character? (If the scene doesn't give you a clear clue to the emotional color of the relationship, use your intuition and create an emotional color for it that you can believe in the given circumstances and in the comic or dramatic tone of the scene. In contemporary texts, the tone can be both drama and comedy at the same time, so you've got to be smart enough to catch, and play, the particular tone of that writer.)

At the beginning of the scene, what's my character's point of view? Hostile? Loving? Friendly? Competitive? Supportive? Humorous?

How and why does it change, if it does?

What do I want (what's my objective)?

How high are the stakes?

What's standing between me and what I want (what's my obstacle)?

What does my character do to try to overcome it (what are my intentions)?

Answering these questions helps you to make choices about your interpretation to help bring the character to life. The following chapters will give you additional tools and techniques to bring to any audition or performance. Above all, trust your impulses and intuition. Fly with them in the audition. Don't waste your time worrying. Be creatively active. There is a complete list of questions on page 305 to help you prepare for a full performance or when you have a longer time to prepare for an audition. The more times you go through these questions for different parts, the more your technique will grow.

5

INNER IMAGERY: THE LIFE WITHIN

In the previous chapters we've analyzed in technical ways how to break down a text. These tools will work for every role you ever play. We've also started to look at interpretation, which includes choosing your own way of expressing your character's superobjective and active intentions. Script analysis helps you digest the script so that you understand it as the writer wrote it. The interpretive choices you make, including how you express your superobjective and active intentions, come from how the script affects you personally and how it fires up your imagination. The next step is to use your imagination to fill in the flesh and blood of the character. This is what helps you create an *internal life* for that character that makes the person you're playing live.

What do I mean by an internal life? I mean the thoughts, feelings, memories, and inner decisions that may not be spoken. When we look into the eyes of actors giving fully realized performances, we can see them thinking. We're interested in what they're experiencing that may never be spoken, that quality of nonverbal expression—which is as much a part of the characters as breathing and as real as what they say and do. This is their internal life. It helps us believe in the characters and care about them.

How do you create that internal life? One way is through *inner imagery*—your internal pictures that play through your mind as you speak.

If you ask me, "Where did you go to high school?" my inner movie starts playing. Birmingham High School in Van Nuys, California, was built as a military hospital during World War II and the hallways were sloped to accommodate soldiers in wheelchairs. By the time I got there, the walls were painted a bright shade of coral. It was a combined junior high and high school, so when you walked down those sloping halls, you saw little kids in seventh grade and older teenagers who were almost adults. It was so full of hormones I don't know how it didn't just explode. As you can see, my images of Birmingham High are very specific. And they're not just abstract images, they affect me sensorially—I can *see, touch, taste, hear,* and *smell* them—and they affect me emotionally as well. If I talk about Birmingham High, everything I say and how I say it is colored by what I see in my mind's eye.

In acting, if you have the line, "I went to Birmingham High School and I almost threw up every day," and you don't have an inner image for it, the line won't have cellular resonance. I'll tell you what I mean by cellular resonance. Inner imagery is the thing that makes the audience plug in to their own unconscious. Obviously they're not going to have the same inner imagery that you as an actor have, but because you have inner imagery, it releases theirs. And if there's magic in the process of communicating from stage or screen to the watching audience, a great deal of it is that. When the actor has inner pictures inside them, it releases the unconscious of the audience to show their inner pictures. In other words, it has a cellular resonance for the audience, and this cellular resonance makes the audience believe you're not acting but living. But as you'll see, it's not important if your inner pictures are personal memories or if you make them up out of your imagination; what's important is that you have them.

In Tennessee Williams's play *Sweet Bird of Youth,* which was made into a film that I've listed on your *required* video viewing, a fading movie star, Princess Cosmonopolous (Geraldine Page), has a vivid speech to Chance Wayne (Paul Newman), a younger man on the make. Princess's "comeback film" has just come out and she assumes it was a flop. In her speech, she relives the night of the premiere: "There's a thing called a close-up. The camera advances and you stand still, and your head, your face, is caught in the frame of the picture with a light blazing on it and all your terrible history screams while you smile. . . . After that close-up, they gasped. . . . People gasped. . . . I heard them whisper, their shocked whispers. 'Is that her? Is that her? Her?' . . . I made the mistake of wearing a very elaborate gown to the premiere, a gown with a train that had to be gathered up as I rose from my seat and began the interminable retreat from the city of flames, up, up, up, the unbearably long theater aisle, gasping for breath, and still clutching up the regal white train of my gown, all the way up the forever . . . length of the aisle, and behind me some small unknown man grabbing at me, saying, 'Stay, stay!' At last at the top of the aisle, I turned and struck him, then let the train fall, forgot it, and tried to run down the marble stairs, tripped of course, fell, and rolled, rolled."

As she talks, interspersed with flashbacks of the premiere, we *see* her eyes and, through them, her brain, *remembering* this humiliating nightmare—the gasp at that close-up, her flying through the aisle to get out, the man trying to stop her, her hitting him, her tripping, her rolling down the stairs, "like a sailor's drunk whore . . . Hands, merciful hands without faces, assisted me to get up after, after that? Flight, just flight, not interrupted until I woke up this morning." Williams's writing is intensely visual, intensely emotional, but it is Geraldine Page, through her own inner imagery, who makes it live.

If you've never worked with inner imagery, I suggest you find a monologue with descriptive imagery or a passage from a book that's very descriptive. It's vital for actors to read excellent fiction so they can exercise their ability for making movies in their mind's eye by bringing to life in their imagination what they're reading. A good example is Frank McCourt's sensorially vivid autobiography *Angela's Ashes,* about his childhood spent in poverty in Ireland and New York City. *Angela's Ashes* is filled with richly detailed images. As you read it to yourself, you experience the world McCourt describes, you *see* it, you *smell* it, you *taste* it. Imagine the icy cold streets McCourt walked down as a child, the smell of the boiling potatoes, the dank coldness of the apartment, the nauseating medicinal smell wafting through the rooms, and the unbearable vision of babies' corpses. The images that come into your mind as you read my description right now, and your sensorial responses to them, could be usable as your inner imagery if the description were part of a monologue.

Please don't tell me that you don't want to go to these painful places and see these horrible images because it upsets you too much. Just close this book now and don't be an actor. Why am I saying that? Of course you should be upset. Of course you should weep. As well as laugh your ass off. Acting represents all that human beings experience, and if you want it to be "nice," you will never be a serious communicator of the human experience.

Although not all scripts have the vivid imagery of Williams or McCourt, every script contains dialogue where your character will talk about things they've seen, done, or have otherwise experienced that you must bring to life when you deliver the speech. There are two ways you can do this: you either imagine it as the writer describes it and thereby give the lines an inner life or you find a personal experience of your own that you can match to the writer's imagery to bring it to life. Both can work exceedingly well. I'm going to start with the first technique.

The effectiveness of using imagination to build a powerful belief in the writer's imagery was brought home to me life-changingly when in a class I played Elyot in a scene from Noël Coward's *Private Lives*. Early in the play, Amanda and Elyot, now on their honeymoons with their new spouses, reminisce about their own honeymoon. Amanda asks Elyot, "Do you remember waking up in the morning, and standing on the balcony, looking out across the valley?" Elyot replies: "Blue shadows on white snow, cleanness beyond belief, high above everything in the world. How beautiful it was." I had only seen the hills of Encino dotted with tract homes, so I worked directly with Coward's imagery. I visualized the blue shadows on white snow covering a magnificent mountain that I created from scratch in my mind. As I learned the lines, I allowed that image to join me—to come into my mind's eye—and I did the same thing when I rehearsed with my scene partner. And lo and behold, as I was performing the scene in class, the image joined me vividly and my eyes filled to the brim with tears.

Maxwell Anderson's verse play *Winterset* is about a son avenging what he believes to be the wrongful execution of his father and his father's best friend. It is based on the real story of two Italian immigrants, Sacco and Vanzetti, who were wrongfully executed for murder. In *Winterset*, the son, Mio, has a speech that starts, "When I was four years old we climbed through an iron gate, my mother and I, to see my father in prison. . . ." That's just one sentence, but look at the imagery it offers for you to imagine for your inner movie: "When I was four years old, we climbed through an iron gate, my mother and I, to see my father in prison. . . ." Okay, how big were you at four years old? *Climbed*—there's a word for you! What was it like to *climb through an iron gate*? What did the iron gate look like? Did you touch it? What did it feel like? Were you holding your mother's hand? What was your mother's attitude? What did you feel? What was the terrain like under your feet? You *saw* your father in prison: what did his face look like? What was the position of his body in the cell when you first saw him?

Many actors believe (and are taught) that their imagery *must* come from their own personal life. I think this robs them of the possibility of being deeply moved and affected by something that is different, and perhaps more complex, than their own life experience. Our life experience is powerful, but none of us has lived everything. So when I say imagine it as the author wrote it, I'm inviting you to open the door to emotional riches as young children do automatically, because they have so little experience and such easy access to their imaginations.

Inner imagery is part of our everyday life. We speak to someone and say, "Yesterday I had lunch with my sister," or "I just came back from England," or "We saw this fantastic Bruce Springsteen concert." Those are just lines. What brings them to life for the people who are hearing them are the subliminal images that are waiting to join us in our minds as we describe the events because we actually experienced the things we're talking about. In acting, it doesn't matter whether you *actually* lived it or you imagine it fully, because if you imagine it in detail in your imagination, and you commit to believing it, it is *as if* you've lived it. It's yours forever. When you're sitting at a dinner party hearing a story about someone else's life, what captivates you is not only the words they're saying but the energy in their eyes as they recall it in front of you. Believe me, if they just said the words and didn't join them with their memories, you would be starting to pour yourself that next glass of wine.

Mio's speech in *Winterset* is filled with description, but if you don't have inner pictures for what you're describing, your performance will be dry for the audience. Even with Maxwell Anderson's words, and even if you have a beautiful voice when you say them, what will touch the audience, what will really give you human power, is the chemical-electrical experience of feeding your body a sensorial image and responding to it as you send your ideas. In that sense you are your own acting partner.

Mio says his speech to Miriamne, a beautiful young woman to whom he's attracted but whom he needs to push away, because he feels romance will weaken his desire for vengeance for his father's death. In this speech he tries to express to her why he cannot love:

When I was four years old
we climbed through an iron gate, my mother and I,
to see my father in prison. He stood in the death-cell
and put his hand through the bars and said, My Mio,
I have only this to leave you, that I love you,
and will love you after I die. Love me then, Mio,
when this hard thing comes on you, that you must live
a man despised for your father. That night the guards,
walking in flood-lights brighter than high noon,
led him between them with his trousers slit
and a shaven head for the cathodes. This sleet and rain
that I feel cold here and on my face and hands
will find him under thirteen years of clay
in prison ground. Lie still and rest, my father,
for I have not forgotten. When I forget
may I lie blind as you. No other love,
time passing, nor the spaced light-years of suns
shall blur your voice, or tempt me from the path
that clears your name—
till I have these rats in my grip
or sleep deep where you sleep. . . .
I have no house,
nor home, nor love of life, nor fear of death,
nor care for what I eat, or who I sleep with,
or what color of calcimine the Government
will wash itself this year or next to lure
the sheep and feed the wolves. Love somewhere else,
and get your children in some other image
more acceptable to the State! This face of mine
is stamped for sewage!

It's a vivid and disturbing monologue. You may have had a traumatic experience of your own that you could use to make this speech truthful in performance. That's called *personalization* or *substitution*: saying the author's words while sensorially connecting to a specific memory from your own life that will emotionalize you in the way the play calls for at that moment. But I'm asking you not to go to your own experience right away, unless it just seizes you as you read the script. If that happens, of course you should grab it.

But I've chosen this speech precisely because what happened to Mio is so extreme and uncommon that it's unlikely to evoke personal images for you. Rather than turn yourself inside-out trying to find parallels or near parallels from your own life, start with your imagination to build a belief in the imagery Anderson gives you. Once you create your own inner pictures for everything you talk about, you will have the memories that the character has and you'll be living a specific life, Mio's life as you interpret it.

As an actor, however, you're not just using inner imagery to give life to the writer's images—you're calling on that imagery to fuel your objective. Mio is not simply recounting what happened to him as a child, he is also *trying to make Miriamne go away,* even though he is deeply attracted to her and deeply lonely.

Mio's superobjective is *to avenge my father's death at any cost.* Why do I say *at any cost*? Because, ultimately, he dies for it. His objective in this monologue is *to get Miriamne to understand why he can't be close to her.* His feelings for her, which he expresses eloquently later in the scene, are an obstacle, and Mio has to try to overcome this obstacle by painting himself as dangerous and incapable of love.

When he says, "I have no home nor love of life," even though you as an actor are looking at the actress playing Miriamne and may be saying to yourself, "My God, I love her mouth" or "I love her hair and I want to kiss her passionately and have her hold me," at the same time you have to believe yourself when you say "I have no house, nor home, nor love of life, nor fear of death. . . ." The more you want her, the more you must wrestle yourself away from that want. So the more you feel the attraction, the deeper the commitment to push her away.

There's another element to the speech, too. Besides using these memories to try to push Miriamne away, as Mio you're saying to yourself, "*I* must remember these memories myself in order to stay away from this love, because it will take me off the path of my vengeance, which is my life's mission. For I loved my father so deeply, and because he was wronged by bigotry, ignorance, and injustice, if I don't right this wrong, I have no right to take my next breath."

If you perform Mio's speech without inner imagery and just play an active intention—Mio *pushing Miriamne away* or *lashing out at himself to demand that he remembers his commitment to his father*—my deep belief is that the audience will never entirely believe that you've *lived* the words you're saying. If you don't have inner imagery for it, the speech becomes a kind of romantic, poetic indulgence. Just words with no inner resonance. When you do your work on the inner imagery, you may find that the words you first use to describe your active intentions change because your intentions become more emotional and real to you. For example, instead of *pushing Miriamne away,* your active intention might become *to degrade her, to demolish her, to nail her with my truth.*

Now let me make a very vital point: *once you've done the imagery work, you don't have to consciously bring it up during performance.* Of course you can if you need to or want to, but you will find that in most cases it will automatically join you like an eager child as you play your active intentions because you've rehearsed with these images. If you're playing Mio, it will join you as you *try to shock her, to confront her with the ugliness of my life*—or whatever you pick as your active intentions. Let me repeat: work on the imagery consciously as part of your homework, work on it in rehearsal, and then it will simply be a part of your performance.

Now, suppose you're working on the character of Mio and you do want to use personalization or substitution. Perhaps your father or another beloved member of your family died of cancer, and it was wrenching; maybe the touch of his hand the last time you saw him in his bedroom could be the inner image you use when Mio says, "My father held out his hand." It doesn't have to be his touching you with his hand; it could be a kiss the last time you saw him alive. Even something as simple as feeling the texture of the sheet or pillow on the deathbed might be enough to catapult you into the emotional reality of Mio's speech. Or you might remember an experience that to you as a child *felt* like the death of a parent: your mother and father going on an extended trip or leaving you at school alone for the first time. These are all personal experiences you can use that could fit into the imagery of *Winterset.* But—and this is a big but—*if you think about something personal and it takes you out of the story, it's not helpful.*

I've used personal experiences and memories many times in my acting, and sometimes they've worked very well. However, I will say at this point, without going into a lot of autobiography, my relationships with my family were very difficult, and so sometimes when I tried to use a memory, I shut off emotionally—because the memory was too painful and I wasn't resolved about it. That led me to use the world of imagination, which freed me and gave me emotional access for my acting. Now I can use either personal experience *or* imagination when I need it.

Through the years, as your career grows, you will find your own way. Each job will have its problems that you must solve—and the tools I'm giving you can be used to solve them. I ask you to start by using the images the writer gives you and allowing your imagination to make them real to you because the images are so specific and keep you inside the character and the world of the play. There can be a danger if you try to find a parallel experience in your own life that doesn't really parallel the play emotionally, because your acting work will not correspond with the specific world of the script. Also, your work may either be too emotionally shallow or so overly emotional that it overwhelms the scene. That's another reason I'm asking you to start with the play's imagery.

How do you use your imagination to make the writer's imagery effective for you and therefore for the audience? Playing Mio, you have to imagine the scene of four-year-old Mio going with his mother to visit his father in prison *in detail* so that you make it emotionally affecting to yourself. You have to live it in your own mind. It has to be *sensorially real*—the way my images of Birmingham High School are real to me—so that you can see the experience, touch it, taste it, smell it, hear it.

At four, when Mio's father said good-bye, the child probably did not even understand what electrocution or death were. He felt it through the grief of his mother and father. He got it like a sponge as children do. The more he matured, the more he realized what his father's death meant. And because, as the play tells you, his father and his father's best friend were immigrants, and because Mio is the son of a convicted murderer who was executed, when he says "This face of mine is stamped for sewage," he's saying, "They may have stamped me for shit, but I won't lie like the government lies. I'll clear his name even if it kills me."

In working on Mio's speech, say to yourself: "Let me try to imagine the experience vividly so that I can feel it. Can I imagine what that experience of being dragged to the prison by my mother was like, over rocks, perhaps, or down slippery streets until we reached it that rainy night? Can I imagine what she had dressed me in when I was four years old and how she tried to protect me from the pouring rain? Because we were poor, could she not afford a new umbrella? Did we have a broken one, and did she try to keep it over me so I wouldn't get wet? How did she look with her hair drenched from the rain? Could I see the tears on her cheeks or did they blend with the raindrops? What was my father's death cell like? What did my father look like with his head shaved as he waited to be executed?" You want to explore all of these images but ultimately you may find that one or two are especially exciting emotionally and you may find that these ignite you for the monologue. Any images that come to you that fit the writer's imagery—images from a movie you saw, people you glimpsed walking down a street, a photo from a newspaper, your grandparents, or people completely imagined from scratch—are usable possibilities.

If you build your performance like this, if you create it with as much sensory detail as a real memory, you will be sending that imagery to your partner when you speak. Again, you don't have to call it up while you're acting and say to yourself, *Now I have to think about my father's hand, now I'm going to think about the bars.* That's not your job when you're performing. That is—and I'm repeating this on purpose—for your homework. The actor's job in performance is to send the ideas to this young woman, and because you've created and worked on the inner imagery as though you've actually experienced it, your eyes will play the movie and she will read that and it will be an accompaniment to the text. It will make the text alive, and it will make you alive to your acting partner—which will galvanize her.

Once you have done your inner imagery work, it's there as if you've lived it. In performance, you don't do an acting exercise to call up inner imagery, you play the intention to achieve your objective. I'm going to say it again: some of the images you've been working with as homework will join you in performance. I want to make this absolutely clear because you can get confused in a scene, asking *Do I think of my inner imagery now?* No, you build your inner imagery and it's there. Just as in life when you say "I went bowling with my friends last night and we had a blast," you don't first stop and say to yourself *Oh, now I'm going to think about that experience of bowling.* You've lived it, so all you've got to do is say "I went bowling last night with my friends and had a blast." *The truth is already there in you.* Doing your homework with inner imagery will give you the conviction of truth with everything you're saying.

There *are* certain moments in a play or film, however, where you can consciously bring up an image for an emotional response. Playing Mio, you may decide, for example, when you're talking about seeing your father in his cell to call up in your mind's eye the image of your father's shaved head in the prison because it provokes you to anger or to tears. That's a specific *emotional trigger* for a specific emotional response at a given moment, which I'll discuss in detail in Chapter Seven.

There's another technique I'm going to introduce you to that you work with in rehearsal to create a particular emotion or quality of feeling and that joins you in performance: the *"as if."* An "as if" is a combination of imagination and personalization; it's something from your personal life that *could* happen but has *not* happened and you imagine it *as if* it had. Many actors work with "as ifs" all the time and, once again, as long as it doesn't take you out of the circumstances of the script but rather invests you in them emotionally, they're without doubt one of the great tools that have been invented for acting. If a play or film requires you to have a reaction of grief or shock or hysteria and nothing in the script provokes you to this intense emotion, an "as if" will solve the problem.

Suppose the script says you walk into a room and see a dead body or something else equally horrifying. The camera's on you, but you're literally looking at nothing because the dead body's filming tomorrow. Or you're filming against a blue screen because there are going to be special effects that they will put in later. You have to react *but there's nothing there to react to*—it's all up to you and your inner imagery.

If I were the actor in this situation, I might use an "as if" with my beloved cat, Noir. It was violently windy yesterday as I was driving along thinking about "as ifs," and I asked myself what would happen if the windows broke in my house and my cat was cut in half and I came home and saw her body in two parts and saw her face with dead eyes. I started to get very emotional. I didn't want to go there. I didn't even want to think about it, but I thought if I imagined that while I was acting, it would really affect me, which is what makes it a good example of an "as if."

Some actors say, "I don't even want to think about those painful things happening to people I love because it puts bad vibes into the air." In my opinion, that's nonsense. You use people or things in your work *because* you love them, so it's not negativity, it's a celebration of love. If a scene calls for me to express grief, and I imagine my beautiful cat in peril and dying, I'm showing the audience the depths of loss, the depths of love. You can't stay clean and tidy and be an actor. You've got to use imagery of things that upset you, things that make you laugh, things that arouse you sexually, things that crash through your inhibitions. As Bobby Lewis said to a young actor playing Hamlet, "You think Hamlet's real? It's a story. But it's real if you believe it and make it real."

Making it real to yourself is part of the actor's job. You have to commit to every word you're saying, and that's what inner imagery helps you to do. So you either have to create from your imagination the imagery that the writer gives you, make that real and believe in it, or you have to find personalization or substitution that fits the script, or you have to find an "as if" to bring you to the emotional place you need to be. The truth is, you'll probably use all three. But, again, *you must believe something*—and the something you believe has to be *specific*. When you talk about your own life, you don't have a *general* picture of the things and people you're talking about; your high school, like mine, isn't just some generic high school somewhere out in the void. *Everything* is specific. Only bad actors are general; life never is!

The specific inner imagery you use is part of your interpretation and part of what makes you unique. Everybody who knows me knows I am an aficionado of the great Lena Horne. She once said, "Many young singers were brought to me to try to find an aspect of my style that they could use. But the one thing they could never copy was what I thought inside. That was mine." When she worked on a song and rehearsed it a *hundred* times—literally—not only was she phrasing it and breathing it, she was seeing things in her imagination and her memory to make the song come alive.

Great dancers have inner imagery, too. I saw the most extraordinary video of a famous Russian ballerina, Galina Ulanova, who danced *Romeo and Juliet* on film at fifty-two years old, playing the fourteen-year-old Juliet. The camera very rarely goes close to her face but when it does, even her eyes look fourteen because of what she's thinking. Her face is older, of course, but her inner imagery made her move with such youth and so much lushness and innocence that she *was* Juliet. Watching her, I felt I was watching a great actress dancing.

People in the theater still talk in awe about Laurette Taylor, who, in 1945, originated the role of Amanda Wingfield in Tennessee Williams's *The Glass Menagerie* and raised the bar of acting for the next generation of actors. She died before I could see her but when I started studying acting I would hear about her incredible subtlety and naturalness. Uta Hagen said she went to watch Laurette Taylor's performance four times to try to figure out her technique for being so believable in everything she said and did, but each time Uta Hagen became so completely absorbed in the play that she forgot she was watching an actress and believed she was watching a woman named Amanda Wingfield live. Uta Hagen complained that she never learned a damned thing from Laurette Taylor because she could never catch her acting!

There are tens of thousands of people who perform but some people stay forever in our memory and become part of the history of our profession, and my belief about them is that they are deeply, deeply connected to inner imagery, and that without it, you become what I call a hack. As Stella Adler said to us again and again when I studied with her, "It's not the lines, it's the life."

6

BATTLING ACTING TEACHERS: DON'T GET CAUGHT IN A SENSELESS WAR

In the 1930s, Lee Strasberg and Stella Adler were members of the Group Theatre in New York, which influenced acting for the rest of the twentieth century and into the twenty-first. These two legendary teachers became enemies because of their differing perspectives on the uses of life experience and imagination in acting.

At the Group Theatre, Strasberg taught a famous exercise called *affective memory*, which came from the great Russian acting teacher Stanislavsky and his colleagues. In the 1950s, when Strasberg became affiliated with the Actor's Studio in New York, affective memory became a fundamental exercise of what came to be known as Method acting or the Method. (Because so many people are confused about the term, I'd like to point out that *Method acting* is simply that—one method of approaching a role. There are many approaches; as Eli Wallach, a member of the Actor's Studio, commented when he was eighty-eight years old, every actor has a method.)

Affective memory is a tool for calling up an unusually intense personal experience to stir up emotions when you need them for a role. You sit or stand and begin the exercise by breathing and relaxing your muscles; then you re-create your experience by recalling the *sensory details*—the feeling of the air on your face at the time or the way your pants clung to your legs or your dress to your body because it was hot in the room, the smell of the perfume your mother wore or the aftershave lotion your father wore, the taste in your mouth from the peanut-butter-and-jelly sandwich you'd just eaten for lunch, the sound of a car honking its horn outside.

As you go deeper, eventually you get to the moment where the emotion (or *affect,* in psychological terms) emerges. Maybe it's the sweet smell of the perfume or the uncomfortable stickiness of your pants against the back of your knee or the way your dress was too tight and cut into your armpits or the blaring sound of the honking horn outside your house that becomes the trigger for the intense emotion of the memory. The goal of the exercise is to know that you can use that sense memory to create that emotion when you're doing a scene in a play eight times a week or for the twenty-fifth take in a film. This can be an excellent way of working. But it's just *one* technique; it's not the *only* technique.

In the Group Theatre, Strasberg became preoccupied with doing the affective memory exercise, and Stella Adler began to take great exception to it. She and other members of the Group, such as Bobby Lewis, Harold Clurman, and Sanford Meisner, felt the actors' overemphasis on sense memory during performance took the actors out of the world of the play. In other words, the actors' involvement in their own emotional lives became more important than the play itself.

Stella was so upset by this, and by the fact that certain actors began to court their own misery as if that would make them better artists, that she went to see Stanislavsky in Paris and trained with him. Stanislavsky—responding, of course, to Stella's report—said that what Strasberg was doing was not, in fact, what he taught. He felt that Strasberg was underutilizing the *physical action* of the scene, the *active doing*—the intentions. He also said that actors could use their imagination as well as personal experience to evoke emotion.

So Stella came back to New York and told Strasberg he was misrepresenting Stanislavsky's ideas. And she began to teach what she had learned from Stanislavsky, emphasizing the physical action of each scene and the actor's imagination. She also emphasized what was particularly interesting to her: the ideas contained in every script.

Many years later, when Strasberg died, she came to her class and said, "I'd like a minute of silence. A man of the theater died today." The class took a minute of silence, then Stella added: "And it will take a hundred years to undo the damage that that man has done to the theater."

I think that's cruel and untrue, myself, since Lee Strasberg contributed some beautiful actors and performances to the theater and to film. Stella Adler, as much gratitude as I have for her teaching, also made some mistakes. Some of her actors were so concerned with the big ideas of playwrights and with hitting the big emotional peaks—she was always urging actors to bring their emotion to the size of the play—that sometimes they pushed emotions that they didn't have and hurt the believability of the plays. As a teacher of the next generation, I revere both Stella Adler and Lee Strasberg, but I disagree with their dogmatic view that acting had to be seen *their* way as the *only* way. I also suspect that toward the end of their lives, they were in agreement to a great extent, but they were too proud to admit it.

Not long after Strasberg's death, Stella Adler called Anna Strasberg, his widow, and said, "We should have talked . . . we should have talked." Later she wrote Anna a note, "In history there are battles that now end in love."

The misunderstandings and ego conflicts between talented and passionate people have gone on as long as ideas about acting have been discussed. All the exercises and techniques of the master teachers have value. In any creative group there will be some conflicts and sometimes those people split into factions and form new groups. History often blows the reasons for a split out of proportion. People who weren't even there pick up the debate and embellish it, and before long, rumors and misrepresentations are passed down as facts.

Today there are still teachers who are fighting the same old war when it's clear that both life experience and imagination can be useful tools for the actor. *It's about what's best for the actor and for the script.* This is why I don't ally myself with any one way of thinking. I share a collection of techniques, some that I've created and some that I learned from the teachers to whom I've dedicated this book: Stella Adler, David Craig, Uta Hagen, Sanford Meisner, Kenneth MacMillan, Tim Phillips, Charles Nelson Reilly, Warren Robertson, Sam Schacht, and Jim Tuttle. And since I continue to study, I'm always adding new ideas to this collection.

As an actor, you are what's important and the script is what's important. You want to use whatever techniques help you to become the most specific and alive in a part. Each actor is different, so I don't quibble with a wonderful actor who says "I never use anything but memories from my life" or one who says "I never use anything but my imagination"; who am I to say to a wonderful actor that either is incorrect? But not all actors can effectively work only one way or the other. So I'm saying, make yourself available to all the possible techniques and ideas to make yourself grow as an artist. You don't have to take sides. Be independent and find your own way.

Recently, the writer and director David Mamet returned to the battlefield with his book *True or False*. Mamet makes the huge assertion that sense memory, inner imagery, and creating a history for your character are all useless and, he says, destructive. In essence Mamet says that actors should forget all other techniques and tools and just stand there, have an objective and an intention, and say what the playwright wrote. Mamet says there's no such thing as a character or a character arc; there's just you delivering lines. The Method, he says, is "nonsense" and "hogwash." He throws out Stanislavsky and all other teachers who came after him and were interested in his techniques, including Stella Adler, who taught, among others, Brando and De Niro; Lee Strasberg, who taught, among others, Kim Stanley and Al Pacino; Uta Hagen, who taught, among others, Geraldine Page; and Bobby Lewis, who taught, among others, Meryl Streep.

Erasing the tools of sense memory, inner imagery, and creating a history for the character would destroy the very fabric of the plays of Shakespeare, Ibsen, Strindberg, Chekhov, Anderson, Williams, Miller, Albee, August Wilson, and every other playwright—including Mamet himself. Without some kind of specific inner imagery, you could never sustain the audience's interest, their belief that you are living or have lived what you are talking about. Alan Arkin, in discussing his performance as George Aaronow in the film version of Mamet's *Glengarry Glen Ross,* said that he went deeply inside the character of Aaronow and found his inner life. Arkin explained that if he had listened to Mamet's comments about how to play Aaronow, he would have failed in the part. (Mamet didn't direct that movie, but he was on the set.) Arkin used the very tools and techniques Mamet dismisses in order to make Mamet's character fully alive.

Mamet insists that the playwright has already done all the work. He gives lip service to the importance of acting in the moment and working off the other person's behavior, but he assumes that playing only objectives and active intentions will keep actors more in touch with the verbal aspects of their role, which he considers paramount.

In fact, this position is a catch-22. Mamet seems to believe that because you are you, you automatically have access to your emotional palette, and that it will all happen on the stage, in the moment, without your doing any kind of inner work.

Of course there is misuse of Stanislavsky's work. In certain classes, actors have been reduced to blithering idiots by remembering trauma; actors start to compete over how much trauma and pain each one has and how much emotion they can display. When you hit that terror or that grief and you sob and scream, it's very powerful and it moves people, but if a teacher professes that having wide access to your emotions is the most important part of acting, you're lost before you begin. Your emotional life is your personal palette of colors that you can use to interpret a part, but you can't start interpreting before you understand the play—and honor the writer's words.

I've taken classes that emphasized personal emotional release. I'm grateful for the work I did in those classes because I was repressed and I needed to explode that repression and break through. But that wasn't acting, it was just a step toward acting. It multiplied the number of colors I have on my palette. The more colors you have available to you, the more wide-ranging and nuanced choices you can make. Learning to act is learning how to make the choices.

In one of the final scenes of *Streetcar*, Stanley rapes Blanche. Stanley enters the scene with joy about the upcoming birth of his child, and it's the way that Blanche speaks down to him, as she has done since she arrived, that provokes him to consume her. The actor's job in that role is to understand and feel what it means to Stanley to have a woman belittle and humiliate him, and then for her to try to steal the most precious possession in his life, the jewel in his crown, his wife, Stella. The play is so well written that just the way Blanche treats you as Stanley *could* provoke you to rage without any affective memories, "as ifs," or personalizations. But if the play *doesn't* provoke you, you'd better have a technique that puts you in touch with something you can use that stimulates you with your own rage and fear.

I'm going to share with you something I would use if I were playing Stanley (a bad idea). But if I were, I'd use the memory of my third-grade teacher standing me up in front of the class because I'd teased one of the girls. My teacher humiliated me, repeatedly telling me that I was a terrible, bad boy until I turned bright red and began to cry. I've never forgotten that moment. One trigger I remember from that trauma is touching the cold steel underneath my desk with my hot red face when I tried to hide my head so no one would see me weeping. A second trigger is seeing the white handkerchief with embroidered flowers that the teacher always used to stop the postnasal drip that flowed out of her perpetually red nose. Watching in my memory the handkerchief being brought up to that nose and patting her nostrils in a phony-aristocratic way would give me all the rage I need to destroy Blanche. The reason this affective memory is so stirring is that the parallels are very close: like Stanley, I was humiliated by a phony-aristocratic woman. Again, it doesn't matter if you use personalization or imagination or a combination. Audience members only know what lives.

Sidney Lumet's great film of the 1960s, *The Pawnbroker,* is about Sol Nazerman (Rod Steiger), who runs a pawnshop in Harlem. Sol cannot allow himself any emotion because he is afraid of feeling the pain of his family dying in the Holocaust. He's so emotionally dead that at one point in the film he actually impales his hand on a nail to see if he can feel. The only person he begins to care about is his young Hispanic assistant, Jesus Ortíz (Jaime Sánchez). At the end of the movie, the pawnshop is robbed, Jesus gets shot, and, as he's dying, the pawnbroker is holding him in his arms. In those days, in black-and-white films, they used chocolate syrup for blood because it was the right consistency and would photograph like blood. When Steiger was being interviewed about his career, he talked about *The Pawnbroker* and about the chocolate syrup, and the extraordinary moment when he was holding his dying assistant. Steiger explained that he did an "as if" with the chocolate syrup to make it blood—but not just any blood. Steiger's "as if" was that it was his daughter's blood, and even as he talked about it in the interview, he started to sob.

When the young man dies, Steiger is so anguished that he opens his mouth to scream but no sound comes out. The interviewer asked him about this. Steiger said that he hadn't intended for that to happen, he had had the full intent to scream, but at that moment in that take in the movie, he remembered the famous painting by Munch of the silent scream, and Steiger said it was God—it came to him at that moment of the take, he opened his mouth to scream and suddenly he saw that painting in his mind's eye and couldn't make a sound. It's a fantastic instance of imagination and personalization and acting in the moment coming together, because the chocolate syrup is, in fact, not blood but *if* it were, and *if* it were your daughter's blood, then you would scream, except at that moment his unconscious brought forth Munch's painting and something in the actor deeply said, "This is grief beyond sound. It is the same grief that I feel for the six million who died, for my family who died. There is no sound that's loud enough or horrible enough to express it."

If you're a young actor, you may be asking yourself, "How do I find my way to make choices like that?" My answer is that you try in good classes and in professional situations. You work on many different plays and many different scenes from those plays, you work on inner imagery and intentions, you do everything I'm telling you and you work and work and work. I'm very adamant about this: you're not simply *entitled* to be an actor—you're not an actor just because you call yourself one—you earn it. And you earn it by working.

What I'm teaching you with all of this work is to use your intellect to reach your emotions. You don't use your intellect to be clever, that's not what acting is about; you have to reach your emotions so that you can use them in the service of the play, and if you're not reaching and activating your emotions with the choices you're making, then you have to make other choices. Even if your choice is brilliantly created in your mind, if it hasn't affected your heartstrings so that the character's music is playing, then it's not working. Likewise, if you're just a bundle of emotion without real ideas about how to play the part so that it illuminates the writer's ideas and makes the character full of human behavior, then you haven't done the work of acting.

I began this chapter by talking about the war between Stella and Strasberg. As an actor you've really got to get past prejudices that may have been handed down to you, past even thinking that there's one right answer. You've got to say, "If I am good at what I do because I use all the tools and techniques available to me and continue to be curious to learn others, I will get my just deserts, I'll get remuneration and ultimately I'll get respect. Where I really want to go is to this other place where I live with all artists close to God."

Even though this may sound pretentious to some people, it isn't; acting is a spiritual quest to touch human beings. In the chapter on inner imagery, I talked about how the chemical-electrical experience of feeding your body a sensorial image and responding to it gives you power as an actor. When I saw Vanessa Redgrave's magnificent performance in Ibsen's *Ghosts* in London, it seemed as though there was a glow around her body.

She literally looked electrified. I don't think this is an impossibility. Since we are made largely of liquid and chemicals and electrical impulses, it seems entirely possible to me that in the right performance, when you are "plugged in," you would create a kind of energy around you.

One night when I was teaching, I was in an absolute rage because of something that had occurred in my personal life, and I also felt a lot of fear, partially because I was in such a rage. A student came up to me later, and said, "Did you know you were glowing?" I said, "What?" He repeated, "You were glowing." In truth I was in agony, but I was so plugged in emotionally and my concentration was so keen that something electrical happened to my body that was visible. I'm sure that that's what happens when actors are 100 percent concentrated; they're not just figuratively electrical, they're literally electrical.

When the actor is that alive and that focused, it draws the audience's focus and connects to something in them. Whether you believe in telepathy or extrasensory perception or auras, there's something that we see as audience members watching a great performance that goes beyond just a person speaking words and moving. We see the person living, and we see the person living very intensely, and they do seem to throw off light.

That's what I want you to do in your performances; I want you to be illuminated.

7

EMOTION ON DEMAND:
FINDING YOUR TRIGGERS

The degree of your commitment to gaining what you want in the scene (your objective) is the degree to which the audience is moved. Don't make the mistake of thinking that you will move the audience simply because there's water coming out of your eyes. As the Group Theatre alumnus and teacher Bobby Lewis said so humorously, "If crying was acting talent, my aunt Bubba would be a star."

One of the great things I learned from Sanford Meisner was that emotion is the result of active doing. The fierce passion to get the money from the other character, to get love from them, to be forgiven by them, to incriminate them—all justified objectives—will *cause* some kind of emotion. As an actor, it's not your job to judge the amount of emotion you're revealing as good acting or bad; it's your job to commit and concentrate and invest yourself emotionally in getting what you *need*. The inner imagery that you work on as homework, which makes everything you say and do as your character real to you, is part of this commitment and concentration.

In the play *Runt of the Litter* by Bo Eason, Jack is the younger brother of a great athlete. In one scene, Jack lets a baseball hit him in the face in order to get an automatic walk to first base because he's afraid he won't actually be able to hit the ball. The older brother, Charlie, who senses that Jack may have done this in order to be part of his gifted athletic world, looks at the bloodied eye, and says to Jack, "Did you let that ball hit you?" *Runt* is a one-man show, and Bo played every role. Thus, he was his own scene partner, playing both Jack and Charlie. At that moment in the play, as Charlie he had to imagine seeing his brother's injured eye as he pursued his objective—to stop Jack from mutilating himself in order to win approval—by *confronting him about his self-mutilation*. Bo said to me, "When I took the time to see the image of the younger brother's swollen and bloody eye while I pursued what I wanted, I was deeply connected to my own play. Not only to the words but to what the words mean and what drives my character." Charlie's love for Jack and his objective of protecting him came alive because Bo could see the image of Jack's injured eye in his imagination.

Again, concentration is the key to powerful acting, and what I mean by acting is living. Some nights Bo had tears in his eyes as Charlie asked Jack if he let the ball hit him; other nights he just had deep concern. The power was in how deep his need was to try to protect his brother, not the amount of water from his eyes that could be seen by the audience. The audience experienced his emotion as real because of Bo's creating the injured eye as real to him and his powerful commitment to his objective.

However, in certain parts, you won't have a choice about how intense and explicit to make your emotion, because another character will say the horrifying demand "Stop crying now" or "Wipe those tears out of your eyes" or "What are you so angry about?" or "Why are you so scared?" You can't say, "I don't have it tonight, so I'll just play it subtler." The script literally *requires* that emotion from you. For some actors, this challenge is a nightmare, but like any other acting problem, it's a problem that can be solved. In this case, you solve it by preparing yourself with an *emotional trigger*.

An emotional trigger is the choice that can cause emotion to arise within you when you need it. It is sheer technique, it is inner music, and as an actor you have to have a way of plucking the string within you to make the music. An emotional trigger can be a sensorial memory from your life, it can be an "as if," it can be completely from your imagination, it can be a physical gesture—like clutching your stomach, putting your hand over your mouth, or wiping your eyes with the tips of your fingers. It can be anything at all as long as it will ignite the emotion you need to make the script work.

The reason I talk about a physical gesture at this point is that when you use an emotional trigger, it will probably cause you to do a physical movement. So make sure you trust that impulse, because once you see what your body is doing to express emotion, you can use that gesture to recruit the feeling. I once saw Michael Gambon, a celebrated English actor, cover his face with his hands in a scene that demanded him to cry. I was sitting very close to the stage, and I could see that he did not have the emotion that second when he needed it, but by committing to the physical gesture and the circumstances of the play, ten seconds later the emotion exploded and he was sobbing. Our bodies store emotion, and physical gestures are often the key to unlocking it.

Sometimes students say to me, "I don't cry that easily," and I say to them—not unsympathetically but not particularly sympathetically, either—"Then work at it." What has made you weep: What music? What event in a movie or play, what event in your life? If you cry watching McDonald's commercials, what is it specifically that evokes that emotion? Is it a happy family? When you see a father and son talking lovingly, or a mother and daughter hugging each other, does that make you cry?

There are specific things that trigger specific emotional states in everybody, not just crying but joy, laughter, tenderness, sensuality, anger, and fear. As an actor you have to have a list of things that you know will cause you to be emotional at a moment's notice. Sanford Meisner called this list the actor's golden box, and it really is gold. You can actually create a small card file to record specific triggers that work for you. The golden box might contain a memory of the time your mother slapped your face and made you cry hysterically; the time you became enraged when you stood up to a bully in school; the first time you were sexually aroused on a date; the time you burst out laughing because your uptight uncle tried to cut the roast beef and knocked it off the platter onto somebody's lap. Remember, when you do this work, you must re-create it sensorially. I reiterate: seeing, tasting, touching, smelling, hearing.

The golden box can also be filled with "as ifs"—imagined events that have a proven power to make you emotional. Remember how Rod Steiger in *The Pawnbroker* made the chocolate syrup they used for blood into his daughter's blood? That "as if" was his emotional trigger for the grief he needed to make the scene work.

In a way your emotional trigger is emotionally tricking yourself. You trick yourself into being emotional by staying out of the way and not *demanding* emotion but *inviting* it. You have to use emotional triggers as if you're coaxing a kitten: you can't go over to a kitten and force it to pay attention to you, it'll run away; you have to hold out your hand very gently until the kitten decides to come to you. Emotional triggers are exactly the same. You have to work them as you would rehearse a difficult piece of music over and over again until you master it.

You can work on emotional triggers as homework when you're alone. You can also work on them in public. Say you secretly trigger yourself at lunch with a friend and start weeping. When your friend asks what the matter is, just tell her nothing, and explain that you're working on your emotional trigger. She may think you're insane but you'll know you had a personal triumph. And I mean that you should do exactly this. A seriously committed actor will find their emotional triggers and practice tricking themselves to get emotional, because *it's not magic, it's not about psychology or therapy, it's simple meat-and-potatoes work that you do on a daily basis.*

Actors can be the laziest people in the world. "I went to the gym and called my agent, I'm exhausted. I better go have lunch." A violinist, a professional tennis player, a Wall Street broker, a lawyer wouldn't think of not spending six to eight hours a day or more working on their craft. So don't be entitled babies: acting is a job that you can learn to do well, and it takes an enormous amount of practice to be good at it. Working on emotional triggers is part of this practice.

Maybe what triggers your humor, what really sends you into paroxysms of laughter, is the memory of somebody farting in church. Fine. You can be as antisocial as you want in your imagination. The audience benefits and nobody gets hurt. Choosing the right emotional trigger means knowing yourself, knowing what triggers *you*. Commit to coming up with five emotional triggers for weeping, for example, as well as five emotional triggers for other intense emotions that may be called on for a part. These may be affective memories or "as ifs."

As an actor I had to do my own search for emotional triggers, especially for crying. Even though I cried a lot as a child, as I grew up I became ashamed and clammed up. I couldn't feel and I wouldn't feel. But I longed to be able to, and I knew that in order to be good at acting I *had* to feel. So I did the very homework I'm telling you to do.

One of the exercises I created to break through those emotional blocks is called Memories of Home.

Memories of Home Exercise

Sit in a chair, leave your eyes open or close them if it's easier, and in your mind's eye go back in your imagination to the house or apartment in which you lived for the longest time during your childhood. Start by walking down the street where the house or apartment building was. You'll notice that you will see it at a specific time of day, which I always find fascinating. You never just think of your house at some limbo time; it's either in the morning light or in the afternoon or at dusk. I think the time of day is very emotional for people.

As you walk down the street in your mind's eye, you do a sense memory: the outside of the house looks like this; my feet on the pavement sound like this; the temperature feels like this (I remember it as hot or cold or windy); the air smells like jasmine (or smoke from fireplaces, or garbage from garbage cans out on the street, rotting in the heat); I hear the bell of an ice-cream truck or a siren from a fire engine or the sound of the subway; I taste the salt from the sea breezes (or the soot from a nearby factory or the sweetness in the air from apple trees with apples ready to pick). I see my gate, my fence (is it newly painted? is it peeling paint? is it rusted?). I walk up to my front door and look at it: I look at the color and the texture of the door, the handle, the knocker or bell; I look at the window next to the door.

You see, smell, hear, taste, touch, everything you can remember, then you can actually put your hand out and touch the doorknob of that house, feel the coldness or the warmth of the metal knob, feel the weight of the door and open it. Then imagine the first thing you see after you open the door, which is probably some sort of foyer, and then you begin the Memories of Home tour. You walk through the house to every room, and you remember everything you can, every object, the carpet, the linoleum, the furniture, the painted or wallpapered walls. Some rooms will have more emotional triggers than others.

If a certain room or object frightens you, see if you can stay with the work and dare yourself to explore it. Listen to me now very carefully, because it's important that I say this. I know well that some people's childhoods have intense, painful trauma, and if you know this about yourself, it would be better to do this with a therapist so that you can feel safe. For those of you who have only the normal amount of trauma, press on with your work and continue to look for emotional triggers.

You may find an emotional trigger on your mother's perfume tray, as I did when I remembered a particular bottle of my mother's French perfume with a tiny red bow around the bottle. It was the embodiment of a certain kind of glamour that my mother possessed and it made me remember sadly a time when she was vividly alive. You may find your father's ties are emotional triggers. Don't ever judge or edit what triggers you. Be curious. There is no reason to be ashamed or intimidated by your own responses, whatever they are. They are for you to know and use in your acting.

When you do Memories of Home, you'll be amazed at what you had forgotten and what you can now remember. Be courageous—some things will scare you, some things will make you unbearably sad, some things will make you intensely angry or joyous and hopeful.

For instance, doing this exercise I remembered two plaster-of-Paris Scottie dogs' faces on the wall. I had completely forgotten about them, but as I saw the knotty pine wall of my bedroom I suddenly remembered the two little Scotties' faces, which made me smile. Then I remembered that my brother had a chartreuse fishing rod behind the door, which made me feel sad, because I wasn't part of his fishing trips. Those were two emotional triggers for me: the fishing rod made me sad, the plaster-of-Paris Scottie dogs' faces were bittersweet. I also remembered the comforter I had that I loved because I could envelope myself in it and hide. I remembered its smell, the billowy feel of it, and how I never wanted to get out from under it and get up to go to school. I remembered the marigold yellow curtains that my grandmother had made for my room. I remembered that we had little wooden fruit and vegetable crates that my mother had gotten from the grocery store to put our toys in. I never would have remembered these things unless I had done that tour and really done the sense memories of being there.

If you say to me, "Well, I did that exercise and I didn't feel anything," don't be critical of yourself, but be curious about why this may be so. In my experience, there are several reasons. Houses and families *are* emotional, so it's not that you don't have an emotional response to the home you grew up in. The simplest explanation is that you didn't do the exercise slowly or thoroughly enough to experience the emotions that are there. Or you may be blocking the emotion because of fear. One rule of thumb when working emotionally in your acting: be gentle and kind to yourself but thorough and hardworking.

You may find objects in the Memories of Home exercise that you can use as emotional triggers for your acting work. If you don't, search for other memories. As an actor, if the written circumstances of a script I was working on didn't summon up the emotion I needed and I knew I had to cry, I often used the death of a little puppy I saw run over and that I watched die. It always makes me cry because of the innocence of the puppy's eyes and its look of patience as it waited for something it couldn't comprehend, its own death. It was a small, red Irish setter puppy, its body was quivering, it obviously had internal injuries, it was shitting, and there was blood coming from its anus. It was on a very parched piece of grass by the side of the road. It was my first awareness at ten years old that things that are beautiful and innocent still get crushed and die. The emotional trigger that I used was the quivering flesh and the patience of the eyes, the surrender. Sometimes all I needed was the parched grass around the body and the tears flowed.

This memory was helpful to me at a time when I tended to block painful family memories and therefore couldn't use them effectively for my acting work. I think that the memory of the puppy *is* connected to my family in a very direct way, because my innocence was taken from me in childhood and I was not protected: I identified with that puppy because at ten years old I felt a part of me was dying. But understanding this connection is *not* important for acting; the only thing that matters is that it triggers me emotionally.

Personally, part of my life's journey has been to understand my inner world, and I couldn't have done that successfully without exploring my childhood in therapy. I'm in favor of therapy for actors, because I believe that the more you understand and resolve deep family hurts, the healthier you become, and the less frightened you are of your creativity. Don't make the mistake of thinking you have to continue to suffer in your own life to show the human condition when you're acting. The healthier you are, the better you can use the techniques I'm teaching you.

Getting back to emotional triggers, for physical pain a choice could be "It's as if someone's rubbing my body with sandpaper." You have to allow yourself the sensory reality of how your body would feel if the sandpaper was breaking your skin open. It sounds horrifying, but there are scenes you'll have to play where you'll have to use it or use something else horrifying that triggers you. Watch Dustin Hoffman in *Marathon Man,* as Laurence Olivier, playing a Nazi torturer, drills an exposed nerve in his mouth. Here's the key: for something to be an emotional trigger, the image or the memory or whatever choice you make must not stay in your head; it should urge you to be physical. It has to become a sensory reality because that's the only way it can be an emotional reality. You may not act on the physical impulse, but it should cause one. That's the rule. An emotional trigger has to carbonate feelings and behavior.

You could feel how much Dustin Hoffman, had he not been tied to the chair by his torturer, wanted to push that drill away. And the impulse to push the drill away, which we see in his physical behavior as he frantically struggles to pull his head away from the drill—the only thing he can do—is fully alive because of the specificity of the work Hoffman did to create the pain of the drill hitting an exposed nerve. As powerful is his relief when his torturer, demonstrating the possibility of stopping the torment, applies oil of clove to soothe the pain. Hoffman's behavior was that of a deeply relieved child, almost an infant sucking his bottle. This was truly creative "as if" work for an emotional trigger.

I want to add here that the fabulous teacher of voice and Shakespeare, Patsy Rodenburg, told me that Laurence Olivier's "as if" for torturing Hoffman was that he was tending the roses in his garden, which he did with tender precision. Talk about another powerful "as if"! This is interpretation, the actor's choice.

The second scene of Lanford Wilson's play *Burn This* is done a lot in acting class. The male lead, Pale, has to enter the scene—his first—in a rage. This is not debatable; the author demands that you enter with this emotional condition. Otherwise the play won't work. If you're playing Pale, the first month you may do it great, but five months into the run on a Saturday matinee, after you've given a blistering performance the night before when the audience stood and screamed and laughed, you may find it difficult to pull up that rage. Sometimes the trigger that has worked before doesn't work now. If you're playing Pale, the fact that your usual trigger doesn't work may make you so angry at yourself that you can use that anger as the character's rage. Remember, the audience will never know or even be interested in how you got there. They just want the story. If you're not angry at yourself, you need to have another trigger from your golden box to catalyze that rage. Or you could be angry at your co-star for jumping on your lines or forgetting hers, and you could enter expressing the anger you feel at her. But rage you must have—that is your job in *Burn This*.

There's a famous story about a film in which the two stars had a sizzling love scene onscreen. The reality was that from the first day of shooting, the two stars did have a strong feeling for each other—contempt. Their sex scenes are very hot because they had a passion for each other, it just happened to be hatred. But it was electrical.

In acting, the worst thing to be is indifferent. Sometimes I talk to a young actor who's just done a scene that didn't work because it was emotionally dead. I'll ask him what his approach to his character was and he'll tell me that he was playing his character as a man who was so strong that he didn't care about how people responded to him. *That doesn't work!* If an actor says this to me, I respond, "Well, if your character doesn't care, why is he in the room?" The character may aspire to not caring or try to convince other people that he doesn't care, but there's no drama if he *really* doesn't care.

As an actor you have to find what the character does care about and you have to invest yourself in it emotionally; the writer puts two people there, so you have to care! I'll put that in bold letters: YOU HAVE TO CARE, YOU HAVE TO IMAGINE, YOU HAVE TO TRIGGER, YOU HAVE TO KNOW YOURSELF, YOU HAVE TO BE INTERESTED, CURIOUS, PASSIONATE.

You have to be deliberate and honest with yourself. You have to say, "I have trouble being sexual onstage," or "I have trouble laughing," "I have trouble with grief." These emotions are your palette, that's what you have to paint with, and you can't play scenes that require these emotions without finding a way to trigger them—however painful that may be. As the director Arthur Penn once said, good actors go to emotional places where nobody else wants to go.

I'll end by talking about an actor whose commitment to breaking through his barriers and gaining access to emotional triggers changed his life and career: Michael Clarke Duncan. Director Frank Darabont's company, Darkwood, sent Michael to me to coach for his audition for Frank's film *The Green Mile*. Michael was up for the role of John Coffey, an African-American giant who was the Christ figure in Stephen King's metaphysical drama. John Coffey was arrested for the murder and rape of two little girls in Georgia in the 1930s, not a hospitable place for blacks under any circumstances. I knew full well from reading the script the demands that the role of John Coffey was going to make on whoever did the part. I could tell from Michael's first tape test that he was not in touch with his emotional life. He had been a security guard in Chicago, a bouncer, and a stuntman, and he had appeared in several movies but never in a lead that demanded a deep emotional well. This part needed a gentle giant who appeared physically intimidating and whom other people could believe might be violent.

As soon as Michael walked into the house, he said, "I don't want to be here." I responded, "Well, I hear you, but you're going to have to try to trust me because I'm the guy that's going to get you through the screen test, so sit down." I asked, "What do your friends call you?" He told me they called him Big Mike. I said to him, "Well, Big Mike, you can't play this part," and Michael looked angry and kind of startled, and said, "What do you mean, Mr. Moss?" And I said, "Only Little Mike can play it," and he said, "I don't think I know who that is." I told him that was our problem: we had to find Little Mike.

This intrigued him. I asked him to tell me about himself. He told me about the poverty he came from, the way his mother struggled to take care of him and his sister, how for most of his childhood there was no man in the family, how his mother had to sacrifice. One of the most emotional moments in our work together was when Michael began to express his feelings about his mother. These feelings were enormously powerful, as Michael's relationship with his mother is of the deepest kind of gratitude and love. Michael told me that without her love and support, he wouldn't have survived. He experienced a lot of violence in his childhood because of the neighborhood he grew up in, and a lot of loneliness, but he has and always has had a great relationship with his mom.

He was already big by nature but he made himself bigger by building up his muscles so that nobody could hurt him and so that he could protect his mother and his sister. He had to grow up very, very fast. He remembered the bigotry of the white policeman who made him walk in a dirty puddle so his shoes wouldn't look clean; he remembered a terrible event that happened to his family that he was helpless to do anything about. These memories would just make him flood with tears. He would weep and weep, and he was both exhilarated and horrified in the process of it.

As he wept he'd tell me, "I haven't felt these things," and "I don't know where this is coming from." But we knew we were on to something because he suddenly realized that he had all this emotion.

When we began to work on the role of John Coffey, I said to him, "You've got to carry the pain of the entire world in your eyes. The good news is that you have it. Now you have to be willing to share it." To help him identify and reach his emotional triggers, we would do exercises. He would sit in a chair opposite me, and I would ask him questions about his childhood, what it felt like to be black, fatherless, poor, his love for his mother and his sister, how hard he worked to care for them by being a security guard, his dreams of being an actor and wondering how he would ever get from the Chicago ghetto to Hollywood.

An essential part of the exercise was for him not just to talk about his childhood but to open his heart as he talked, to allow the emotion to come up again and again as he remembered the features of his mother's face, the incident when the white policeman made him walk in the dirty puddle, the terrible event that had happened to his family. As he talked, we were looking for his emotional triggers. Then we'd work on scenes from the film. For example, I asked him to have a specific image that he worked on when John Coffey says, "I'm tired of all the pain and feeling here in the world—every day. There's too much of it, it's like pieces of glass in my head all the time . . . can you understand?" Michael rehearsed with this specific image, and that triggered the emotion necessary to make this a powerful and truthful line.

What makes this moment in the film work powerfully as well was Coffey's intense desire to get Paul Edgecomb (Tom Hanks) to understand that he was in so much emotional pain that, to a certain degree, death would be a blessing. In other words, his objective was to protect his dear new friend Paul, a white police officer, from feeling guilt or grief about his passing.

Michael understood what it was to be an outsider, he understood what it was to be hated because of how you look, he understood what it was to be helpless, he understood what it was to be angry, he also understood what it was to have gifts that most people don't have and that he didn't fully know he had. He also had a dream. By breaking through his personal barriers and accessing his emotions, he was able to use these experiences to create an indelible performance as John Coffey. The price that Michael paid to be able to play John Coffey was to access his own real-life pain.

There's no question in my mind that playing John Coffey was part of Michael's destiny. And I want to say this to every actor who's reading this book: you don't know what's waiting for you. Michael Clarke Duncan obviously didn't know there was a *Green Mile* waiting for him. As he told me, there was no chance in hell he was ever going to star in a movie with Tom Hanks; it just wasn't possible. But he did.

When I met Michael again after the premiere of *The Green Mile*, I asked him how he felt. He answered, "When I used to get into an elevator, people would back away. And now they shake my hand."

8

THE ACTOR'S CHOICE:
CREATING YOUR INTERPRETATION

When the British director Peter Hall called Judi Dench regarding her availability and interest in playing Shakespeare's Cleopatra in *Antony and Cleopatra,* Dench responded, "Who wants to see a menopausal dwarf play Cleopatra?" This was, of course, because in middle age and at around five feet tall, it was daunting for Dench to have to fill the shoes of the most famously glamorous woman in history. Hall's reply was, "Listen, Judi, in the first scene, you'll show us a little bit of Cleopatra. And in the second scene you'll show us a little bit more of Cleopatra. And maybe by the end of the play, we'll see all of Cleopatra." Hall was more interested in Dench's interpretive skills than in her judgment of her physical qualifications. He was talking about the layers of psychological and emotional development that Dench could reveal in her portrayal. A good or great performance is like peeling an onion; in every scene you reveal another layer, something the audience hasn't seen until then. They stay involved because they are constantly learning about and discovering the character they are watching. They can't take you for granted—and it keeps them hooked.

Hall wanted Dench because he knew that he could count on her to bring Cleopatra to human life in a profound and provocative way. He wanted her *particular* peeling of the onion. In other words, he wanted her interpretation.

Why do we want to see great plays like *Hamlet* over and over again? Well, for one reason, they're great plays, but secondly it's to experience actors of each generation who are gifted interpreters of the great roles in these great plays. We hear of Barrymore's Hamlet, Gielgud's, Olivier's, Burton's, Finney's, Nicol Williamson's, Kevin Kline's, Kenneth Branagh's, and Ralph Fiennes's Hamlets; we hear of Sarah Bernhardt's, Judith Anderson's, and Diane Venora's Hamlets. The actor's interpretation of Hamlet is talked about as *that actor's* Hamlet. And you hear critics say, "It's as if I've never seen *Hamlet* before"; "This *Hamlet* is a revelation"; "The most heartbreaking *Hamlet* I've ever witnessed." These publicity blurbs make my point: each actor or actress brought something unique and, in the best cases, startlingly new, to a text many people are keenly aware of and some know by heart. This is the power of interpretation: the power of the *choices* that each actor makes in bringing the role to life.

So far we've looked at three techniques that contribute to interpretation: choosing your own carbonating words for your superobjective; choosing your own words for your active intentions; and creating your inner imagery. In this chapter, I'm going to introduce you to several other useful tools for interpreting a role, some of which I will talk about in more detail in subsequent chapters. These tools are: choosing a private secret for your character; making behavioral choices based on your character's social and economic background; making choices based on your character's blood memory, including choosing an accent; physical choices; finding the humor in drama and the dramatic underpinnings in comedy; making choices in rhythm, tempo, and nuances of meaning in your delivery of lines; and determining the size of your performance. All of these choices ultimately affect your character's behavior, which is what the audience sees and how it gets to know the character.

One of the exercises I do with students to teach interpretation uses popular songs. I'll play three different interpretations of the great Harold Arlen–Johnny Mercer song, "Come Rain or Come Shine." I often use Frank Sinatra's, Judy Garland's, and the saxophonist David Sanborn's recordings, two sung versions and one instrumental. First I read the class the lyrics of the song, then I play the recordings. Judy Garland's interpretation is a kind of a mad mambo, replete with one thousand bongo drums and horns and violins. It is sort of hysterical, while Sinatra's interpretation is bluesy and sad, and David Sanborn's saxophone is almost like a celebration of the blues, an expression of the joy of playing the blues. Each interpretation has a different feeling, although it's the same song.

The first step of interpretation is to study what the writer wrote. The lyrics to "Come Rain or Come Shine" have an obsessive quality, evident from the song's first line: "I'm going to love you like nobody's loved you, come rain or come shine." It's a song of extremes: "High as a mountain, deep as a river, come rain or come shine. I guess when you met me, it was just one of those things"—which I suspect means a passing fancy—"but don't ever bet me, 'cause I'm going to be true if you let me." The lyrics go further; they predict—no, demand—the other person's reaction: "You're going to love me like nobody's loved me, come rain or come shine. Happy together, unhappy together, and won't it be fine." This isn't a question, it's a statement, as the next lyrics show: "Days may be cloudy or sunny, we're in or we're out of the money, but I'm with you always, I'm with you rain or shine." Essentially you're saying, "I'm going to love you obsessively, and you don't have a thing to say about it." There's very little about the other person: with the small concession of "if you let me," it's all about what *I'm* going to do and what *I* have to have. So the first step of interpretation— honoring what the writer wrote—means that if you're singing "Come Rain or Come Shine," you have to honor the lyrics' almost dangerously obsessive quality. You have to understand that if you're singing "happy together, unhappy together, and won't it be fine," you don't even care whether you're happy; you just want to be with this person.

The second step of interpretation is your primitive emotional response to the material. You have to have a reason for singing a song—not just because you have to, for a job—but an emotional reason, a reason to be excited about doing it. As you read the lyrics to "Come Rain or Come Shine," which lines leap out at you and affect you? Where do you have an emotional reaction? Do the lyrics evoke a particular experience in your life? It's the interplay of your subjective reaction with the point of view and content that the lyrics give you that creates your performance.

Obviously, Judy Garland and her arranger wanted to come up with a unique interpretation of a much-sung song. They made the tempo much faster than it was usually played, and in so doing, they brought out the obsessive and insistent qualities inherent in the lyrics and injected them with a hyperurgency, as if she's about to have a nervous breakdown. It's also—on the Carnegie Hall album—quite thrilling. I've talked to people who actually hate this interpretation, but it is very strong, and I promise you it will affect you one way or the other.

The grand saloon singer Sinatra's interpretation is filled with longing and deep sadness. The obsession he expresses is about mourning, not about hope or desperation. This is underscored by Gordon Jenkins's elegiac arrangement, which is filled with weeping strings and cellos bathing Sinatra in his misery. I have heard that when Sinatra recorded this performance, he was in mourning over his relationship with the glamorous 1950s film star Ava Gardner. Sinatra was quoted as saying, "I find my performance of a song in the character of the lyricist's story." His great gift, besides his voice and phrasing, was his ability to make every lyricist's story into his personal story while honoring the lyrics. In "Come Rain or Come Shine," he does this by singing about his own broken heart.

Isn't it interesting that David Sanborn, the excellent saxophonist, could celebrate the obsessive and sensual qualities of this famous song, that he could find so much joy in it, seeming to say, "It may hurt, but what a thrill to love somebody that deeply!" Even in this instrumental version, Sanborn evokes the lyrics in his phrasing with the saxophone, almost like joyous masochism. Three great musical performers putting their stamp—their interpretations—on the same popular song.

When you're interpreting a part in a play, your first two steps are the same as with a song. First, you have to deeply understand what the writer has written. This includes understanding the given circumstances, the objectives, and obstacles that are clearly written into the script. It also means you have to try to understand the ideas that inspired the writer to write the story; the ideas are emotional because they have the writer's passion behind them. Don't be arrogant and assume that you can interpret it before you deeply understand the material. Second, as you read through the script, find what moves you most strongly and make a note of it in the script so you begin to find your own personal reason for playing the part. You may find yourself identifying with your character, which is helpful, but even if you don't, you've got to find something in the script that ignites your own passion.

As you read a script and familiarize yourself with the given circumstances, an inspirational flash might hit you that cracks open the entire role. For example, Helen Hunt had a brilliant idea for interpretation while she was reading and rereading the script of *As Good as It Gets*. She decided that her character, Carol, had a secret. The secret was that she is sexually attracted to Jack Nicholson's obsessive-compulsive character, Melvin, and for the life of her she doesn't know why, and, in fact, is embarrassed by the feeling. That was her private secret. At the beginning of the movie, there's a little moment when they brush past each other in the restaurant where Carol works. Helen told me that at that moment, she was going to look at Melvin and say to herself, "I like him, I don't know why I like him, I think I'm crazy because he's crazy and yet he's attractive to me for some chemical reason that I do not understand."

This secret attraction then forms a basis for their eventually getting together romantically. But it isn't given circumstances; it was Helen's interpretation. Another actress playing Carol might have decided that at that point Melvin irritates her and that she is impatient with him. But the way that Helen saw Melvin, he was kind of an eccentric but lovable kook. This choice made Carol appealing and it set up from the beginning, without being obvious, that something could happen between them. It also gave them a place to go emotionally when Melvin enrages her by saying that it looks as if her kid is going to die; because she had the secret attraction for him, it made her fury that much greater.

For an interpretation of a character to work, it's vital to understand the socioeconomic level of the character: What class are they from? How much education have they had? What were their financial circumstances growing up? What other social experiences—such as racism or prejudice—shaped them? All you have to do is look at your own life and see how important these factors were in shaping your identity and point of view about life. You can't be general about these factors or about their effects on the character; you have to be very specific.

Maggie in *Cat on a Hot Tin Roof* says, "Oh, Brick, Brick, y'know I've been so goddamn disgustingly poor all my life." The word "disgusting" is a major key to understanding Maggie—not just "poor" but "disgustingly poor." Perhaps she was disgusted by the food she had had to eat; the house she had to live in; the smell of the hand-me-down dresses she was forced to wear. We've seen that Maggie's superobjective is economic: *to have so much money that I never have the fear of being poor for the rest of my life.* I suggested earlier that you might imagine yourself as Maggie, watching your mother die in the poor ward of a hospital. The play tells us Maggie was a debutante, that she "came out" in high society, but it also tells us that in order to do this she had to suck up to rich relatives and that she had to wear cast-off clothing. She mentions that when she married Brick she only had two dresses. So another fact about her socioeconomic background is that she came from a poor family *with pretensions*.

How do you translate this into interpretative choices? You translate it into human behavior. When Maggie enters the bedroom and tells Brick, "Well, I just remarked that one of th' no-neck monsters"—Brick's brother's children—"messed up m' lovely lace dress so I got t' change," how important is this to Maggie? If you've been "disgustingly" poor, a lovely lace dress has much more meaning than it would to someone who has always been wealthy. How Maggie carefully holds and cleans that garment, how carefully she hangs it up, tells the audience how much she values her clothes—and that she does not take for granted *anything* of material value. It also says a lot about how she wants to present herself and move up in society; she certainly would never wear a dress with a stain on it. It would remind her too much of her poverty-ridden childhood.

Compare this with Nora in Ibsen's *A Doll's House* in the groundbreaking interpretation by Janet McTeer, who played the role in London's West End and on Broadway. For her first entrance as Nora, McTeer flung her clothes willy-nilly all over the room as she came in from the cold. She threw her coat across the living room, because she knew the maid was going to pick it up. Now, that isn't in Ibsen's stage directions of *A Doll's House,* it is an interpretation by Janet McTeer that Nora, who has been really pampered and treated like a spoiled child, scatters her clothes because that's what a spoiled child would do.

The clarity that comes from understanding the socioeconomic factors influencing your character was brought home to me by Stella Adler's discussion of *Pygmalion* in her script analysis class. She said, "You have to understand what being in the lower classes in England at that time in history meant to an unmarried young woman. It meant that she was either a prostitute or had some menial job, as Eliza Doolittle did, selling flowers, that paid her very little money, and that she lived a life of desperation and the possible terror of falling even lower than she was." Stella learned from doing research that the lower classes of that period could not afford hot water, so they bathed infrequently and when they did bathe it was in cold water. So in the scene in which Eliza is forced by Mrs. Pearce, Henry Higgins's housekeeper, to take a bath, when she screams, "Boohoo!!!!" it's because she believes she will either be submerged in ice cold water or scalded to death by hot water she's never experienced and because, with her exclamations of, "I'm a good girl, I am!" she thinks it's indecent to be naked in front of another person.

When I understood and felt Eliza's desperation and panic at the idea of a simple bath, I began to feel tears running down my cheeks because what Stella taught me was a missing link in my education as an actor. That missing link was understanding how the social and economic level of every character I played helps to define the character and their behavior. Don't think of this as a tool just for period texts. Social class and economic circumstances affect every character you play, affecting how you dress, talk, move, and feel about yourself and the world.

Another aspect of interpretation has to do with the *blood memory* of the character—the nationality, the ethnic roots of the character. In *The Bridges of Madison County* Meryl Streep adopted a specific Italian accent for the role of Francesca, even though word has it that Clint Eastwood, who directed as well as played opposite her, said he didn't think she needed one. But Streep saw it as central to the story and central to her believing herself in the part. Her Francesca has kept much of her Italian self even though she's been living for some time in the American Midwest. Her accent embodies her isolation and loneliness in a community where she is different from everyone else. If you watch the way she struggles for certain English words and uses her body to help her speak, she brings Italy onto the screen. There is something fascinating about that European flavor with the raw-boned American energy of Eastwood that makes the relationship between the characters they play moving and memorable.

When you have an accent—and I'm going to say this several times in this book because it's so important—it's not just an accent, it's a way of life. It affects how you express yourself physically and emotionally. Look at Meryl Streep as Sophie in *Sophie's Choice* and as Francesca in *The Bridges of Madison County* and see how her accent affects her interpretation of these women. Meryl Streep is one of the rare, true great actresses of the cinema; she makes her characters live. As Streep once said, "I never give any character I play less respect than I give my own life."

A vital part of interpretation is the physicalization of a character. Chapter Ten discusses physical choices in detail, but I'd like to introduce the concept here with three examples where physical choices are crucial—and very much open to interpretation.

One of the given circumstances of Shakespeare's *Richard III* is that Richard is in some way physically deformed. In the first scene he tells us:

But I, that am not shap'd for sportive tricks,
Nor made to court an amorous looking glass;
I, that am rudely stamp'd, and want love's majesty
To strut before a wanton ambling nymph;
I that am curtail'd of this fair proportion,
Cheated of feature by dissembling nature,
Deform'd, unfinish'd, sent before my time
Into this breathing world, scarce half made up,
And that so lamely and unfashionable
That dogs bark at me as I halt by them . . .

When Anthony Sher played Richard III in London, he made the deformity the dominant characteristic of the man and therefore the justification for his vengeance and overwhelming ambition. Sher studied spinal injuries and people with deformities for a year prior to his rehearsal of the play. He did drawings of Richard III as a creeping spider with a crutch on each limb. This was an astonishing and brave choice which Sher brought to life. You can find out exactly how he did it in his wonderful book, *Year of the King: An Actor's Diary and Sketchbook,* which includes his drawings and his diary. Contrast this with the filmed versions of *Richard III* by Laurence Olivier and Ian McKellen, both of whom played Richard with far milder physical disabilities.

Actresses playing Laura in Tennessee Williams's *Glass Menagerie* face similar choices. *The Glass Menagerie* was Williams's breakthrough autobiographical play about a young writer, Tom, who must break away from his dominating mother, Amanda, and his psychologically crushed sister, Laura. One of the given circumstances of the play is that Laura has a club foot, but how much of a club foot she has and how it affects her walk is open to interpretation. We also see in the play that Amanda has disabled Laura emotionally by filling her head with the romance of the Old South and by overpowering Laura with her personality. The club foot could be almost unnoticeable physically but so big in Laura's mind that it is the real symbol of her internal damage; she may overemphasize it because it parallels and gives a reason for her phobic shyness. It's in this interplay of psychological damage and physical disability that you as an actress find your interpretation of Laura.

My final example is Dustin Hoffman's Dorothy in *Tootsie.* Dorothy could have been many, many kinds of women. There are lines that tell you something about how she is but there really isn't anything that tells you her carriage, her makeup, her style. Hoffman has said that he based her on his mother, which meant that she was a bit old-fashioned. This worked perfectly for the thoroughly decent woman the script calls for Dorothy to be. Dorothy is direct, decent, honest, sensitive, caring, and strong, and she won't put up with any kind of machismo, but her feminism is genteel at the same time as it's assertive.

Here's another key that can open your interpretation and make the audience want to connect with you: when you're playing high drama, look for where you can find the humor in a scene. What could be more terrifying than the figure of Medea in Euripides's great tragedy? Yet Diana Rigg found uncanny opportunities for humor when she played this mother who murders her children out of revenge for her dallying husband. And watch John Malkovich mine as much humor as he can in every role he plays. His Obie-winning performance as Lee in *True West,* Sam Shepard's indictment of family violence, was a testament to this. The glowering and demanding older brother he played was filled with defensiveness and arbitrary points of view, and Malkovich constantly surprised us with the humor that can come from such rigidity. Brando found tremendous opportunities for humor in the role of Stanley Kowalski, so much so, in fact, that it's said he completely lopsided the original Broadway version of *Streetcar* and made himself so likable that the audience preferred him to Jessica Tandy's Blanche DuBois. Elia Kazan righted this wrong in the screen version and made sure that as charismatic as Brando was, your sympathies went right away to Vivien Leigh's Blanche. By the way, even though the stakes are desperately high for Blanche, Vivien Leigh found opportunities for humor, too. So don't get caught in, "Oh my God, it's life and death and therefore there are no laughs."

The reverse is also true: it's dimensional to find drama or darker tones in a comedy. Robert Morse originated the role of J. Pierpont Finch on Broadway in the Pulitzer Prize–winning musical comedy *How to Succeed in Business Without Really Trying.* It made him a huge star (he was on the cover of *Time* magazine) and he repeated the role in the film. The vibrancy of Morse's performance was created in part by the subtle tones of dark ambition that shimmered under the comic surface. He understood how dramatically high the stakes were for Pierpont's rise to business power. His subversive comic performance was filled with the kind of boyish charm that is usually associated with a young, innocent hero, but Morse's Pierpont was completely amoral, closer to a sociopath than a hero. Morse played this to the hilt, literally turning to the audience and smiling in a conspiratorial way as if he were Richard III confiding his plans to usurp the throne. There was nothing heavy-handed in Morse's interpretation, it was as light as a soufflé, and as piercing as the beak of the character's last name, Finch. Other people have played the role, but nobody ever played it like Robert Morse.

A fundamental part of interpretation is being sensitive to the rhythms of the writer, understanding that Eugene O'Neill has different rhythms from Tennessee Williams, from Shakespeare, from Shaw. Understanding the rhythms and the music and the tempo of each character is vital as well. There are times when you might choose to go against the rhythm of a line and pause in order to make a point—that is your interpretation. But again, you have to be very smart about why you're going to do this and when. If you keep pausing in the wrong places, the audience will fall asleep, because it will seem as if you're waiting for something to happen instead of doing the play. Keep your focus on your active intentions.

Sanford Meisner taught actors never to look at the punctuation in a script. His belief was that it would force you into giving a particular line reading that might not be your own—meaning that you would get stuck in a certain way of saying it instead of following the impulses arising from your intention. It's a good idea to experiment with Meisner's rule, *but be careful!* You might miss something valuable that a smart writer gives you in his punctuation. The essential point is that your reading must come from a real, organic desire to reach the other person in a certain way.

John Patrick Shanley's play *The Dreamer Examines His Pillow* is about a young couple in a highly dysfunctional relationship. At one point, the young woman hurls this accusation at the man. She says, "I'm hearin' shit, I'm seein' shit, I'm smellin' the smoke, somethin's burnin', don't you tell me there's no fire, you *are* hitting on my sister." If you pause during this litany you won't earn the enormous laugh that you should get here. The author put in that accelerating string of commas for a reason. If you deliver the line as, "I'm hearin' shit, I'm seein' shit, I'm smellin' the smoke, somethin's burnin', don't you tell me there's no fire." (pause) "You *are* hitting on my sister," it may work dramatically but it won't be hilarious. And you will also miss Shanley's somewhat surreal blend of dramatic confrontation and unexpected humor.

The impact of tempo was brought home to me by Ralph Fiennes's interpretation of Hamlet's famous "To be or not to be" soliloquy. Instead of the usual hesitant, musing reading, Fiennes delivered the speech as fast as he could muster the words. I found it riveting. Done with so much speed, the speech seemed not to be spoken words but thoughts, as if Fiennes were actually taking us into Hamlet's mind. There isn't a person in the world playing Hamlet who doesn't look at all of those legendary monologues and say, "Christ, how am I going to put my stamp on this performance?" And there's another aspect to the challenge as well: "How am I going to make the audience *hear* this in a new way? Make them pay attention and get something out of the speeches that perhaps they've never gotten before?" Through his creative searching, Fiennes did discover a way to make us come to the edge of our seats with one of the most famous soliloquies of all time. Of course, there were people who roundly disapproved of Fiennes's interpretation, but by God he had one, and it was supported by the text.

Sometimes words or whole lines are repeated by a character in a script. This is a particular interpretive challenge. If you don't bring out the nuances of meaning, the repetition will be emotionally empty. For every line, you always have to ask yourself internally, *Why am I saying that?* For a repeated word or line, you have to ask yourself internally, *Why am I repeating that word or line? How does it clarify my character's psychological development?*

Recently I saw the old tearjerker *Now, Voyager,* a wonderfully masochistic romantic movie. It's about a wealthy spinster, Charlotte Vale (Bette Davis), who is dominated by her sadistic mother and who escapes, after a nervous breakdown, into a romantic liaison with a married man (Paul Henreid) she meets on an ocean voyage. And I think it's important to note here that they never stop smoking. (You'll understand when you see the film why I say this.) There's a moment of epiphany for the Bette Davis character that speaks volumes about interpretation. Charlotte's mother says, in essence, "If you don't live your life the way I want you to, I'll disinherit you." Then the camera makes this wonderful move toward Davis's face as she says, "I'm not afraid, Mother," then the camera moves closer still and she says, as if she's surprised, "I'm not afraid." Look at the line in the script, "I'm not afraid, Mother. I'm not afraid." It doesn't necessarily have to be read like that. But as Bette Davis interpreted it, the first time she says, "I'm not afraid, Mother," is a quiet, confrontational standoff, but the second "I'm not afraid" was discovery and awe. She says it a third time, too, as if she's incorporating that fact into herself and thereby becoming a whole person, finally and forever cutting the cord that bound her to a life of misery. This interpretation is rooted in character and in active intention. The first delivery of the line was *to quietly con-*

front; the second was *to realize with awe;* the third was *to take into my being the strength I have discovered.*

It's interesting to consider what goes right for some actors and wrong for others in the same role. For example, Princess in *Sweet Bird of Youth* has been tried by at least three major actresses, but only one of them crossed the finish line with it. Both Joanne Woodward and Lauren Bacall were famous movie stars when they threw their hats in the ring to play Princess. Both talented actresses did pre-Broadway tryouts, but the productions never came into New York. On the other hand, Geraldine Page originated the role before she became a famous movie star, but she made us believe she was true cinema royalty in the grand tradition. She was helped by Tennessee Williams's writing, of course, and by director Elia Kazan's demand that she play Princess with as much theatrical size as possible while not losing her truth—because the truth of Princess Alexandra del Lago is that her life is a performance.

Size is an interpretive choice: How much energy and intensity will you give your character, and how will that energy and intensity be expressed? I saw Geraldine Page's Princess in Los Angeles in the national tour of the play, and it was galvanizing; she found the truth of the particular kind of old-time movie queen that Princess was. She started the role without any makeup whatsoever and her hair a kind of frizzy mess, so when she said to Chance, "I must look like some kind of Martian," she did. But even as a Martian she had grandeur. It reminded me of the famous exchange in Billy Wilder's 1950 masterpiece *Sunset Boulevard,* in which William Holden, playing a down-on-his-luck Hollywood writer, says to an old-time silent film star, Norma Desmond, played indelibly by Gloria Swanson, "You used to be big." She responds, "I *am* big. It's the movies that got small." Page's performance personified that idea.

Page's Princess, like Bette Davis, spoke with a kind of a broad *a,* as if she'd had elocution lessons. You can hear it in the film version when Princess says, "Chaance, Chaance." There's a kind of flowery theatricality to the way she speaks. Page, with Kazan's support, created that interpretation based on her knowledge of movie history. When Princess was young, studios trained rising stars in elocution and deportment, training that gave them a slightly aristocratic air that made us feel they were a little bit better bred than we were.

Princess is a difficult and demanding role for many reasons. One of the big traps is to fall into a kind of phony exaggeration without understanding that the exaggeration is based on a certain kind of training and a certain kind of lifestyle. By the time we meet Princess, the exaggeration is so much a part of her that she's unconscious of it. We meet her when she's down on her luck and her career is, according to her, on the skids, after what she thinks has been a disastrous attempt at a comeback. She has to convince us of her great fame, and it has to be shown to us in everything she does: how she talks, how she carries herself, her gestures, her phrasing, her handling of garments; it has to be authentic, not played at. I believe that Princess probably came from somewhere in Iowa or Idaho before Hollywood "polished" her, and Page was deeply aware of the roots of the Princess Alexandra del Lago—but she also knew that at the time we meet her, the Princess is more real to Alexandra than whoever she had been before.

Al Pacino starred in several productions of David Mamet's play *American Buffalo,* with different interpretive choices each time. *American Buffalo* is the story of three misfits who have a very odd and inept way of trying to capture the American dream: they try to set up a robbery that goes wrong in funny and sad ways. The first time Pacino was cast as Walter Cole (ironically nicknamed Teach), he played him as a fireball. Pacino later stated in an interview that he could never find a way of doing the role that pleased him until the last time. It was a much quieter performance; Pacino played Teach as a desperately defeated clown, someone with very little hope. Pacino said he finally stopped pushing the part— stopped demanding huge energy—and started to simply inhabit it. He realized that the character was a small man, and giving him powerful size defeated the purpose of the play. I saw the first and last productions and admired his commitment in both. In the first production, his performance was extremely effortful and I was aware of the acting; in the last, I couldn't catch him acting anything. I was just moved.

You have to find something in every script that ignites your own passion. There may come a time in your career when you do an acting job just for money, but don't make the mistake that I've seen other actors commit, which is either to walk through the part with no emotional investment or to comment on their disdain for it in subtle ways. *Don't ever play a part without some personal investment; it's better to get a regular job that's just for money.* If you choose to act without passion it begins to eat away at you; you're in danger of losing the one absolutely essential ingredient for a healthy acting career: the thrill of the challenge to be a better actor.

Even if you're doing commercials to put bread on the table, invest in them. Use the techniques I'm teaching you and find the positive in it. Never underestimate the impact that positive energy has in our business.

If you are having trouble finding emotional heat in your role, go back to the idea that you think provoked the writer to write the script. If your conclusion is that the writer wrote the script just to make money, you can still find a way to challenge yourself and make it fun and avoid contempt. Even in an inadequate script you may find excitement in communicating certain themes. If you read a script that you don't like at all but you see something in the part you're up for that excites you, go for it. Even in a very small part you may hit on an interpretive idea that turns you on. An actor I know, Kent Broadhurst, had a chance at a small role in Mike Nichols's film *Silkwood* playing a malcontented worker in a plutonium factory. In every scene his character was engaged in a boring, repetitive task, and he had very few lines. For the audition, this smart actor brought in a small matchbox, and as he did the scene he pushed the matchbox open, put a tiny ball bearing in it, then pushed it closed, over and over again, lost in the inner imagery he had created for this dour, mean-spirited man. The casting director told Broadhurst when he walked out of the room, "Mr. Nichols said, 'That's an actor,'" and of course he got the part. His commitment to his interpretation won him a great cinematic experience working alongside Mike Nichols and Meryl Streep, and he improved his on-camera skills in the process.

Where does interpretation become misinterpretation? When it hurts the text. In my class, a young actor did a poignant scene from Michael V. Gazzo's play *A Hatful of Rain,* about a young man addicted to heroin after World War II, his wife's discovery of his addiction, and her attempt to save his life. In the scene, the husband, Johnny, tries to apologize to Celia, his wife, for never being home. Johnny loves Celia deeply. He cleans the house, prepares dinner, and brings her flowers in the hopes that she will forgive him—although he is still keeping his addiction secret. She believes he's trying to cover up a love affair. In order for the scene to play correctly, the actor playing Johnny must expose his vulnerability, and although there is a moment where he becomes frustrated over her punishing him with her coldness, you have to walk a very thin line with that anger, because his objective is to gain closeness to Celia, not to push her away. It's the character's feeling of being out of control and containing it because he loves his wife that makes the scene so alive with danger.

At this vulnerable moment, the young actor in my class became so enraged that he brought his fist down with all his might on the kitchen table, breaking every dish and glass that he had so carefully set to seek Celia's forgiveness. Needless to say, the scene was over and could never recover from that indulgence. Like the scene I described in *The Seagull,* the violent action wasn't justified by the needs of the scene and the dialogue didn't support it. When I pointed this out, the young actor playing Johnny turned to me and yelled, "But I had a real moment, I was truthful and passionate," and once again I had to give him the sad news that that was wonderful for him, but the play ended when that explosion of violence was committed.

No matter how successful you become, your job as an actor is to interpret the writer, not to "improve" the work, not to fit it to your preconceptions, and not to tailor it to your self-image.

A very famous actress once called and said to me, "I want you to read this script and help me rewrite it." In the script, the character the actress was going to play had someone murdered. Given the particular character and circumstances, I thought the script provided ample emotional justification for her actions. But the actress didn't want to be seen that way, she thought of herself as a certain kind of movie star that could never do anything that dastardly. Her exact words were, "I have to rewrite this role and you have to help me, because I won't be perceived as heroic enough." When I called to tell her I didn't think the script should be changed, she told me she'd get back to me—which of course she never did. Instead, she made them rewrite the character, and the movie failed. That wasn't interpretation of a part; it was arrogance and insecurity, and her career has suffered enormously for it. Always remember where interpretation ends and the desperation to be loved by an audience begins. And remember that when you serve the script, you also serve the audience and yourself as an actor.

9

Defining and Redefining
Your Relationships

You're preparing to play a part. *How* do you work? You read the script thoroughly at least three times—once as audience, and simply respond; the second time on your lips to get a sense of the language; and the third time you read it out loud to hear the story and language. And starting with the very first reading, you make notes in your script of how it affects you personally and ideas about what you might want to use to bring it to life. If you find personalizations and "as ifs" to create life for yourself, write them in the script with shorthand notes—just one or two words— about people, places, things that you're personalizing or imagining "as if," and write them near the line where you're using them.

Let's say, for example, you're playing the snobbish Gwendolen in Oscar Wilde's classic comedy *The Importance of Being Earnest*. Gwendolen has a scene in which she first meets and pretends to like the younger and more attractive Cecily. In fact, she's intensely threatened by her because Cecily is a ward of the man Gwendolen loves and Gwendolen is afraid Cecily will steal his affections. If you're playing Gwendolen and have had a college roommate whom you disliked and had to pretend you liked, then you have it in spades.

So you would write down your old roommate's name in the script next to your first sighting of Cecily. Then you begin to remember the way you behaved toward her, because that's what you're looking for: that fake niceness hiding that poisonous envy, because she's thinner than you, has better skin than you, and has seven cashmere sweaters for every day of the week. That bitch. Let me clarify: I'm not saying you should think of your roommate onstage while you're acting the play; *you have to work with the actress who's in front of you.* But it might help you to think of a particular moment when you envied your roommate right before you walk onstage, and you would use sense memory of events involving your roommate as part of your homework and during the rehearsal process. You can even imagine your roommate dressed to the nines in late nineteenth-century couture as Cecily would be, fanning herself and batting her eyes at the boyfriend you're afraid she's stealing from you.

This personalization—or substitution—helps you remember organically what it feels like to be insincere and try to hide your venom: how insincerely you flattered her and touched her on her arm affectionately while hating her guts. If you have notes in your script, then when you're doing your homework and studying your part, you're going over all the levels of it at once, so that you're carbonating yourself while you're learning your lines.

Besides writing personalizations, memories, and "as ifs" in the margins, you can write down your objectives and intentions. As Gwendolen, you might phrase your objective "to find out as much information as I can from this unexpected, potential rival"; your intentions might be *to ingratiate myself, to sweetly compliment her, to interrogate her genteelly,* and, finally, *to confront her by emptying my sacs of poison.* Like a musical score, your annotated script helps remind you of the active doings for different moments in the text. It helps you when you're learning the part and also during the long run of a play. If you forget your original choices and start acting on remote control, then you can always go back to what we call the bible, your original script, for notes to remind you.

Do you have to write everything on your script? Some people write in a notebook or in a computer file so they can read the notes to themselves separately from the script and experience the emotion of their choices as they read them. Other people imagine their personalizations and "as ifs" vividly but don't write them down. That works for them. I suggest always writing down your objectives and intentions next to your lines. But everybody's different. The vital thing is not to shortchange yourself by being sloppy and vague. Demand specificity so that it's always there in as much detail as in life and therefore makes you boil inside.

On your first reading of the script, you can immediately identify each character in the simplest way as "my mother, my sister, my husband, my wife, my son, my daughter, my friend, my boss." But that's only the beginning. You also have to define in every scene who the other character is to you *emotionally* and how that changes from scene to scene. This is called the *redefinition of a relationship.* As you read the script, keep asking yourself, *Who are they to me* now *emotionally?* Then write the answer at the top of each scene. It may change within the scene three or four times, but you must have a point of view of how you're starting the scene in relationship to that person. With your notes at the top of the scene, you'll be able to say, "Oh, that's right, *that's* what they mean to me now. They're no longer my potential lover, they are my adored lover whom I would die for and want to spend the rest of my life with."

Use highly charged adjectives and explanatory phrases to bring your relationships to life. For instance, you might say about a character who is your sister, "This is my jealous, rat bastard sister who just betrayed a confidence to my mother and I hate her fucking guts," or about a character who is your husband or your wife, "This is the love-of-my-life husband (or wife) who's cheated on me our entire marriage and I just found out about it and I will never forgive him (or her)." Both these statements describe your relationship in specific emotional terms; they give you a point of view that helps you start the scene with a strong emotional charge toward the other character.

Now let's say that in the next scene your cheating husband begs you to forgive him, and you finally break down and tell him you've loved him your whole life and all you want is for the marriage to continue. So at the start of the next scene he is still the love of your life but, because of his infidelity, you are terrified that he'll leave you. You emotionalize the *redefinition of the relationship* scene by scene with emotional language and with specific images—internal pictures like finding your spouse in bed with someone else or finding their love letters to someone else. All you have to do is say the sentence and remember the image and you immediately know who they are to you.

Emotionalizing and writing down the redefinition of relationships scene by scene is especially vital for films, because you will film out of sequence. You need to have instant access to your feelings toward the other character at any given point in the shoot. This is incredibly helpful when you're doing the last scene of the movie first and the middle of the movie two weeks from now and the first scene on the last day of shooting. This sounds ridiculous but I've been there when it happens. Your notes will tell you exactly what you want to project when the camera starts to roll.

Another part of your homework is to physicalize these emotional reactions to the other character. Say, for instance, that you're frightened or enraged by someone. As preparation, use that emotion to activate your body in a kind of dance. What I mean by *dance* is a series of physical gestures or movements. For example, you find a series of physical gestures or movements that express your feelings toward *"my brutal, tender, sexy, heartbroken, cold-hearted husband."* You do the dance as homework, but the day of the shoot or before you go onstage, you might do that dance again because if you remind your body of the physical behavior catalyzed by your emotions, you will bring this into the performance.

Sometimes all you have to do before your entrance is visualize the movements from your dance in your mind's eye or physicalize it subtly— do a small version of it—and you will be out of your head and into your body. Through the dance you make the relationship real to you and to your body, you make it visceral. Sometimes, too, you may find a gesture in your dance that will become part of your character's physical reaction to the other character.

Your character's point of view toward another character may be redefined several times within one scene. Sometimes the script makes these pivotal redefinitions very evident. Sometimes it takes real work to figure them out. It's fascinating to watch on film the face of an actor change because internally they've redefined the relationship with the other character in the scene from trust to mistrust, from attraction to repulsion, from friend to enemy. If you have these redefinitions clearly inside you, the muscles of your face will *automatically* reveal the change in increased or decreased muscular tension. This can be extraordinarily subtle, but in a close-up it's wondrous.

A prime example of this is Nicholas Ray's frightening psychological film noir, *In a Lonely Place.* Gloria Graham plays Laurel Gray, a young actress who begins a romantic relationship with Dixon Steele (Humphrey Bogart), who is suspected of murder. Because Laurel saw the girl who was murdered leave his apartment, she tells the police that he didn't do it. But it's not that simple—because he could have left and killed her later. Worse, as Laurel becomes romantically involved with him, she observes him almost kill a man over a trifle, and her face registers her lessening trust and growing suspicion and terror, and Dixon's face registers his reaction to her reaction with fear, helplessness, and fury. By the time she finds out his innocence, it's too late: her lack of trust, her pulling away in fear, creates so much rage in him that he nearly does become her murderer. Their romance cannot survive these redefinitions.

Don't finalize your emotional map too soon. During rehearsals, you may find you've left something out; for example, you may realize for the first time that another character says something that hurts your character. Then you have to go back and draw a new inner map that includes the new emotional redefinition. Sometimes these kinds of discoveries are made in a preview of a play or later in the run, or in the filming of a scene. That's why it's important to stay open and to always *really listen* to whoever is speaking to you and take nothing for granted, no matter how many times you've rehearsed and played a scene.

In *The Green Mile,* when John Coffey is brought into jail and has to relate to four white guards, he is gentle and so polite, but what is shimmering underneath that, which Michael and I built, was, "If I make a wrong move, they will hurt me." At the opening of the scene, Michael didn't define individual relationships between John and each policeman because he didn't know them yet; he related to them collectively: "They are policemen whom I fear, who have power over me, who have hurt me in the past and will hurt me again if I do anything wrong." He is actively looking at the policemen in that scene, and saying to himself, *Who could be on my side? Who's safe and who's dangerous?* One of the guards is a sadist, the other three are kind. And the guard played by Tom Hanks is exceptionally kind, but Coffey doesn't know that yet. The relationships are redefined within each scene, and scene by scene, as he gains more knowledge.

When actors don't understand this, they may play only one emotional perspective in the relationship—"I'm angry" or "I'm hurt" or "I'm sad"—and it's *never* that simple. I worked with a gifted actress in my class who was playing the woman in a scene from Harold Pinter's *Betrayal.* In life, the actress often saw herself as a victim, so her choices in her acting work were frequently sensitive, and tearful, coming from the point of view of being attacked or victimized, as if she were asking, *How could you do this to me?* This led her to leave out crucial elements of Pinter's woman, Emma: Emma's betraying self, how she betrayed her husband and her lover, how she lied, how angry she was, how manipulative she was. When

I confronted the actress with this issue, initially she got upset and a bit defensive, because in asking her to recognize the character's dark side I was also asking her to recognize her own. I tried to help her take off the mask of the victim role so that she could reveal honestly the character's anger and manipulation. As upset as she was, she was also, thank God, fascinated and interested and ready to grow as an actress, and indeed she did. It changed her career and it changed her life.

I'll have more to say about self-knowledge—your relationship with yourself—later. For now, in defining and playing your relationships with other characters, be aware not to leave out aspects and feelings of the character you're playing because you are uncomfortable with them personally.

What are the possibilities of any given relationship? Relationships are multileveled, multilayered, multicolored: as an actor you are looking for those things that make a relationship faceted like a diamond. If you say to yourself, *I love my wife, and I could never have a moment when I hate her,* you may be depriving yourself of the opportunity to make the character you're playing more fully real. We all have a loving side and a dark side and to deny it or want to deny it cripples you as an actor.

If there's great love in a relationship, be curious about where you may resent the other person or be thin-skinned regarding them. Loving someone is to some degree being dependent on them, which means it's not okay for you if they leave. If you're dependent, you're vulnerable, so you love them but there may also be a chunk of resentment: you fear that if they leave, a part of you will die. It's well-known that in some long-term marriages, one spouse dies and soon the other spouse dies as well. The surviving partner can't stand the world alone, but that doesn't mean the entire relationship was all roses; there may have been terror in it, anger, possessiveness, and any number of other little monsters. There are moments in scripts as well as in life that will be uncomfortable because you judge them to be inappropriate. Regardless of your own judgments or those of others, feelings are not realities. Perhaps you can feel a moment of awareness of your teenage child's sexual attractiveness. Of course you would never act on that awareness, you would never betray them in that way, but it doesn't mean you didn't have the feeling.

In Edward Albee's play *The Goat,* a man has a sexual relationship with a goat, literally. Bill Pullman played the man so beautifully; he really made you believe his romantic infatuation and longing for this four-legged beast. He, as an actor, did not judge it; he explored it. And that's my point: don't judge your humanity, be curious about it, and find in yourself the truth of all the characters you play, both the light and the dark.

In defining relationships, you're telling an emotional story about your character. It's a story you have to make your own in order to make it live. The information the author gives in the script is always just a skeleton. By this I mean it has no flesh and blood, no matter how great the writing is—and I'm talking about the great writers: Shakespeare, Strindberg, Ibsen, O'Neill, Williams, Miller—it's a skeleton until you identify your personal understanding and visceral connection to all the specifics of your character and all their relationships with the other characters in the script.

Let's take Williams's *The Glass Menagerie* as an example. From the script we know certain things about Tom's relationship with his sister, Laura. We know the sadness he feels toward her, the protectiveness he feels, but the script doesn't tell us how those feelings developed. Tom and Laura don't reminisce about their childhood, but they had one. And we do know that their father, a traveling salesman, disappeared one day; Tom says at the start of the play, "He fell in love with long distance." So in order to add specificity to their closeness at the time dramatized in the play, you could build the conversation Laura and Tom had when they discovered their father had left the family. You can also build the kind of humor that they share with each other about their mother's eccentricities. We have evidence of Tom's dry wit throughout the play, and Laura's intelligence is revealed in her behavior toward Jim O'Connor, whom Tom invites as "a gentleman caller" for his sister.

A helpful exercise that I give my students is an in-character improvisation, which is staying in character and creating your own dialogue in an event that's separate from the play. This exercise helps you to find behavior and specific emotional colors in your relationships with other characters. I'll tell you how to do the exercise, and I'll use *The Glass Menagerie* to illustrate.

In-Character Improvisation

Read through the script you're working on and identify a key relationship with another character. Then identify the critical issues in that relationship. Keeping these critical issues in mind, begin to imagine scenes from the past and present that aren't in the script but are connected and important to fleshing out the relationship and fleshing out events that the characters talk about and/or participate in in the script.

Now, with your scene partner, choose one of these imagined scenes that your intuition tells you would be helpful to your playing the character, and improvise the scene in character. Make the same kind of full commitment to playing it that you would if it were scripted.

Initially, you may feel resistant to doing this, but once you get the hang of it, it will be a technique you will use forever, because it solves problems and creates usable, interesting physical and emotional life that you can bring into performance.

Using *The Glass Menagerie,* you could do an improvisation of Laura talking to Tom about her glass menagerie. Or of a humorous conversation they have together about their mother's eccentric Southern affectations. This can lead to behaviors that you then incorporate in glances at each other and physical gestures during the play. Even an in-character improvisation of Tom and Laura playing a card game together could help you define particular behavior that would help you to truly believe this brother and sister's closeness and need for each other.

As you work on in-character improvisations, you will see how they contribute very specifically to developing your character and your character's relationships when you go back to rehearsing the text. You will find that your performance has new life because, through these improvisations, you will have developed ways of looking at each other, touching each other, laughing or crying with each other, and you will increase your investment in your character and the relationship.

In my experience, rehearsing a play for four weeks over and over again without any in-character improvisations makes it harder to open the door to experiencing human life in the given circumstances, unless the director asks questions of the actors that encourage them to go deeper into the behavioral aspects of the relationships. If the director doesn't do this, you have to—because the play depends on the audience's believing that the relationships are real, that if characters have known each other, those relationships existed before the curtain went up, and that the behavioral idiosyncrasies of those relationships are indelibly true to life.

In *The Glass Menagerie,* the audience has to believe that Tom and Laura care about each other, and they can only do this if the relating they see you do on the stage is truly familial. How is Tom's relationship with Laura affected by her physical impediment? As Tom, you might say to yourself, "I feel protective of Laura, because I am a man, she is my little sister, and we have no father, and part of a man's feelings toward women is a primitive instinct to protect them." But it's impossible for Tom to heal the damaged leg or damaged psyche, so his feelings of tenderness and protectiveness are mixed with helplessness and guilt; he's physically whole and she's not. Being continually provoked by their mother to assume the role of the family protector ties him miserably to a feeling of responsibility for problems he never created and cannot solve.

Added to this is Amanda's cloying, fantastical idea of what female energy is. Tom sees that she is molding Laura into something that won't work in the real world, which only pushes Laura further into fantasy. His helplessness to solve this problem, realizing that he would have to give up his own life to protect Laura, and that even then he might not succeed, makes him painfully rip himself out of the house and abandon Laura. The destructiveness he sees in his mother is revealed in his lines in the middle of the play: "You ugly babbling old witch," and, in the same scene, "Every time you come in yelling that bloody damn 'Rise and shine, rise and shine,' I think how lucky dead people are."

By being specific about the day-to-day interior relationship between Tom and Laura—which in-character improvisations will help you with—the actor playing Tom will understand the wounded heart that says to Laura at the end of the play, when Tom has already left home, "Oh, Laura, Laura, I tried to leave you behind me, but I am more faithful than I intended to be." He reveals to the audience that he cannot stop thinking about his sister, that she haunts every step he takes. And this is why the last line of *The Glass Menagerie* is so wrenching: "Blow out your candles, Laura," Tom says, which I believe means, "You will have no real life, and it breaks my heart, but I must say this to you, forever. In order to find my life as an artist, I must say good-bye." I think it's valuable to know that Tennessee Williams was haunted his entire life by a mentally ill sister, Rose, who was in an institution until she died.

In *The Glass Menagerie,* it's easy to see how Laura needs Tom, but you must see it from the other side of the equation, too: How does Tom need

Laura, what does she give him? I suggest that Laura validates Tom through her appreciation of him, and also that she supplies a loving tenderness that nourishes him in contrast with his tormented relationship with his mother, Amanda.

If you're playing Tom and you're defining your relationship toward Amanda, you might say, "My mother, Amanda, is the chain around my neck, who will not let go of my throat and my genitals, who I tolerate because I have to." You will find your own ways to describe your relationship to her, and you may even find a place for admiration and an odd affection, because crazy as she is, and crazy as she makes you, she's doing the best she can. But as Tom you can never forget that she's dangerous, because she would allow you to give up your art—your writing—in order to protect her and Laura.

The play leads up to the last scene, in which we see Tom in the present, by himself on a city street. Up to this point we've seen a series of scenes from his memories of his past, and these memories inform us in a very emotional way about the present, the present of Tom's telling us what he's left behind and the price he's paid for going off on his own. Unless the play involves us with the relationships in this family and makes us care profoundly, we won't care about the ending, either.

So far I've talked about defining and redefining your character's relationships with other characters. But there's another question you have to ask: What is your character's relationship with him- or herself? Neil Simon's play *Chapter Two* is about a widower, George, who remarries. George's new wife, Jennie, undergoes a major transformation in her relationship to herself and therefore her relationship to George. During the play, Jennie takes a lot of hostility from George because he is still grieving about his first wife's death and is guilty that he survived. He can't bear to be happy. We find out that he's ruined their honeymoon and on their first day back, he continues to bait her into arguments. Near the end of the play, Jennie has finally had enough and tells him off: "I feel better than I felt when I thought there was no one in the world out there for me, and better than I felt the night before we got married and I thought I wasn't good enough for you, well I am, I'm wonderful, I am nuts about me and if you're stupid enough to throw someone sensational like me aside, then you don't deserve as good as you've got." If you're playing Jennie, you need to show first her bad relationship with herself and her inability to stand up to men, then her growing inner strength (the play tells you she's been in therapy) as she faces the possibility of losing the man that she adores, and finally, you need to show her discovering and celebrating her own value.

In *Sophie's Choice,* the movie based on William Styron's novel about a young writer, Stingo (Peter MacNicol), who meets a couple, Nathan (Kevin Kline), an American, and Sophie (Meryl Streep), a Polish immigrant, after World War II. Meryl Streep's interpretation of Sophie's relationship to Nathan is almost like he is a rock star and she is his groupie or he is a guru and she is his devotee. But what colors much of their relationship is Sophie's relationship to herself and to her traumatic past. She responds as a kind of adolescent girl with such glee and gratitude toward him that she can hardly contain it; it's as if she is able to be a free child with him, but it has an edge of hysteria that comes from the terrible guilt Sophie has for being alive. It's almost as though she is *sneaking* joy in her relationship with him. Streep brings a poignancy and a danger to that relationship. I think the idea that she is stealing joy is true, because Sophie is frantically running from her guilt and stealing joy that she feels she took from her little girl, who was murdered in the Holocaust because Sophie, who could save only one child, chose her son and gave her daughter up. With Nathan, she becomes like that daughter, like a giggly little girl, but it is a guilt-ridden, desperate pleasure. Thus, her relationship with her murdered child is part of her relationship with Nathan. Another thing that's interesting about Sophie's relationship to Nathan as interpreted by Streep is that it parallels her idolatry of her father, which was shattered when she found out that he was a Nazi.

Sometimes defining your relationship with a character that's not even mentioned in the script is essential in filling out a performance. This is part of the flesh and blood that you as an actor must add to the skeleton the writer provides. In *As Good as It Gets,* Helen Hunt had to define her relationship with the husband who'd fathered the child and then left them both, even though Carol never talks about him. This was one of the things Helen and I realized she needed to explore in order to fully understand her relationship with her son and her desperate need for money, which came from the fact that she was totally on her own financially.

Helen created in her imagination in detail who her ex-husband was, what her relationship with him was like, and why he had abandoned them. Answering these questions about Carol's prior life helped Helen to invest emotionally in Carol's given circumstances. Only knowing about her relationship with her ex-husband could Helen walk into the apartment as Carol. Is it the apartment where they lived together? Did he leave her there? There are ghosts in places, and she had to know if there were ghosts in that apartment for Carol—which meant defining her relationship with her ex-husband.

Good actors are good detectives, and don't make the mistake of believing people who say, "You don't have to do back story for your character." Asking and answering questions about the character's past will never hurt you and it will often help you enormously.

Some scripts are so much about a relationship that the actor has to invest that relationship with extreme passion for the script to have maximum impact in performance. Sometimes the script hands you the whole relationship on a plate, and all you have to do is commit to adding flesh and blood to the skeleton. In Shakespeare's *Romeo and Juliet*, the relationship, including the background of their warring families and friends, is in the script from beginning to end, and the relationship between Romeo and Juliet is unambiguous: from the moment they set eyes on each other, they are in torrid infatuation, and external obstacles only serve to intensify the cementing of their hyperromantic bond.

In Shakespeare's tragedy *Othello*, the relationship between Othello and Desdemona is far more complicated. External events provoke internal obstacles in Othello that make their relationship emotionally searing and tragic. The play opens with Othello, a Moor and a military leader, already married to the young, aristocratic, European Desdemona. She is an assertive, adventurous, passionate woman, and at least in the beginning, you feel that Othello is proud of those qualities. But in Act 3, Scene 3, Iago, one of Othello's soldiers, insinuates to Othello that Desdemona has possibly been unfaithful. Ignorant of Desdemona's innocence, and willing to believe the manipulative Iago, Othello begins to interpret things Desdemona says and does as proof of her betrayal of him; he is convinced of her guilt by his own jealousy and by the circumstantial evidence that Iago produces, a handkerchief that Desdemona supposedly had given to Cassio, one of Othello's soldiers—Othello's favorite, in fact—whom Iago says was her lover. At the end of the play, Othello strangles and then smothers Desdemona.

As an actor playing Othello, if you wonder why Othello doesn't ask Desdemona directly about Iago's accusation or believe her denial that she's been unfaithful, you're overlooking many inflammatory and very real reasons for this. Othello considers Desdemona his subordinate. You have to build your rage with an understanding of the unequal relationship between men and women as well as the racism of that time, both of which, sadly, persist among some people today. Othello's weakness is his pride, and, perhaps, out of his own personal reverse racial prejudice, he sees Desdemona as an aristocratic white trophy, his bounty for his military prowess. You also have to take into account how hot their sexual relationship has been. When you look at all these facts, you begin to see how mortified, hurt, and enraged Othello would be at the very idea of his wife's infidelity, especially since Iago says it's with Cassio, one of Othello's own men, and a white man at that. Othello's belief in his wife's infidelity speaks of a deep insecurity in him, and, perhaps, what he endured in humiliation as an African as he rose through the ranks of the military.

You have to answer the question, Why is Othello so prideful that he won't directly ask Desdemona, whom he passionately loves, whether or not Cassio was her lover before he kills her? You have to ask yourself and personalize why, and you have to find a set of specifics for yourself that make you connect to the relationship viscerally and, therefore, behaviorally. And believe me, Othello's fantasies of the sexual relationship between Desdemona and Cassio are painfully and extremely erotic because of his awareness of Desdemona's passion toward him. The more specifically and graphically you imagine what Othello must imagine, the more you can begin to understand why he is so blinded, why he finds it intolerable even to ask the question, and why he not only murders Desdemona but attempts to have Cassio killed without ever asking him directly about the affair. You have to get down and dirty because that's what makes people behave in violent and extreme ways. You have to constantly redefine Othello's relationship with Desdemona throughout the play, because in some scenes it changes line by line as he tortures himself trying to calibrate the possibility of her guilt.

In his excellent book *Audition,* Michael Shurtleff says that every scene is about love. I think he means the celebration of love, the need for love, the absence of love, the yearning for love, the betrayal of love, the missed opportunities for love. And not just love between men and women but the love between all human beings. *Othello,* a play that ends in the murder of the beloved, is about love. Indeed, Othello says in his last big speech at the end of the play, he "loved not wisely but too well." And "too well" means obsessively, desperately, without any ability for discernment. Once Iago tempts him with the idea of infidelity, Othello is gone—because Iago mirrors back to him Othello's worst fear in his relationship with Desdemona. It's Othello's madness, but you must build *why* that relationship drives him to such heartbreaking and horrifying decisions.

Sometimes life gives you a gift: your relationship with the other actor mirrors the relationship between the characters you are playing. This happened for Hank Azaria in *Tuesdays with Morrie,* when he played opposite Jack Lemmon. *Tuesdays with Morrie* is a television movie based on Mitch Albom's autobiographical account of his visits with his elderly mentor, Morrie Schwartz, who was dying. When I worked with Azaria, he told me that one of the things he wanted to do as Mitch was to reveal an emotional vulnerability that he had never had an opportunity to expose before, because he usually played comic parts.

Although Azaria didn't know it, Lemmon himself was suffering from cancer. There was a vulnerability Hank saw in him and that Lemmon saw in Hank that made their relationship to each other needful, alive, dimensional, and poignant. Hank admired Lemmon as Mitch admired Morrie; he was touched by Lemmon's availability and openheartedness as Mitch was touched by Morrie's openness. And thus Hank was helped to portray the love, empathy, and, ultimately, loss, of a man he respected and grew to love. It's the kind of beautiful miracle that sometimes happens in theater and film.

Remember that you *always* have an emotional stake in your relationship with the person you're playing opposite, even if your character claims indifference. In George Bernard Shaw's *Pygmalion,* which Lerner and Lowe turned into the musical *My Fair Lady,* Professor Henry Higgins takes on the cockney flower girl Eliza Doolittle as a project to prove to his friend Colonel Pickering that he could teach even a guttersnipe how to speak proper English and she could then pass herself off as a lady. Higgins says he has only a scientific interest in Eliza—in other words, that he's unaffected by her personally. But the emotional current that builds throughout the play and makes us care is the fact that although Higgins doesn't understand it, he becomes emotionally involved with her and volatile when she talks about leaving him. If the actor playing Higgins doesn't invest himself emotionally in Eliza, the play is dry and will not work and the audience will not care. We have to feel Higgins's creeping affection for Eliza as the play goes on. At the end of Shaw's play, Eliza says to Higgins, "What you are to do without me I cannot imagine," and that is not dry. Shaw meant you to feel the incalculable loss of Eliza's humanity to Higgins's life; he also wants you to pull for their union, which does not take place in the play. Because Shaw is a great writer, there are clues in the text to Higgins's emotional involvement despite his disclaimers, and you'd better pick them up! As philosophical and sociological as George

Bernard Shaw was, what finally makes him great is that all of his characters have a human heart.

It may seem obvious to you that Higgins is emotionally involved in Eliza but I've seen performances where Higgins was played so arch and icy that the actor missed the fundamental relationship in the play that causes this icy figure to thaw. In these performances the ice never did thaw and Higgins became shallow and brittle. Just as you can't play passivity as an actor, you can't play indifference—you can play trying to be above feeling, trying to make the person feel they're being dismissed, *but that's because of feeling in the relationship, not because of a lack of it.*

There's one more relationship that as an actor you have to define, and that's your relationship with the audience. I like to tell my classes a famous story about Alfred Lunt and Lynn Fontanne, two of the greats of the American theater for more than four decades. Lunt and Fontanne were married, and they often acted together. One of their great techniques was being able to talk to each other at the same time, overlapping lines, and doing it in a way in which the audience could hear both of them clearly. It always delighted the audience. They were legends in their own lifetimes, but they always worked as hard as they did at the beginning of their careers—which is the main reason they were legends. When they were appearing in a play on Broadway or on tour, they continued to rehearse between performances, perfecting the smallest detail or behavior or line reading. I saw them live in *The Visit* when I was fifteen years old on their last tour; I'll never forget the way Ms. Fontanne, in a fiery red gown, sat on a balcony, holding a long cigarette holder as she looked down upon her prey, the man who had broken her heart when she was a young girl; or the terror in Mr. Lunt's eyes when he was being attacked by a mob about to murder him through the diabolical manipulations of the woman in the red gown.

One of the Lunts' great hits (later made into their only film) was *The Guardsman,* by Ferenc Molnár. During the Broadway run, Mr. Lunt could count on getting a huge laugh at a particular point in the play when he was facing away from his wife, who was playing a famous actress, and asked her for a cup of tea. One night he didn't get the laugh, and afterward he said to Ms. Fontanne, "Did you do something tonight that you've never done before? Because I didn't get the laugh." She said, "No, I never move on your laugh lines." The next night, he delivered the line and once again he didn't get the laugh. He went backstage and said to her, "You're moving or you did something, because I didn't get the laugh again, so make sure you're perfectly still." She assured him again that she would never move on his laugh line. This went on for about a week and finally he stormed backstage, and started yelling, "Why are you against me? Why do you want me to fail? You're jealous of me getting the laugh!" And she said, "Alfred, if you want the laugh, stop asking for the *laugh* and start asking for the *tea*."

The lesson here is that in order to have a healthy relationship with the audience, you don't try to get the audience to love you, you don't try to get them to laugh or to cry, you just play the reality of the scene. Even someone as gifted and dedicated as Alfred Lunt fell into the understandable intoxication of encouraging the audience to love *him* and, without meaning to, he abandoned his character, his relationship, and the play. Every actor learns this between one time and a hundred times in an acting career: don't court the audience, play the play!

10

DESTINATION, BUSINESS, AND GESTURE: CREATING PHYSICAL LIFE FOR YOUR CHARACTER

When Helen Hunt came to work on her audition for *As Good as It Gets,* she told me that the director, James Brooks, wanted her for the role but was afraid that her intelligence was too much in the forefront of her personality. Brooks worried that the audience wouldn't accept her as a career waitress without other aspirations. He sent her away to do homework to prove him wrong.

What I suggested to Helen was a technique that was created by the teacher Michael Chekhov: to find the center of energy in the character's body. I asked Helen, what does your character do for a living? She told me she was a full-time waitress. I asked her where the center of her body's energy was as a waitress. Her answer was, "My feet." So I suggested that she pull all of her energy into her feet, as far away from her brain as she could get, and we agreed that she should try to walk as though her feet were the main energy of her survival. Almost instantly, the walk for Carol Connelly was born. Her feet turned out to the side and although her walk was strong, it was almost a waddle. Needless to say, Helen got the part. In other words, once the choice was made, a physical character was born out of a technique that bypassed the brain and went directly to body impulse. As this example shows, sometimes something as simple as finding the character's physical life based on the character's job can be the key to finding physical behavior for the entire performance. This walk becomes the character's walk, and because you're doing it, it changes your point of view—the way you see and interact with the world when you act the part.

There was another dimension to Carol Connelly's walk: the actor's personal experience. While Helen was working on the part, a close relative was dying. She told me she felt she was charging down the hospital corridors like a general in the army, as if her energy could save her relative's life. She related that purposefulness to Carol's desire to save her son's life in the film.

Just as you are physically alive and expressive of who you are every moment of every day, as an actor you must make your character physically alive and expressive in their way.

I want to emphasize this because I find it's missing in many of the actors who come to study with me. You have to learn how to discover your character's physicality and deem it as vital to your craft. Some actors believe that if they experience something emotional themselves, then it will be communicated to the audience automatically and that alone will make the audience feel connected to them emotionally. *Wrong!*

Emotion unconnected to physical life doesn't reach the audience and doesn't teach them about the human being they're watching. Even if a character is deeply physically repressed, it's the physical repression—the absence of movement—that illuminates the interior of the character. In an extreme close-up, your inner imagery and thoughts can be enough to connect an audience to you emotionally, but once you're in a medium shot, or if you're on the stage, you better find physical life associated with that emotion to express it.

When I observe young actors who start in television dramas or films and have never been on a stage before in a demanding role, I am appalled and amazed by their helplessness, their inability to choose interesting physical behavior that engages the audience's imagination and emotions and helps to clarify the author's intent—the actor's job. They stand on a stage saying their lines as if they're waiting for a bus that never comes. It's as if they're expecting a director to give them a technique for physicalizing a character that they should have learned before they started working professionally.

The three primary ways of creating physical life for your character are *destination, business,* and *gesture.* Physical destination on a stage or soundstage is where you move your body to, how you move it (for example, Helen's walk as Carol Connelly), and why you move it. Moving your body around a stage helps the audience feel and understand what you say out loud (text) and what your character holds back (subtext). Business is any kind of activity that engages your body in something other than moving from one place to another. Sometimes you create physical business to be interesting and to fill in a space where the writing lacks excitement, but the business you create must always make sense with your character development and with the text. Business can also illuminate text and subtext, as does gesture. Gesture, as I mean it, is an unspoken, bold physical choice that may or may not be repeated throughout the play or film; gesture is psychological, and it helps the audience to understand something about the character's inner life.

To be creative and exciting with the tools of physical destination, business, and gesture, you must deeply understand the material you are acting and begin to see your body as an exquisite conduit directly connected to the audiences' guts. You want to heat up the minds and feelings of the audience, and nothing does that better than unique, idiosyncratic, specific human physicality.

In *Boys Don't Cry,* Hilary Swank as Teena Brandon has a gesture that sets up her entire performance. Teena looks at herself in the mirror in her jeans and cowboy boots and tips her hat as a young man would to a young lady, with gallantry and a wink. This private moment filled with joy confirms her own belief in her masculinity and makes us root for her. We wish her a happy life in the sexuality she is choosing to impersonate.

Truly embodying a character takes you beyond the mechanistic way that the terms *destination, business,* and *gesture* are sometimes used. During the time I worked with Hilary, she cut her hair blunt and short, lost a good deal of weight, worked out at the gym to build muscle, and chose to live as a boy for a month until she could pass in society as a young man. She stuffed her crotch—which in the world of cross-dressing, the world she was entering as Teena Brandon, is called packing—and walked as an older adolescent boy, using her shoulders with a kind of swagger. Hilary had been recently married and her husband, Chad Lowe, agreed to introduce her as his younger brother when they went out together.

She was shocked by what she discovered. Hilary looked so androgynous that no one could tell which sex she was, so people tended to avoid her and look at her disapprovingly. This was extremely painful to her and made her understand the isolation and loneliness that Teena Brandon had experienced her entire life. Hilary had always been seen as an attractive young woman with a beautiful body; she had great ease relating to other women and to men as a woman. Once that identity was masked, she began to believe the life of Teena Brandon. Living as a boy in this way took courage and commitment, but it was the only way Hilary could gain insight into Teena Brandon's courage and commitment and also into Teena's joy. Hilary also experienced the joy any actor feels when they have successfully transformed themselves. She was absolutely determined to succeed, and succeeding meant a 100 percent commitment to a physical choice that changed her entire view of the world. And, as Hilary said, "If I couldn't believe myself as Brandon, how in the hell would the audience believe me?"

One of the physical behaviors we discovered for Teena Brandon as her "male" self, Brandon, was how she sneaked looks at the men around her to see if they believed she was one of them. She kept checking out their reactions, and as they accepted her, Teena's confidence as Brandon grew. One of the most touching and creative aspects of Hilary's performance is Brandon's gentle, chivalrous courting of Lily Tisdale (Chloë Sevigny), the woman he falls in love with, and his courtesy to all the women he meets. There isn't a scene in *Boys Don't Cry* that Hilary and I didn't break down and explore with physical choices before the cameras ever started rolling.

With Michael Clarke Duncan in *The Green Mile,* one of the important choices Michael and I came up with for the introduction of the giant John Coffey was his frightened, childlike exploration of the eyes of the prison guards to see which one might strike him first. We added a gesture, too: he offered his huge hand to the guards as if to say, "I am no threat to you. Please don't hurt me." The gentleness of this gesture established in the audience's mind a tremendous tenderness and vulnerability that contrasted with Coffey's huge body and face. It was as if John Coffey was gently reaching out to the audience as well as the guards, saying, "Please don't hurt me."

Helen's, Hilary's, and Michael's performances have in common a strong sense of physical self that contributed to the audience's understanding of the inner emotional life of the characters and identified them from the moment they hit the screen. My challenge is to get you excited by this part of your acting. Since I am dramatic and theatrical by nature, I use provocative and stern attacks, but that energy is passion generated by my watching life and watching great actors who learned from life the art of physical acting. So now you challenge me back and say, "All right, fine, but how do I learn?" First lesson: observe life. Second lesson: observe the best acting you can find.

Begin by spending an entire day being aware and keenly observant of your body, how it feels and how it moves. What do you do when you get up in the morning? What's the first thing you do? What's the second thing you do? How do you get dressed for the day? How do you walk out the door? Where do you go? How do you behave when you're "doing nothing"—just waiting in a line?

Every day I wait in line at my neighborhood coffee shop for my morning fix. Some mornings I'm very sad and mad because I've woken up from a dream that upsets me or I'm just in a lousy mood. I don't want to talk to or see anybody. I put on my dark glasses and my baseball cap, I grab my *New York Times,* and walk into Peet's Coffee. There are hoards of people there, also waiting for their fix, and I hate them, and I stand in line, and I want to be invisible. I don't want to be there, but I do want my coffee. So I enter the shop (lugubriously), get in line (resentfully), I shift my weight (impatiently), and move up (oh so slowly) toward nirvana, my coffee. Notice that my physical destination has an emotional point of view that is described with an adverb, saying not only where I move but emotionally how I move (lugubriously, resentfully, impatiently, oh so slowly). On those days, my business is shifting my weight, pulling away from people who get too close, burying myself in the *New York Times* theater section, and pulling my baseball cap down around my eyes. If a camera got a close-up of my eyes, it would capture my sadness and anger, but it wouldn't be as interesting as seeing how I try to hide those feelings through my physical behavior. Of course, on days when the sun is shining and the birds are singing in my heart and life goes well, I enter (jauntily), without my sunglasses, I wave and smile (exuberantly) at the people I know, and wait (patiently) to be served.

Besides observing yourself closely, be keenly observant of others. Keep a notebook with you at all times, and as you discover an interesting behavior that catches your eye, record it. Laurence Olivier, England's reigning acting king for over half a century, kept a file in his head of behavior he had seen (he didn't have to write it down because unlike most of us he had a photographic memory). As he worked on a role—and he played hundreds—he would remember a behavior and incorporate it into his performance. I personally don't understand any actor who ever gets bored. There is so much to learn, to see, to understand, and to give to the audience, and there is so much to learn about this amazing physical body that we have been blessed with that helps us reveal the human condition. How can we ever be bored?

To learn by observing brilliant physical acting, watch these performances: Vanessa Redgrave in *The Loves of Isadora, Julia,* and the television movie *If These Walls Could Talk;* Nick Nolte in *Q and A, The Prince of Tides*, and *Down and Out in Beverly Hills;* Anthony Hopkins in *The Remains of the Day, The Silence of the Lambs*, and *Amistad;* Daniel Day-Lewis in *My Beautiful Laundrette, The Last of the Mohicans,* and *My Left Foot;* and Meryl Streep in *Sophie's Choice, Death Becomes Her, Cry in the Dark,* and *The Bridges of Madison County*. Watch these actors' performances without sound. Wow!! Believe me; see a performance once with sound and once without—it is a revelation.

Notice how different the same actor can be in different performances largely based on their choices of physical life. A great deal of Anthony Hopkins's performance as Hannibal Lecter in *The Silence of the Lambs* is in close-up, because the director is examining the internal world of a madman. And because Hopkins's inner thoughts are so alive and private, they pull us into the film. But it's not just what you can see in his eyes; it's how he holds his body and moves his head that reveal who he is. A particularly riveting physical moment is when he lifts his head and exposes his nostrils to the camera to catch the scent of the body lotion that Clarice Starling (Jodie Foster) used before she came to him that day. He is a cannibal, and in that one physical, animal gesture, there is no doubt in our minds that we were looking at a connoisseur of flesh.

Hopkins has said that he played Lecter as if he were a head waiter in a restaurant. He had the costume designer tailor his clothes tightly to his body, giving him an appearance of elegance and formality—for this was a head waiter in a high-class restaurant, even though he was caged in a jail. His carriage was straight, tall, and refined. He acted with his whole body even in close-up. He added to this the voice of Hal the computer from *2001: A Space Odyssey,* a disembodied, mechanical voice. These are creative choices, deeply connected to the author's intent and expressed by a gifted actor through his physical instrument. And let me not leave out the important fact that he had joy doing it, and that this added an even more sinister quality to his character because we could feel his joy. This was a man without guilt or conscience, who was only interested in his own sensual, murderous pleasure.

When you watch Hopkins's work as John Quincy Adams in *Amistad* you will observe how old he seems at the beginning of the film, how much effort it takes him to move his crippled, aging body. After Adams resumes his legal career, defending a slave who had led a violent mutiny on a slave ship, the energy returns to his body and movements, and he seems to lose twenty years. I have talked to people who didn't understand Hopkins's performance and who accused him of not being consistent with his physical choices, but Hopkins understood an old man's thrill coming back to life for something he believes in, and how this makes him young again.

Then watch Hopkins as Stevens, the almost cripplingly repressed butler in *The Remains of the Day.* He has very little expressive physical life, but we feel his desire to move. Hopkins understood that you cannot play repression as *absence;* what he played was holding down the need for human contact and repressing it with all his might. And so we feel the emotion and sensual pleasure that hc cannot allow himself to have. When his father dies and he's looking at his corpse, all he can do is touch him with one finger, not even his whole hand. If that isn't the sadness of repression, you tell me what is.

Two stage actors I admire who are not household names but who do terrific work are Cherry Jones and Michael Hayden. Jones gave a career-making performance on Broadway in *The Heiress,* and part of its great success was her absolute bravery in physicalizing the inner turmoil of a rejected daughter. When Jones as Catherine Sloper entered in the first scene to greet her abusive father, she covered her stomach with one arm and clutched at her dress as she tried to be the dutiful daughter he demanded. Before she ever spoke a word, we saw her clutching, terrified desperation. This was a daughter begging for a father's love that would never come, and she broke your heart. In the second act, she grabbed her other arm behind her back as if she were trying to straighten her own spine. And by the end of the play, she stood elegant, rigid, and cold, arms at her sides, a human being who had given up all hope of love.

In Hayden's breakthrough performance in the musical *Carousel* both in London and on Broadway, he portrayed the swaggering braggart, Billy Bigelow. When Julie Jordan, the young woman with whom Billy falls in love, sings to him, "I always say two heads are better than one to figure it out," she's talking about life; Billy snaps back, "I don't need you or any-body to help me figure it out, I got it all figured out for myself." For the rest of the first act, Hayden's Billy Bigelow clutched his skull, tapped at his temples, and seemed to be trying to wake up his brain. This is what I term a *psychological gesture,* repeated so the audience understands what the character never allows himself to admit in words: that Billy Bigelow doesn't have a clue how to figure out anything.

There's an aspect of business and psychological gesture that deserves special attention: the *private moment*. A private moment is a moment alone on the stage or screen when you do something that you wouldn't want someone else to watch. I mentioned Hilary Swank's moment in front of the mirror in *Boys Don't Cry*. A private moment always reveals character. In *Orpheus Descending,* before Vanessa Redgrave as Lady Tor-rance went to make love for the first time to Valentine Xavier, the young man who has awakened her from years of loneliness, she smelled under her armpits. I was very taken by this private moment, because it wasn't particularly alluring, but it was very earthy. The fact that she wondered if she had BO before she walked in to have the sexual and spiritual connec-tion of her life created a certain primitive, honest privacy that humanly connected us to her.

Before there were "talkies," there were silent films. When you watch, and you must, Charlie Chaplin, Harold Lloyd, Buster Keaton, Greta Garbo, and the young Lillian Gish you will be moved both to tears and to great laughter by their intense emotion and deeply expressive bodies.

When students in my class fail to ignite a scene with physical behav-ior, I ask them to stop talking and do the scene without words. Almost in-stantly the scene becomes clearer to them and to us, because they have to understand and physicalize the wants and needs underneath the dialogue. Do this as an exercise. Take a scene and work on it with a scene partner without saying the lines. How can you make your scene partner under-stand your wants and points of view by how you move and behave with your body and how you handle objects? This takes time, patience, and dedication. Remember: every human being moves specifically based on class, education, nationality, gender, and psychological baggage. Without the dialogue, you have only your physical behavior to embody these char-acteristics and to pursue your objectives.

I also sometimes ask students to physicalize the point-of-view exer-cise I gave you in Chapter One, "Given Circumstances." Let's go back to Melvin in *As Good as It Gets*. I said that you could express his point of view as, "My name is Melvin Udall and the world is a terrifying, vicious, unfair, desperate mine field in which I must get them before they get me, and I must keep control of everything in my life so the world doesn't explode into chaos where all the germs will get me." Now physicalize these descriptive words, almost like a dance. How would you express *terrifying* with your body? How about *vicious*? *Unfair*? How does your body *protect itself* from germs? When you look at the video of the film, notice how Nicholson as Melvin avoids touching anyone as he walks down the street, as if touching them would literally make him die. Notice specifically how he walks, the gestures that show us that Melvin considers contact with other people dangerous and that the world is a filthy place. Come up with your six descriptive words or phrases for any character, then physicalize them. Remember that in performance these physicalizations can be used broadly, moderately, or very subtly.

Class, education, and social standing powerfully shape physical self-presentation. The playwright Harold Pinter is helpful to work on to develop specific physicality, because all these factors exist in his characters in blistering ways, and because his dialogue demands to be punctuated with physical behavior. In *Betrayal,* Pinter's bitter, vicious, and sad commentary on a certain terrible relationship in upper-class British society, the first scene is between two ex-lovers. They meet in a bar they used to frequent, so the place is hot with memories. They are both married and had an adulterous affair with each other for seven years. The affair has been over for two years. To make the circumstances more dangerous, the man is a business colleague and the best friend of the woman's husband, Robert. What he doesn't know at the top of the scene is that she is about to separate from her abusive husband and has told him in detail about the affair—although the truth is, the husband knew two years before. Quite a rat's nest. She is looking to see if her ex-lover still has romantic feelings for her; he is terrified that his wife may find out about his indiscretion and equally terrified about the reaction of his supposed best friend and colleague, whom he betrayed. The woman has called him out of the blue. He is fearful; what does she want? He might be excited to see her, but he is definitely nervous.

There are plays and films like *Betrayal* where the dialogue is so riveting that too much movement damages the material, and in those cases, specific, subtle choices are even more important. At the top of the first scene in *Betrayal,* the two ex-lovers are seated at a table and the man gets up once and goes to the bar for another round of drinks. Other than that, they sit and talk, period. The two characters are holding back certain facts and feelings that are painful and frightening. So every small action and shift of position—when and how they pick up a glass, take a sip or down the drink in one gulp, suddenly cross or uncross their legs, make tentative or bold, direct physical contact, move forward in their chairs, sit back, or turn their heads away—tells what the characters are feeling and not saying. There is one moment in the scene that is delicious for the actress, and the only moment when she is not watched by the man. He goes to the bar to get a drink and she is left alone to reveal to the audience her sadness or terror or anger or hopefulness. Will she adjust her hair? Take a drink? Light a cigarette? Take out a handkerchief to dry her eyes because she's suddenly started to cry? All of this is the actor's choice; the key is that every movement must be specific.

What are her inner thoughts as revealed by her physical behavior? What are his? "Does he think I am still attractive?" "I wish he would hold me." "Does she want me back?" "Will she tell my wife?" "Why hasn't my friend Robert called me? What the fuck is going on?" "Should I bring up things from the past?" "She looks sad." "He looks cold." "Oh God!" What you do physically, how you do it—how big, how fast, how slow—is all vital. The wrong movement at the wrong time and Pinter is dead.

Don't be a killer!

Let's talk for a moment about how different acting situations affect your work on physicalization. In a stage play, before you open you have eight hours a day for four weeks to discover the physical life of your character, on top of the time that you have for homework. In many feature films, and in all television movies and dramatic series, you have no rehearsal time. You show up, they put you in a costume, point the camera at you, and say, "Go there. Do this." In the worst-case scenario, where there is a time and budget problem, they want you to do it one or two takes, and if you don't make any major mistakes, they'll say "Print!" and move on.

A great deal of filmed television drama is done in medium shots and close-ups, and the blocking is done by the director, which is the reason some young actors who have only done television are so helpless onstage. Even though you don't get a lot of chances to do physical work in TV, sometimes just bringing a hand into a frame or moving your head a certain way or handling an object can achieve a lot.

In making feature films, some actors enjoy the improvisational exploration of a scene without rehearsal, and some find it a nightmare. The more homework you do on physical expressiveness before you show up for filming, the more ideas you will be able to bring to the director. If he likes your suggestions, he may even adapt the blocking or camera movement to include them.

The key to destination is that whenever you move, it has to be for a reason you believe in. The old joke, "Why am I crossing to the refrigerator?" answered by the irritated director, "Because I'm paying you," is only funny to people who don't understand the importance of justifying emotionally whatever you do. Whether it's for stage, screen, or television, you bring in your ideas, and don't ever let any director tell you that they're not valuable, because if your ideas are coming from a deeply felt and thought-out justification, the director should—and the good ones will—see them as a gift of gold.

If you have a small part in a film, don't discuss your physical choices, just do them. If the director doesn't like them, believe me, you'll hear about it. If your ideas are not accepted, don't take it personally, don't throw a tantrum, do what the director asks you to do—that is called being a professional—and do your best to find something in yourself that can motivate what is being asked for. (For more, see Chapter Twenty-one on stage, screen, and television.)

I believe that the reason we still love James Dean today is that he was so accessible emotionally and that his emotionality was always put into physical behavior. In *East of Eden,* when as Cal Trask he punches his brother, Aron (Richard Davalos), during a political melee, Dean gives one of the greatest punches in cinema history. I think it's based on two things: one, that he studied with Katherine Dunham, a famous dance teacher whose technique was largely based on Afro-Cuban movement, which was very sensual (many of the actors at that time in New York took these dance classes, which were done to live drumming); two, that he meticulously studied cats, who are always in a state of releasing tension. So when he picks that punch up, seemingly from the ground, and punches his brother, he follows through the movement and seems to go all the way to infinity.

I think he was able to do this because his body was so free, since he did so much physical work in his early training to uninhibit himself. And you would be wise, actors, to lose your false pride and get to a jazz class, a ballet class, or any dance class that makes you move in a way you're not used to. It's very well known that football coaches have asked their teams to take ballet classes for grace and flexibility. Learning new ways to use your body opens up your range of physical choices in playing characters and gives you the courage to make choices that you'd never have dreamed of before. It also opens up the range of characters you can play.

An actor who made his career on physical movement is John Travolta. His physicality in *Saturday Night Fever* is the stuff of legend. But what I find particularly interesting in that performance is his use of an object as he makes moves on this elusive girl whom he's trying to impress in his sleazy, macho way. He betrays his vulnerability through the movement of his hands, watching them as he moves his ring up and down his finger, almost taking the ring off and examining it as though it was a work of art or a great scientific project, because the truth of it is he's too shy to let her see how much he likes her, and how afraid he is that she might reject him.

Sometimes, as in Travolta's use of the ring, physical business can be multilayered and reveal character in profound and unexpected ways. Twenty-five years earlier, Marlon Brando paved the way by picking up Eva Marie Saint's delicate, gauzy glove and putting it on his big, meaty hand in *On the Waterfront*, saying with that physical business, "I can't touch her. The closest I can get is to put the glove that was on her hand on my hand." It's a famous physical moment in film, because it seemed like the first time a real, virile leading man did something that delicate, and that's why Brando was Brando.

In *Dead Man Walking*, Susan Sarandon as Sister Helen Prejean made a very powerful and almost classical Greek-tragedy choice at the end of the film. As the murderer Matthew Poncelet (Sean Penn) is dying by lethal injection on the other side of a glass wall, she reaches out to him with her whole arm. Such stage-worthy physicality is rarely seen on film because actors are often afraid of being thought of as too theatrical. But because the stakes were so high, she earned the right to that bold choice, and it was authentic to her character's high spirituality. Sending love through her eyes was not enough; she had to reach to him and send love from her heart down her arm and out through her fingertips, so he could see the love. It's one of the most moving physical choices I've ever seen, and, because of it, she allowed the man, although he was a murderer, to die with grace and forgiveness.

I want to say a word about the director Elia Kazan, who directed Dean in *East of Eden* and Brando in *On the Waterfront*. Kazan's understanding of physical characterization will always stand the test of time because

Kazan was an animal of the theater who moved into film and retained rich, passionate, truthful physical expressiveness. I believe working in the Group Theatre in the 1930s with the greats of the American theater at that time, and living through the Depression, when human beings had to claw their way to survive, stamped his artistry with brave and unique style. Propelled by the desperation of his immigrant past to find a way to succeed in America, Kazan grew up as an artist, and one of the ways he did it was through directing his actors to find physical metaphors for their intense internal life. You cannot watch a Kazan movie without being startled by the brave physicality of his actors.

In *Splendor in the Grass,* which is so much about flesh, sensuality, and sex, he bombards you in the first frame with Natalie Wood as Wilma Dean Loomis and Warren Beatty as Bud Stamper clutching each other in the seat of a car and kissing passionately, seeming to want to devour each other. Beatty's character is so aroused and so frustrated that she won't go all the way that he smashes open the door of the car and gets out. Kazan moves the camera to water rushing violently and dangerously over a fall. This shot was a physical metaphor for the danger and tragedy to come. And I'll never forget Barbara Loden as Beatty's doomed sister, Ginny, running down a rain-splattered street on a bitterly cold New Year's Eve in a little slim dress with her heels clicking on the pavement, running to oblivion.

And lastly, Kazan's direction of Jessica Tandy as Blanche DuBois in the stage version of *A Streetcar Named Desire.* There is a moment when Blanche explains to her beau, Mitch, that she was complicit in the suicide of her homosexual husband. Blanche says, "The only unforgivable sin is deliberate cruelty, and it is the one thing that I have never, never, never been guilty of." But of course we know she has been guilty of it, and so does she. And just before Jessica Tandy finally told the truth to Mitch, she clasped her hand over her mouth as if she were willing the cruel statement to be pushed back down her throat. I saw this moment when she re-created it in an interview on television. It was physical, psychological, and powerful, and whether Kazan directed her to do that or she created it, it was under his guidance that the behavior was born.

Speaking of *Streetcar,* let me make a quick point. Brando as Stanley Kowalski makes a simple cross, and as he does it, he fiddles with his watch. It's not profound business, but it gives him a little touch of elegance, which is fascinating and slightly subversive to what we think of as Stanley's brutality. And if you want to see, to my mind, one of the most hilarious, creative, and awe-inspiring moments of physical business ever done, watch Laurence Olivier, in Alfred Hitchcock's *Rebecca,* talk on the phone, propose marriage to Joan Fontaine, butter a biscuit, put jam on it, drop the jam on his dressing gown, scoop off the jam from his dressing gown, put it on the biscuit, and eat it. I rewound the tape five times to watch this in utter awe. It's technically brilliant, and it's also subversive in a character we otherwise think of as a perfect gentleman. But Olivier always said, "If I play a beggar I look for the king, and when I play a king, I find the beggar."

Let me finish with one last example of great physical acting: Janet McTeer's white-hot performance in Ibsen's *A Doll's House.* I have said to my friends and students, "You know, if you had told a producer that the biggest hit drama on Broadway next season would be Ibsen's *A Doll's House,* he would probably have laughed you out of his office." But McTeer, who is six foot one, and whom nobody would have cast as Nora Helmer, knew she had a great Nora in her to give, and she found a director who shared her vision. Once again, like Cherry Jones in *The Heiress,* before McTeer even said a word, Nora was already vividly alive. For her first entrance, a frantic, overgrown, seductive child seemed to fly through the door, wildly throwing down her coat and scarf and packages as if she knew an adult would pick them up. I described this in the last chapter, but it was just the beginning. Freezing, huffing, and exhilarated from her Christmas shopping in the brutal Norwegian winter, Nora then ran to the samovar for hot tea, touching it momentarily to warm her freezing hands, like a delighted child. We knew from her overexcitement that there was a hysterical, overstressed girl holding down a volcano, and when McTeer exploded in the last scene, screaming the birth of women's rights at her shocked husband, her body became completely still, focused, and dangerous. Then she suddenly got up and began to prowl the stage with rage and grief, a wild animal trying to pulverize her home, her cage, her doll's house.

The night I saw this performance, McTeer had, I was told, a 104-degree temperature. She had a serious case of the flu and had obviously taken an antihistamine. Her mouth was dry, and she had cups of water placed all around the stage. Each time her throat dried up, she would grab a cup and drink the water, never stopping the intention of a scene or making the audience feel uncomfortable. Somehow she integrated the movement effortlessly. The problem was, she was losing her voice. By the end of the play it was almost gone. I don't know where she found this voice, but a growl came out of her throat as she screamed, "You have done a great injustice to me, Torvald!" It was so primitive that the audience gasped. For as she fought to give her all as an actress and survive, that served as a metaphor for Nora's struggle, and it seemed to me—and I don't believe I am overstating this—an epic performance.

11

BACK STORY AND BIOGRAPHY:
BELIEVING IN YOUR
CHARACTER'S LIFE

When you see a performance that rivets you, it is because you be-lieve that what you are watching is actually *happening* in front of you. When the character enters, you have a sense that they are coming from a life that has been lived fully prior to this moment. They were born, grew up as part of a family, had an adolescence, became an adult, and some-where along the way an event or a series of events propelled them to en-ter the specific situation in which you meet them, with a specific goal or superobjective. This prior life is the character's *back story* or *biography*. Even if the back story is not in the script, creating one can help ignite your performance.

Here's an example from my own career. I was cast in a play about a sweatshop in New York at the turn of the century, playing a penniless Russian immigrant, Leonid. In the play, Leonid worked alongside a num-ber of women whose very livelihood depended on the small salary paid to them for the sixteen hours a day they spent bending over a sewing ma-chine and being yelled at by the big boss if the work was not done fast enough. My character stood up for the women in a very heroic way. He always protected them, regardless of the cost to himself. In fact, he eventually lost his job because he could not bear to stand by when the son-of-a-bitch boss mistreated a woman.

The script never explained what drove Leonid. I knew that I needed a trigger that would enrage me every single time a female was abused. So I asked myself, what could make me feel that incensed, that passionate, that militant about protecting women? And suddenly I had an image of a very big burly man standing over a beautiful young woman, striking her and pushing her into a radiator in a drunken rage. The young wife's head was cracked open, and she bled to death, clutching the hand of a young child. My character was that young child. When I investigated this fantasy, I smelled the cabbage she was cooking for dinner, I saw the twisted face of my imaginary father coming home late and drunk, and, most of all, I heard the sickening crack of that poor woman's head hitting the radiator, her moaning and clutching my little hand as she died. Well, that was all I needed. Every time that boss came near a woman, I sprang to my feet and let him have it!

It wasn't enough for me to simply have an intention, an active verb—for example, *to attack, to protect, to bully back, to annihilate, to strike back*. All these intentions were usable, but I needed my back story to make it explode; the back story gave me the emotional justification to stand up for these women at any personal cost. It enabled me to *live* inside my character's skin.

I've already talked about creating a back story for Maggie in *Cat on a Hot Tin Roof* to make your performance sizzle. Maggie's superobjective is economic security: *to have so much money that I never have the fear of being poor for the rest of my life*. I suggested a possible reason Maggie feels this way is that her mother died in agony because she couldn't pay for medical treatment. Again, this back story is not in the script; I imagined it based on Maggie's line "You've got to be old *with* money, because to be old without it is just too awful."

For this back story to work for Maggie, it's not enough to know it intellectually, you have to visualize it and build it sensorially so that you *feel* it. You have to see the peeling green paint on the walls of the public hospital where your mother died, smell antiseptic mixed with urine in the halls, feel your mother clutching your hand, saying, "Don't ever die like I'm dying, Maggie," and begging you to get her more morphine because she can't stand the pain. You have to build it with specific details so that it makes you weep, so the audience feels the truth of what you're saying when you tell Brick, "You've got to be old *with* money, because to be old without it is just too awful."

One of the reasons Michael Clarke Duncan was so riveting in *The Green Mile* was the back story we created together: John Coffey had been beaten so often, had come so close to being lynched, that when he was taken into that room with a bunch of white men, he knew the blows were coming. He had to overcome his terror and his certainty that there would be a beating, which he did by trying to keep things peaceful. He played against his seven-foot-three height and he was extremely kind, obedient, respectful, and friendly to the guards. If you remember the scene, there were scars all over his body when he walked into the prison. The back story was especially alive in Michael, because he had personally experienced police brutality in his childhood, and he could use this to bring Coffey's terror to life. This terror was pulsating underneath his stillness, it was alive in him as he searched the eyes of the guards for someone who might be friendly to him.

Michael and I didn't just create a history of racial antagonism and physical harm for John Coffey, we went deeper and created a full biography. The biography included the fact that Coffey's parents were lynched when he was a baby and he was brought up by his maternal grandmother, who had dropped dead in front of him. After that he had run away and grown up in the wilderness, far safer among the animals than among human beings. Out of his desire to escape from all his personal losses, out of the threat of continued violence from white society, we found the story of how he recognized his inherent powers, in particular with the fireflies that circled around him every night.

When I first read the script of *The Green Mile,* I was aware that this could be a critical stepping-stone for an actor who was lucky enough to get the role, and I would have felt that I'd failed as a coach if Michael and I weren't thorough in our examination of the character's entire life, past and present. By the time Michael entered the movie, he knew John Coffey's past so deeply, and was so connected to his own past abuse, that it seemed to me as I watched him enter that his skin was quivering with anticipation of violence toward him.

Sometimes part or most of the back story is in the script. If you watch *Midnight Cowboy,* you will notice that in the beginning you are shown highly traumatic events from the childhood of Joe Buck (Jon Voight). Joe is a victim of incest and gang rape and his mother is promiscuous; he is abandoned and poor. Because *Midnight Cowboy* is adapted from a novel, there was a rich back story for the screenwriter to work from, and you are given vivid reasons to understand why a seemingly decent and good-natured human being succumbs to the depths of degradation as the adult Joe Buck does. *Midnight Cowboy* is the story of a search for connection, the search to love, to care, and to be cared about.

To play Joe Buck, you have to understand deeply that a great many people spend most of their lives reacting to their childhood; if that childhood is abusive, they will self-destruct in some way—unless they do something to heal themselves. From the flashback memories the script describes and perhaps others you build from your imagination, you have to create for yourself the events that have prevented Joe from being in touch with any realistic goals for a decent life. But you also have to create from Joe's past a childhood hunger for validation and attention that draws him to Ratso. Ratso Rizzo, a complete opportunist, is surprised, and finally forced by Joe's loyalty into some form of decency and closeness with Joe. We know nothing about Ratso's biography from the film, but his name alone should make your imagination go flying into a very exotic and troubling back story that includes the whys of his physical disability and the ways it affected him growing up.

In playing a role, you must *never* judge your character, good or bad, unless in the writing the script specifically demands as part of your character that your character judge themselves. If text doesn't demand this, then don't make a judgment.

It's a basic rule of acting that villains always have a justification for their actions that makes their behavior tolerable, and sometimes completely acceptable, to themselves. If you want to read the back story of a serial killer and can bear to face the unimaginable experiences that form a murderer, read *The Shoemaker: The Anatomy of a Psychotic* by Flora Rheta Schreiber. I recommend it even though it is excruciatingly painful to read, because the cruelty done to the serial killer as he grew up makes you face the inevitability of his violence, and it will give you an understanding and compassion that is necessary for the artist to have. If you're playing a heavy, find reasons that are emotionally justifiable to you for taking whatever actions the character takes.

Here's a final example of how helpful it can be to create a back story that affects you emotionally for a significant moment in a script. It's from the painfully tender scene at the end of J. P. Miller's *The Days of Wine and Roses*. Kirsten, the alcoholic ex-wife of Joe Clay, comes to see Joe and their daughter, begging to be accepted back into the family. We have learned from earlier scenes that Joe himself was an alcoholic, and that he was the one who started Kirsten drinking because he didn't want to drink alone. During the course of the play, however, he has found his way to AA, while she has become a promiscuous drunk. Now Kirsten arrives at their tiny tenement apartment and begs Joe to take her back—except that she refuses to stop drinking. Joe says to Kirsten, "I can forgive you, I can try to help you, but I don't know if I can take you back. I don't know if I can forget enough." And she responds, "You're talking about them— Yes, there were plenty of them. But they were nothing. . . . I thought they would keep me from being so lonely, but I was just as lonely, because love is the only thing that can keep you from being lonely, and I didn't have that."

Two students in one of my classes recently did this scene. The woman had done her homework but the man had not. So when he said, "I don't know if I can forget enough," it was dry as cardboard, but when she said, "There were plenty of them," you knew she had picked up strangers in bars and fucked them all night and the next night went out to another bar and picked up somebody else. If you're playing Joe, you've got to have an image of walking into the apartment and finding her having sex with another guy, drunk out of her mind, and you either leaving silently in grief and shame so they won't see you or dragging the other guy out of the bed and throwing him out the door, with his clothes after him. If you don't have a specific back story in your imagination connected to this—as you would in life—an event that was almost unbearable to you, then you can't play this scene with Kirsten with the emotion it requires.

I want to add that when the actor brought the scene back after working on his back story and filling in the inner imagery, instead of being cardboard, Joe was flesh and blood and overwhelmingly moving. I try to stay as objective as possible when I teach, but when I saw this scene after the work he did on it, it was so filled with real depth and human feeling that I put my head down and wept.

12

The Animal Exercise:
Expanding Your Behavioral
Choices

One of the greatest interpretive performances I've ever seen was in the Berliner Ensemble's production of *The Resistible Rise of Arturo Ui* by Bertolt Brecht. The play is a satire about Hitler's rise and fall. Martin Wuttke, who played Arturo Ui, literally started out as a dog. When the curtain came up, he was facing the audience on a slab of concrete on all fours, with no shirt, his body painted a kind of opaque white. With food coloring, his tongue had been made an incredible blood red, and he was salivating and panting—like a big, murderous, starving, vicious, drooling dog. The first ten or fifteen minutes of the play is all information delivered by the other characters and he remained at the side of the stage as a dog, watching intently the audience's reaction as well as the action on stage. As he began to become the Hitleresque character of Arturo Ui, he rose to standing, but he kept the bark of the dog in the way he spoke, so he barked his words, and that became Arturo Ui's voice.

Wuttke took an animal exercise of a specific dog—what I saw in his performance was a German shepherd—found its behavior as a four-legged creature and then kept aspects of the dog for his two-footed human character, including being hyperalert and breathing fast. By keeping the bark, he gave us an extraordinary and insightful interpretation of Arturo Ui as a mad dog. It's one thing to hear a dog bark; it's another thing to watch it become a person who was a monster like Hitler. Whenever I hear a speech of Hitler's now, I hear the bark in it. This is a talented actor, really using his imagination and the animal exercise to help him paint the worst of mankind.

The Animal Exercise

Pick a specific animal and learn all about its behavior. You can go to the zoo, watch documentaries, and read books about the animal; if they're domesticated you can watch them in your everyday life. Study their breathing patterns, their musculature—where the most powerful muscles are for attacking and eating prey and running from predators—how they eat, defecate, urinate, have sex, and what kind of alertness they have when not in captivity. Study the sensory perceptions they need for survival, which can include extraordinarily intense smell, hearing, seeing, tasting, or touching; remember that any animal you play is either prey or predator or both. If you visit a zoo, you can also study the sadness of animals in captivity. You'll probably think of mammals first, but don't forget birds, snakes, fish, or even insects as possibilities for a particular character.

Once you know the behavior, then bring it into class, create as much of the habitat as you need onstage, and live as the animal for a period of five to ten minutes. If this is not an exercise your class does, you could videotape yourself at home. When you see the tape, do you believe yourself as the animal? When you do, pick certain characteristics—like the breathing, hyperalertness, and bark of Wuttke's dog—and use them as part of your physical behavior for a character.

The animal exercise helped me to create the part I now think of as my most successful work in the theater: Little Harp in *The Robber Bridegroom,* a Broadway musical based on a novella by Eudora Welty. The show is about a small, wonderfully outrageous town in the South that Ms. Welty created to tell the story of a glamorous robber who became a folk hero and lover to a young woman named Rosamund, the daughter of an evil stepmother and a very rich and naïve father. With the help of the director, Gerald Friedman, I was able to create Little Harp using all of my shadow self, all of my antisocial impulses—and some I had never thought about before playing this bizarre and wonderfully comic character.

Because the play was an ensemble piece, we were on the stage for the entire two and a half hours. We played not only our main character but also animals and trees. During one of our first rehearsals, Friedman asked us to pick a specific animal to use for the scenes that took place in the forest. Since Little Harp was filled with rage, I picked a rattlesnake, because I found out that rattlesnakes are born blind and that their mother leaves them after three days. I figured that would really piss you off. I slithered on the ground and I flicked my tongue to sense what was around me, and out of that rattlesnake grew the walk of Little Harp. I walked with my knees bent as low as I could possibly bend them, which gave my character, a predatory bondage-freak rapist, a slithery quality and a sensuality I had never been able to reach in my work up till that point. The animal exercise freed me.

Later, we were also asked to pick the specific kind of tree or plant we would embody in the forest. I chose a weeping willow. And having chosen the weeping willow out of my instincts, I realized that the character of Little Harp was so extremely perverse because of a deep hurt. In rehearsals, I discovered that Little Harp rarely bathed and that he had fleas. Another idea that came to me was that Little Harp was inflated with his own importance. He carried his brother's head around in a box—and the brother's head talked to him (this was a fable, after all)—but when he wasn't with his brother, he was left to his own mental capacities, which were, to say the least, minimal. However, I've observed in life that many people that I would consider ignorant can be unbelievably judgmental and self-righteous. So the entire rehearsal process—the animal exercise, the tree exercise, making a decision for Little Harp to believe that he was incredibly smart, giving him fleas, and having to deal with the extreme heat of the Mississippi summer, which made me irritable and very itchy—created very specific behavior for my character. I added to that a very broad Mississippi accent.

The last choice I made for my character was the conviction that the title character—the robber, played memorably by Barry Bostwick—was the only thing that stood between me and my chance for world fame; if I destroyed him, the title of the play would be *The Robber—Little Harp*. My point of view that I was smarter than any of the other characters in the play turned out to be highly comical because all the actions that I did were so incredibly stupid. Whenever in performance I felt out of touch with my character, I would remind myself of my initial technical work. When I reconnected with the thought and behavior of that blind little abandoned rattlesnake, the part came alive again.

If you're interested in exploring a role through the behavior of an animal, I suggest you rent James Foley's *After Dark My Sweet*. Jason Patric plays Kevin "Kid" Collins, an ex-boxer who is mentally ill and homeless. You'll notice that Patric enters the film in a desert, leaping off a rock in an unmistakably simian way. His arms are gorilla-like and seem to weigh more than the rest of his body. His walk is aggressive and predatory, and the tempo is extraordinarily fast, as if he were running away from something. He is like a frightened animal, eyes flashing and darting. It is all very chosen, very committed, and bravely executed.

Patric worked on the role for a year prior to filming and he had Jim Thompson's novel on which the film was based to help him with his preparation. For me, the physical choices he made to be animal-like were startlingly effective, down to the way he observed Rachel Ward's Fay Anderson while they were having sexual relations, which was electric in its combination of mistrust and eroticism. This characterization rightfully ignited his career.

There's also an interesting choice by Charles Laughton, the great British actor who also directed one magnificent film, *Night of the Hunter* (don't miss it!). When Charles Laughton played Henry VIII, he showed the king's mental disintegration at the end of the film by portraying him as eating like a starving ferret, using his front teeth as razors, with eyes blazing madness.

13

PLACE: THE RICHNESS OF WHERE YOU ARE

Stella Adler used to say, "Where you are is who you are." What did she mean by this?

If you observe your behavior throughout the day, you'll see that if you're hanging out talking to a close friend at the gym, your body language, your expressiveness, is different than if you were talking to that same friend at a dressy restaurant over lunch. If you go from the restaurant to your bank, from there to the library, then for a jog, and then out to dinner at the beach with friends or your significant other, you'll observe that your relationship to the space you're in—whether it's small or large, formal or informal, who's in the place, what the place means to you emotionally, psychologically, philosophically—changes your behavior, even your breathing. Whether we are normally conscious of it or not, we are always affected by where we are. Our deportment, our manner, even our choice of language adapt to the setting.

Let's look at what place means to the characters in the film *The Hours*. The apartment where Clarissa Vaughan (Meryl Streep) lives is not especially large, yet there is a feeling of Clarissa's wandering through its few rooms as if she were lost. Look at the 1950s suburban tract house that Laura Brown (Julianne Moore) lives in, the kitchen where she is making the cake. There is an antiseptic quality to the house: it's very clean and very impersonal. The imposing English home of Virginia Woolf (Nicole Kidman) seems almost like a hotel. But as different as all these places are, there's a sense that each woman is wandering through a desert, that she is alienated from her own home.

Notice, too, that when Virgina Woolf walks into the kitchen of her house, she becomes like a shy, apologetic yet resentful child. Simply walking into that room fills her with trepidation and anxiety, and it takes great effort for her to do it. As an actress playing this role, you would have to make a choice along the lines of, "When I walk into that kitchen it's as if I'm walking into a courtroom where they think I'm guilty and I have to prove my innocence." Virginia overcompensates for her fear at one point by acting bossy to the cook; she does it to overcome her anxiety because to her, her own kitchen is such a place of danger, because she senses the negative judgments of the cooks. And what's moving about the scene is that she reveals courage; after all, it isn't courage unless you're frightened.

Carson McCuller's play *The Member of the Wedding* is set in the kitchen of a big old Southern house. In the play there's a special relationship between Frankie, a thirteen-year-old white girl, and Bernice, the African-American cook who works for her family. We see the kitchen where Frankie and Bernice talk during the various phases of Frankie's turbulent adolescence. Frankie goes into the kitchen and gets fed on every level: it's where she gets mothering. Frankie goes there to express to Bernice her longings and frustrations about being an outsider, lonely and awkward and so desperate for connection that she wants to join her uncle and his bride on their wedding night. Frankie's parents were killed when she and her brother were young children and she's been raised by relatives. Bernice is her confidante. The sad thing about it is that in that household, Frankie could never get the nurturing and love from anyone else that she gets from Bernice in that kitchen—and Bernice knows that. But as Frankie matures into a young woman and starts to have a social life, we see through her behavior that from a needy childlike thirteen-year-old, clutching at Bernice and relishing her time in the kitchen, Bernice and the kitchen become what she wants to escape. In fact, it seems as though the place makes her skin crawl. So as we talked about redefinition of relationships throughout a script, there's also redefinition of place. By the time Frankie sees Bernice for the last time, she is a self-involved older adolescent who feels that in escaping the kitchen she's escaping prison. Frankie leaves this place of nurturing, probably never understanding until years later the incredible value of Bernice and that big, warm kitchen.

As an actress playing thirteen-year-old Frankie, you could imagine the kitchen and Bernice as a huge, comforting pillow. You want to lean back and stretch in it, literally place your body against the refrigerator, the table, the cabinets, even go to the sink and put the water on to take the summer heat away. As Frankie gets older, you could redefine the place by imagining that everything in that kitchen makes you itch or is too hot to touch. You have to keep moving—the opposite of the pillow. Finally, the kitchen becomes a prison with bars that's getting smaller and smaller. You gasp for air; you will suffocate if you don't escape.

As an actor you *always* have to ask yourself how you feel about the place your character is in. *Who's Afraid of Virginia Woolf?* takes place entirely in George and Martha's living room. How do George and Martha feel about that room when they walk into it? How do their guests Nick and Honey feel about it? One of the great things Edward Albee does is to make the room so alive that it's almost a character in the play. As the curtain goes up, Martha defines her relationship to the place: "What a dump!" The irony is that she neglects to take responsibility for making it that way. That's because, from her perspective, she's making a comment on the higher class of living that George hasn't provided for her.

The room is messy; it's filled with liquor bottles, old magazines, newspapers, and books. It's where George and Martha stage their psychological orgy, if you will. It's the place where they pull out their dirty laundry. When Nick and Honey enter, the room is intimidating and foreign to them, it's a place of old-school academia which they aspire to; Nick has just begun to teach at the university where George has long been a professor and where Martha's father is president. What is taken for granted by George and Martha is intimidating to Nick and Honey. If you're playing Nick and Honey, what is in this living room that attracts your eye and how do you judge the different things you see, pro or con? To George and Martha, that place is obviously home, and it's also where they tear each other and other people apart. To Nick and Honey, who are innocent of this at the start of the play, it's where they've come to network.

As an actor in the play you have to ask, "What does the place mean to me in terms of creating possible behavior for my character?" George and Martha treat the place like an old shoe, it's comfortable, they slop in it—or, more specifically, Martha slops in it and George tolerates her slovenliness, but you could interpret George's irritated tolerance as a symptom of his wishing the place were cleaner and better organized. Nick and Honey see the living room as a bridge to their future so they're very polite, even diffident in it. As you read their dialogue at the beginning of the play, you can almost feel them sitting up straight on the sofa, putting their best manners on—probably seeing the dust in the corners and trying not to stare at it. It's clear that the place where George and Martha live is not taken care of and is therefore a metaphor for the lack of care for each other and themselves.

In Pinter's *Betrayal,* the ex-lovers Jerry and Emma meet in the pub where they used to meet secretly when they were having their extramarital affair. The place is rich with memories: it holds their history with each other. It's a hot place for them, an emotional place. As an actor playing Jerry or Emma, you have to sit in that pub and look around and have memories come back to you just as they would in life. There's the table across the room where you once held hands. There is the table where you had a terrible fight. Your physical focus cannot always be on your partner, and that is why *endowing*—investing—particular places in the pub with memory gives you other focuses that will feed you as an actor. It also gives the audience unspoken nuances of the characters' past relationship.

Because in *Betrayal* the place is vital to memory, as an actor you can make great use of the *fourth wall.* This is the downstage wall between you and the audience, which doesn't exist physically but needs to exist in your imagination for a full performance. When Jerry or Emma look out at the fourth wall, what do they see? Is there a window? Is there a garden outside the window, a lovely garden that used to make them feel romantic? Or has the garden been turned into a parking lot? Or perhaps the fourth wall contains the doors to the bathrooms where Emma went to cry her eyes out so Jerry didn't see, or where Jerry used the pay telephone to call his wife and lie to her about where he was. I have heard some actors say, "Oh, I don't believe in the fourth wall, it doesn't work for me. I want to feel and use the energy of the audience." Once again, if it works for you, fine, but don't throw out the possibility of trying to endow the fourth wall with images that stimulate you to deeper feeling in the scene.

How do I *live* in the space is the question you must ask yourself as an actor; why did the writer place me here and what is my job in living in this place? What behavior can I find that grows out of my relationship with the place?

Consider the role of place in *The Diary of Anne Frank,* the famous play based on the diary of a thirteen-year-old girl murdered by Nazis in the Holocaust. The entire play is set in the tiny attic in Amsterdam where the Franks and four other people were forced to hide because they were Jewish. The attic is a tiny thread that holds them between life and death. It is the whole world to these people; outside the window is where they could live if they were free, but they are not, so they have the impossible task of trying to find some privacy in this too-small space. The place is filled with mounting fear and frustration, yet Anne and Peter, two teenagers, find a corner to be alone together and begin their budding romance, a step in the natural progression of life that Anne will never get to complete. So this tiny attic is both their prison and their safety. At certain times in the play, Anne and Peter are so enraptured with each other and with the idea of being in love that they transform the attic into a place that's as romantic as a garden in spring. Even though their lives are in danger every moment, their infatuation makes them and us believe in the possibility of their future together.

In Frank Perry's film *The Swimmer,* which was based on a novella by John Cheever, Burt Lancaster plays Ned Merrill, a man who travels through a suburban neighborhood stopping only to swim in his neighbors' pools. His life as he knew it is disintegrating and he is internally lost. Place becomes powerful in *The Swimmer* simply because *there is no place for him;* he is an outsider going from visit to visit to visit, from one swimming pool to the next. Watching it makes you feel very lonely. The lack of a place where he feels connected is vital to his character because he is searching for it and never finding it. Unless you've had an experience of losing a place you've lived in and felt connected to because you had to move or because of a financial crisis, or you've experienced a mental crisis where you've become a stranger in your own home, you might have trouble identifying the kind of emotions and behavior that this kind of anxiety about place creates.

Let me give you what is to my mind the most searing image of displacement: I saw a small collie running frantically down a highway, unable to stop running and panting, for it had lost its master and knew instinctively it was in great danger. It didn't know where to go, it just kept moving. It was sheer panic. If you were playing a role where a loss of place is so crucial, you have to create an image or "as if" or a back story to affect you. Sometimes one photo of a lost child in the newspaper could do it, but find it you must.

In *Cat on a Hot Tin Roof,* Williams makes it very clear that Maggie and her husband, Brick, are in the bedroom where the former owners of the house, a homosexual couple, slept together for many years. To be sure, this was not an idle choice on Williams's part. The 1950s, when the play was written and set, was a time of great repression, shame, and secrets regarding politics and sexuality, personified by the HUAC hearings. The head of the FBI, J. Edgar Hoover, kept files on certain homosexuals with evidence that those in power might be able to use against them, even though Hoover himself reputedly was a secret cross-dresser and was inseparable from a male companion for more than forty years. Talk about hypocrisy. Tennessee Williams blew the lid off sexual repression and changed the face of theater by talking honestly and openly about homosexuality and sexuality in general. Remember, this is the era when Elvis Presley could only be photographed from the waist up on *The Ed Sullivan Show* so the audience wouldn't see his undulating pelvis! If you do the play, researching the period will reveal all this to you. You'll see how Williams titillated and shocked the world with his frankness and opened people's eyes.

As I said, Brick and Maggie's bedroom in Big Daddy's mansion has the built-in memory of the gay couple who lived and died there. Against this backdrop, Maggie tries desperately to make Brick interested again in her ("You were such a wonderful lover to go to bed with") after she has raised the specter of a love affair between Brick and his closest friend, Skipper. This is the sore that Maggie keeps picking at and this bedroom is really the site of everything she has to conquer, because whether or not Brick had sexual feelings for Skipper, he feels guilty and complicit in Skipper's death, and this guilt is colored by the question of homosexuality. Williams could not have picked a more emotionally loaded place for Maggie's desperate attempt to bring Brick back to life.

Look at the way Williams uses place in *Streetcar* just to emotionally ignite Blanche's entrance. When Blanche, in a dress that Williams tells us is more suited for "a summer tea or cocktail party," gets off the streetcar named Desire and looks around the neighborhood with disbelief, Stanley and Stella's neighbor Eunice asks her, "What's the matter, honey? Are you lost?" Indeed, Blanche *is* lost, and if you're playing Blanche you better understand how seeing the dingy place in which your sister lives affects you.

It's like a punch to your stomach, and you can barely find your breath. Blanche says with incredulity to Eunice, "Can this be her home?"

As bad as the place looks to Blanche when she first sees it, of course it gets worse as she walks into it and learns the truth of Stella's situation. So this opening scene sets up the conflict of the entire play. As an actress it is your job to have a fantasy, an image of this place that is in exact opposition to what it is when you finally discover it. Otherwise you won't capture the improvisational feel of Blanche's discovery and her terror at seeing it in reality. If you expect a charming flat in the French Quarter with a beautiful wrought-iron balcony with flowers spilling over it and lovely curtains in the windows, the lack of all of that will be devastating, and more devastating still will be the smell of the train tracks that permeates the apartment, and probably with it, the smell of the cattle that the trains carry. Playing Blanche you constantly do your best to cope with the place, which you do by trying to change it into something more refined—and failing. Blanche comes there *to find a safe place;* as the play goes on, she must find a safe place to get away from that place.

In *Barefoot in the Park,* Corie and Paul's new apartment doesn't have a phone or anything else in it when the play starts. They are starting their life as newlyweds and they have to add the phone, lights, and furniture to create a world. The apartment is very hard to get to—you need to walk up five flights of stairs to reach it. There's no elevator. Every actor who enters the front door of that apartment must convince the audience that they have walked up those five steep flights. By the time they get into the apartment, they are out of breath or their legs ache or are threatening to give way or they have some other physical behavior that is the result of that torturous climb. Talk about a sense of place! One of the things that made the play a smash hit, and that Neil Simon provided for the actors, was the opportunity to define their own relationships to the unseen stairs and make an entrance that was uniquely exhausted and shocked for each character.

Corie has picked the place, so in that sense it's hers, and she's often in the position of having to defend it. When Paul asks her where the bathtub is, she responds hesitantly, "There is no bathtub."

PAUL: No bathtub?
CORIE: There's a shower.
PAUL: How am I going to take a bath?
CORIE: You won't take a bath, you'll take a shower.

PAUL: I don't like showers, I like baths. How am I going to take a bath?

CORIE: You'll lie down in the shower and put your feet over the sink. . . . I'm sorry there's no bathtub, Paul.

Given who Corie is, whatever anyone else has to say about the apartment, she responds by trying to adjust their perception so that they won't be critical. She tries to make them see the place as positive and wonderful. But it's not wonderful. She made a mistake, but she's going to keep saying it's wonderful no matter what.

This is Corie's problem on a larger level. She doesn't face reality and she doesn't care enough about her husband's needs even to have warned him before they moved in that the place didn't have a bathtub. In the play, Corie begins to learn to be more aware of Paul's needs, and Paul begins to learn to be more flexible and more playful. So the apartment says a lot about their relationship.

The Green Mile gets its name from the color of the linoleum that is on the floor leading to the electric chair. Most of the film takes place in the same location, on death row. One of the character choices that the film explores in terms of place is that John Coffey is too big for his cell, so he always had to bend down to get into it, which is a metaphor for the bigness of his spirit and special gifts that are too big for the outside world and certainly too big for the small jail cell. This was the director Frank Darabont's intention. In fact, even though Michael is six feet five inches, Darabont put him in special shoes with very thick soles and heels, raising him to seven-foot-three so that John Coffey dwarfed everything around him.

As I've said before, for John the jail starts out as a place of incredible fear, coldness, and isolation, but because of his true innocence and spiritual beauty, Paul Edgecomb (Tom Hanks) and some of the other guards treat him with kindness and begin to believe in his special healing gifts. As this happens, the place begins to warm up. There's an incident when Paul gives John a plate of cornbread as thanks for healing a severe urinary infection and giving new life to his sexual relationship with his wife. John asks, as if he were Paul's child, if he can give some cornbread to Eduard Delacroix (Michael Jeter), one of the inmates that he particularly likes and not give a piece to the wicked and sadistic "Wild Bill" Wharton (Sam Rockwell). Paul makes it clear that John can do whatever he likes, and the look on John's face proves that the jail has become a safe, warm home and the friendly guards have become almost like a family.

Each prisoner has his own space, and the space is defined by the temperament of the prisoner. Just as John's cell becomes a safe, warm home for him, the cell that holds "Wild Bill" Wharton is like a cage for an animal. Once again, behavior toward place—in this case the individual prisoners' physical behaviors in their cells—expresses their emotional reaction to the place. Their physical behavior includes how they stand, sit, or lie on the cot, how they react to the confinement, and how they relate to the bars that hold them in. To help the actors and the audience feel a variety of moods, as well as to contribute to character development, Darabont and the director of photography, David Tattersall, worked tirelessly to find different angles and lighting that would accomplish this. Their investment in keeping that single location alive visually was enormous.

Place also affects John Coffey when he's being brought out of the prison to heal the warden's wife, who has cancer. As John is freed and walks to the truck in which the guards will take him to the warden's home, he looks up and sees the sky full of stars for the first time since his incarceration, and there's a change in him that feels like a kind of birth. When he walks across the grass for the first time in a long time, everything seems full of wonder—the grass under his feet, the air he breathes, and the infinity of the sky.

One of the most striking things about Michael's acting is his delicacy as he walks into the bedroom where the dying woman is suffering in bed. John is in the house under the suspicious eyes of the warden, who has a gun, but John, a huge black man in the home of this mistrustful and highly agitated white warden who could shoot him in an instant, takes his place not with fear but with confidence. He's much too big for the bedroom, yet he walks into it with enormous gentleness and a sense that he has the right to be there. As he walks into this place of privacy, a white couple's bedroom, the most private room in their house, he does so with complete innocence. He sits on the bed and, in order to heal the woman, he has to kiss her on the mouth and, with his breath, although we don't quite understand it at the time, suck out the cancer and infect himself. All of this is done with enormous kindness, patience, and certainty.

John feels people's pain so acutely that he reacts solely to her pain and his desire to heal her. Whatever sense of place we as an audience might bring to that scene—what we know about segregation in the South at that time, how we fear the white warden might react to John's going into his bedroom and kissing his bedridden wife—John Coffey has his own reality and there's no place for fear in it. During that sequence, he is not a black man in the South entering the bedroom of a white woman whose husband can kill him on the spot; he is a healer entering the room of a sick person he feels compelled to heal. It is a masterful choice on Michael's part not to react to the place but to the person in the place—and the place makes the scene that much more tense for the audience.

I hope this chapter inspires you to always be interested in asking of every place your character is in: What behaviors can I create in response to that place that make the story emotional and alive for the audience?

14

Cold, Drunk, Hot, Sexy:
Using Sensory Work
for Character

A young actor, a student of mine, was in a film that took place in the mountains, after a plane crash, where the extreme cold was an important given circumstance. One of the realities of the location where the film was being shot was that the morning temperature was freezing, but in the afternoons it would get quite warm. My student noticed that as the day progressed, some of the actors were forgetting that it was supposed to be bitter cold, that their voices and rhythms were slow and summerlike and their bodies were too relaxed. When he pointed this out to the director, the director said offhandedly to the company of actors, "Oh, yeah, don't forget that it's cold out."

One of the most important aspects of creating a believable performance is the behavior that stems from the sensory realities of a scene. If it's freezing, it affects everything you do and how you do it, from how you hold your body to how you speak. This is work that actors should do on their own. Never forget this rule of thumb in the acting business:

nobody in the audience praises or blames the director for your performance; they praise or blame you, the actor.

In Akira Kurosawa's beautiful film *Dreams,* one of the episodes takes place in the snow, and all the actors are dressed in parkas and snow boots. It was filmed on an indoor set where the temperature was between 80 and 90 degrees during shooting, but you could never guess that from the believability that the actors brought to experiencing the frigid temperatures and the behavior that that called for.

Elia Kazan was brilliant in bringing sensorial realities to life in his films. He was one of the first directors to film largely on location instead of on studio soundstages, and he chose the dead of winter in New York City to shoot his classic film *On the Waterfront,* a story of dockworkers who were forced into long hours and poverty wages due to the greed of the big bosses who fought the start of unions. It has been stated many times in analyses of the film that you could see the actors' breath in the cold air and that led to a tremendous sense of involvement in the raw circumstances of the story. Kazan said he didn't like filming in California because everybody looked so damned healthy, and he wanted and felt he needed the pallor of all the hungry actors who tried to survive in New York.

One of the iconic moments of all acting on film is the moment when Marlon Brando as Terry Malloy picks up the sheer, delicate glove that Eva Maria Saint as Edie Doyle has dropped on the ground, and puts it on his own big meaty hand in order to find a way to be close to her. It seems so odd and out of character for this ex-prizefighter and uneducated dockworker to long so completely for this young woman that he would allow himself to put on this feminine article. The fact that it was freezing out, and you could see that it was, and that it was having an effect on Brando and on Eva Maria Saint, made this possible, because the actors and the director were sensitive to the characters' need for warmth physically and emotionally. The air Brando exhales as he puts the glove on bellows out in white clouds, metaphors for tenderness, isolation, loneliness, and hope.

In Kazan's film *Splendor in the Grass,* there's a scene that takes place on New Year's Eve in the midst of a brutally cold Kansas winter. Barbara Loden as Ginny runs wildly down the rain-slicked street in her skimpy white dress, enraged and crying because her father has rejected and humiliated her in front of the guests at the family's New Year's Eve party. You can almost sense the tragic fate of that character by the sound of the delicate high heels clicking on the wet pavement and the sight of her thin, sensual body running against time. Again, Kazan has given the actress sensory realities to affect her behaviorally, and his filming of the bitter cold makes you feel truly frightened for this lost, unprotected young girl.

For Loden, the sensory work in this scene involved her being drunk.

Loden's character, Ginny, is an alcoholic who always has a flask with her. She tries to get her brother, his girlfriend, and everyone around her to lose their inhibitions and join her in flamboyant, sexual abandon—her way of responding to her severely repressed mother and dominant, narcissistic, and contemptuous father. As an actor, what are the sensory realities of being drunk? It's different for every person's chemical makeup. Loden chose a drunkenness that made her body like a rag doll, as if she had no bones to hold her up. She seems to be falling into everyone, looking for someone to support her. At the same time—as in the scene just before her flight down the street—she can become belligerent and attacking. Loden's careful exploration of these specific reactions to the alcohol in her body was based on her script analysis and interpretation of this doomed flapper. Her specific sensory work helped the actress to reveal the character's pain, isolation, and rage.

During the last year of his life, James Dean did two very different and creative examinations of drunks, one at the beginning of *Rebel Without a Cause,* and one in *Giant.* In *Rebel,* Dean's volatile, drunken adolescent goes from almost fragile infantilism into a volcanic rage, including making his voice into a police siren in the opening sequence of the film. In *Giant,* the character's weepy, sleepy drunkenness was used as a vehicle to explore the wasted life of a man who was riddled with competitive rage, and who became a pathetic and broken old man. Look at these films to see what Dean did physically to embody two very specific drunken characters.

As an actor playing someone who's drunk, you have to first understand what alcohol does to the brain and then how it affects your muscle responses. For the most part, it slows you down, although there are some people with a different chemical makeup that alcohol actually speeds up. The script will help you to decide on the kind of response your character has to alcohol or drugs. People say, "Oh, he's a lovable drunk," meaning that the alcohol reveals an expression of warmth, kindness, and the need for physical affection in the person, as opposed to "Oh, he's a mean drunk," about a person who starts fights, baits people with sarcasm, and explodes with pent-up rage. Martha in *Virginia Woolf* is a sloppy, slashing drunk, while George is an acerbic, controlled, intellectually deadly drunk.

Alcohol can increase your sensitivity to touch, or it can make you numb. Drunkenness also goes in stages according to the amount of alcohol you've consumed and your individual sensitivity to it. Some people can drink enormous amounts and barely show any sign of having had a drink. Other people quickly lose motor control, get dizzy, and throw up. All of these behaviors can be created through sense memory if you have had any experience that would produce these responses.

For my own sense memory work, I'd draw on the time when I got blindingly drunk on tequila. After my friends and I left the bar, we went to a screening of *On Golden Pond*. I felt that my head was the size of a very large pumpkin. As I went to the candy counter and ordered a jumbo Diet Coke, I made a terrible mistake. When the man behind the counter gave me the gigantic plastic container of soda, I misjudged how close my hands had to be in order to actually hold it, and I watched, in slow motion, the epic amount of liquid fall through my hands and drench the entire candy counter, including all the popcorn. When the man announced sternly that the candy counter was now closed, I began to laugh hysterically, walked into the movie theater, sat down, listened to the first music of the title sequence, and began to sob my guts out—which shows how quickly emotions can change when you're in the state of inebriation. Look at all the colors of my drunken behavior—all the specifics—that I can explore in sense-memory work and bring to my performance.

That said, you don't have to ever have had a drink in your life—or a recreational drug, for that matter—to do this work. You can research the effects of alcohol—or drugs—on people by reading books on the subject, by going to AA meetings with respect for the members' anonymity and listening to people's stories, or by talking to an alcohol or drug counselor. You can go to a bar any night of the week and watch people getting progressively drunk. Once you know the specific drunken—or stoned— behavior that the writer seems to suggest for your character, you have to use acting techniques to provoke those behaviors in your body. This involves finding where in your body tension is released or increased by the particular stimulant or depressant that your character has ingested.

Let's say you're going to play a character and you want to give them the same kind of drunken looseness that Loden used in *Splendor in the Grass*. How do you this? If you've never been drunk, were you ever injured enough to be given Demerol or Vicodin or laughing gas? Have you ever had a deep-tissue massage that left you completely relaxed, almost floppy? If so, you can do an acting exercise to re-create the sense memory and the overall physical effect.

The Memories of Home exercise in Chapter Seven is a way of doing sense-memory work to help you discover your emotional triggers. The exercise below uses the same tool to bring back a physical sensation, which may also provoke an emotional response. The more you do sense-memory work, the more you will be amazed at how memories are stored in your body, waiting for you to activate them. If you do daily sense-memory work as homework, you will be prepared for whatever you need to do in a performance—whether you have to come up with a toothache, symptoms of the flu, or be raging drunk. It's money in the bank, and it will pay off time and time and time again.

If you don't have the discipline to do this work by yourself, recognize that and find a class where it's done properly, and get your practice in. For more help, read Edward Dwight Easty's excellent book on sense memory, *On Method Acting.*

In Los Angeles I taught four nights a week for thirteen years and we did a half hour to forty-five minutes of sensory work at almost every class. There is an actor I won't name—there's no point—a television star who was about to break into A movies in a big way. He came to my class to audit, which is something I didn't normally allow but did as a special favor to him after we had a cordial and creative meeting. Without asking my permission, he brought a friend with him, and I naïvely allowed them to sit in. They found the sense-memory exercise difficult and, instead of trying to work, they giggled their way through the exercise and neglected to pay for the class. I'm telling you this not because of the money, which was a small amount, but because of the lack of ethics and the lack of commitment. This actor got his break and starred in a film and was so artificial and physically tense that he acted himself out of a career. He had his chance, but he threw it away because he was not truthful to himself about what he was missing technically as an actor.

All sense-memory work starts with a muscle-relaxing exercise. If the TV star had committed to working on his weaknesses, he wouldn't have appeared on film as a stiff soldier in a part that asked him to be free and sensual and appealing. He had worked out until he was buff, but his perfect body had no appeal because he was so clearly uptight. I'll talk more about this in Chapter Eighteen on relaxation. For now, here is the exercise re-creating a physical sensation that you can use in performance.

The Physical Sensation Exercise

Choose a physical sensation that you want to work on: toothache, sitting in a warm bath, sunbathing, intense cold, being sexually excited, postcoital pleasure. The possibilities are endless. Choose a monologue that you've memorized to use with the physical sensation. It doesn't matter if the monologue calls for this particular physical sensation, it's just text to use for the exercise.

Turn off the phone and all electronic devices that produce noise and learn how to embrace and explore the power of silence. Silence gives us a medium in which we can get to know ourselves and our instrument intimately—and that is essential to acting.

Sit in a comfortable chair with your eyes open or closed and concentrate on your breathing for about five minutes. Notice your inhalation and exhalation; don't try to change your breathing. If it's shallow, be aware of it and allow it to move down into your diaphragm. You'll start to be sensitive to the sounds of birds, cars, people outside, and even the creaking and settling sounds of your floors and walls. Being aware of these sounds is the beginning of teaching yourself how to ready your instrument for a sense-memory exercise.

Now begin to be aware of where in your body you are holding uncomfortable tension. You may be so used to holding this tension that you don't even feel the discomfort until you get quiet and take the time to observe it.

You can start looking for tension at the top of your head or at your feet, it doesn't matter. Then go all the way through your body checking to see where the tension is hiding. Once you've located it in your forehead, chest, jaw, eyes, stomach, feet, tongue, or anywhere else, inhale into that tightness, and on the exhale gently ask the muscles to let go. You may have to repeat the inhale and exhale several times before the muscle actually releases. Just be patient and concentrate. Once the muscle has released, you'll move that part of the body with more freedom and expressiveness. Be open to the release of tension also releasing different emotions: laughter, tears, anger, or whatever feelings come up.

Once your muscles are released, if your eyes are closed, open them. You are now ready to begin the next part of the exercise.

If you are re-creating a physical sensation that you've experienced in your life—say, intense cold—first you have to fully experience with your five senses the feeling of comfort of sitting in your chair in your warm room. Then choose a particular time when you remember experiencing intense cold. That way you'll know the specifics of where the cold is coming from and what parts of your body are exposed more than other parts.

Re-create in your imagination where you were when you experienced this intense cold. It's important to use all five senses since you don't know which senses will most powerfully trigger the memory.

What did your surroundings look like? As you allow yourself to see in your mind's eye where you first experienced the cold, the room you're in when you're doing the exercise will begin to change and take on your inner visual. That's when the work begins to live. It's important to understand that the images come and go, but stay with it, and continue exploring your five senses to experience the cold.

What did your surroundings smell like? When you breathe in, do you feel the cold air coming into your mouth, throat, chest, and lungs? One of the things that you experience when a particular part of your body feels cold is that it tends to make your whole body cold. If the back of your neck is exposed to a cold wind, you'll feel the temperature in your body drop.

One of the things that allows you—and eventually the audience—to believe that you're cold is that being specific about *where* you're cold causes specific physical behavior: pulling your coat up around your neck, trying to pull your hands inside your coat, keeping your face away from the icy wind. Remember, cold makes you want to move to warm yourself up. It creates energy, as opposed to heat, which slows you down.

Then, once you have created the cold, start to speak the monologue you've chosen out loud. Don't act it; just say the words simply. See how your voice and body are affected by the physical sensation that you've created through the sense memory.

Once you have finished the monologue, sit quietly, releasing the sense memories that have created the physical sensation, and just breathe and relax. Then you are ready to re-create another physical sensation if you want to.

The reason it's vital for you to do the sense-memory part of this exercise with your eyes open is that you will almost surely be keeping them open onstage! There's no point practicing sense memory without making it practical in performance. If you were in the play *K-2*, which takes place entirely on a freezing mountain, you would have to act cold for two hours—while performing all your other tasks.

The more you do this exercise, the more adept you become at sensory work. When you're preparing for a part, use the exercise to work on the specific physical sensations you need. Then try out and refine each sensory choice you are making by rehearsing with it at home before bringing it into rehearsal. You'll find that if it's the right choice for the moment in the scene, the physical sensation will join you easily.

It's important to know that sometimes you can create a physical sensation for yourself sensorially in an instant. Let's say you have to grab the handle of a pot on a stove and burn your hand. Simply imagining the pot handle as a sharp knife cutting into your skin—an "as if"—might make you react at that moment exactly as you have to. Or if, in that moment, you believe that the handle is as hot as a burning coal, obviously that will work, too—and remember, the second you feel the burning, the next instant is the behavior of how you are going to make your hand feel better, which makes the whole sensory reality believable. The point is that sometimes a physical sensation is so accessible to your imagination that you can immediately create the behavior you need.

If I said to you right at this moment, someone stuck a pin in your eye—react! That's how quickly you can believe it. Remember: sense-memory work is not magical; it's just sensorially remembering sensations you've already experienced or can imagine in an "as if."

Say you've never been drunk, so you decide to do the Physical Sensation exercise to access the time you took a painkiller like Vicodin or Demerol after some kind of intense pain, because you want to use the sense memory of the warm flood of physical well-being released by the drug to create loose, expansive drunken behavior.

Once your body is relaxed, your next step is to work with all five senses to start bringing back the intense pain that caused you to take the painkiller in the first place. Let's say you had an excruciating back injury. Being specific about your physical discomfort is the only way to truly understand the effect the drug has on your body and how grateful you are for it. Where is the pain located? Is it a sharp stab or a deep ache? Is it constant or do you only feel it when you move a specific way? Does it stop you in your tracks? Where were you when you felt the pain? What time of day was it? What do you see? Hear? Smell? Taste? Touch?

Once you are reexperiencing the pain, you can begin to use the five senses to remember the Vicodin (or other painkiller) and its effects. How does the tablet look, how does it taste on your tongue, how does it feel as it moves down your throat? What happens in your body as the pill began to take effect? Can you let go of your effort to brace yourself against the pain? Are you eyelids getting heavy? Is your tongue getting thick? Have you lost the energy or the desire to control your muscles?

Once you begin to respond sensorially to the physical memory, your behavior will begin to change if you believe yourself. Don't judge your responses, explore them. Stand up and begin to try to walk a straight line, as if you were trying to take the sobriety test on a highway. You can turn the walk into a kind of dance in which you find gestures and movements that reveal the lack of inhibition brought about by the drug. You can use these movements later in creating your character.

If you've never had an experience that you can use for sense-memory work for drunkenness, find an "as if" to put you in touch with the particular behavior you need. For example, imagine that your head weighs ten more pounds than it does and that your eyelids have tiny weights on them that you keep trying to lift up. Build this "as if"; recall a time when you struggled to keep your eyes open. Then add extra weight until your eyes seal shut and your head falls forward involuntarily.

There's a wonderful "as if" that Tennessee Williams gives Alma in *Summer and Smoke*. She has experienced an intense anxiety attack with palpitations and has taken a sleeping powder to ease her. As it starts to take hold, Alma says, "I'm beginning to feel almost like a water lily. A water lily on a Chinese lagoon." Exploring this imagery physically, letting it seep into your body—the sense of floating without any resistance—might be enough to provoke the behavior you want in the scene.

The sensory realities of Ginny's drunkenness in *Splendor in the Grass* are part of her emotional condition. In the New Year's Eve scene I described, Ginny is running through the freezing night, which usually would present another set of sensory realities. However, to Ginny, it's a flight to freedom, and she's so drunk she doesn't even react to the bitter cold. We react for her. This is not sloppiness on the actress's part; it is chosen character work and sensory work based on her emotional and liquor-ridden state. It is perfect for Ginny's given circumstances.

A few years ago, however, there was a film (which I will not name) that made an awe-inspiring sensorial mistake. I use it as a negative example in my class. A young woman was beaten severely by a big thug and afterward had a large cut and bruise on her mouth. When the leading man entered the next scene, he kissed her passionately. She made no response whatsoever to the obviously excruciating pain that kiss would have caused her. At that moment, the movie ended abruptly for all of us who were paying attention. A couple of scenes later, someone must have reminded her about the injury, because she began to react to the pain, but by then we had lost all belief and caring.

Contrast this with the extraordinary sensory work in *Bonnie and Clyde,* directed by Arthur Penn, where for the first time I felt the body's price when a bullet—explosively propelled lead—shoots into flesh. Both Gene Hackman and Estelle Parsons as Clyde's brother and sister-in-law respond so believably in their shock and pain when the bullets enter their bodies, and in their incapacitation and the deterioration of the areas in which they have been injured, that as the audience you physically recoil and want to look away. I'm alarmed at seeing violence in films treated as a game where the consequences are portrayed like cartoons. It is dangerous to society and it increases the possibility of our young children using guns, ignorant of the reality of what they're doing or deadened to the true responsibility for inflicting pain and death.

We've talked about cold. Now let's talk about heat.

Laundry and Bourbon by James McClure is a one-act play about two women, Elizabeth and Hattie, who live in the Texas desert. It takes place at the height of a brutal summer. Again, the weather is a central character in the play. Elizabeth says: "I like this land but sometimes it gets too hot and burnt for people. It's still too wild and hard for anything to grow." Later she comments: "Look at that cloud. Look how it's throwing a shadow across the land. God, doesn't that shadow look peaceful gliding over the land? Doesn't it look cool? It reminds me of a cool, dark hand stroking a hot surface. Lately I felt so hot and hollow inside I wanted something to come along and touch me like that." The play has a lot to do with both women's unfulfilled desires and Elizabeth's fear of abandonment. Their memories of past summers are filled with sexuality and lost youth. The desire for relief from the heat becomes a metaphor for the desire for relief from the sadness and stifling frustration of their lives.

Laundry and Bourbon demands that the characters be physically uncomfortable from the heat—clothes sticking to your skin, perspiration collecting on the back of your neck, underneath your hair or along your hairline, or the burning sensation of a drop of sweat in your eye. You can't playact that, you have to create it. You have to know where the sun is in relation to where you're sitting; what time of day it is; and the overall sensation of heat all over your body. This may sound difficult, but it's a technique that becomes stronger and more usable as you practice it. I'll say it again: only bad acting is general; life never is.

Examine your body's reaction to different weather conditions during the year, then use that behavior for a character. But never think in clichés. To this point, you *must* listen to Stravinsky's *The Rite of Spring*. Some of the rhythms are violent, demanding, and almost scary, not your stereotype of springtime; it makes you recognize not just the sweetness but the violence of nature bursting alive. In terms of nonclichéd specific behavior, I have a friend who sweats from his armpits in torrents, and is always lifting his arms to try to get some fanning motion to cool himself off, even inside in winter if he is extremely anxious. When you commit to exploring, practicing, and using sensory work it is endlessly creative.

Shakespeare's *A Midsummer Night's Dream* takes place in a forest where young lovers sleep, awaken, and transform. Some of the characters are fairies with magical powers, and they use these powers to manipulate people's emotions and bodies in various ways. While the lovers are asleep, the fairies sprinkle them with love juice in order to create mischief by making the lovers switch mates. So one of the sensory demands for the young lovers in *Midsummer* is to wake up and suddenly be in love with, and enormously sexually attracted to, someone who heretofore you had either dismissed or were actually hostile to. You have to wake up completely intoxicated with that person, loving their eyes, their lips, and everything else about them. It's like being zapped by Cupid's arrow.

The smell of gardenias is very potent, and for some people filled with sensual desire. That smell or another smell that affects you in that way could give you the behavior you need to play one of these young lovers. You can do sensory work to imagine that the person you're suddenly attracted to has the fragrance of a hundred gardenias, and you want to get close to them and inhale that voluptuous smell. Again, this is where you have to know and be honest with yourself about what turns you on sexually and romantically. It might be a particular human smell that turns you on, the smell of someone you are involved with now or were involved with in the past. Conversely, if you have to play repulsion, the smell of bad breath, strong BO, or dog shit might do the trick.

Sexuality is a very complex emotional-physical response and quality that people exude. Stella Adler said, "You're either sexy or you're not," but I don't believe that. Obvious physical attractiveness is only hot for a short period of time but passionate need, honest sensuality, and exploring of your own nature sexually without shame can make you very desirable regardless of what you look like and what age you are. When you are doing an intimate sexual scene, of course you should use what's attractive about the other actor—it's a biological reaction that you can use creatively in your performance—*but don't confuse it with a real relationship.*

What happens in a situation where you have to be intimate with another actor and you're not attracted to them or they actually make you sick? Search out and find one aspect of them that you find attractive if you can or that reminds you of someone that you've had a great heat for, or you use an "as if" or a personalization and invest yourself fully in that belief. This would be the perfect opportunity to do the sensory work of a smell that turns you on as I suggested above, or even a sense memory of a specific sexual act that you've done with someone who really excited you. If you need inspiration, remember the story of the two stars whose sexual heat onscreen in a movie was generated by their contempt for each other. Intense hatred or disgust in the hands of talented actors can be transformed into seeming lust. Perhaps the lust that these actors showed on the screen was their lust to obliterate the other actor with their own momentous sexuality; they turned themselves on and aimed themselves like a heat-seeking weapon.

One of the techniques you can use to create a character sensorially is to play a condition of weather. Glenn Close said so beautifully, "When you enter, you must disturb the air," and she did this brilliantly in *Fatal Attraction* as Alex, who has an affair with a married man and then stalks him. She played the role as if she were a gust of wind, breezy at first, then turning into a hurricane.

Cecily, in *The Importance of Being Earnest,* could be played as a dewy spring morning. If you're using a condition of weather to play your character, you explore it with your senses. What are the properties of a dewy spring morning? Freshly mowed grass, twittering birds, blossoms in bloom, the air is fresh and invigorating, and everything is new. Listen to the sounds of that morning, smell the smells, feel the touch of the air and the dew on the petals, see the dew like sparkly diamonds that make everything shimmer and the clear blue sky that makes you feel as if everything is possible and positive. How does physicalizing a dewy spring morning make you carry yourself? How does it make you walk? What tempos and rhythms and tone of voice does it create in you? Does your voice ever twitter like the birds? It's as if every time you take a breath, you smell the sweetness of roses. When you write in your diary, do you write with curlicues and hearts and underline special words with breathless excitement, and clutch the diary to your breast and kiss it, because everything is so pleasurable?

In Dianne Wiest's absolutely sensational performance as Helen Sinclair, the overaged diva actress in Woody Allen's *Bullets over Broadway,* she played the entire role as if she were in a snowstorm. Her voice seemed to be in a perpetual state of deep freeze and at times she took deep breaths as if she were trying to catch her breath in the cold. It was correctly over the top, exactly what the role required.

You can also use work based on any of the five senses to help you create a point of view of your character. You could imagine the taste of a very sour lemon in your mouth. In fact, if you do it right now, your salivary glands will go into immediate action. If you keep working on it, the sourness will make your face show a kind of disapproval and disdain that may be perfect for embodying this element in a character you're playing. The cliché of smelling a raw onion—especially if you're also holding it—can contribute to your portrayal of a tearful character, or someone with a cold, although I suspect this particular choice would work better for a character in a comedy. If you're playing a character who has a mental illness and is so disturbed that he or she cannot really hear what others are saying, you could do sense-memory work of hearing an incredibly loud bell ringing in your head, which would automatically make you jerk and make you try to create physical behavior to stop the sound.

The sense of sight can help you create a character experiencing life with an enormous sense of discovery. I've talked about Frankie in *The Member of the Wedding,* who is thirteen at the beginning of the play. At that point, Frankie is filled with enthusiasm for so many things she's discovering for the first time. When I was a young actor creating characters with that kind of enthusiasm for the world, I would rediscover my aesthetic excitement for each color I saw—the primary blues, reds, yellows, and greens, and I would feel the absolute joy of seeing and examining the gradations and enormous array of delicate pastel hues. All you have to do is go to a museum and see the great French Impressionists to see how you can rediscover your own sense of wonder at what your eyes can take in. And certainly watching Vincente Minelli's *Lust for Life,* with Kirk Douglas as Vincent Van Gogh, you will see the eyes of a great painter seeing the wonder of nature and transferring it to canvas in a very disturbing and thrilling way.

How a character reacts to light can deeply inform their behavior. Two great examples are Blanche in *Streetcar* and James Tyrone in *Long Day's Journey into Night.* Blanche has the famous line, "I never could stand a naked lightbulb—any more than I can a rude remark or a vulgar action." Blanche puts a Chinese lantern over the naked lightbulb to help hide the stark reality of where she is, not only in Stella and Stanley's dreary apartment but also in her life. She is especially sensitive to how light will make her look, because she's obsessed with aging. One of the first orders she gives to Stella is, "Turn that over-light off! Turn that off! I won't be looked at in this merciless glare." James Tyrone wants his family to keep unnecessary lights turned off in their house; on the most mundane level this is for financial reasons, but O'Neill makes it clear that on a more profound level, Tyrone wants to leave everything unexamined and in the dark.

Whenever you walk onto a set, be sensitive to objects that catch your eye in a special way, for you may find physical business or spontaneous emotional reactions that you can use immediately on the day of the shoot or that you can incorporate into your character's behavior in a play.

Sensory realities and sensory work lead you to many explorations and discoveries that can illuminate the characters you are playing. If you've never worked with these tools and techniques, now is your chance. It will be discovering a whole new world.

ENDOWING OBJECTS, PLACES, PERSONS, AND EVENTS

What did your first bicycle mean to you? The record or CD you wore out in the ninth grade? Your first car? Your first baseball mitt? What about your first pair of high heels? What about the orchid you pressed in a book from your first prom? Or the photo of the girl you took to the prom wearing that orchid? Look around your house. I guarantee you it's filled with objects that glow with emotional heat. That's the reason the Memories of Home exercise I suggested in Chapter Seven works—because the objects you sense memory from your childhood home are still emotionally charged. They have a history, *your own history*.

The Personal Object Exercise

Here's an exercise I do in my class to help actors find their emotional relationships to objects. We start with a relaxation exercise, like the Release exercise in Chapter Eighteen. Then I ask, "Allow yourself to remember an object that was given to you in childhood that you can hold in your hands. Let it drop into your hands. Begin to create it in your imagination as if it were there—the look of it, the smell of it, the taste of it, the texture of it, the sound of it." By sound I mean the object scraped or tapped against another object. Sometimes, if an object is a locket or a necklace or a ring or a religious symbol, you might have fondled it or even put it in your mouth while you were thinking, without realizing it, and now the taste of it will come back to you—whether it was metallic or glass or wood—and your tongue will feel the shape of it in your mouth. The point is to use all the senses you can to recreate this object. Then I ask the actors a series of questions while I ask them to keep the object alive in their hands. The visual sense—visualizing it in your hands as if it were actually there—is extremely important at this point in the exercise. Then you ask yourself as you're looking at the object and exploring it, *who* gave you the object? *When* did they give you the object? *Where* were you when you got the object? *What time* of day was it? What were you and everyone else in the memory wearing? What are the sounds you can recall? And the smells?

I then instruct them, "As you explore the object in your hands, feel the weight of it, the texture of it. Hold it in one hand, then the other, and play with it, exploring it from every angle visually. Sometimes you will allow yourself to remember a small nick in the object or you will remember when it was new, when it was perfect. The visual memory of it will sometimes even time travel from seeing it when you first got it to seeing it later, when it's aged. How has your feeling toward the people who gave it to you changed since that time? What is it that you've left unsaid toward this person or these people? On your lips, silently, or, if it's comfortable to you, out loud, talk to these people while you hold the object in your hand and see how that affects you." I next ask, "Where is this object now? Do you still have it or has it been lost? If it's been lost, what would it mean to you if you could hold it now?"

Finally, I ask—and this may seem odd, but it's gotten great response from actors—"If this object had a voice, what would it sound like? And what would it say?" That's truly making that object live. Actors have said to me that when they've allowed their object to have a voice, the object came to life, and said, "I've missed you. Where have you been? Why did you throw me away?" Or, more humorously, "You fucking son of a bitch, who do you think you are to treat me so badly!" The first response might make you cry, the second might make you laugh—and that's the goal: responsiveness.

For some people, doing this exercise with religious objects—like a cross or a mezuzah—can bring up very rich emotional responses, but never judge or try to alter your responses because you think they're inappropriate. Be interested in your response, and keep all judgment away. I've also had students work effectively with objects as diverse as a beach ball, football, baseball, a pair of stockings, a toy bear, a cereal bowl, or a pair of cuff links. Sometimes objects that you think will bring up sadness instead open up joy or gratitude—and vice versa.

Whatever emotion comes up, be curious and patient, and keep exploring the object sensorially and the *images* that join you as you do the exercise. If you keep working with the Personal Object exercise as part of your daily regimen, it can become part of your golden box. When you need to create a particular emotional moment for a character, simply touching or visualizing the object will trigger the response you need.

I've also had students tell me that they've used the Personal Object exercise in the waiting room before an audition to give themselves a feeling of confidence and well-being and access to open emotionality. Even during an interview at an audition, conjuring the weight and texture of an object in your hand can ground you and focus you.

One of the most powerful uses of an endowed object was in the film *The Object of Beauty*. I suggest—no, I demand—that you rent this film because of a particular moment in it that is a perfect example of an endowed object in a text. In the movie, the object of beauty is a small Henry Moore sculpture that belongs to Jake (John Malkovich). He doesn't love the sculpture; he plans to sell it as a means to an end. The character likes to live in very high-end hotels, and one of the hotel maids discovers this small sculpture and falls in love with it. She sees its beauty, not its monetary value; she sees the purity of the artist's intent. She steals it and then suffers the pain of losing it. Toward the end of the film she finds it where her boyfriend has hidden it in a junkyard. Her finding it is one of the most gorgeous moments of endowing an object with meaning, because when she finds it, it's "as if" she's found her lost baby. The tears just flow from her eyes, her cheeks turn pink, and she holds it as if it's her own small child.

Your job as an actor is to find for yourself the emotional meaning of *every* object, person, place, and event in the script that your character talks about or relates to. There are two steps to this process. First ask, What does the object mean to my character emotionally? Second ask, What can I use to provoke that emotional response in *me*? Sometimes identifying with the given circumstances your character is in is enough to elicit the emotional response that is required from a prop, but, again, if it isn't, you need techniques to help you.

To provoke the maid's reaction to finding the small Henry Moore sculpture in *The Object of Beauty,* I described an "as if" that an actress might use—the "as if" of "It's my very own child, my precious baby, that's been lost." If I had this acting problem to solve for myself, I might add to this, "It's my precious baby who has an illness and if I don't find her immediately, she will die." I've raised the stakes for myself to give my choice urgency so that the moment I pick up the object, the emotion would have a particular quality of intensity, pain, relief, and gratitude.

If you're playing the maid, you've got to find your own "as if." It could be the "as if" of a pet that you love; it could be a beloved brother or sister; or a lost and grieved-for part of yourself. It could be a substitution: for example, if you actually lost something that was valuable to you, like one of the personal objects we talked about earlier. (Remember, one of the parts of the Personal Object exercise was my asking, "Where is this object now? Do you still have it or has it been lost? If it's been lost, what would it mean to you emotionally if you could hold it now?")

When the maid who finds the Henry Moore sculpture picks it out of the trash heap, she grasps it and looks at it to see if it's been injured, as if it were actually human flesh. Remember, actors, the prop department gives you objects, but they are dead until you endow them.

In the film *Stanley and Iris,* which starred Jane Fonda and Robert De Niro, Stanley's father dies, and when Stanley, who is mentally slow, is given the artifacts of his father's life in a shoe box, he finds a watch. Stanley picks up the watch and within seconds De Niro floods with tears. There's no question that the actor endowed the watch with some kind of memory—because the *character* did. What could the memory be? The moment he saw his father pick out the watch in a store? Or the night when his father said to him, "One day this will be your watch," and how he never thought he'd have to lose his father to get it. Choosing the specific memory is your work as an actor. You have to endow the object with meaning *before* the performance. Then in the moment you don't have to think about your choice. When you touch the object, it comes to life for you.

Even the history you build for the watch has to affect you emotionally; it can't be dry. It's no use to you if you write it down nicely or imagine it if it doesn't arouse feeling and provoke behavior in you. It's useless to be a "good student" who sits at home and imagines the history of an object as if you were writing a master's thesis. You're job is to be *subjective*—to make choices that work for the script and for you. I'm repeating this again and again because I struggled with endowing objects at a time in my life when I wanted to avoid experiencing my acting emotionally. I would make choices that were intellectually pleasing but never reached my heart, so all I did was get to talk about them with the teacher after they hadn't worked.

I cannot give you a better example of an endowed object or a more thrilling one than the "mistake" that happened during a performance of *Chéri,* a play by Anita Loos starring Kim Stanley and Horst Buchholz in the story of a wild affair between an older woman and a younger man. One scene takes place after the couple has made love. They are in a post-coital reverie, and the young lover is eating an apple. One night during the scene, Horst Bucholz accidentally dropped the apple on the floor. Kim Stanley, without skipping a beat, picked up the apple and began to kiss and lick where the young man had bitten into it and molded this right into the scene. You have never seen a more romantic, erotic, desperate, and human example of passion than that "mistake" that Kim Stanley turned into art. She didn't *think* about endowing the object, it was second nature to her; she was so invested emotionally in the relationship that his mouth on an object aroused her to immediate action.

Good artists always push boundaries, and when a talented actor comes along who takes that extra step into the vulnerability of human needs, it jolts the audience into feeling. There is a singular moment of object endowment when James Dean as Cal in *East of Eden* tries to help solve his father's deep financial problems and, on his father's birthday, delivers a big wad of money wrapped in tissue paper with a ribbon around it. He does this with the fervent hope of finally gaining his father's love, which has eluded him his whole life. When the father rejects the money, because he feels it is war profit and therefore tainted, Dean makes the choice of taking the money and trying to literally press it into his father's body. As the money falls and his father won't pick it up or accept it, he hangs his arms around his father's shoulders and sobs, then he runs out of the room, crying out against the rejection and turning his need for love into hate. Dean endowed that money with all of Cal's hopes and dreams of obtaining his father's love.

In another scene in *East of Eden*, Jo Van Fleet plays Cal's mother, who left him when he was a small child to run a brothel. When as a young adult Cal tracks her down, she tells him to get out, because she can't stand being close to the son she abandoned. She touches the safe in her office, puts her head against it, and begins to twirl the lock as if it's the only thing she can trust. It's a supremely lonely moment, because you understand that the only thing this woman is close to is cold, hard cash. And this is brought home even further by the way she writes out a check and folds it crisply, as one used to paying people off, before handing the check to her son, whom she hasn't seen in all these years. Ironically, this check is how Cal eventually makes the money he tries to give to his father. So money becomes a substitute for love. Clearly, Kazan wanted us to understand that this woman knows how to barter, knows how to sell, but not to love. The mother's safe, the check she writes out—the only gift she's ever given her son—and the package of money Cal tries to give his father are all emotionally endowed objects.

A League of Their Own is a film about a women's baseball team during World War II. Throughout the film, women on the team keep getting telegrams from their husbands telling them that they're coming home or from the war office telling them that their husbands are dead. So when a woman gets a telegram, she never knows what it will say, and the apprehension is, therefore, great. One moment in the film, they learn a telegram has just been delivered, and the camera pans the faces of all the women on the team. They don't know who the telegram is going to. Geena Davis, who plays Dottie Hinson, has a little pendant around her neck, and she picks it up off her neck and holds it. You can tell by the way she picks it up that her husband gave it to her, and as she touches it she's praying that the telegram won't be for her, saying that he's dead. She's clinging to her husband by touching the object.

In *Sweet Bird of Youth*, Princess says to Chance, "Well, sooner or later, at some point in your life, the thing that you lived for is lost or abandoned, and then . . . you die, or you find something else. This is my something else." She is talking about the drug hashish. In the movie, watch Geraldine Page when she's saying this. Watch how she inhales the comfort she feels from "her friend," the hashish; she takes it into her lungs as if it's a lover. The hashish is an endowed object because Princess has made it so important for her survival. The important thing about what Page does is to particularize the hashish in such a way that it is her life-saver and she is grateful to it as she would be to a doctor or a lover who administers relief or sexual fulfillment. That's the genius that was Geraldine Page.

Hilary Swank in *Boys Don't Cry* endowed her cowboy hat with joyful meaning as her character, Teena Brandon, looked at herself in the mirror, using the hat to complete her image as the new young buck in town, Brandon Teena. The way she handled the hat, it became a symbol of her gallant masculinity and her successful gender transformation. Later in the film, alone in a bathroom, Teena has to use a Tampax. She has to take it out from her satchel and look at it and be reminded that she has a vagina. As she looks at it, it's as if she's saying, "This is a foreign object but I am being forced to use it, and it is my enemy"—the Tampax, the female anatomy being her enemy, her woman's body being her enemy. The Tampax makes her have to face the fact that she's not a boy, so it's a heavily endowed object.

Sometimes you'll have an instinct to touch or handle a part of your costume or a prop or part of the set in a certain way, even when the script doesn't specify it. You endow the object with special meaning for your character so that it makes you more specific and alive in the material. Trust these instincts, they are very good. If you're an actress playing a character who has a scene in her kitchen, say, and there are no specifically endowed objects, and you're talking to your husband while you're drinking coffee out of the same cup you do every day, serving breakfast on the same plates, using the same frying pan, then every single item in that kitchen can be an endowed object to your character. Let's say you're nervous about something you're going to do later that day, and drinking from your particular cup makes you feel better. The cup is comforting because you've endowed it with the warmth and protection of home.

Say you're in a play and you're supposed to be surrounded by antique furniture, which, needless to say, will really be cheap reproductions. You must endow the cheap wooden reproductions as if they were real antiques. You would handle them with great delicacy, you would sit in the chairs and sofas carefully, you would look at them with great pleasure if you were a character who would respond to them aesthetically. However, don't make the mistake of treating the furniture in a period play like Christopher Hampton's *Les Liaisons Dangereuses* as antiques. To the characters, they are not antiques, they are their regular sofas and chairs. They sit in them and handle them in a certain way because of the style and manners of the day, not because they're antiques. If a piece of furniture is especially cherished in a play, as in August Wilson's *The Piano Lesson,* which is about an old piano that has generations of history and is central to the emotional life of the leading character, you must endow the furniture almost as a living ancestor, which means that you will touch it with special affection and respect, as you would a person.

Again, if you're putting on a diamond necklace but it's really just a rhinestone prop, you endow it with value by the way you look at it and handle it. That's how the audience experiences it. During the filming of Steven Spielberg's classic suspense movie *Jaws,* the mechanical shark kept sinking in take after take. Nevertheless the actors had to endow it with the fear they would feel if it were a real giant man-eating shark. When you're angry at the prop, it's difficult to believe that it's going to eat you, but you've got to convince yourself—whether through imagination or personalization or "as if"—so that you can react to it as if you are truly afraid.

With today's technology, acting in films often involves endowing a blank blue screen as if it's something very specific, which will be put in later through the magic of special effects, say a tornado in the film *Twister.* Helen Hunt, who played an expert on tornadoes, told me that when she had to see the twister that, in fact, wasn't there at the time of shooting, she had to call up images that would make her feel awe and fear. In *Gladiator,* much of the environment of the coliseum and the spectators was created later through technology, yet the actors playing gladiators had to film their scenes as if they were really in that place with that crowd. If you want to act in films, it's vital to have the ability to endow with your imagination a place or an object that's not there at all. Use the techniques I discussed in Chapter Five, "Inner Imagery," to help you do this.

In my class I often use a scene from Williams's *Orpheus Descending* to help actors learn about endowing a prop. The play's leading male character, Valentine Xavier, always carries a guitar, which he calls his life's companion. He says to his leading lady, "It washes me clean like water when anything unclean has touched me." He tells her the story of the autographs from great musicians who have signed his guitar, and each one is

like a special part of his family. Time after time, I have watched young actors bring in that scene without having worked on the history of how
those great musicians signed Val's guitar. It angers me that they abused
Williams's writing by not doing their homework, and I sternly send them
home to do it.

I tell them to specifically imagine going to a club, hearing "Blind"
Lemon Jefferson or some other great musician past or present who has
thrilled them, and being transfixed and moved by the way he plays so that
as you're listening, you weep and then go backstage and ask him to auto-
graph your guitar. When the actors bring the scene back after they've
done the homework, their performance is radically transformed. As they
touch the guitar and the autographs of the great musicians Val has encountered, the entire scene starts to glow with meaning.

Let me share with you a life-changing experience that I had with an
innovative genius named Jerome Robbins. Nothing I had ever seen in
the theater excited me or moved me more than *West Side Story,* which
Robbins had directed and choreographed. Several years later I was auditioning for his new musical, *Fiddler on the Roof,* and on my third callback,
Robbins said to me, "I don't think *Fiddler* is going to work out but I'd
like you to be in my Broadway revival of *West Side Story*." He cast me as
Big Deal, one of the street gang, the Jets. One day Robbins came in to
watch a run-through and was seated in the middle of the orchestra of the
Winter Garden Theater, where he observed us and took notes. We were
all understandably nervous and when he walked on the stage after we
completed the run-through, he said, as only Jerome Robbins could, "If
you think the shit I just saw on this stage is going to open at City Center
next week, you're out of your fucking minds!" We all looked at him in appalled silence. Then he said, "Now let's go to work and fix it."

Jerome Robbins educated us about the sensory realities of street kids
who lived in tenements and had never been to the country. In the dream-
ballet sequence of "Somewhere," the kids are catapulted into the country
and dance joyously. There was one particular dance step that we'd been
performing like a bunch of chorus kids in *42nd Street.* Robbins passionately explained to us that these kids are kicking their heels into the soft
earth for the first time in their lives, and when they swing their leg to the
side, they are smelling the earth that their heels have opened up. He went
on to give us that kind of specific imagery for every step of the ballet. Ultimately, we didn't *dance* the ballet; the sensory imagery that we endowed

the choreography with *made* us move. Opening night we stopped the show for three minutes. It's a thrill I can still feel to this day throughout my body.

In *The Days of Wine and Roses,* Joe and Kirsten have a little girl whom they talk about but who doesn't appear onstage in the play. In the final scene I've discussed before, Joe says to Kirsten, whom he's trying to save from dying of alcoholism, "There's a little girl who'd love to wake up tomorrow morning and have you make breakfast for her." Last night in my class an actor played Joe and when he said that line, his performance was extremely shallow. I asked him, "Did you create for yourself a real little girl who wakes up in the middle of the night screaming for the mother she never gets? A little girl that you have to comfort when she wakes up like that?" That's not in the play, but it *is;* you can't say, "There's a little girl who'd love to wake up tomorrow morning and have you make breakfast for her," if you haven't built her in your imagination. The actor had never done this work, that's why his performance was so superficial.

As an actor, you have to endow the little girl with the kind of emotional importance that a child has to a parent who loves her. You have to say to yourself, "I've got to build that little girl in such a way that she has a specific voice, that she cries for her mother in a specific way that I've heard, and that she clutches me when she wakes up from a nightmare with deep loneliness because she misses her mother." Then there will be a little girl with a history that affects you emotionally and behaviorally; in other words, she will *live* when you talk about her.

I want to share with you an example of endowing people and, simultaneously, endowing an event, that came out of my work with a young actor on the role of Chris in Arthur Miller's *All My Sons.* Chris has an important scene with Ann, who had been his dead brother's fiancée. Chris loves Ann but is deeply guilty about allowing himself any pleasure with her because of the atrocities he saw in World War II and because she was engaged to his brother, who did not survive. Chris recounts to Ann the fact that he had lost most of the company of men he had led during the war. He tells her a story of a young soldier who gave him his last pair of dry socks before the soldier was killed. He is trying to express to her how selfless his men were, how courageous they were in protecting each other and him, and that because they were protecting each other instead of saving their own skins, they were massacred.

If you're playing Chris, in your homework, you must create that platoon specifically when you talk about it—and by specifically I mean you can use your best friends as if they were in that platoon or the guys from your high school basketball team or you can remember the men in the film *Platoon* or any other people to whom you give faces and personalities and beating hearts. You also have to create the specific soldier and the event of his giving you his last pair of dry socks: how the day was cold, rainy, and muddy, and how he came into your tent to offer this gift to you. If you don't create the specific day and soldier in your imagination, the scene will have no emotional impact; the audience won't feel the blood and death that Chris has to feel. The audience should pay a price for watching *All My Sons,* and if they don't, we as actors have failed to do our job.

In Mike Leigh's film *Secrets and Lies,* there is a great scene in which Hortense Cumberbatch (Marianne Jean-Baptiste), a black woman, says to Cynthia Rosse Purley (Brenda Blethyn), a white woman, "You're my mother, I spoke to you on the phone," and Cynthia says, "That was you . . . No, no darling, you've been dialing the wrong person. . . ." The whole screen is filled with their faces and the scene lasts for about five minutes, an eternity on film, without the camera ever moving from them. After the white woman has vehemently denied that she could possibly be the mother of a black child, you see her thinking back on her sexual past, and there's a moment when you actually see her remember the night she went to bed with a black man. (It is clear in the film that the baby was taken away from the mother immediately after she was born.) That is an endowed event, an endowed back story that she had repressed. It's so exquisite because you can literally *see* the exact moment when she remembers that black lover and how startled she is. Brenda Blethyn had an image of that memory that was so specific you can almost see inside her brain as it surprised her; you can't fake that. How did she do it? Maybe she thought, *Well, how many men have I had sex with? There was him and there was him and there was him. They were all white. And then there was . . .* And then she realizes it. You see this happening in her eyes and on her face and you see how up to that instant she has blocked that event.

I'd like to end with a story about the actress Laurette Taylor, whom I've mentioned as inspiring Uta Hagen, Geraldine Page, and many other actresses and actors of that generation with her performance as Amanda in *The Glass Menagerie.* During one of the fallow periods in her career, Taylor was doing a stock production of Shaw's *Candida,* a play about a woman who wants to be needed by her minister husband and makes him jealous through her dalliance with a young poet. As the story goes, the actors playing the husband and the would-be lover were perfectly dreadful, and yet Laurette Taylor's performance was described not only by the critics but by everyone who saw her as incandescent.

When a friend of hers came backstage and asked, "How can you be so good with actors who are so bad?" Laurette Taylor replied, "Oh, I believe they are great. They are just having problems showing it. And every night, I go on the stage to support them and give them the energy to be great." In other words, she *endowed* them with a talent that they were in fact lacking but that she believed in and *needed* to believe in to play her part successfully. What made this choice so especially right for the play was that the actress saw how much the actors needed her in a way that mirrored the way her character in *Candida* is looking to be needed. Instead of complaining about having to work with inferior actors, she just endowed them with great talent and love, and played that. That's why we still talk about Laurette Taylor to this very day.

16

THE MOMENT BEFORE:
STARTING THE SCENE WITH LIFE

In this brief chapter I want to focus on a subject I've touched on without naming it: *the moment before*—the time immediately preceding your entrance. I discussed it in regard to Janet McTeer's entrance as Nora from the cold Norwegian winter in *A Doll's House,* and all the characters' entrances up those five flights of stairs in *Barefoot in the Park.* Creating behavior based on a moment before makes you more involved with your character, and it involves the audience, too. They care because you have built their belief that you have a full life offstage. That's why it's a mistake not to do the work that's required to build what happens to you *right before* you walk into any scene on a stage or on a film set.

The set for Eugene O'Neill's play about lost souls, *The Iceman Cometh,* is a bar. In the 1999 Broadway production starring Kevin Spacey, each character made an entrance suffering from his own particular hangover. When you are a dyed-in-the-wool alcoholic, the only thing that counts is your next drink. Every alcoholic has a certain tolerance for the amount of liquor they consume, but at a certain point you either have to sleep or pass out. If you're playing one of the customers in *The Iceman Cometh,* then *the moment before* is the moment before you enter the bar. If you are staying in a fleabag hotel upstairs, you know that every morning you are close to that first drink. Your body literally *needs* the alcohol because the blood sugar content was high when you fell asleep but now that you've awakened your body is trembling; not having a drink for hours, your blood-sugar level has gone down.

There are specific physical sensations when you wake up with that kind of a hangover. You are nauseated, your head aches, your mouth is bone dry, and possibly you have defecated or urinated in your bed. Walking down a flight of stairs or a hallway to get to that bar is the longest walk of your life. Your body is screaming, *Get me that drink and get it to me now!* Depending on your age and the severity of your hangover, you'll walk from your bed to that bar in a certain way based on the physical obstacles that your particular quality of hangover puts in your way.

Every character entering the bar in *The Iceman Cometh* comes from that kind of moment before—the moment before they get their first needed drink. Some of the characters don't mind being seen as hungover, others disguise the fact and try to pretend that they are in some state of sobriety, but the physical, sensorial obstacles are there even if you try to hide them—for example, your hands may tremble but you pretend the quality of joviality and clearheadedness. If you're playing one of these characters and you want to enter on shaky legs, with a lack of equilibrium, maybe imagining you have pebbles in your shoes would make you walk carefully the way a drunk with a hangover might. Alfred Lunt actually did use pebbles in his shoes when he starred in Friedrich Dürrenmatt's play *The Visit,* to give him a sense of imbalance and terror as he backed away from a mob set on killing him.

The degree to which you need that first drink in *The Iceman Cometh* is affected by how much pain and discomfort you are in and how that first shot will begin to alleviate that pain. In life, we are always on our way *from* somewhere *to* somewhere else to accomplish something. That's why the moment before is so important when you're entering a scene; without knowing specifically what the moment before entering was, and bringing that experience into your performance, the performance will lack real depth and truth. We come from a specific point of view based on our literal moment before.

Let's look at Nina in *The Seagull.* When Nina makes her first entrance, she has run from her parents' estate to participate in Treplyev's play. She is frightened and excited. We find out later in the script that she had to sneak out of the house after having had a terrible fight with her parents concerning their disapproval of her associating with bohemians. Perhaps she desperately ran through the forest to make sure she was on time for her performance. (One of the first things she says after she enters is, "Am I late?") Perhaps she stumbled and fell and has dirt on her face and leaves in her hair, and is brushing them off and catching her breath as she enters. This is not about being overly fussy or busy; this is about the specificity of the life with which the character walks into the play. Why is that a helpful moment before for Nina? Because Nina wants to shake off her family, she wants to wipe them away and enter a new and glamorous life. The behavior is rooted in the character's psychology and in the given circumstances, and though the audience won't consciously be aware of it, the idea that she feels as if she's escaped a prison will be illuminated by how she enters.

If the script doesn't specify or give you clues to a moment before, you could have a good creative time coming up with one on your own. In Uta Hagen's book, *A Challenge to the Actor,* she makes a very good case for having your preparation consist of cultivating the opposite emotion from the one you will call upon when you start the scene. For instance, if you're going to walk in and discover a dead body, you might prepare your moment before as returning from an enjoyable walk in the park on a lovely spring day; you might even walk in with an ice-cream cone. In these circumstances, the discovery of the dead body would certainly shock you, because it's the last thing you expect to find.

Sometimes the script gives you many clues for your moment before, as in Lanford Wilson's *Burn This.* Pale is first heard screaming obscenities at someone and then desperately screaming Annie's name outside the door of her loft. He walks in with a bandaged hand, talks nonstop, and later announces that he did a couple of lines of coke and "it don't affect me." When he is asked about the injury of his hand, he tells the story of how he had to bust a "son-of-a-bitch" because he was not given the understanding he needed and deserved.

If you're playing Pale, you could make the choice that you did cocaine in the elevator on the way up to the apartment. This makes sense since midscene he says he's taken coke. Obviously he's keyed up and you could justify it any way you want, but it could well be that he's just taken drugs, and playing that choice would give you the edge you need for your entrance. Given the fact that he's intimidated by and attracted to the woman he's about to see, his dead brother's dance partner, he could easily have felt the need for drugs immediately prior to his entrance. We don't know whom he shouted to outside the door, but if you're playing Pale *you* have to know, and the playwright helps you enormously by giving you a fight outside the door that the audience can actually hear. I mentioned in the chapter on emotional triggers that Pale *must* enter in a rage and that you can't equivocate about this. All the choices you make about your moment before for Pale have to feed into this rage.

Here's one of my favorite examples to illustrate what choice in acting means and how using specific sensory work for a moment before can bring a scene to roaring life. Kim Stanley and another gifted actress played Masha in two separate productions of Chekhov's *Three Sisters.* I'm going to focus on the romantic and sensual scene between the ill-fated lovers Masha and Vershinin, who enter a living room having just come from a carriage ride in the snow.

In the first production, when Masha entered the living room, the scarf that was over Kim Stanley's head was damp from the snow, as was the part of her hair that the scarf did not cover. She entered the scene filled with vitality and humor and excitation, and made her way over to a fireplace, warming herself, and drying her hair. She was excruciatingly alert. As she talked to Kevin McCarthy as Vershinin, she folded the wet scarf and put it on the grate to dry, and as her hand brushed the hair from the back of her neck, she moved around to catch the warmth of the fire. Her whole body seemed to be flirting, literally in heat, warming up and finally boiling. The scene is beautiful on the page, but the actress's very specific use of the heat of the fire and the wetness of her hair and scarf, and her decision to draw attention to her neck and breasts as she was moving to catch the heat of the fire, was so alive and sexy, you wanted to take her on the floor yourself.

The other actress, who in her career has done many fine pieces of work, was swathed in a gorgeous Russian winter costume, smothered in fur, and looked quite glamorous as she entered as Masha, but the scene did not come alive in the thrilling way that it needs to. It was not erotic or romantic, passionate, longing, or funny, all of which Kim Stanley's and Kevin McCarthy's was—because they had created their moment before so specifically. Walking into that warm, inviting living room from the cold and snow outside triggered their physical desire for each other and their longing for closeness. They used the moment before to make the moment of now sensorially alive. The attention Stanley gave to warming her hair and neck, seemingly doing it for her own comfort but truly doing it to intoxicate the man she's in love with, was human and extremely private and, therefore, universal.

In the other production of *Three Sisters,* the actress didn't seem to be coming in from anywhere but offstage. There was no moment before. There were costumes to suggest the cold weather outside, but the actors didn't invest specifically, and the difference sank the scene. You have to do the sensorial work and the probing into the carriage ride before their entrance to help the play come to life. This is part of your work, the actor's work. Chekhov did his, and I think we will agree he did it very well. But reading his words can't make your heart beat the way Kim Stanley and Kevin McCarthy did in Lee Strasberg's production of *Three Sisters.* For the heat of the scene was intensified by the way McCarthy watched Stanley's flirtatious behavior, by the way this ignited their passionate and wild embrace. Stanley wasn't indulging herself to flirt with the audience. Her sensory behavior was directly connected to her objective—to drive him mad with passion—and was also connected to her task of warming herself after the cold, damp carriage ride. Words are very powerful, but they are more powerful when the senses are added. If the characters have come in from a carriage ride on a cold, snowy night and the actors don't make us believe that they did, why should we believe anything else they say and do in the scene?

And this, again, is my answer to David Mamet's indictment of sensory work as useless. In the right hands, the specific use of sensory work intensifies the meaning of a scene and brings the writer's world alive onstage. I fight for the intelligent and committed dedication to these ideas, for, used appropriately and explored through the play—not separated from the text but connected to it—they can lead to uncompromising truth.

17

MOMENT TO MOMENT: IT'S ALWAYS IMPROVISATION

The first time I heard the phrase "moment to moment" was in Sanford Meisner's acting class when I was nineteen years old. At that point, I had no idea what it meant or how crucial it is to good acting. *Moment to moment* means that you don't miss a moment, that you're so *present* in the scene, monologue, or soliloquy that you never miss a truthful impulse within yourself. It means that if you're acting with a partner, you are so connected to them, so focused on seeing and listening to them, that you never miss a truthful response. When you're acting moment to moment, you're in the *now* emotionally; you never get lost in your own thoughts instead of listening to the other actor; you never become self-conscious and start to wonder how you're being received by the audience or whether you're doing what you planned. Moment to moment is about *investigation,* it is about *exploring* a choice in performance, not simply repeating it from rehearsal; moment to moment allows you to discover the scene fresh every time as if for the first time. Moment to moment means being alive to yourself in the *now* and to the other person in the *now*.

This does not contradict the idea of doing complete and vivid home-work on the text and on your character—it is in addition to the technique and tools I've given you. Doing your homework gives you a foundation for your moment-to-moment work. Once you have done your script analysis, created the back story for your character, and have chosen active intentions based on their wants, then you use moment to moment as the performing technique that keeps you alive and improvisational onstage or during the shooting of a film. If you've done your homework thoroughly, the impulses that come to you during your moment-to-moment per-formance will always be appropriate for your character and connected to the story.

It was this moment-to-moment quality of discovery in performance that Laurette Taylor possessed as Amanda in *The Glass Menagerie* that made Uta Hagen say she couldn't catch her acting. As David Craig, one of the greatest musical theater teachers of all time, said about singing a song, "Songs don't take place now, they take place in the *now* of *now*." Great moment-to-moment acting takes place in the *now* of *now* and it is that hy-perfocused energy that makes the audience believe anything could happen.

To be moment to moment, you have to be available to your own im-pulses and to what the other person gives you. This means to be without an inner censor, to be wide open. Good actors say, "I'm open, just hit me the tennis ball and let's play." Indeed, I tell actors to watch tennis because it is one of the most specific moment-to-moment sports. The other person hits the ball to you and you have to instantly decide how you're going to hit the ball back. You don't know what's coming; you have to stay in the moment and watch like a hawk or you'll miss it. Tennis players are so trained in what they do and so present in the moment that that decision is intuitive. If you watch tennis, you'll understand moment-to-moment acting.

One of the keys to "playing tennis" in acting is listening. I often repeat to my classes a great quote from Geraldine Page: "If we could only listen to each other on the stage like the animals in the forests do—as though our lives depended on it." Listening, truly listening, to the idea that the other character is sending to you, and the nuances of how they are send-ing it, provokes you into your performance, so you must listen every time you act as if for the first time. Literally, you must believe I have never heard this before and I have to investigate it, understand it, and find out how it affects me. Then and only then will I discover my next mo-ment in the scene. In life, how can we know what to say and how to say it if we haven't truly listened to what has been said to us? We all know people who have a hard time listening to us, and we generally find them incredibly dull.

If you lose concentration during a performance, truly listening can ground you and bring you back. When you're acting in a film, if you listen fully enough the editor may feature your performance because your listening may be a lot more interesting than the other person's speaking. Most importantly, listening keeps you involved—catching the idea from the other person and responding because you got it. Whether in film or onstage, truly listening and being affected by what you hear propels you forward to all of your next moments and adds to the peeling of the onion of your character.

Strindberg's one-act play *The Stronger* is about two women competing for the love of one man. The wife of the man talks continuously for about twenty-five minutes while the mistress remains silent for the entire play. Strindberg's title is really a question: Who is the stronger? The woman who has to speak and spill her guts or the one who listens and makes silent decisions she never reveals in speech?

Plays and films are heightened reality, they are about critical times in people's lives, so characters listen to each other because they need to get information, even if they misunderstand what the other character is saying—which is often the point. Even when a character doesn't listen or only half listens, the actor needs to know why they're not listening and where their attention goes. And the failure to listen is always a provocation to the other character. As the go-go dancer Chrissy says in David Rabe's *In the Boom Boom Room* to her lover, Al, whom she feels isn't hearing her, "You listen to me, what I'm saying, because I am very uptight, because I am worried over my life." Within the same scene she says several times, "Are you hearing me? Are you listening to me?" She also screams this at her parents. She is desperate to be heard and ultimately goes to the most self-destructive lengths to *make* the people around her listen.

At nineteen, I was so frightened of myself that in scene work I could very rarely put my attention on anyone else. As much as I wanted to be heard, it was very difficult for me to truly listen. I was so busy listening to the thoughts roaring inside my own head and waiting for my cue that my acting was the opposite of moment to moment—I was moment minus moment; I wasn't present enough to be actually affected by another person's behavior. Also it was difficult for other people to understand me even if they were listening, because I spoke so quickly it was as if I were mainlining Benzedrine. Meisner picked up on this when I studied with him.

Meisner created the Repeat exercise to help beginning actors to lose their self-consciousness and begin to look outside themselves and to find their spontaneity. An essential part of good acting is reacting; this exercise gives you a real experience of spontaneous reaction if it is taught properly.

The Repeat Exercise

Two people sit in chairs facing each other and each observes the other. One of you will start the dialogue by saying aloud what you *see* about the other person. For example, "Your forehead is creased" or "Your lips are tense." The observation must be an objective fact—not something you think about them or project onto them: "You are sweating" as opposed to "You are nervous." The other actor will then acknowledge the observation by repeating it. If you've said, "Your forehead is creased," they repeat, "My forehead is creased." You would then repeat again, "Your forehead is creased." When they repeat "My forehead is creased" the second time, you note if there are any subtle changes in the way they say it, and when some behavior of theirs catches your attention or some behavior of yours catches their attention, that person introduces a new line of dialogue describing that behavior.

For example, if the other person's saying "My forehead is creased" and the absurdity of repeating that line to each other makes you laugh, then the other person might see this, and say, "You are laughing," and you would agree heartily, "I'm laughing." Interesting things can happen in this exercise: right after you say "I'm laughing," you might start to weep and then the other person would say, "You are crying"—and they might burst into tears as well.

If you stay open and observant, you'll become hyperaware of your subjective response to the person sitting opposite you. You may be attracted to them, you may not like them, you may think they're a terrific actor, a terrible actor. The discipline of the exercise is never to comment verbally on your subjective judgments but just on what you actually see in front of you. If you leave yourself alone and don't try to manipulate or censor your emotions, your emotional response to the other person, and theirs to you, will come out anyway as you say what you see—and it will be authentic. In other words, what you feel about what you see about the other person as well as in their behavior creates an emotional reality in the moment. The point of the exercise is to be authentic—which means to *not* act but to discover in the moment.

The Repeat exercise makes you confront your fear that if you stay truly alive in the moment, you're going to lose control over how you present yourself. If you're alive in the moment to your own impulses and to what the other person is giving you, you might get angry and you might blurt out your line or you might weep or you might get sexual, something might happen that ordinarily makes you embarrassed in life—but that's the gold in acting! Even your authentic embarrassment becomes an important and interesting part of your performance. That's the moment when the audience feels, "Yes, that is really how life is. I've had that experience myself" or "I hope I never have that experience."

I want to be clear about allowing impulsive moments in your work. Remember that I said if you do your homework conscientiously, your impulses will work for the character and the text. But if you don't do your homework diligently, then you might very well have impulses that sink the scene. Remember the young actor playing Treplyev in *The Seagull,* who hit Nina? That was the actor's desire, not the character's desire. And the young actor in *A Hatful of Rain* who destroyed the kitchen table? The character he was playing wanted his wife's forgiveness, so he would have to contain his rage. It is as if these actors were playing tennis without knowing that their objective was to get the ball over the net to the other side.

To drive this home, imagine that two prizefighters in the ring felt so angry that they started to box in the aisles of the arena and punched each other silly all the way out onto the street. Part of what makes a prizefight exciting is that they have to contain themselves within the bounds of the ring—which is the same thing as moment-to-moment acting within the given circumstances of the text.

I'm very happy that Meisner was my first teacher, because this is a great way to start learning the craft of acting. In fact, before you come to a teacher like me, who is deeply into script analysis, structure, and character, it would be smart to take a course from a really good Meisner technique teacher and to learn the sense of being in the moment and solid in your freedom of impulse. When you do the Repeat exercise, you're not a character, you're literally you, you don't have to worry about dialogue because one of you is always creating dialogue.

Once you've learned the Repeat exercise in a Meisner technique class, get together with an acting partner and do the exercise at home. Something happens in this simple moment-to-moment exploration that is totally organic, which is why Meisner created the exercise. He didn't want people to "attitudinize" their acting—to cop an attitude—to *pretend* they're angry, to *pretend* they're funny, he wanted the work to be organic, to grow out of real impulses in the now.

Sadly, recently I've heard a number of actors make fun of the Repeat exercise because they confuse simple with simpleminded. Again, I think if it's taught correctly—and by that I mean with a focused concentration on the actors being truthful to what they're seeing—it is helpful and a solid beginning to a lifetime of truthful acting.

One day in Meisner's class, he got so mad at me that he did something very cruel. He stood me up in front of the class, he took his index finger and poked me in the chest very hard, and I reacted. He said, "That's moment to moment!" And he backed me up all the way to the wall until I was sobbing. He assaulted me and humiliated me in front of the class, and I never forgave him for his sadism. But I've always been able to separate his neurosis from the brilliance of his teaching, and he was, in his own way, trying to get me to be truthful in my moment-to-moment reality. He called this the *pinch-ouch*. The moment is the pinch, the reaction is the ouch: pinch, ouch, pinch, ouch; action, reaction, action, reaction.

One of the biggest obstacles to moment-to-moment acting is having an idea of how you should come over to the audience, an image of yourself that you want to project. If you're wondering, *What if they don't like me? What if they think I'm fat? What if I look silly doing that?* you can't be in the moment. You're stuck in a preconception of yourself that doesn't allow you to use yourself in creative and different ways.

There was an aspiring actor in my class who was extremely viable commercially and every agent in New York was trying to sign him. He was a former athlete; he exuded a certain glamour and made sure that he dressed the part every day. One day in class, I asked him to do a physical task in the scene he was performing. The task was to clean up a messy room for a reason that was important to him. He said, "I don't see any reason for doing that." And I said, "Well, it's to teach you how to move on the stage in a way that's authentic and to make sure you don't get caught posing." When I said this, he turned red and started to laugh, and he answered, "I don't pose and I don't clean rooms for any reason." When I mirrored back to him that his face was red, he turned purple, and said, "I don't know how my face could possibly be red since I feel completely at ease," which then made the class laugh because they could see the color of his face. I did everything I could to try to help him to be humble and human in the moment instead of continuing to portray himself as a character of infinite perfection. For this actor, the idea of playing anything that might embarrass him or make him look less than perfect was humiliating and impossible for him even to try. Needless to say, with all of his attributes and the business literally pounding on his door, his career began but ended abruptly. Instead, he became a banker. Enough said.

For good actors who stay in the moment, there are no mistakes. Earlier I described how Kim Stanley picked up the apple that her young lover had accidentally dropped and sensually kissed where he had bitten into it. What she did was so erotic and romantic that she turned what could have been a disaster into a new expression of excitement in their relationship. That is the point of moment-to-moment acting—you *are* living, and therefore a so-called mistake is turned into real human behavior that you and the other actor are excited to respond to. In film acting, the takes are so short that all they have to do is catch lightning in a bottle—once. So mistakes that enliven a performance may be immortalized for eternity. I know many actors who say, "I can't wait for something unexpected to happen so I can improvise and discover something new."

Now, here's an example of what can happen if you're not playing moment to moment. When Alec Baldwin played Stanley Kowalski opposite Jessica Lange's Blanche in *Streetcar*, he went to make an exit and the door jammed and he couldn't get out. He ended up walking out the fourth wall, and the audience laughed because the fourth wall had been established as the wall of Stanley and Stella's apartment. Baldwin's next entrance was through the jammed door, and this time he kicked it in—to delighted applause. He later said courageously that if he'd really been in the character of Stanley moment to moment, he would have kicked the door down the first time it jammed. But he went into his head, so he left the stage as an actor who had faced a malfunctioning door, and then came up with the idea of what his character would really do. He humbly commented that he was disappointed with himself because he had taken the audience out of believing in Stanley and the story.

There's a story I like to tell about Jeremy Irons and Glenn Close on Broadway in Tom Stoppard's *The Real Thing,* a play about the terrors of marriage. The story goes that after they were playing eight shows a week for a solid year, they were doing a Saturday matinee and after the first act Irons said, "I'm so sorry, I'm just played out, and I don't have any juice left." And she said, "It's not you, it's me. I'm dead. I don't have any impulses left. Let's go back to the second act and change all the blocking." So they both went out after the intermission, and Irons said, "Just promise me you won't do anything you did before." She agreed, and apparently the performance just exploded, because neither of them knew where they were going to go on the stage or what they were going to do. They literally forced themselves back into moment to moment. Brave actors both!

Meisner used a great image for moment-to-moment acting. He said it's very similar to being on a tightrope; you've got to concentrate and balance yourself all the time or you'll fall, you've got to balance in the moment, you can take nothing for granted—it doesn't matter what happened in performance last night, tonight is a complete new discovery, and I mean this even if you've played it three hundred times. To paraphrase Meisner, the stage is not for amateurs. An amateur would never step on a tightrope and risk his or her life with no net the way a true actor will, knowing he or she could fall at any moment. But really it's the openness to falling that is so important, because in a sense actors do have a net—the net is having done your homework, having the text of the play to act, and each other to work off. Just for now, as you're reading this book, imagine a tightrope walker high, high, high above the ground with no net below them, every single footstep and forward motion has absolute concentration and dedication to the *now* of each footstep, and nothing can be taken for granted. Again, it's the precariousness of being in the *now* of *now* that makes a performance vibrate with light.

I'm going to talk about another important aspect of moment-to-moment work: pauses. As I've said, the writer demands a certain tempo and rhythm for the text to work at its best. Pauses are part of the rhythm of the line; silences are part of the rhythm of the scene. I've mentioned one of my favorite plays by Harold Pinter, *Betrayal.* Pinter's style is characterized by pauses; his characters often take time between lines, but it is never arbitrary. It is always for an emotional reason. In other words, the pauses are moment to moment. One of the jobs of the director and actors is to understand the inner life—the mind of the characters, why they're *not* speaking—and the physical behavior that may go along with it. Pinter's silences drive the story forward if you fill them correctly. If you don't, they're just dead stage weights. And if you don't fill them, you shouldn't be doing Pinter. His silences are *filled* with life. They are silences in the midst of intense emotional events between people: "What if he leaves me?" "I'm afraid they're going to hurt me." "I'd like to knock the crap out of her." "I'm afraid they're going to have sex with my wife." "What if tonight's the night I die?" These questions reverberate in Pinter's silences. If you're in one of his plays, you're on that tightrope doing moment to moment within the rhythm of his lines. In rehearsal you examine the silences and find out why they're there, what their content is, and how the pauses help the story move forward. You begin to feel the rhythm and to know how long to live within the pause and fill it with life before the next line.

What if there is an absolute demand from the director and/or the text that you take no pauses, that you must work in a specific, fast tempo? You still have to do moment-to-moment work. To give you a front-row seat to make the case, there is a play, *The Red Peppers,* that Noël Coward wrote in the 1930s about a husband-and-wife vaudeville act on a second-rate circuit right before motion pictures killed vaudeville. *The Red Peppers* is high comedy and as everyone who knows comedy will tell you, comedy is about rhythm and correct tempos. The husband and wife, George and Lily, begin the play by doing a musical number in which the wife drops a prop on the stage and "mucks up the whole exit," after which they both run offstage and begin to undress and redo their makeup for the next number. So they enter into the dressing room out of breath from the exertion of their act and she is guilty and he is furious. When I was a teenager I got a record album on which Noël Coward and Gertrude Lawrence, his friend and marvelous leading lady, performed these roles.

What I was taken with and learned so much from was how quickly they picked up their cues—barely taking time between lines—how you could feel that they were out of breath from the energy that their characters had spent on the stage and now they were expending more energy getting ready for their next musical number, and all the while using still more energy jabbering at each other. It's clear that these two people live to argue; if it weren't this, it would be something else. The end of the argument is when finally George, having had enough of Lily's excuses, says to her, "Lily, it doesn't matter *how* you did it or *why* you did it, you *did* it!" Lily's reply is, "Well, all right, I *did* it." And George's final triumph is, "Well, don't *do it* again."

Just reading this you can feel the rhythm and tempo with which it must be played to pay off. It's the speed with which these characters top each other that creates the comic fizz. But it's vital for you to realize that even if the writer or director demands certain rhythms and tempos from you, you still have to be moment to moment and grab from each other the *truth* of each second. That's what gives it life!

Moment to moment is the inner life, the emotional life, the discovery of life; it's why it's so joyful to act the imaginary circumstances every time for the first time. If you're moment to moment in performance, you are open to things that you weren't expecting to happen. I call it catching the wave. You surprise yourself; you go into the scene with the willingness to surprise yourself.

I caught the wave one night when I was playing Big Deal in the City Center revival of *West Side Story*. After the lead character, Tony, had been killed by the rival gang and his body was being carried offstage, I happened to catch the eye of Joe Bennett, who was playing Action, another member of the Jets. Joe and I just looked into each other's eyes and started weeping. We caught the moment and we came offstage and said, "My God, we were the Jets and our friend had been murdered." We discovered the truth of that moment together for the first time, after we'd already been playing for audiences for three weeks. It was an epiphany to me to be on a stage in front of an audience and to catch a silent moment from another actor in character and break down emotionally. It was then that I knew my Meisner training had paid off.

18

RELAXATION AND
OVERCOMING FEAR

Actors work their entire lives to relax in front of an audience. Michael Chekhov was an actor and teacher in the Moscow Art Theater who came to Los Angeles in the 1940s to act and teach. I like to quote his statement about relaxation in acting: "An actor should be a volcano in a completely relaxed body." By this he meant that the body should be as relaxed as possible and the emotions inside should be ready and available to boil. Although I believe this is true, Chekhov's statement can be misleading if you misinterpret it.

To be completely relaxed in front of an audience is impossible and undesirable because deep concentration creates a certain healthy tension, an energy that flows through the body. The healthy tension comes from the desire to accomplish your task—your objectives: I *must* get what I *need*. When I say *healthy tension,* I mean the same tension that the high-wire artist has as he crosses the taut rope between two towers. The high-wire artist's body is not stiff with tension but is released and concentrated on a task that must be performed or he will fall.

One factor that makes relaxation a complex subject is that we talk about being relaxed or tense to describe our emotional state and also our muscular state. Sometimes we feel emotionally tense or keyed-up, which we may call tense, but our bodies are more relaxed than we're aware of, and other times we are unaware of emotional tension but our bodies are carrying our stress, resulting in muscular tension. As actors, it's our job to be aware of the difference and to help ourselves to release emotional and muscular tension that can interfere with our performance.

Believe me, opening night of any play or the first day of shooting any film—or the day you shoot your big scene—carries with it a certain extra tension. You get through it the best you can—in ways that I'm going to share with you—but to expect yourself to be completely without tension is an unrealistic demand. And remember, unrealistic demands you place on yourself only add to your tension!

The physical tension we carry in our bodies often begins in childhood. When you are trying to hold back tears, anger, joy, or humor as a child, you have to force your facial muscles, your stomach muscles, and other muscles to stop your natural impulses. When you try to hold back emotion, you swallow it, affecting your throat, your chest, your shoulders, and your abdomen. When you have a bad self-image, you may stoop and carry an apology in your upper body. There is a lifelong connection between emotion repressed and the physical consequences of repressing it. Most of the time, we're not aware of the physical tension we carry until we get a headache, a backache, a neck ache, a stomachache, or some other signal we can't ignore.

There's a wonderful old adage, "What you are speaks so loudly I can't hear what you're saying." As actors, we must be aware of the physical image we're presenting because that is the physical embodiment of the characters we play. The minute that your body walks on a stage or in front of the camera or into an audition, people are already responding to your carriage, your facial expression, and your physical energy. If you're like most people, you hold your breath when you're frightened, and when you hold your breath, it automatically causes muscle tension. The most helpful thing I can say to you about tension, whether you are onstage, filming, or in an audition, is to keep breathing—*don't hold your breath!*

The thrill of acting is in the amount of aliveness you bring to the characters you play. If you examine an ordinary day in your life, you will see that physical tension in your body ebbs and flows. You wake up and stretch, because certain muscles have become tense from the position you've slept in; you feed yourself and get energy from the food; you go to work, which can cause you to have other muscular tension from extreme concentration, from the position you have been sitting in, or from a problem you confront with someone you're working with; you break the tension of work with lunch and, hopefully, refresh and reenergize yourself; you go back to work, go out for a night's entertainment with friends, then go to sleep and begin the cycle again. Tension, release, tension, release, tension, release.

In the same way that the sun comes up in the morning and sets at night, the natural cycles, from light to dark, cool to warmth, work to relaxation, sleep to waking, make life interesting. Life changes, it has tension. As people with our own individual historic tension, even when we are released we may be only partially released. For example, I tend to hold tension in my throat, chest, and stomach, and even when I'm doing something relaxing, often I'm still tense in these areas. But because I've worked on being aware of my physical tension, the minute that tension crops up in these places, I release it through breathing into where the tension is and on the exhale allow the muscle to let go. To become creatively relaxed as an actor, you must go through an examination of where your body holds unwanted tension. You must also be observant of where others hold tension in their bodies because observing them will help you to delineate physical behavior for the characters you play.

The places in the body that are famous for holding tension are the jaw, the throat, the chest, the stomach, the hips, the sphincter muscle (tight ass), knees, hands, feet, shoulders, and back of the neck. In other words, your whole body! This is the tension that you want to do your best to get rid of. One reason drinking and smoking and drugs are so difficult for people to give up is that they don't know how to release physical and emotional tension in other ways. Releasing tension is one of the primary beneficial effects of meditation.

All you have to do—and I recommend that you do this—is sit in a café for an hour observing people walking by and you will see different people's bodies holding tension in different places. They walk with stiff legs, with their head jutting forward, with their shoulders rounded and crunched, or they lead with their chest puffed out. You'll see this in certain men as they swagger down the street wanting to appear powerful and macho. The female equivalent to this is women who broadcast their sexuality by leading with their breasts and undulating their hips. These extreme defense mechanisms are used to try to control others, and they are generated by fear and sometimes hostility. It is not the same as a natural exuberance or confidence, nor is it sensuality that comes from enjoying one's movements without self-consciousness. With natural exuberance, confidence, and sensuality, the body is muscularly released and not held in an attitude. A muscularly released body is far more attractive than a body stuck in one attitude—and for an actor being stuck in one physical attitude means that your career is likely to be stuck and limited to type casting.

As you are sitting reading this book right now, be aware of where in your body you are holding tension right this second. Is it in your back? your neck? your jaw? your throat? your shoulders? your stomach? And I ask you right now, are you fully breathing? I teach all my students the Release exercise, which I suggest you learn and do on a daily basis.

The Release Exercise

Sit in a chair as you do at the start of the Memories of Home and the Personal Object exercises. As you allow yourself to breathe naturally and deeply, allow yourself to become super-aware of where your obvious muscular tensions are located. Start with the muscle that you feel is most tense. Breathe into the muscle and on the exhale ask the muscle to relax and allow it to let go of the tension—*awareness of tension, breathing into it, and breathing out to release.*

Let's say the tension you're most aware of is in your throat. What muscles are involved? How tight are they? You can, if you want, bring your hand or hands up to touch or massage the area as you breathe into it, and hold them there as you breathe out and ask the muscles to let go. You may have to do this several times as you feel the muscles release. You may feel emotion start to rise in you as you become conscious of the tension and release it, since often the tension is unexpressed emotion stored in the muscles. So don't be frightened if you feel you want to laugh, cry, or get angry. Allow the emotion to express itself in sounds and movement as you keep breathing and allowing muscular release. Move through your body and be acutely aware of even the most subtle tension. Give each muscle that you're aware is holding tension the amount of time and breathing it needs to release before moving on to the next. As you work on this exercise on a daily basis you will start to be conscious of subtle tensions in your eyelids, your scalp, calf muscles, ankles, toes, the back of your tongue. Exploring and releasing these tensions is excellent care for any person but absolutely mandatory for the actor. The exercise should last a minimum of fifteen minutes, and of course you can do more.

I learned the effectiveness and the necessity of this technique personally in the back of a New York taxicab several years ago. I was on Park Avenue at 6:00 P.M., the height of rush hour, and I was late for an important appointment. My shoulders had risen up to my ears because *I was trying, with my shoulders, to get the cab through the traffic faster.* Absurd, of course. My body became so uncomfortable in this position that I was forced to be aware of it, and by doing the Release exercise I began to let my shoulders move down to their natural position, which, believe me, was quite a long way to travel! Finally, my shoulders hit bottom, and once they did I immediately began to sob. This was an epiphany for me in understanding the connection between holding muscular tension and releasing emotions.

Relaxation exercises are often part of acting classes. I've heard some acting students be critical of them, and this is because of ignorance and fear. When students are judgmental about relaxation exercises it's because they're afraid of what they will find when they release their own muscles or they don't see what it has to do with their acting or the exercise is being taught incorrectly and indulgently. What I mean by *indulgent* is saying to actors that relaxation is the main objective in acting or making it seem that doing a scene with some physical tension means you have failed. This is nonsense. As I said, some degree of physical tension will always be present. The key is to make an effort on a daily basis to become acquainted with your tension so that it doesn't stop you from performing the character fully and richly.

If you need more help to release yourself physically—which will also help you to come alive emotionally—find a good teacher of the Alexander technique. In fact, I recommend this whether you feel you need it or not. The Alexander technique deals with physical awareness. As you become aware of the specific places where you hold your tension and release it, you will find that the power of your physical presence—and this is the point—increases in a way that can change your career. The accompanying emotional release will send fresh energy flowing through your body and also is a great means of decreasing depression.

Once your body is muscularly released, then you can begin to choose specific areas to *hold* muscular tension in order to reveal a character. Watch the end of *The Silence of the Lambs* and observe how Anthony Hopkins as Hannibal Lecter walks away from the camera on his way to, as he says, have a friend for dinner. You'll notice how jauntily and sensually he expresses the character's extreme confidence and pleasure in his predatory pursuit. Nothing in his body is held, it's all released. Then watch him play the repressed butler Stevens in *The Remains of the Day*, where every muscle seems tightly held. That's how we know it's the actor's *choice*. Stevens is a man who is 99.9 percent overtly physically unexpressive, with volcanoes burning inside; he is unaware that his extreme commitment to *not* being physically expressive speaks volumes about his psychological terror of his own emotions.

If you read a scene superficially, it might seem as if it calls for you to be relaxed, but be sure you haven't missed the underlying tension. It's the tension, the conflicts, the obstacles in a very quiet scene that make it potentially so riveting and that, along with the characters' objectives, move the story forward. In Howard Sackler's play *The Great White Hope,* which is about Jack Johnson, the first black heavyweight champion of the world, there is a lovely scene between Jack and his white lover, the aristocratic Eleanor Bachman. Jack, having returned from an evening swim after the couple has made love, lies in bed with Eleanor as they caress each other. Jack is playful and sensual, Eleanor is suffering from sunburn—the first clue of distress. Jack pours champagne on Eleanor's back and she screams in shock from the cold champagne on her hot skin, then they giggle and play like two teenagers.

On the surface you would say the characters are relaxed, but the truth of this scene is that when the play takes place, in the first decades of the twentieth century, it was illegal for a black person and a white person to have a sexual relationship; as the play makes clear, it seems as if the whole country is against their romance. Eleanor has a small monologue in which she expresses the desire to get so tanned that she looks Creole, in other words to become closer to Jack's skin color. Then Jack hums the blues. Eleanor asks if Jack is tired of her, and he reassures her that although he's tired of many things, she's not one of them. Jack responds, "Everybody know I done gone off Cullud women, I has too, 'cept for my momma." The scene at times is very quiet and the characters' bodies are in a state of release after sexual intimacy and after Jack's swim, but it is also filled with fear, dreams, and longed-for transformation. At the end of the scene, when Jack and Eleanor are enfolded in each other's arms and very still, federal marshals barge into their private cabin and Jack and Eleanor are arrested.

The scene's language is light and playful and then melancholy. If you read the play and are meticulous in your analysis of the different subtle transitions of what the characters express about themselves and their wants of each other, if you have done your homework exploring the time in which *The Great White Hope* takes place, a time in which the majority of white people didn't want a black world champion boxer and physical danger threatened black-and-white love relationships, and if you're specific about Eleanor's sunburn and how it makes her body uncomfortable and how Jack tries to soothe her first with champagne and later with a lotion, then you will begin to understand how much underlying tension there is in this beautifully written "relaxed and quiet" scene. This illustrates the point I made earlier about the healthy tension that comes from characters pursuing their objectives with what I would call in this scene a painful and quiet passion. If you are too physically relaxed in this scene you will destroy the dramatic tension that must be there, the dramatic tension of still waters running deep.

In case you think that "still waters running deep" is a mood—and I've said you cannot play a mood (remember, *mood* spelled backwards is . . .)—it is really not a mood. First of all, the waters are *running*—so they are moving. Secondly, they are moving in a particular direction and underneath the surface; they are moving in the direction of the characters' wants.

Again, the point of relaxation is not to be slack or limp or sleepy but to allow the energy to flow freely and vitally through your body. A good image for the release of energy you are aiming for is to think of it as being like the blood that flows through your body, which is pumped by your heartbeat. There's nothing to stop the flow of blood, and when there is, you get ill.

Perhaps the emotional state that creates the greatest amount of physical tension for actors is fear—fear of public humiliation. What if I forget my lines? What if I give a bad performance? What if everyone sees my terror? What if I throw up? What if I become completely dysfunctional? Or, probably the worst of all possible terrors, What if I shit in my pants? What if I do any one of these things and get fired? For most actors in this state of fear, death would seem preferable.

It can seem to you that you're putting yourself in a very vulnerable position every time you act or audition. After all, you are your instrument, so everybody *is* looking at you and listening to you, and you may decide to feel that they are judging you positively or negatively. Whether they're judging you or not is none of your business. I'm not kidding. In my view, you are *not* in a vulnerable position. Your job is to give the best performance or audition you can. If you concentrate on your acting tasks and are more interested in your creative contribution than in your fear of being judged, you will be doing the work you need to do to give a good performance or audition.

We all like and to some degree need outside validation. It feels wonderful. But if that's your main preoccupation, I can assure you that the validation will be a very long time in coming. Why? Because you cannot fully commit to your choices and explore them moment to moment if in every moment you are waiting for some kind of validation from outside yourself. When you split your concentration between your acting work and your fear of negative judgment, you are never wholly showing your talent, and, by the way, you are making sure that you have no pleasure in your creative experience.

The excitement in acting is allowing yourself to explore the circumstances you're in and having fun playing them, and if a director or a casting director gives you an adjustment, instead of defying them or feeling criticized, you get the pleasure of trying it a new way. Resistance doesn't help you. Being open and trying to find the truth of the scene and interesting choices for your character is the name of the game.

As I mentioned before, fear is a feeling, and one of the best ways to get rid of fear is to concentrate on something else that you can fully commit to, and one of the first things you should fully commit to is, as I said, breathing. Stella Adler used to say, "Fear is like a little pug-nosed dog that keeps barking at you, but it's only a little dog with a big bark. All you have to do is kick it and it goes away." She also said that you have to talk to fear, and what you say to fear is, "I need you in order to survive in my life. I have to know what fear is. But you are not my mind. You are not my heart. You are not my creativity. You are not my soul. You're just fear. So take your proper place in my life, you don't run the show. You're just fear." I think that is brilliant because it's about autonomy.

If you say, "I'm victimized by my fear," what you're really saying is "I don't want to combat it, I want to be overwhelmed by it so I can avoid my power and my passion and my joy." If this angers you as you read it, you're exactly who I'm talking to. You have not found, nor have you been truly interested in finding, how you combat your fear. You have to be assertive about grappling with this problem that all performing artists have. That's why in Barbra Streisand's comeback to live performance at Madison Square Garden, which was taped by HBO, she was shown backstage before the concert doing meditation breathing. She didn't let her fear stop her.

Is it scary to perform or audition in front of other people? If you're shy, yes, it can cause you anxiety. If you expect or demand perfection from yourself and you're afraid of making a mistake it can cause you anxiety, too. You may shake, your heart may pound, your palms may sweat. Fine. We've all been through that. You may even fear that you're going to die. But you're not going to die, and if you do, well, the fear will be over.

If you're specific in your work and nervous at the same time it can give your performance a kind of shimmer, because your internal stakes are so high, but it all goes into your performance and works for you. Singer/actress Diahann Carroll used to say that when she opened on Broadway in a musical, she would lose her hearing—not so good for a singer since you have to listen to the orchestra. Fear can do unbelievable things to you, but there is such a thing as human will. It's saying to yourself, *I've got to understand my particular physiological reactions to fear and I have to find techniques to help me get through it so I can succeed.* Carroll, despite her extreme reaction to fear, certainly found the will and the techniques to overcome it and gave excellent performances in such musicals as *House of Flowers* and *No Strings.*

Sir Laurence Olivier went through a period later in his career when he was frightened that he might forget his lines on stage. His fear was so intense that he asked the stage manager to request of the other actors that they never look him square in the eye because he felt he would lose concentration. But he got over it and continued to work. So however frightened you may be, you are far from alone, and many stars who you might think couldn't possibly be fearful have, in fact, revealed that they've been literally terrified. And yet they continue to work.

All of the work that you do in analyzing the text and committing to choices is your *protection* against fear. Remember Stella's advice to recognize that fear is only a small part of you and to talk to your fear and put it in its place. Then review and concentrate on your choices, immersing yourself in your character's given circumstances and desires and your inner imagery, and go out there and do it, because let's face it, you want to, or you wouldn't be in the business of acting.

You also need to find specific ways to take care of yourself when you're afraid. A therapist once suggested to me in a session right before an opening night, when his entire office was vibrating with my fear, that I buy presents for all of the cast members, and it was a big cast, about twenty-five people. I spent the entire day going to a nursery and buying each actor a small plant for their dressing room and lugged all twenty-five plants up the stairs into all the different dressing rooms. By the time I was ready to open, I was too exhausted to be scared. I just had enough energy to focus on my work and give a good opening-night performance.

Another technique I've found helpful is to do a simple exercise of breathing love in and breathing fear out. Don't judge this as New Age or corny. Try it. As you inhale, say silently to yourself, *I'm breathing love into my heart,* and as you exhale, say, *I'm exhaling fear.* Do this at least ten times and I guarantee it will change how you feel, not the least because it slows your heartbeat down. And, of course, it guarantees that you are breathing!

I was coaching an actor whose family lived in Australia. He was going in to the network for a final callback to star in his own television series and I went with him. He was young and inexperienced and filled with nervousness. I suggested to him that he think about his brother in Australia to whom I knew he felt very close. At that moment, he pulled out his cell phone and actually called his brother in Australia. They chatted for about five minutes, and it calmed him down and made him feel connected and loved. He went in and got the job—because he took care of himself.

So the lesson here is that you are only a victim of your fear if you are passive about finding ways to confront and solve the problem.

There are two schools of thought about whether you should clean your instrument out of the particular day's emotion and start from scratch, from a sense of neutral relaxation, before a performance or audition, or whether you should bring whatever happened to you that day emotionally into your work. Neither school is saying that you should keep muscular tension that has nothing to do with your character. The first school of thought believes that you should rid yourself of anger, sadness, or too much adrenaline, and calm yourself down into a relaxed state and then build the exact emotion you need for your entrance into the first scene. The second school believes that you don't clean the instrument of whatever happened emotionally to you during the day, you use it as gasoline for your performance. That's why you hear some people say, "She gave a very angry performance tonight," or "He gave a melancholy performance tonight," meaning that the performances stayed in keeping with the text but varied in emotional tone. I've heard that Mike Nichols always says, "Bring your day with you."

I believe that it depends on the person. Some people like channeling the emotion of their day into the work and can modulate and focus their emotion to fulfill the character's needs. This type of person can use a frustrating day comically and truthfully to ignite her performance as Billie Dawn in Garson Kanin's *Born Yesterday,* a comedy about the awakening and maturing of one of the theater's classic dumb blondes, or use the same frustration to play the darker tragic character of Medea. But perhaps you're the type of person who gets emotionally stuck and has a hard time working through emotions like anger or sadness, and a hard time letting go of your personal reaction to what happened to *you* that day. Then you would benefit by doing a relaxation exercise and either letting yourself grieve the sadness, or, if you're stuck in anger that distracts you from your character, dissipating that anger by doing physically aggressive movements—punching, kicking—followed by a relaxation exercise. What you'll find is that underneath most anger is sadness or fear.

If you're the second type, the key is to free up your instrument to be available to different types of emotion so that you're not stuck in just one. If you don't unblock your emotions before a performance, you are in danger of being closed and fake. This is why it's so helpful to know your own inner world. Sometimes just being social with other people before a performance can get you outside yourself and help you. If you know yourself well enough, you will discover whichever techniques work best to prepare you to act. Remember, you never have to be stuck. But some days are easier than others.

Should you do a relaxation exercise to release muscular tension before every performance and audition? The answer is yes, but only to a degree. Once you have learned your body's specific tensions, you'll get so good at recognizing and then releasing them that you begin to do it without conscious attention. Releasing tension becomes a way of life rather than an exercise. It's very much what cats do all day long; they are constantly aware of and releasing tensions. They won't tolerate being tense. So emulate cats, they are wonderful teachers.

But until you become adept at finding and releasing physical tension, do the Release exercise daily, just as you work out physically and vocally—a subject I'll discuss in the next chapter—and just as you do the acting exercises I suggest. If you feel you're physically tense before a performance or an audition, find a quiet place and do the Release exercise. You can do it in your parked car or in the waiting room before an audition or, before a performance, standing outside of camera range or in the wings or in your dressing room.

The Release exercise also puts you in a very receptive state for rehearsing the emotional triggers or sense memories that you are going to use in your audition or performance. Sometimes it's enough just to begin the sense-memory work. Then, when you see that your instrument is responsive and the emotions are alive and accessible, you might want to stop the exercise. This keeps you revved up for your audition or performance. It's different for everybody: some people never run out of emotion and can access it as often as they want; other people prefer to save it and just use it when they need it. You have to know the kind of animal you are. Some actors don't like to do sense memories right before a performance because they feel that the work they've done at home will join them when they need it. Again, you have to find out what works for you.

Actors who seem to the audience to be exciting and electrically alive seem to be fully physical even when their whole body isn't visible. One of the great physical performances is Meryl Streep in *Sophie's Choice.* Alan Pakula, who directed the film, used many shots of Streep's entire body because she was so expressive as Sophie, jumping like an excited child or in languorous sensuality with Kevin Kline, also a tremendously physically expressive actor, as Nathan. And yet there are many close-ups of Streep, too, and one of the things that gives them power is your awareness of her entire body, knowing that it's expressing itself even though you can't see it.

Elia Kazan said that the difference between Marlon Brando and James Dean was related to this exact point. In *East of Eden,* Kazan filmed Dean as Cal Trask in as many full-body shots as he could possibly get, because Dean was so expressive with his body that it spoke to the audience in powerful ways emotionally and psychologically. Whereas with Marlon Brando in *A Streetcar Named Desire, On the Waterfront,* and *Viva Zapata,* he photographed him mainly in medium and close shots because Brando's power seemed to emanate from his upper body and face.

The last idea I'd like to share with you is that if you're emotionally alive while you're filming but your body feels tense to you, and you are self-critical about that, you may be surprised to see how good you are when the scene is cut together. The director and the editor may use close-ups of you, and your eyes may be so filled with need and desire or another emotion that brings the story to life that the close-ups carry the scene. This is one of the reasons why they say an editor can save an actor's performance. I'm giving you this information to help you avoid unnecessary suffering when you finish a day's shooting and you hate what you've done. There's another point as well: what makes the close-up work is your intense concentration on your acting tasks, which may have been overzealous and caused your body to be physically tense but which registers in a positive sense on your face. In film, you never know until you see it. But if you concentrate instead of giving in to your self-judgment and fear, your concentration is likely to pay off.

19

VOICE, ACCENTS, AND
BLOOD MEMORY

When I was getting ready to move to Los Angeles to open my acting studio in 1989, I got a phone call from a Mrs. Dixon, a renowned vocal coach who had heard that I was going to teach in Hollywood. Mrs. Dixon was about to retire. She took me out to dinner and urged me to tell the next generation of young actors that 80 percent of their performance in a film is on the soundtrack.

Young actors, particularly on the West Coast, often don't feel that they have to have strong and flexible voices. They know they will be heavily miked for film and television work, and they've also been misled to believe that their performances will be primarily visual because we're always told that film is a visual medium. But one of the reasons some careers don't have longevity is that work on the voice has been relegated to the province of live theater and the vocal element of film acting has not gotten its due respect. Mrs. Dixon saw this negative trend growing and was concerned about it. When you think of Katharine Hepburn, Bette Davis, Paul Newman, Humphrey Bogart, Richard Burton, Anthony

Hopkins, Harrison Ford, Jack Nicholson, Goldie Hawn, and Denzel Washington, you can't separate their visual power on the screen from their vocal distinctiveness on the soundtrack.

Voice is so important for film work that Woody Allen stopped production on two movies to give his leading ladies time to find their characters' voices, and it took both films to a higher comic level. Mira Sorvino's high, squeaky Minnie Mouse voice defined her as Linda Ash, the hooker in *Mighty Aphrodite*. Dianne Wiest's deep, resonant contralto, which she used so hilariously, defined her as Helen Sinclair, the grande dame of the theater who kept entreating her young paramour, "Don't speak," in *Bullets over Broadway*. These actresses chose these voices the way you make choices about the physical behavior of your character.

Laurence Olivier's performance in his stage and film version of *Othello* was largely based on his vocal choice for the character. Playing a Moor who is a general, a commander of men, Olivier trained diligently so that he could drop his voice an entire octave, creating an entirely new sound for Othello, one that he had never used before. That's what excited Laurence Olivier about acting: transformation.

Leonardo DiCaprio plays the legendary Howard Hughes in Martin Scorsese's *The Aviator*. While I was working with Leo on the role, he read many books about Hughes, pored over newsreels, and listened to audiotapes of Hughes to learn as much as he could about the man. Hughes spoke in an entirely different register than Leo does, and this presented a vocal challenge. In every coaching session we did for the film, Leo disciplined himself to speak in the more nasal tones of Hughes instead of in his own lower and more resonant tone. To do this, he had to change the center of his vocal production from his chest into his head. He practiced this during the rehearsal period nonstop as we worked on the specifics of the role so that when he acted the part, the sound was as natural to him as if it were his own speaking voice. Through listening to the audiotapes, Leo also learned that publicly, at least, Hughes did not inflect much emotion in his voice. This was an important clue to playing his character and to the difference between his public and private persona. By connecting the voice he used to his own emotional instrument, and using it to express the various choices he made, Leo was able to allow his voice to inflect emotion in the private scenes while maintaining a subtle nasality that defined Hughes's well-documented voice.

A wonderful comic actor who's had a great success in television is Brad Garrett from *Everybody Loves Raymond*. Everything about Brad has a unique largesse about it, including the sound of his voice. His deep and resonant voice is so distinctive that it's a power in itself, and it completes the package of his tall, hardy presence. Brad's voice is so distinctive that when I coached him for the role of Jackie Gleason in the television movie *Gleason,* it was impressive to me to watch him move into a different vocal territory. Brad had watched episodes of *The Honeymooners* for years and because he's a great mimic—as many good actors are—it wasn't difficult for him to capture the idiosyncratic way that Gleason spoke. But like Leo, Brad wasn't just impersonating the vocal qualities of another person, he was able to hook up the sounds to his own emotional life, so his speaking seemed utterly authentic. While taking on the rhythms and vocal tonality of Gleason, he retained his emotional truth in the center of his vocal choice.

Close your eyes and listen to Dustin Hoffman in *The Graduate.* Benjamin, the role of the college graduate of the title that made Hoffman a star, sounds almost monotone because the character doesn't want anyone to know what he's feeling. But his inner life is so turbulent that little emotions creep into his voice—breakthroughs of hysteria and whining and pleading. Later in the film, the character begins to have more vocal dimension and strength, because Benjamin starts to claim his right to express what he feels. Contrast this with another vocal performance of Hoffman's in *Rain Man,* where Hoffman played an autistic adult who, because of his autism, did not have vocal variety or expression. In between these two films, Hoffman challenged himself again vocally in playing characters of both sexes with different vocal qualities in *Tootsie.*

It is shocking when you hear the voices of some so-called adult actors, particularly on television, that sound adolescent and without nuance, depth, and color. It's fine to sound youthful, but the voice has to have tone and variety to keep the audience interested on an aural level. Some actors speak so quietly—again particularly on television—that they don't make a vocal impression at all. Sometimes it's hard for the audience even to hear their lines, although they're miked. This is often done with the purpose of seeming conversational and "natural." But often it's an affectation of naturalness and it deprives the actors of full expression and stops them from being as interesting as they could be if they had the desire and the technique to use their voices in more creative ways.

Some actors have a voice that is very distinctive but limited. There are many examples of young women with childlike voices that help to make their careers early on. The problem is that they become famous for having a trick voice that they become stuck with. What starts as an asset can end up a liability.

The voice should take on the sound of the emotion you're revealing in a part. When you hear a baby cry, it is very piercing and can be unbelievably unnerving because nothing stops the sound of them expressing their needs. They don't hold any muscles to restrict their sound, they let go completely from their belly, and they make this absolutely free and wide-open sound. Then life does its ugly job and babies start to hold their breath, hold muscles, and stop speaking from their body because society and experience begin to limit them. To one degree or another, we've all gone through this process. Some of us come out of it vocally better than others.

So as an actor, what do you do about your voice? First, you have to recognize what kind of a voice you have. Are you one of those people who is largely identified by their voice? Can you use your voice in different ways or do you find that it's stuck in one register or another? Do you have a small voice and difficulty projecting? These are things that you have to find out by trying to use your voice in different ways.

Can you do something about your limitations? Absolutely. You can work with a good vocal production coach on specific exercises to train your voice so that it has power, flexibility of tone, range, emotional connection. You can learn how to breathe deeply so that you are capable of doing some of the long passages in Shakespeare, Ibsen, Shaw, Strindberg, Williams, August Wilson, or John Patrick Shanley, to name a few of the playwrights who demand strong vocal ability, without having to take extra breaths that weaken the meaning of the lines and stop the flow of the scene. The point of getting vocal training is so that you *can* make choices. You don't want to lose your distinctiveness, you want to increase your options because in the long run, this will enrich your career.

Vocally, it's vital that your throat and neck muscles are relaxed, that the tongue is relaxed, and that you understand that you speak on the air and not on a lack of air. You have to train yourself to relax your upper body and then concentrate on filling your diaphragm. You need to become sensitive to how much breath you need for a speech and rehearse it as you would a dance, meaning that you have to have an awareness of where to breathe and how much breath reserve you need to have for a given text. Where you take a breath depends on your interpretation of the text as well as your need for breath.

The resonating cavities that are in the cheek area parallel to your nose and your upper head resonance bring the voice forward and you should train and exercise specifically for producing more resonance on a daily basis. When you go to a good vocal coach, they will give you exercises to improve your resonance. One of the best exercises is simply to use air to vibrate your lips, making sure that your jaw is relaxed at all times. Having a tense jaw and using the wrong muscles in your neck and throat and breathing improperly—breathing from your chest instead of your belly—gives you vocal problems. If you breathe from your upper chest, you automatically tense your throat, raise your larynx, and tense all the other muscles that need to be relaxed for making focused and healthy sound.

Different roles have different vocal demands, and some roles that are especially vocally demanding require specific exercises to prepare you for them. You may have to do these exercises not just in rehearsal but every night before you go onstage or as a warm-up for your voice before you film. Start your vocal exercises gently and avoid pushing it; don't try for big sounds until you're warmed up. Doing vocal exercises properly takes patience but it will pay off for you in big dividends, particularly when you have to perform eight times a week in the theater or in a film in which you have to yell or scream. It's yelling and screaming in a part that gets people into big vocal trouble. It's important that you work on your voice as soon as possible and that you take it seriously, because if you don't I promise you that someday you will get a part that you are vocally not equipped to play and you will be at the throat doctor every day in order to give your performance. It's happened to a lot of film actors who have made the transition to theater quickly without the right foundation, and to singers with great natural voices who have never learned sound vocal technique.

As a young actor, I trained intensely for singing, but I took my speaking voice for granted as being okay—and did everything wrong. I breathed through my upper chest as I spoke and sometimes gasped for breath. I didn't discipline myself to breathe diaphragmatically because when I did, I felt so vulnerable. I didn't like the emotion that came from breathing properly so I breathed improperly in order not to feel. Obviously, my early life as an actor is a perfect example of what not to do vocally. Not breathing from your lower torso is bad both for vocal production and emotional freedom.

It was a revelation for me to work with the sublime Patsy Rodenburg from England, a master vocal coach and interpreter of Shakespeare. The specific and rewarding exercises Patsy taught me put me in touch with how vital it is to warm up the voice and the body together for performance. When your whole body is connected to making sound, your emotions automatically begin to join you. Patsy's exercises for producing a healthy voice filled with emotion and air capacity are described in detail in her three excellent books, *Working with the Voice, The Right to Speak,* and *The Need for Words.* Working with the information in these books and the best vocal coach you can find will set you on the right track. If you can sing, don't confuse that with your vocal control as a speaker the way I did. They're related, but they're different, so you need to work on both, because one doesn't give you automatic ability for the other. One of the things that studying singing can give is strong breath support that you can then learn to apply to your speaking voice.

Many of my students have expanded their vocal range and strengthened their tone because in my classes I relentlessly badger them to do so.

There's another aspect of vocal performance I want to talk about: accents. Don't ever underestimate the importance of complete commitment to an exact accent for a role you're playing. This specificity will not only make the audience believe your character as they hear it, it will add to your interpretive ability in a role. By using your tongue, lips, and jaw differently from what you're used to, and introducing new melody and rhythm in your vocal pattern, you will automatically have different physical impulses from those you've had before, and these become part of your characterization. They can, in fact, become the foundation of it. You'll experience this yourself when you begin to work specifically with an accent.

Two brilliant actors who can help you to understand this are Daniel Day-Lewis and Meryl Streep. Look at Day-Lewis in the film *My Beautiful Laundrette,* where he plays a gay British street tough; *A Room with a View,* where he plays an aristocratic British fop; and in *The Last of the Mohicans,* where he plays a powerful Native American leader. He'll astonish you with his vocal and physical variety, and you'll see the relationship between the two. Look at Streep in *Sophie's Choice, The Bridges of Madison County,* and *Cry in the Dark*—Polish, Italian, and Australian, three very different women.

Actors make significant breakthroughs because of one performance that is so specific it catches the audience's eye and they become intrigued by the actor who created it. At the beginning of his career, Robert Duvall was cast in a play, *The Days and Nights of Beebee Fenstermaker,* by William

Snyder. In it, Duvall played a young Texan adrift in the big city. He had one scene at the end of the play, and it launched his career. Before rehearsals, Duvall went to Texas, and tape-recorded three different accents from three different regions. The first day of rehearsal, he presented the tapes to the director and said, "Pick one." I love that story because it proves how actors can empower themselves and make choices that produce results that change their careers.

As I've said before, life is never general, only bad acting is. Yet so many actors, the first time they come to my class, do a scene with some kind of general Southern, New York, or British accent—and are confronted by me with the wonderful news that they have a lot of work to do. Ultimately, serious actors take on the challenge of being dedicated to absolutely authentic, specific dialects. This work quickly reveals to them physical impulses for their characters that would never have arisen if they hadn't committed to specific dialect work because, again, how we speak affects our entire behavior. They find themselves using their imaginations more courageously and less mentally as they make intuitive choices that come out of the entirely new way they're speaking.

If you're stumped on a specific accent, just make a phone call to a shop in a region your character lives in and ask questions and tape-record the call. Or, better yet, take a trip there as Duvall did, and study by looking and listening and taping. In major cities there are teachers who specialize in coaching actors for various accents. As a backup, there are recordings, films, and even novels in which characters' dialogue is vividly written in the exact accent you might need. All of this can be part of your research.

Neil Simon, one of the most prolific writers of stage and screen in the last forty years, mainly writes about an urban Jewish experience. It's not a joke to say you don't have to be Jewish to play him, but you do have to understand the blood memory of Jews to play his Jewish characters authentically just as you have to understand the blood memory of any nationality you play. Blood memory is a concept Stella Adler felt was absolutely necessary for actors to grasp. It is related to language and accent; it means understanding the history of the people your character is descended from and the land they come from because that's how their language was born and, to some degree, how they became the particular person they are when the script takes place.

Stella said that each of us as actors has the blood memory of our ancestors. My father's mother was from England; my father's father was from Odessa in Russia; my mother's mother came from the Deep South. What I have observed in my own acting is that I have an affinity for characters with roots in England, Russia, or the South. This isn't to say I haven't had fun working on Irish or Italian characters or that I couldn't do them very well. It's just that my blood memory usually makes the others that I mentioned easier and—I'm only speaking for myself now—seems to help me understand their internal emotional life, and to reproduce their accents, much more quickly. But let me add to this that you may find yourself working on a part that is very far from your blood memory, with an accent unlike that of anyone in your family's past, and you may find yourself resonating so powerfully to the emotional dynamic of this character, which includes their behavior and accent, that it will shock you. My advice to you when that occurs is, run with it and be grateful! That's why I said you don't have to be Jewish to play Neil Simon, but to play him well you certainly have to understand the specific Jewish people he writes about, who are first- and second-generation Jews from Brooklyn and the Bronx, and you have to have a feeling for the way they talk.

There is an inflection that is specifically heard as a Jewish lilt. It's a kind of music as unique and vivid as an Irish brogue or a Southern drawl. If you grew up in a Jewish family where the influence of the Jewish European culture was still felt, you know exactly what I'm saying. If you didn't, the lilt of the comic raconteur Jackie Mason certainly personifies it, as did Lenny Bruce, the rebel comic of the 1950s, both of whom you can hear on recordings. You can hear the lilt in the comics Billy Crystal, Larry David, and Robert Klein as well as in Barbra Streisand and Bette Midler. A large amount of humor in the Jewish tradition stems from terror, suppressed rage, a love of language, and a huge desire for freedom and mobility that was denied to most Jews in most of the European societies they came from. There's also a Jewish tradition of fatalism, encompassed in the phrase "You should be so lucky" or "Go know," and the inimitable shrug of the shoulders that says, "It's beyond me, it's up to God." It helps to understand all of this to play a character in Simon's trilogy, *Brighton Beach Memoirs, Biloxi Blues,* and *Broadway Bound* as well as in his other works, including *The Last of the Red Hot Lovers* and *Prisoner of Second Avenue,* which focus on Jewish characters. It is exemplified in Richard Dreyfuss's brilliant comic turn as Elliot Garfield, a young Jewish actor, in *The Goodbye Girl.*

Similarly, in addition to learning a New Jersey or a Sicilian accent to play a mafioso character, it will help you if you understand the origins of the mafia. This will inform your characterization and make you understand the incredibly fierce clannishness within the family, the complete mistrust of everything outside the family, and the violence. These qualities come from a time in Sicily when the government was so corrupt that the peasants were starving to death and had no political rights whatsoever but were at the mercy of whatever was doled out by the hierarchy. There was no real justice for the common man. The lower classes formed a vigilante group that allowed them to get food, water, and other necessities, which eventually turned to crime, even violence and killing. You can see how these people felt justified in protecting their families against a government that had no compassion or human decency. This was handed down generation after generation as the immigrants came to America and treated this government with the same contempt and turned crime into big business.

If reading this chapter has excited you to immediately take on a role that challenges you vocally, demands that you learn a new accent and the blood memory of a new character, then you're home free. But I suspect that some of you will resist working in these areas, and I want to address your laziness and/or fear and demand that you work on expanding your vocal size and on finding the accents that relate to your own blood memory and on characters that require you to grow, even if it isn't comfortable. Being a good actor is not about being comfortable, it's about having a vision of your own potential and having the desire to learn about and appreciate many other cultures that you can illuminate through your work. Actors are citizens of the world and can bring different cultures to people who have never experienced them before. Actors are also time travelers who can bring to today's audiences plays from centuries before and make them come to new life. I think audiences need this now more than ever. To realize your potential as an actor, you can't limit yourself by making yourself or your world small.

20

An Actor's Tipsheet
for Comedy

There is an old adage, "Dying is easy, comedy is hard." Although comedy *is* hard—because it takes timing and a particular kind of responsiveness to and creativity with the text—some actors are born comedians; while their comic instincts can be honed, they intuitively know how to be funny. For other actors, comedy is an art to be learned. Whichever group you fall into, in this chapter I'm sharing with you specific tips to help you develop your skills for comedy.

FIND THE RIGIDITY IN THE CHARACTER YOU'RE PLAYING.

A classic theory of comedy that has proved very useful to me is that much of comedy is derived from rigidity. When you think about the great television sitcoms from *I Love Lucy* to *The Honeymooners* to *All in the Family* and *The Mary Tyler Moore Show* and up through *Seinfeld*, *Frasier*, *Everybody Loves*

Raymond, and *The Larry Sanders Show,* you'll see that the leading characters in these shows have very strong points of view that we count on weekly.

Lucy is always making mistakes with Ricky and having to bear the consequences. We count on her confusion and lack of judgment, her insatiable desire to prove she's right, and her inevitable downfall. When we think of Ralph Kramden in *The Honeymooners,* we know that in every segment he's going to become very frustrated and angry about something, and, finally, scream, "To the moon, Alice!" In *All in the Family,* Archie Bunker's very name tells us he's set up immovable defenses. All the people around Mary on *The Mary Tyler Moore Show* are set in their attitudes—Lou, Rhoda, Phyllis, Ted, the Happy Homemaker—and Mary is always trying to make peace amidst all these strong, often inflexible personalities. The two brothers on *Frasier* positively pride themselves on their rigidity; Raymond in *Everybody Loves Raymond* has rigid masculine habits that his wife, Debra, is always trying to cure him of, and Raymond's mother, Marie, and father, Frank, are clashing titans of rigidity. *The Larry Sanders Show* luxuriates in exploring three major narcissists vying for their needs and desires to be front and center at all times. Their extreme anxiety and sense of playing for the highest stakes make this comedy an antisocial classic.

There's an enormous comfort in observing these rigid points of view on a weekly basis from our living rooms and anticipating the next emotional car crash that is waiting for the characters. We're at a safe distance and the benign ending allows us to enjoy the drama of the conflict and the discomfort it causes. The truth of comedy is that it's usually about pain, and we are grateful that it's somebody else who's going through these trials and tribulations and not us. Of course we see ourselves—with all our own rigidities, pretensions, extravagances, and balloons just waiting to be pricked.

In Molière's play *Tartuffe,* one of the main sources of comedy is in the character of Orgon, who believes that his friend Tartuffe is a spiritual icon. Although Orgon is given many clues that Tartuffe is a poseur and a charlatan, he refuses to acknowledge it. He is so extreme in his denial that his wife, Elmire, is forced to prove it to him once and for all in one of the most hilariously funny and uncomfortable scenes in the history of comedy.

Elmire places her husband under a table covered with a cloth and tells him to hide there until he hears the sexual advances that she knows Tartuffe will make. But her plan goes riotously awry when Orgon still resists acknowledging the truth of Tartuffe's debauchery and his wife has to come up with more and more excuses to elude Tartuffe's grasp. Elmire's desperation at her husband's dumbness and refusal to be wrong as Tartuffe is trying to make love to her causes her to be so explicit in her need for help that anyone would help her—except for Orgon, who stays in his hiding place until it's almost too late, refusing to believe that Tartuffe would cuckold him, because his need to believe that he's right makes him ignore what he's hearing.

No one is more rigidly obtuse and self-inflated than Peter Sellers's Inspector Clouseau in the *Pink Panther* movies. Clouseau is never wrong, at least from his own perspective. At the end of *Return of the Pink Panther,* in which Clouseau makes a complete buffoon of himself while never admitting to any mistake, he says, with complete authority, "I *always* knew the murderer was her, and now I must take my leave, *au revoir,* everyone," and instead of walking out what he thinks is the front door, he walks into the hall closet—and, in a masterpiece of comic timing, stays there. All the people he's said good-bye to are just watching the door, waiting for him to exit, but he doesn't. About a minute later, he throws open the closet door with great panache, throws his scarf around his neck, and blurts out, "Stupid architect."

When you approach comic texts, find the rigidity of the character you will be playing and the physical behavior that you can create from that rigidity. And then watch, too, to discover whether the character's rigid point of view begins to soften and change. In those cases, an element of poignancy is introduced into the comedy. The comedies that touch your heart usually do so when the characters begin to see and admit their rigidity and begin to respond more empathically to others.

This is the secret of James Brooks's film *Terms of Endearment.* Garrett Breedlove, Jack Nicholson's debauched, uncaring astronaut, and Aurora Greenway, Shirley MacLaine's desperately narcissistic and seductive aging Southern belle mother crash into each other and, because of circumstances, *must begin to change.* These circumstances include Aurora's daughter, Emma's (Debra Winger), fatal illness, which demands that Aurora put her focus on her daughter instead of herself. MacLaine's hairstyle changes from artificially flaming gold to the salt-and-pepper truth of her fifty-plus years and Nicholson's astronaut is forced to feel her pain and vulnerability and becomes vulnerable himself. One of the reservations some people had about this film was that it started as a hilarious comedy and turned into a bittersweet story about loss and how it demands us to change and mature. I heard people say, "What a manipulative ending! Why did they have to introduce cancer and death in such a funny movie." And the answer is, of course, life can be very funny and, in one second, turn tragic, and although we may not like the reality of this, the fact is that it's true.

ALWAYS PLAY THE HUMAN TRUTH AND BELIEVE IN THE CHARACTERS' STAKES.

Whether you're in a drama or a comedy, you always have to play human truth. That's why, for example, Mike Nichols, a superb comedy director who originated the Broadway productions of many of Neil Simon's smash hits, often chose actors with a big range. It was Nichols who cast George C. Scott in *Plaza Suite,* although Scott was best known for dramas. Nichols knew that, as I've discussed, the stakes in Neil Simon's comedies were sky high, and it was the degree of savage commitment that the actors brought to these stakes that made the comedy so funny. Opposite Scott, Nichols cast Maureen Stapleton, an actress known for her dramatic ability. In the final act of *Plaza Suite,* Nichols directed these two fine actors as desperate parents who, on the day of their daughter's big wedding, find that their daughter has locked herself in the bathroom of their suite in the Plaza Hotel in which the wedding is about to take place. The degree of angst and desperation that George C. Scott revealed as he tried to get his daughter out of the bathroom and down to the wedding was performed with the kind of ferocity that Scott would have brought to playing King Lear. This overwhelming passion was what made it so side-splittingly funny. Stapleton, who always found the humor in drama, was also committed to the drama in this comedy. Neither actor played attitudes—they weren't trying to court the audience by being funny. They played it as if their lives depended on it, with true desperation. And that, along with Neil Simon's circumstances and lines, made it hilarious.

TAILOR YOUR ACTING CHOICES TO THE STYLE OF THE TEXT AND THE PRODUCTION.

All comedies require that you play the human truth but each requires its own way of playing the truth. *Tartuffe* cannot be played in the same style as *Plaza Suite* or *Terms of Endearment* or *Everybody Loves Raymond*—and not only because you're wearing period clothes.

Molière set *Tartuffe* in his own era, the seventeenth century, a time of extremely elaborate and formal dress, manner, and social codes. Everything was about the impression you made on an external level, and because Molière lived in the court of the king, he was at first applauded and then hated for revealing the lies and hypocrisy of the society he wrote about. Molière's social satires do not plumb the depth of human emotion in an obvious, realistic way, but you must find emotional depth and complexity in his characters in order to bring them to life, because it's there to be explored. Many of his characters are stylish and formal; that is part of how they present themselves. But if you play their physical style and manners without real human need and the truths that underlie them, it becomes just an arch presentation.

I've even seen a very dark and brooding production of *Tartuffe,* where Tartuffe was played as so oily and evil that the play was filled with a kind of desperation and terror, which is the subtext of the comedy. The director challenged the actors to interpret the characters from a much darker view and made the comedy mordantly, almost bitterly, funny. This was an artistic choice. One of the exciting things about being an actor is working with directors who have a unique and unusual vision and exploring a text from there. The actors in this production of *Tartuffe* forced us to see the psychologically primitive nature of their characters' needs that was impossible to hide beneath their external finery. So although behaving with the style of the court is essential to acting Molière's plays, there is a range within that style to bring out different interpretations.

As you've seen from my previous discussions of it, Noël Coward's *Private Lives* has a high degree of stylish glamour that stems from the characters being extremely wealthy, well-bred English men and women in the 1930s, who choose to spend their time bickering wittily amongst themselves and exploring their neurotic obsessions. The first time I saw the play, it starred Maggie Smith as Amanda and Stephen Elliot as Elyot, the former spouses who meet again on their honeymoons with their new mates. Smith played Amanda as a vain, self-involved, manic, temperamental, desperate femme fatale and played it for high farce, with grand physical gestures and facial reactions that bordered on attitudinalizing and came right up to the edge. She was a great success in the role because she is a gifted clown, and she found high comic energy in Amanda's jealousness, possessiveness, and excessive need for control and for romantic attention. And, on her best nights, she included her great love for Elyot, her ex-husband. On all nights, she expressed the truth of the excesses of Amanda's character, and that's what made us delight in watching her. Both her physical and vocal style were exaggerated and extravagant, but the performance worked because Smith connected it fully to Amanda's *need* for Elyot's undivided attention.

In the more recent London and Broadway revival starring Lindsay Duncan and Alan Rickman, the *acting style* was less extravagant and more intimate, because Duncan and Rickman concentrated more on the subtext of their helplessness in their need for and obsession with each other. The relationship between the two ex-spouses was naturalistic, subtle, filled with real, poignant attraction and longing. This was a much more emotional production. Although it was set in the same period, it made the characters more real and less exotic, fanciful, and farcical. You couldn't get two more different interpretations of the play. Both found different qualities to bring out from the text. Both productions received an immense number of laughs, but for different reasons, and in different ways. Some people preferred one, some the other, but both interpretations worked.

Certain scripts *demand* broad comic choices, as in Mel Brooks's films *Blazing Saddles* and *Young Frankenstein*. Played with less zeal and less comic inventiveness, they would have fallen flat. Look at the high degree of passion and the commitment that Peter Boyle as the Frankenstein monster, who walked as if he had trees for legs, put into his tap-dancing duet with Gene Wilder in top hat and tails. Boyle danced as if he thought he might be Fred Astaire—but with a complete inability to move gracefully or sing lyrics intelligibly. The enthusiasm he brought to his vain commitment made it hysterically funny and poignant at the same time, and helped to define the unique comic style of the film.

COMIC BEHAVIOR REVEALS CHARACTER.

Maggie Smith's interpretation of Amanda, as I've said, was filled with highly extravagant comic gestures, but it was grounded in the basic truth of the character's needs and what's going on between her and her ex-husband. If you are an actress playing Amanda, you might focus on her extraordinary vanity, and decide to show your best profile to Elyot at all times. This could involve always finding the best lighting, making sure you always allow the slit in your dress to open to show off your legs, and to perhaps have your hand brush your lips and your hair in ways that suggest how you would like him to touch you. These are just ideas for physical behavior but taken to extremes they can start to have a lot of humor as well as sensuality.

In Elyot's case, the way he takes the cigarette out of his solid silver cigarette case and taps it can reveal a certain kind of impatience as well as an avoidance of eye contact with Amanda; perhaps it is her eyes that are fatal to you in terms of falling for her again. Or perhaps you make sure that your voice has a dominant quality so that she won't try to usurp your power as you're sure she's going to try to do. Again, comic behavior is built on real, human reasons that the audience can recognize and not just to try to encourage laughs and to show off. Early in rehearsal, in grounding your performance in truth, you can go through a stage where your rehearsal process doesn't necessarily concern itself with being funny because you are simply going for the truth. Then you begin to find the behaviors that come from that truth that are funny—like Amanda always finding the best light or Elyot tapping his cigarette case in an impatient rage. In most comedies, the stakes become very high and it's the passion of your needs that are part of the comic structure of the text that begin to percolate the comic behavior in you and, eventually, the laughs from the audience. If we don't believe that Amanda and Elyot were once married to each other and that they discover in front of us that they are still madly in love, then there is no *Private Lives*.

Let me add that there are very gifted comic actors who will say in a rehearsal period, "We need a funny bit here so that we can get a laugh." There is nothing negative about this way of thinking, because a good comic actor will always base these "funny bits" on some kind of truth.

I was lucky enough to learn one of these "funny bits" when I took over for Lenny Baker in the Broadway musical *I Love My Wife*. In one scene, my character, Alvin, had a great deal of trouble falling asleep. Being unable to go to sleep when you want to is not particularly funny in itself. However, the machinations of blaming the pillow for your distress and eventually beating the shit out of it *is* funny. Forcing the sheets around the contours of your body to the point that you end up looking like an Egyptian mummy because you think it will help you go to sleep, ramming your head into the pillow ten times to make the pillow take the exact shape of your head before you lie back on it, and, finally, kicking all the sheets off the bed and throwing the pillow on the floor and lying there, panting and exhausted by your failure to sleep is funny. This section of the play had no dialogue whatsoever, but nevertheless it brought the house down with roars and applause because it was related to the truthful anxiety that Alvin was suffering in his fantasies about being unfaithful to his wife and took it to extreme comic heights.

Noises Off, an ensemble farce by Michael Frayn about a fifth-rate theater company in the English provinces, demands broad and vital commitment, meaning the characters wear their needs desperately on their sleeves to the point that everybody in the play seems to be about ready to have a nervous breakdown. The play is about theatrical people making humiliating mistakes in front of the audience of the play they are appearing in and also backstage in their personal lives. Although absolute high energy is required to make the comedy effective, the mistake you can make, because it's farce, is to think that you will be funny if you act frantic and use general excessive force rather than exploring each comic moment in terms of the high stakes and desperation of your character. Even in a farce, you have to play with full truth and commitment and to let inventive comic behavior grow out of that.

Characters in sitcoms can also be played more broadly and usually require more physical, vocal, and facial largesse than those in television dramas—but again, this is not an excuse for a lack of truth in your work. Again, a great deal of comedy is frustration, confusion, anger, and pain, and if you know that that's the underlying truth of the scene, and you have developed a comedy persona for your character, you will be able to twist that truth into a funny take in the situations that the comedy script requires, because your comedy will be based on the truth of the character's needs and defenses.

One of the richest sources of comedy is reactions—how your character reacts to another character or to a given situation—and these reactions are often silent. Kelsey Grammer and David Hyde Pierce were wonderful foils for each other on *Frasier*. We relish their reactions to each other playing the snobby psychiatrist siblings because their imperiousness rings so true, and though it is exaggerated for comic effect, you never for one second doubt its truthful origins. Reactions are also the source of much of the comic fizz of *The Larry Sanders Show,* where Garry Shandling,

Rip Torn, and Jeffrey Tambor work off each other like an intensely dysfunctional family.

Like all comic behavior, much of reacting is timing, and timing grows out of what the character is going through. The minute that Inspector Clouseau takes to walk out of the closet isn't simply taking a certain number of beats until he exits. Although actors may actually count out the beats before they do an action or say the next line, those beats represent *the thinking and feeling process* of the character. In Clouseau's case, those beats are the time during which he has realized it's dark, he's not outside, a coat is hitting him in the face, all around him are other clothes hanging on hangers, and that, therefore, he must be in a closet. He turns, finds the doorknob, and it comes to him that the reason he's made this apparent mistake is someone else's fault—where it's obvious there should have been a front door, there's a closet door; clearly it's the fault of the stupid architect! In this instance we don't see the thinking process, we experience it indirectly through the minute it takes for Clouseau's exit and his great panache in offering his explanation, "Stupid architect!" as he moves on. This is timing—and it's all an expression of the truth of his character.

The late great Jack Benny, star of radio, television, and films, including the classic *To Be or Not to Be,* with Carole Lombard, was famous for his timing. The character of Jack Benny that Benny played on radio and TV— the persona he created for himself—was notoriously cheap. Perhaps his most famously timed reaction was when a thief held him up, threatening, "Your money or your life," after which Benny takes an enormously long pause, with his hand to his chin in deep concentration. Finally, in exasperation, the thief screams again, "Your money or your life," to which Benny replies, "I'm thinking, I'm thinking!" It was a masterful deadpan comedy style honed for years in vaudeville that came from the truth of a penny-pinching man really having to think because of his problem parting with his money.

Again, my desire is for you to understand clearly that what's funny must always be from human truth. And what I mean by human truth is human feeling. When my therapist asks me what I'm feeling and I move into my head to figure it out, she patiently asks me, "Are you feeling glad? Mad? Sad? Scared? Or ashamed?" It seems so simple and yet it's incredibly profound in terms of living and, therefore, acting. These five emotions are underneath every comic choice—as well as every dramatic choice— you will ever make.

ALL COMEDY ACTING IS ENSEMBLE ACTING.

A cardinal rule of acting in comedies (and dramas, though it seems to come up more in comedies) is that you have to play in the same style as the other people in the cast. This may seem like an obvious statement, but trust me when I tell you that some actors are insensitive to playing in the style of the production and can capsize the comedy by playing their characters with too low an energy for the rest of the players or taking unnecessary pauses and slowing the train down to a standstill as the comedy dies. Conversely, actors can play at too high an energy to mesh with the other players. In *Private Lives,* you can't take the Amanda from the first production and put her in the second or vice versa, nor can you exchange the Elyots of Stephen Elliot and Alan Rickman in each other's productions. Elliot played Elyot as a dapper, impatient, confident boulevardier, while Rickman played him as morose, jaded, and ready to slit his wrists and somehow also was able to convey a wry and witty nature.

Jerry Zaks, the Broadway director of such hits as Neil Simon's *Laughter on the Twenty-third Floor* and the revivals of *Guys and Dolls* and *Little Shop of Horrors,* tells an amazing story of how playing an inappropriately low energy can sink the comedy. When he was a young actor replacing Austin Pendleton, the original Motel, the tailor, in *Fiddler on the Roof,* Zaks as the character Motel had to ask for the hand of one of Tevye's daughters and was consistently rejected and humiliated by Tevye. Tevye was still being played by the master actor-performer-tragedian-clown Zero Mostel, who had originated the role. The first night Zaks took over the role, in the scene where the timid Motel finally stands up to Tevye and tells him off, right before Zaks began to speak he heard Mostel growl under his breath, "Give it to me! Give it to me!" After the performance, Zaks stormed off to the stage manager and complained that Mostel was giving him acting notes during the performance. The hapless stage manager turned to him and said, "Well, he's Zero Mostel, there's not a helluva lot I can do."

The next night, as Zaks got ready to deliver the same passionate monologue, Mostel growled even more insistently, "*Give* it to me!! *Give* it to me!!" Once again Zaks complained to the stage manager to no avail. The third night, Zaks was in an absolute rage as he walked onto the stage for the confrontation scene. Mostel growled, almost loudly enough for the audience to hear, "*Give it to me!!! Give it to me!!!*," at which point Zaks roared his declaration of independence from Tevye, and suddenly the house came down in screams, laughs, and applause.

Mostel gave Zaks a look as if to say, "Now, schmuck, you did it right," and Zaks learned an incomparable lesson for achieving the correct intensity for this comedy. Mostel intuited that Zaks wouldn't play the stakes high enough for the scene to work as well as it could. *Fiddler on the Roof* takes place in a Jewish village that was under siege by anti-Semites. Motel's love for Tevye's daughter blooms in this world where violence and death are everyday possibilities. These circumstances demand of the performers incredible amounts of vitality, because the stakes are so desperately high.

TEMPO IS CRUCIAL. WHEN IN DOUBT, GET ON WITH IT.

Another lesson that Zero Mostel taught Jerry Zaks was just to get on with it, with the proper intensity for your objective and intention. As an actor, if you're working on comedy and you're not getting laughs, this can be one of the reasons. When I coach actors in comic roles, I always suggest to them that they get on with the line and don't stop the ideas until the scene *demands* a pause. Someone once asked Maureen Stapleton what good acting was. Stapleton said in her wonderfully smart-ass way, "Fast." They went on to ask her, "What is great acting?" She said, "Faster." Obviously, take this with a grain of salt but never forget it when you're doing comedy.

For a lesson in speed, see Katharine Hepburn and Cary Grant in the classic 1930s screwball comedy film *Bringing up Baby*. She plays the madcap heiress who will try anything and he the repressed zoologist who is careful about everything and shocked at his own attraction to someone so out of control. It's very clear when you realize the baby in the title is an enormous leopard—the beast of his own attraction. Watch how these two sublimely quick and alert performers play off each other—as if they themselves are animals always on the alert for danger. It's the sense the actors convey of the possibility of going over the cliff at any moment that keeps you on the edge of your chair and keeps you laughing. In *His Girl Friday,* Cary Grant and Rosalind Russell have more dialogue than any movie ever made—and I'm not kidding. You will simply plotz when you see it. And they say it faster than you can almost get it, but not so fast that you don't. And that's the point.

By fast, I don't mean rushing. I mean picking up your cues unless you have a damned good reason for taking a pause. For instance, like waiting for a laugh—which is something you have to learn about if you're doing live theater or three-camera comedy. And it's something you have to feel and intuit, though one rule I can give you is when you get a good laugh in a scene in the theater, you allow the laugh to reach its height, and just as it begins to descend in energy, you come in with your next line. And you never lose your concentration or your character while you're waiting for the laugh. The laugh should tell you, if it's correctly earned, that the audience is engaged with you, that they're having a good time and that you're on the right track.

One more addendum to the fast rule: you cannot be fast until you know what you're saying and why you're saying it. That's why script analysis is as vital to comedy as it is to drama. Comedy is no excuse for superficiality. You have to take comedy as seriously as if you were playing *Hamlet*.

LEARN HOW TO PUT OVER A JOKE.

Jokes are written with a setup and a punch line. In *Barefoot in the Park,* after an evening on the town during which Corie made a spectacle of herself at the restaurant, Corie says to Paul, "Do you know what you are? You're a watcher. There are Watchers in this world and there are Do-ers. And the Watchers sit around watching the Do-ers do. Well, tonight you watched and I did." Paul replies, "Yeah . . . Well, it was harder to watch what you did than it was for you to *do* what I was watching." You have to emphasize the right words in the setup and punch line to make the joke work. Sometimes, as in this case, the writer italicizes certain words to tell you to emphasize them. But if you only emphasize "*do*" in the punch line, you're not getting the full effect of these two people trying to one-up each other. For maximum effect, you have to emphasize to different degrees all the words I'm going to italicize: "Do you know what you are? You're a *Watcher*. There are *Watchers* in this world and there are *Do-ers*. Well, tonight, **you watched** and **I did**." "Yeah . . . Well, it was harder to *watch* what you *did* than it was for you to *do* what I was *watching*." Of course this emphasis must be supported by your desire to win the argument because you feel unloved and unsupported, which means that the emphases are the *character's* emphases, not the actor's. In other words, you have to learn how to hit the right words in character for the maximum comic payoff and believability.

Much of three-camera television comedy has jokes with the same sort of setups and punch lines, and you have to understand the technique of hitting the right words in each if you want to work in that medium. And I'll tell you something frightening right now: after the first read-through of a three-camera sitcom, if the producers don't think you're funny you'll find in the next read-through of the script that half of your character's lines will be written out. So it's vital that you are educated about where to find the comedy in a line and in a scene *before* you sit down at a table and read it for the producers so that you can protect yourself from the insecurity and the fear that some producers in Hollywood are notorious for. You must learn to hit the right words, stay humanly truthful, and stay in character. Watch the best sitcoms and observe how the leading actors deliver their lines and extract as much humor out of every line they have to say while they're pursuing their objectives with their intentions. *Will and Grace* is a very popular sitcom largely because of this. One of the added strengths of this show is how much comic mileage the series regulars get out of their gestures and voices, and the joy you feel in their performances as they commit to their choices.

Certain scripts for films and plays also contain lines with words that need to be subtly emphasized, but not hit over the head, in order for the interchanges to truly pay off comedically. Sometimes hitting a word just loudly enough for the audience to catch it can get a roar that will amaze you, and you will say, "But I played it effortlessly and I didn't expect to get such a big laugh," and therein lies a great lesson. You don't always have to work hard, but you have to work intelligently. Lastly, the audience will surprise you and laugh in places you never even thought were funny and teach you where the true comedy gold lies in your performance.

COMEDY IS A PHYSICAL ART.

Comedy theorists have pointed out how much of comedy is based on the physical—the ways that the body betrays us with its awkwardness, waywardness, and inappropriate demands, and of course how the physical world seems booby-trapped against us. Many of the examples I've already given are of physical comedy—from Orgon hiding under the table, refusing to believe that his wife is being seduced by Tartuffe, to the bit of battling with the pillow that Lenny Baker created for the character of Alvin in *I Love My Wife*. Watching silent comedies is a wonderful tool to learn about comedy's physical side, because being an *entirely* visual medium, all these films have to be funny with is physical behavior.

In his silent films, Charlie Chaplin creates imaginative physical behavior that is idiosyncratic, surprising, and completely truthful for the given circumstances he's in, which are usually harrowing. Because there is no dialogue except for occasional dialogue cards between shots, Chaplin's physical behavior, his face, and his body, have to reveal all of his inner thought processes and feelings as well as his actions. A perfect example of his effectiveness in the use of physicalization of comedy is in *The Gold Rush*, where the Little Tramp he plays is starving and eats his shoe on a plate, imagining the laces to be a bountiful mound of spaghetti. There is a bereft delicacy and an enormous physical agility in Chaplin's silent work. When you watch it, you will be amazed to see how funny and emotional he is.

Buster Keaton's silent comedy comes from Keaton's seeming never to quite fit into society. The society seems, in its own way, to be filled with madness. Keaton often looks like an extraterrestrial being dropped into the middle of an insane planet where he is surrounded by inmates from an asylum doing comically bizarre physical business, and he's often confronted with danger not only from humans but from machinery. Nevertheless, with a still and bewildered face, he manages to cleverly maneuver his way through every difficult obstacle that is thrown at him. Keaton's comic stunts are so physically difficult it's hard to believe they're not cinematic tricks, but indeed they weren't, which is why Keaton is called by some film aficionados the Jackie Chan of silent film. Woody Allen is a great admirer of Keaton's. Watch Keaton's work and see how it inspired the marvelous physical comedy of Allen in *Sleeper*.

LEARN FROM THE MASTERS.

I believe that Sid Caesar and Imogene Coca in the 1950s set the pace for almost every other comic performance in the next decades. Caesar and Coca, in an ensemble that included Carl Reiner and Howard Morris, and supported by writers the likes of the young Mel Brooks, Woody Allen, and Larry Gelbart, did a weekly television series, *Your Show of Shows*, that has been captured on tape for posterity. Every week the show featured a satire on a famous movie or style of movie—silent films, foreign films, melodramas—as well as comedy sketches based on everyday life. The actors were asked to play *live,* not just in front of the studio audience but in front of the home audience of millions, for each ninety-minute weekly show. This involved different comedy styles, accents, physical behaviors as well as singing and dancing. Watch "Ten from *Your Show of Shows*"; the range of characters Caesar, Coca, and the rest of the ensemble play is so extensive and surprising it will take your breath away, and the physical and vocal choices they make are courageously extreme, even by today's standards. Learn from them the commitment to a brave comic choice and how actors can feed off each other and encourage each other's brave choices.

The style of Woody Allen and Diane Keaton in *Annie Hall* and *Manhattan* is a more naturalistic kind of comedy that exemplifies tormented, neurotic urbanites. Its naturalistic quality is based on the truth of the way people like this often talk, but it is heightened by the intensity of the compulsions of the characters and how they struggle to find language, only to find out that what they're feeling seems to have no words to truly express it. The movies are about intellectuals and would-be intellectuals who are emotionally adolescent and are using big words and ideas without coming to any conclusions that actually work for them. We laugh at how characters who speak with such intelligence can sometimes seem out of touch with what they are feeling and, therefore, be at a loss for words. Learn from these films how intense anxiety can lead to the behaviors of verbosity, narcissistic self-effacement, and self-dramatizing paranoia—and still stay comic.

In *Bullets over Broadway,* Allen has created a successful farce (no easy task) peopled with a certain type of Broadway theater and gangster personages of the 1920s, and the performances uniformly are exactly what I meant by an ensemble style that complement each other. They are all grandly theatrical, even John Cusack as the aspiring playwright facing his first big chance at success and Chazz Palminteri as the theatrical savant mobster who's there to caretake his boss's tragically untalented girlfriend (Jennifer Tilly), who has a part in the show because the mobster funded it. Cusack and Palminteri seem to be playing in a lower key than the actor characters, but when you watch closely you see that their intensity matches the emotional intensity of the theater people internally, although externally it is played more coolly. Every single character in *Bullets over*

Broadway is motivated by intense desperation and hunger, personified by the impossibly funny turn of the matinee idol (Jim Broadbent), who cannot stop eating and by the end of the film becomes a blimp.

In many of Jim Carrey's performances, he exemplifies an outrageous, zany, slapstick kind of comic delivery in which he uses extreme physical body language and even facial grimaces to heighten his comic interpretations of roles. Carrey came to the movies when there was a dearth of this kind of ability, and because he was so gifted at it, and so brave in making a full commitment to it, he became a superstar with the films *Ace Ventura, Pet Detective* and *The Mask*. Learn from him, as from Sid Caesar, how to make a bold comic choice, stay truthful to the need of the character, and take the choice to an extreme with no apology.

Hugh Grant made his trademark a deadpan, urbane, witty, comic delivery. He plays in a sarcastic, even sardonic, easy style, not unlike a modern version of Cary Grant's. Learn from his performance in such films as *Four Weddings and a Funeral*, *Notting Hill,* and *About a Boy,* how to underplay comedy and thus to make it appear effortless, by a subtle use of low-key energy, and how, despite a certain reserve, to make the audience care by allowing us to see shyness and fear underneath an urbane facade.

Since his early work on *Saturday Night Live,* Eddie Murphy has used his phenomenally broad range of comedy characterizations in a variety of styles, from the hyper but still naturalistic comedy *48 Hours* to the extreme characterizations of films like *The Nutty Professor,* in which he played multiple parts with different appearances, behaviors, and voices, to *Bowfinger,* which falls somewhere in between, and in which he played a hot Hollywood action star and his nerdy brother. Learn from Murphy the art of interpretive transformation and how to amp up or nuance down your comic style, depending on the material.

Steve Martin runs the gamut from dark intellectual humor to inspired silliness. He gave one of the all-time best physical comedy performances, along with Lily Tomlin, in *All of Me,* in which her character's high-society-matron soul tries to take over his male body with hilarious results. Watch Martin's intense physical struggle not to be taken over by Tomlin's character's spirit and watch him fail as the strength of her spirit overtakes him. Learn from Martin's performance how total commitment to absolute physical behavior totally convinces us of the truth of one person taking over another's body, and makes us laugh at the same time.

NEVER ALLOW ANYONE TO TELL YOU WHETHER OR NOT YOU CAN PLAY COMEDY OR WHAT TYPE OF COMEDY YOU CAN PLAY.

Only *you* can make a decision about you and comedy, and you make it based on your own sense of humor and whether or not you are hungry to learn about how to be successful at comedy. If you're not drawn to comedy and you really can't find the humor in life, it's a perfectly legitimate choice to stick with drama, but make sure you try comedy, because your drama is twice as effective when you find the jokes—and because you may surprise yourself.

I've had students who didn't appear to have any comic ability whatsoever—until they connected with something that was specifically funny to them in a particular character and therefore could find behavior to express it. For example, I worked with an actor who excelled in dramatic plays and had grown weary of playing sad, tragic parts. I gave him a scene from Neil Simon's *The Last of the Red Hot Lovers,* in which he played a middle-class Jewish married man in the "swinging '70s," who believes the sexual revolution is passing him by and is therefore intent on having an extramarital affair, using his mother's apartment in Brooklyn while she's out of town. This actor was so intent on the truth of his fear of his mother finding out what he was doing, that any time a woman touched a table or glass, he immediately cleaned it, sometimes using Windex and rubber gloves. His commitment to his guilt and fastidious cleanliness brought the scene hilariously alive, but in a very human way.

LOOSEN UP AND DON'T BE AFRAID TO MAKE A FOOL OF YOURSELF.

The particular comedic quality that you can bring to your work has to do with your own taste in comedy and your willingness to work diligently at it. If you are blocked or inhibited, take one of the excellent improvisational comedy classes that are offered around the country and learn by practice not to be afraid to be silly and make an absolute fool out of yourself.

While you can't let anyone label you funny or not as an actor, you also have to be aware and realistic about what might be your limitations or your lack of experience in exploring your comedic gifts. If you don't make people laugh, generally speaking your comedy is not working. I saw a performance of *Tartuffe* in which a very well-known actor pushed and sweated and grunted his way through the role, trying with every muscle in his body to be hilarious. The audience sat dumbstruck and exhausted and barely laughed at all.

I was sitting in a seat that allowed me to see him when he exited off-stage. As he went into the wings to dry his perspiring brow, he turned to his dresser and made a disparaging gesture toward the audience, as if it were our fault that we didn't laugh. He wanted us to laugh because he wanted our positive approval and attention; his problem was that he neglected to give the great part of Tartuffe its full and powerful due. He neglected to play the play. It's like the classic story about Alfred Lunt and Lynn Fontanne that I told in Chapter Nine. As Fontanne famously said, "Stop asking for the laugh and start asking for the tea."

21

STAGE, SCREEN, AND TV:
SIMILARITIES, DIFFERENCES, TRAPS

There is a terrible disease in show business today: if you're very young and commercially viable, you can make several hundred thousand or a million dollars a year on a television series. I have nothing against television. Witness the first-rate writing and acting of contemporary classics like *The Sopranos, Six Feet Under, Sex and the City,* the *Law & Order* series, and *ER.* Having said this, the problem is that if you are bought and sold that young, you may have the illusion that you're already an accomplished actor and that illusion may well stop you from working on your craft.

I tell my students, go and do television, do films, but do a play a year, minimum. Always go back to the theater. Why? Because in the theater you have to speak and be heard, sustain long and complex scenes, capture the audience's attention and hold it for an hour and a half or two hours or more. No one says "Action" when they want you to begin or "Cut" when they want to end a take; no one calls for another take where you get a chance to do it better. On the stage, you have to stand and deliver, with no excuses and no breaks, moment to moment, for the entire performance.

Career survival, over the long run, depends on your commitment to developing a command of your craft. As I write this I am working with a tremendously talented young television star who is about to make a transition into a film role that will require enormous range and technical skill. He became a TV star based on his raw talent and handsome appearance, with very little training. He came to me because he had to reveal more of himself than he'd ever shown before and he humbly explained that he didn't know how. We worked on creating a back story for his character, discovering inner imagery, and developing a list of creative intentions scene by scene that caused him to use unfamiliar parts of himself. In our work together he has found a wider range of colors and emotions on his actor's palette, and it has ignited his desire to try things in his acting that hadn't even occurred to him before. After our coaching session, he galloped out of my apartment on fire with a host of new ideas.

My joy in teaching and coaching is trying to create a bridge for actors to cross over to a better and deeper use of their talent. Every actor needs support to grow, and that support has to come first from themselves and then from directors, teachers, coaches, and other actors. In television dramas and movies and feature films, economic pressures require the work to be done very quickly. To actors especially, this can seem rushed and even unfair.

Films rarely have a rehearsal period. As an actor, when you show up on the set, you have to have studied your character and broken the script down as thoroughly as if you've already gone through a rehearsal process so that you're ready for immediate filming. You also have to be facile enough to work very fast on your feet because you may find they've cut a scene or added one that they hand you when you get there. In television sitcoms, you have a four-day rehearsal period that starts with the first table reading and travels through blocking rehearsals, rewrites, and final script, and shoots twice on the fifth day, sometimes with live audiences for both performances, sometimes once in dress rehearsal and once before a live audience. In theater, you generally rehearse for four weeks except in stock, which is much faster and more intense, where you can rehearse for as little as one week. Theater also often has previews before the official opening.

What this means is that the theater is an actor's medium. The rehearsal process gives you the opportunity to study and explore the play scene by scene eight hours a day with other actors and a director. It gives you a place to try out your homework and to discover new choices—

some given to you by the director and others inspired by your own experience of and reaction to the other actors.

Perhaps you come into a rehearsal and find that the person opposite you is playing their part in a way you never anticipated. They could be more comedic than you'd thought or more melancholy or more aggressive. Your responses are necessarily going to change and be affected by this new energy. The rehearsal process gives your character a chance to grow and define itself before performance—which prepares you for the new growth and redefinition that occur during the run of the play.

Every time you do a new role, regardless of the medium, you have an opportunity to gain new muscles: to apply yourself in new technical ways; to interpret a new and different kind of character than you've played before; or to do a similar character with a new interpretation. Maybe you've become a star playing action heroes in movies and get cast in similar roles time and again. If you choose not to phone in your performance—by which I mean merely repeating the same choices you've made before—even when you're cast as an action hero again, you can still find opportunities to take a leap forward, to interpret your character in a more idiosyncratic, unique way, perhaps with more humor or vulnerability. But what the theater gives you, because of the rehearsal process, and also because the performance is nonstop, is a laboratory designed to develop your craft.

Working on the stage is the best training ground I know for growth as an actor, but don't make the mistake as some movie stars do of going straight to Broadway without prior work in the theater. You need experience to know how to sustain a long performance, you need to understand the rhythms and transitions of doing a live play. You need to understand the phrasing of language when there's no one on an editing machine to help clean up your mistakes and pace your delivery. One of the most important technical things you need to learn in the theater is when to take a pause and when not to. I saw a Broadway production of a classic American play with a gifted movie star who took such long, unnecessary pauses and used such slow tempos that she added fifteen minutes to the play and made it seem like a kind of dirge. I saw another Broadway production of another classic American play with two talented movie stars who did not know how to build their characters and get inside the play.

My point is not that these actors shouldn't have done theater but quite the opposite: these truly talented people owed it to themselves and to their audiences and to the texts to have done much more theater prior to entering these deep waters. We are all entitled to have failures in our careers. Indeed, you can't grow into true excellence without falling on your face sometimes. Being an adult means to be able to challenge yourself with the confidence that even if you fail you still have value. It's a terrible burden to believe that if you try and fail, then you're worthless. That's not true. If you try and you fail, you learn something. One of these movie stars who failed on Broadway went on to do another play much more successfully. As hurt as she must have been, it did not stop her from continuing to work on her stagecraft because her talent and her desire to use that talent were greater than her hurt. In Rudyard Kipling's great poem "If," he speaks of "triumph and disaster" and calls on us to "treat those two impostors just the same." If you take this sound advice, you will reject the grotesque American idea that everything is a competition and that there is only one winner. Good competition is healthy, but when winning becomes your identity, it stops you as an artist, because it stops you from taking risks, since you're more interested in winning than in growing.

But you need to be smart about taking risks and make sure you don't have false confidence that is actually naïveté tinged with arrogance. To prepare yourself to go from film or television into live theater, find a good, strong scene-study class, pick a play you want to work on in class, and then work on every scene your character is in from the beginning to the end of the play. Don't make the common mistake of choosing only the big epiphany scene at the end of the play in which all the strong emotions are revealed. You need to learn how to build a role from the first, more subtle and hidden parts of the character and how to creatively *hide* emotions through different behaviors before revealing them. You'll learn more about creative choices that way than you will by doing fifty scenes from fifty different plays. Once you've experienced working in a class where it's safe to explore and you've worked through an entire role, you are ready to go to an Equity-waiver or small theater and begin building your facility for live stage performance.

Of course there are exceptions to every rule: Cher, who had no legitimate theater background except in high school, gave a very good performance on Broadway in *Come Back to the Five and Dime, Jimmy Dean, Jimmy Dean,* directed by Robert Altman. But let us not forget that she came to the play with enormous live performing experience on the nightclub stage and in the live taping of her television shows, which also involved her creating characters.

Antonio Banderas and Hugh Jackman both started out in theater in their native countries and returned to the stage in the midst of thriving film careers and caused sensations on Broadway. And also, in case you don't know it, here is a litany of just a few of the current and recent movie stars who were discovered in the theater: Bruce Willis, Robert De Niro, Al Pacino, Meryl Streep, Liam Neeson, Daniel Day-Lewis, Robert Duvall, Ralph Fiennes, Glenn Close, Robert Redford, Barbra Streisand, Jude Law, Kevin Spacey, Gene Hackman, Dustin Hoffman, John Leguizamo, Denzel Washington, Whoopi Goldberg, and Mel Gibson. From live standup and improvisational comedy, the list is endless, but just to name a few: Jim Carrey, Eddie Murphy, Robin Williams, Adam Sandler, Will Ferrell, Ellen DeGeneres, Lily Tomlin, Tracy Ullman, Chevy Chase, and Richard Pryor. Many of the stars in these lists go back and forth between live performing and film and television work.

Sally Field made the reverse journey after she came to television stardom playing *The Flying Nun*. She stunned everyone when she went on to study with Lee Strasberg and gave a career-making performance as a schizophrenic in *Sybil*. She won her first Academy Award as Norma Rae, and then made her Broadway debut in Edward Albee's *The Goat*. She gave a superb performance playing the distraught wife of a man who had turned to bestiality. I don't know what Sally Field did to prepare for this role but by the time she opened, she certainly had the acting and vocal chops and the ability to fill the stage.

In ballet, it was a tradition to put little ankle weights on the dancers as they train so that it would be a bit more difficult for them to do the exercises. When they finally removed the weights, the dancers flew. Similarly, the theater techniques I'm asking you to learn and work on so diligently will make you more powerful in all media. You say, "I'm not interested in Shakespeare." I say, "Well, what's wrong with you? He's the greatest playwright in the history of the theater. You *must* try it." You say, "Chekhov bores me." I respond, "That's your fault. Nothing's boring about Chekhov. He's an astounding playwright with unbelievable insight into the human condition." People have told me they didn't like the film *The Hours* because it was a downer. I tell them, "That's not *The Hours*'s fault. That's your fault. You're lacking something." That something is sensitivity and compassion for people who are different than you or the courage to face feelings that you don't want to experience.

As I say to all my students, "When you're lazy and when you're cowardly, I hate you." And as I say to other actors when they attitudinalize emotions instead of acting truthfully and simply or when they push emotion in a scene and don't trust themselves, "I'll kill you." As bizarre as this sounds, they actually get it. I talk in these overly dramatic ways not to be cruel but simply to bring home the point, "It's not okay to be lazy. It's not okay to settle for mediocre work. It's just not okay."

A student said to me, "Your class is too stressful. You make too many demands. I don't want all that stress. I had hives when I had to put up a scene." "Good," I told him. "You do recover from hives. They go away. *But bad acting never does*." If you do a bad performance on television or film, it's there forever; if you do a bad performance onstage, people remember. The only way to recover is to work on your acting skills and grow, even if it means you get hives.

I bring all this up here because it's relevant to what theater gives you. Theater is filled with great roles! And the theater is not against aging. As you grow older, some great parts that you couldn't play earlier open up to you. Let me just name some of the magnificent actors who went back and forth between theater and film into their old age. Ruth Gordon, who at seventy-two years old won the Best Supporting Actress Oscar for her indelible work in *Rosemary's Baby,* said at the Oscars when she received her award, "I can't tell you how encouraging this is for a girl." The audience was helpless with laughter for about two minutes. Sir John Gielgud was seventy-seven when he played the butler flawlessly in the film *Arthur* and won the Academy Award. In fact, he went on acting until he died at ninety-six. Then there's Jessica Tandy, who in her eighties won an Oscar for her performance in the film *Driving Miss Daisy,* and Geraldine Page, who, shortly before she died, won an Oscar for her starring role in the film of Horton Foote's *The Trip to Bountiful,* and, finally, Sir Ralph Richardson, who, at eighty-five, costarred in the film *Greystoke: The Legend of Tarzan, Lord of the Apes.*

Students who want to transition between theater, film, and television often ask me how acting differs in these three media. Let me start by discussing the size of physical choices. Theatrical performances often have to communicate to an audience of eight hundred to fifteen hundred people, so physical choices can be larger and bolder—that's one of the things that makes theater so exciting. For example, in *The Great White Hope,* James Earl Jones gave a career-making performance as Jack Johnson, the first black world heavyweight boxing champion. The physical expressiveness and athletic power that Jones brought to the role was supersized—pounding his chest, strutting in triumph, then carrying his dead wife in his arms like a biblical hero as he screamed his grief. His performance reached the upper balcony of the Broadway theater, but because it was rooted in truth—which all physical choices must be, regardless of size—it also played to the audience in the orchestra sitting only several feet away from him. You will understand the power of this bold physical performance when I tell you that Muhammad Ali saw the play many times and was witnessed onstage, long after the audience and most of the cast had left, pounding his chest in an understanding of and agreement with the truth of what it takes to be a world champion.

Of course in small houses, performances have to be scaled down proportionally, but they can still be bold. There's a famous story about the theater and film actor Robert Preston, who made such a gigantic hit as *The Music Man*. When Preston toured in shows, he played many different theaters of different sizes. The first morning in a new town, he would walk onto the stage, stand in the center, and extend his arms toward the ceiling with his eyes focused at the back of the house. In his imagination, he would grab the sides of the proscenium arch and bring it around his shoulders. Then he knew how much energy he had to use to fill that particular theater.

In motion picture acting as opposed to dramatic filmed television there is the opportunity for an extra element of energy and expressiveness simply because the screen is big. When you think of major film stars like Jack Nicholson, Meryl Streep, Robert De Niro, Daniel Day-Lewis, Brad Pitt, Julia Roberts, and Denzel Washington, they can be very subtle in their close-up work, but in a medium shot or a long shot, they have an emotional ferociousness that excites us because it has a size that we rarely see on dramatic television. Even a film actor as minimalistic as Clint Eastwood—and let us not forget that Eastwood came directly from years of television—at crucial moments in his early Westerns and in the Dirty Harry films found a snarling, vicious, antisocial expressiveness that caught the audience's attention.

Historically, television actors were limited by the small screen because key moments were so often photographed in medium shots (from the waist up) and in close-ups. Especially in the last decade, however, the possibility of doing more physically expressive choices has opened up for television drama series actors because there are more medium and long shots (which capture the entire body). This is both because the technology exists to facilitate this, and also because the public has become more sophisticated in its visual appetites as a result of cable television and music videos. It seems to me that the chances for bold, expressive physical choices are generally given to the guest stars on filmed television dramas because they are seen only once, or a limited number of times, and don't have to sustain a long relationship with the audience. They can be more extreme—or even off-putting as their character may demand—without wearing out their welcome.

Vocal performances differ with the medium as well. In live theater, you *must* have strong vocal ability and an awareness of the vocal energy you need to fill the theater. Do a Robert Preston and stand on the stage. Look at the size of the house and the distance to the last row of seats, taking into account configurations like theater in the round or three-quarters. How much physical and emotional energy do you have to have to be heard by every member of the audience? Then stand there and practice speaking to be heard in that particular space.

Don't, however, mistake what I'm saying to you as a reason or an excuse for developing a style of work that has a shout in it or a vocal or muscular tension that makes the audience feel you're pushing the performance at them. While keeping this in mind, a key element of being successful in acting in general, and especially in the theater, is sending your lines to your acting partner with enough vitality and breath to get the complete idea across, which includes getting to the last word of a sentence without running out of energy, focus, or intent.

I'm continually surprised by how many beginning actors drop their vocal energy at the end of a line. This is becoming epidemic in television dramas. Sometimes they seem to trail off into a whisper and significant words are being missed by the audience. Actors suffering from this syndrome seem to be talking to themselves, not to the other person. I say time and time again in my classes, "The scene is not about *you*. The scene is about the story and sending your ideas to your partner so that they can understand and feel what you're saying and can give a full response and send their ideas back to you."

Some teachers allow young actors to do work as if there were a microphone right near them. In the name of training for television and film work, these actors learn to feel that if they raise their voice, they will be phony and actory. This is destructive because it is a fallacy. This phony, whispery naturalism takes us down the road to aural somnambulism. It drains the clarity and the nuance out of vocal interpretation and, in fact, is not natural but an affectation that makes all these young actors sound the same. It is the vocal expression of noncommitment.

The absolute opposite is true of the best sitcoms, where the leading roles are played by actors with incredibly distinctive voices. Whether you realize it or not, it's their voices and their energy that makes us respond to them, and the same can be true in dramatic television if people are trained to respect their voices and use them with color and subtle tonal changes. It is true that sitcoms allow for broader, more theatrical characterizations, while filmed dramas require smaller visual and vocal choices, because key moments are often photographed in close-up and the actors are closely miked to reproduce natural speaking. *But smaller choices do not have to be less varied or less interesting; they just have to be more subtle.* If you want to watch two television actors in a filmed drama that play with vocal expressiveness, watch and listen to Christopher Meloni and Mariska Hargitay in *Law & Order: Special Victims Unit.* Watch tapes and CDs of *The Sopranos, Six Feet Under,* and *Oz,* and notice the exceptional vocal work of the actors, most of whom have experience in the theater.

If you use the theater to develop your voice and your vocal expressiveness, then you do have to learn to adjust your voice to the demands of a microphone when you're doing film or television. But you don't want to lose the internal richness that makes for an expressive vocal performance. You can't be as loud when there's a microphone up your nose, but to make the mistake of having no tone and no variation will rob you of interesting readings. Your voice can convey as much emotion subtly as it can loudly.

I was never more aware of this than when I saw Robert Duvall's performance in the film *Tender Mercies.* After his daughter has been killed in a car crash, there's a long shot of Duvall saying the pivotal line, "You see, I just don't trust happiness—I never did, I never will." At this moment I started to cry, even though I could hardly see his face. The scene was devastating because of what I heard on the soundtrack—how Duvall's voice was affected by the emotion he was feeling and how deeply his voice conveyed his broken heart. I went back three times to study this film because I wanted to understand the power of vocal film performance at its best. I suggest you do the same.

Now let's talk about another technical reality to being in film and television: how you use your face. Some actors rely on their face to express feeling. They squinch it up, they bug their eyes, they talk from tense jaws, and they literally lean on the muscles of their face without being aware of it. To be a leading player in feature films, television dramas, and even in certain roles in theater, there is a quality of stillness and simplicity that you must have. It's called *presence*. Particularly on film, whether on the large or small screen, that presence must be conveyed through the eyes and not by the larger, voluntary muscles of the face. You'll often notice in memorable screen performances that the face stays very still. The performance seems to emanate largely from the actor's eyes and the subtle muscles that respond unconsciously to the intention the actor is playing. This is not about being stone-faced and self-consciously minimalistic, it's about economy and subtlety. What's thrilling on the screen is to see someone with enormous emotion in them contain it and then send it through their eyes to the audience.

Certainly, some parts are more expressive facially than others, especially in comedy. And every actor has different strengths and weaknesses. But one thing remains true whatever the role: *when a camera is close to your face, stillness becomes mandatory*—not a holding of tension but allowing the camera to come into you as you relax your face completely without any extra tics or grimaces that put a wall between you and your audience.

If someone tells you that you're *indicating your performance,* this is what they mean: you're using your face or body to signal your feelings to the audience instead of actually feeling them. I reiterate here Uta Hagen's great statement, "Don't show me your point of view, have one." It's helped many actors who've studied with me because I stole it from her, but I always give her credit. Indicating your performance is a bad mistake, whatever medium you're working in. It's for amateurs. It's terrible in the theater, regardless of how big the theater is, and it's abominable on film because the camera is so close that it reveals just how fake you are.

One of the things that *Saturday Night Live* does in its sketches is attitudinalize human behavior. This cartoon reality can be very funny. In the classic Marx Brothers' comedies, Groucho Marx would raise and lower his eyebrows to indicate sexual excitement and we laughed—but his vocal delivery was very subtle and deadpan. Jim Carrey, Steve Martin, Eddie Murphy, and a host of other comedic film actors also attitudinalize and strike grimaces and eccentric poses, but, again, they are all able to simplify and play truthful scenes, so don't mistake what I'm saying. In certain comedies, yes, you can make big attitudinalized choices, but not in a drama, and not in most light comedies.

One of the prerequisites for being a good actor is having good taste and being smart enough to know how far you can go with your choices in a particular medium. Let's look again at James Brooks's *Terms of Endearment* because it might seem to you as if Shirley MacLaine's and Jack

Nicholson's performances are antithetical to what I've just been saying. But they're not. Both their characters, Aurora Greenway and Garrett Breedlove, are rigid personalities with enormous eccentricities stemming from defense mechanisms that come from fear. When Nicholson's Garrett says, upon realizing that Aurora is going to be hard to bed, "I think we're going to have to have a lot of drinks," MacLaine's Aurora squishes her face like a sour lemon. She does this to defend herself against her excitement about this man wanting her, to try to maintain an illusion of her refinement like a zany Blanche DuBois.

One of the most fascinating aspects of this film is that as the characters are confronted with serious and painful obstacles, their faces become more still, softer, and translucent. Forced to face excruciating realities, they shed their usual defenses and attitudes. This is a wonderful film to study because it's the best of comedy acting and it does have attitudes in it, but these attitudes are based in emotional defenses and not in playacting an *idea* of comedy; they're real to these people. Some human beings do strike attitudes, so you can see why I'm being cautious with you and why I'm saying to you that you have to be very smart in your acting choices. Again, by choices I mean your interpretation of the character—which, of course, is everything in acting.

Television series pose a unique challenge: playing the same character in different situations week after week. When you regularly watch network filmed dramas, you are aware that the leads are people who generally play with a low-key energy or, if they are intense as characters, mostly they contain their intensity and only occasionally let it flare. But however low-key they may be, they change emotional tones in very delicate ways that keep us riveted by the different facets they reveal as they explore the psychology of their character. These actors' work is meticulous in its detail; they are constantly making choices instead of phoning it in.

ER is one of the shows that consistently does this well. I am always interested in and surprised by the main characters on *ER* because I actually believe they have lives outside of the hospital, and I believed this even before the series showed us a glimpse of those private lives. On the other hand, there are successful filmed drama shows that shall remain nameless where the leads are so redundant week after week that I can't imagine why anybody tunes in except for the human foible called the need for familiarity.

Meticulous choices in acting are crucial in every medium. Meticulous choices are specific emotional points of view about everything you say and do. They are intelligent choices that are fueled by an emotional understanding of where your character is in their life at every moment. They are choices that you are excited about and care about and that are challenging to you as you work on your text. Meticulous choices are vital in feature films and filmed television dramas because the camera can come so close to you. As an actor who's a series regular, being specific will stop you from repeating the same facial gestures every week because what your face and eyes express will have to do with the specific images and intentions that you are playing. Being economical—which means trusting yourself to make very simple, truthful choices instead of being busy and overly elaborate in a misguided attempt to be interesting—will draw the audience toward you more than you may realize. Holding things back creates interesting transitions on your face and it registers well in close-up, because what is hidden causes the audience to want to figure you out. In other words, you may be clear about how your character is feeling toward another character at a certain moment, but you choose to hide it, and that energy plays on your face in a way that creates fascination. When you finally reveal the hidden feeling, whether it be attraction, anger, or fear, it's all the more powerful for the audience because you struggled with it before you revealed it.

One of Sanford Meisner's greatest sayings was, "Don't cry or get angry unless you've done everything you can to hold it back." Meisner was interested in behavior and he wanted actors to understand that *there's a lot that happens behaviorally to your body and your voice before the emotion explodes.* Holding back emotions until you can't repress them anymore is human reality, and it also gives you more to act. Again, this is a useful technique for stage, screen, or television. If you're clear about what you feel and choose to hide it in a certain behavior that's human and believable, that's very different from not knowing what the hell you're feeling or doing. In filmed television dramas, that vagueness—which is really bad acting, meaning that it's general and not specific—shows up very clearly when the camera comes in on your face and your eyes are blank, revealing that your brain is blank as well.

Obviously, this is true for film work, too. This was proven to me in the screen tests for *The Green Mile.* Three very talented actors screen tested for the role of John Coffey and I was invited to view all the screen tests before the final choice was made. The actors were asked to do three different scenes from the film. Each scene was filmed four times. So we watched the first, second, and third scenes twelve times each with each of the actors. On the second take of the second scene that Michael Clarke Duncan did, the camera pushed in toward his eyes for an extreme close-up. Because Michael and I had worked diligently and specifically on what he needed from the other person in the scene and how he felt about dying, his eyes were filled with so much pain that he won the role in that moment.

When you're silent in a close-up, it's your job to be aware of how that close-up advances your character in terms of the story that's being told. What does it tell the audience about what you're thinking and feeling? Well-filmed stories don't have empty moments. If you're not clear about what you must deliver in a close-up, you must confer with your director to clarify that particular moment of storytelling. If you don't learn this lesson of specificity and you become very successful, you can fall into the clutches of your own narcissism and demand close-ups that have no meaning. Such close-ups merely slow the story down and make the film appear bloated.

If you get a part in a TV series and it lasts for seven to ten years, and you are doing the same character week after week, how do you stay alive and challenged in your work? You give it everything you can. Give the writers new ideas for your character, be disciplined and committed, find unusual or provocative choices that you haven't done before that illuminate your character and are still in keeping with it. Build in your imagination what your character's daily life is like offscreen. This will give you more specific points of view about what happens to you onscreen. If you do these things, you won't view being a series regular as a creative prison; instead, you'll be using your good fortune to grow in the role. And do plays during your hiatus!

Dennis Franz, who plays Detective Andy Sipowicz on *NYPD Blue,* has used the role to examine every nook and cranny of Sipowicz's internal and external life. Franz gave a classic performance that proved the power of having a volatile emotional inner condition and holding it back with specific active behavior. It occurred in the segment in which his character's son, also a policeman and with whom he had had a rough emotional relationship, is killed in the line of duty during a shootout. The entire story shows Sipowicz taking care of his responsibilities for burying a loved one. He goes to identify the body at the morgue, he tells his ex-wife about their son's death, he makes funeral arrangements, and he tries to find the culprits in his son's murder. As a viewer you feel that this is a man whose blood is literally leaking from his heart during every chore he must accomplish.

Franz had the meaning of his son's life so specific in his internal world—the depth of his love and the grief for the loss of that love—that you couldn't tell from moment to moment if he was going to burst into tears or if he was going to crack and become violent. He never did either of these things. He simply did the jobs he had to do and, in the last scene, he walks into a bar, asks the bartender for a bottle and three shot glasses, and starts to drink himself into oblivion as the camera moves out. I can't remember ever watching an actor portray with such depth the loss of great love that only a parent can have for a child. It could have been a Greek tragedy, but it was contained in the detective's world that Sipowicz lived in and portrayed on the small television screen.

As pressured and fast as the filming of a feature film is, filmed television dramas can have brutally short shooting schedules that demand sixteen-hour to a mind-boggling twenty-two-hour days! Of that sixteen to twenty-two hours, you may wait thirteen or fifteen hours to do your scene. I want to warn you about this because concentration, preparation, and an ability to conserve and use your energy correctly are crucial to your survival as an actor. You can't count on getting more than one take for your performance. There will be coverage—meaning a master shot (which gets the entire scene from a full-body perspective) and various shots the director chooses to cover the scene—but there may be only one take from each angle. Having scared you, I also want to add that often there may be more than one take, but if you're just starting out and are suddenly confronted by this nightmare, don't say you haven't been warned. Be professional; don't look for fairness or support. That is not what professional situations in show business are necessarily about. If you get another take, terrific, but don't count on it or be upset or throw a tantrum if you don't.

Acting in a three-camera television sitcom—sitcoms are almost always shot with the three-camera technique and dramas are shot primarily with one camera—is as close to theater as television ever gets and, therefore, sitcoms can be a great training ground for both theater and film. Even though the producers and director can and do call for retakes after the show is taped in front of a live audience, you should commit to it like a play where there are no retakes. That way you get the energy going and the rhythm going and the heat between the characters; it's rather like a trapeze act, only with a net, the net being the possible retake. But remember, as an actor, especially if you're a guest on the show, *you* don't generally get a retake just because you want it. If the producers and director like what you did, or if they find it acceptable, it's in the show as is—one more reason for being as prepared as possible when you get there.

Let me add that you can get hired having worked on a script that you find has been completely changed when you show up for the first day of rehearsal. Not only that but your character might be completely different. Those things you cannot prepare for, but you must have an ability to run with them. Being positive, hardworking, and a team player gets you a lot further in advancing your career than being difficult, snotty, self-important, or argumentative. This is not to say that you shouldn't stand up for yourself when your instincts tell you that you're being threatened in some real artistic way, but even then, be a colleague, not an adversary.

As with theater, in sitcoms the time to try things and bring your ideas to the set is during the rehearsal period. This holds true for guest actors as well as regulars. You may have ideas for physical business that the director welcomes. Some shows—not all—are even open to guest actors' suggestions for lines. You have to be sensitive to the vibes around you. There are writers and producers who are so protective and controlling about their lines that every "the" and "and" not said is an affront. You will get notes about this and you must respect it or it will work against you. If you find a line particularly difficult to say—and this is the case in all media, except with classic plays, of course—discuss an alternative and you'll be told if you can change it or not. I've seen young actors who were not educated in script analysis ask for changes or cuts too quickly, when in fact the lines are not only useful to their character but important to the story development. So be very careful and intelligent before you judge that a writer's work would benefit by changing; sometimes it's *you* not looking deep enough. As a guest actor, be respectful of the other actors and don't suddenly pull something new on them during a live taping. The reason for this is that if it works, it's your lucky day and everybody will pat you on the back *but* if you try it and it bombs and ruins the live taping of that scene, your reputation can turn to mud.

I just came back from directing the national tour of *The Syringa Tree* by Pamela Gien, a play that I helped to develop and that, happily, has had a great success in New York and internationally. The play has a cast of one—an actress who must play twenty-six characters in the story that spans three generations of white and black South Africans during and after apartheid. The technical demands vocally and physically are enormous. When I had to recast the New York production in the second year of its run, over two hundred actresses were seen for the role. What astounded me in the audition process was how unprepared and uncommitted certain actresses from Hollywood were. These actresses came from the worst possible philosophy: if I show up, look pretty, and kind of know what I'm doing, I'll have a chance at this part. Only twelve out of the two hundred were sufficiently professional in their attitudes and technically prepared enough to even be considered for this challenging role.

In casting the national tour, we were lucky enough to find two excellent New York actresses, Gin Hammond and Eva Kaminsky, who agreed to tour the country, each playing four performances per week. In the last leg of the tour, both of them told me in separate conversations that the experience of playing this role and the demands that it made on them had refined their techniques and changed their work habits forever. Both actresses had strengths and weaknesses, as every actor does. Because playing twenty-six roles requires so much specificity to differentiate each character's voice and body, and so much stamina to do it, they surpassed their own idea of themselves as actresses.

One of the actresses had a moment when there was a possible laugh that kept eluding her. I told her that it was because she did not have an inner image for what she was supposed to be witnessing on the stage. At that particular moment, she was playing a young child witnessing the birth of an infant. She had to make a sound when the baby emerged—a sound that would express fear and surprise that the baby didn't look rosy and beautiful but rather bloody and blue. The actress thought that the line—"And then the baby . . . Eoou yew!"—would be enough to garner the laugh. But it wasn't. When I confronted her on her generality during this moment, she went back to the drawing board, found her own personal image of what that newborn looked like, and got the laugh.

The theater's demands are extensive and consistent, eight times a week. Over the year these two actresses developed their tools on a nightly basis and these tools are now highly sharpened and will move into their motion picture, television, and theater careers. My demand that the actress have a specific image for what she was witnessing—one of the techniques she had to employ throughout the ninety-minute play—focused on just one moment, but it taught her a lesson that will last her whole life.

I often tell my classes that the theater is a life raft for actors. Because there are so many Equity-waiver theaters and community theaters in major and even smaller cities, there are always plays to audition for and be in. If there aren't any theaters where you live, there's still a way to take charge of your own artistic growth. It's called home theater. Pick a play you like, get a director, and cast it with actors you respect, go into rehearsal for three to four weeks, and present it in your house and serve dinner and after the performance do a question-and-answer session for the people you've invited. You don't even have to make dinner. But don't underestimate the rewards of home theater. And don't do the play just once, play it three or four times a week for a month. Just call all your friends and demand that they come and spread them out over the entire performance schedule. Believe me, they'll be delighted. And I'm not kidding when I tell you to go into a full rehearsal period as though you were doing a professional production. This is what it's all about: commitment, regardless of where you're doing the play; it's the same work whether you're in your own house or in a professional theater. When you're not being paid to act, there's no reason or excuse for you not to be acting in theater, even if you do it in your own house.

I began this chapter by talking about the problems you may encounter if you're young and suddenly become a well-known actor without having a foundation in the craft. Meryl Streep acted in forty plays at Yale before she ever hit the New York theater. The rest is history. If you become well-known to the television audience at eighteen, the theater is your life raft for developing and deepening your skills. If you don't happen to get public exposure at eighteen—if, as with most actors, it takes a great deal longer, decades even—the theater sustains you, teaches you, and keeps you ready. The theater keeps your instrument and your heart alive so that you can live on stage, screen, and in television. One final note: Edie Falco played in repertory theater for twenty years before she came to the screen in *The Sopranos*. I think that says it all.

22

How to Work with a Director
or Be Your Own Director

There's a wonderful story about Mark Rydell, the excellent director of *On Golden Pond* and *The Rose,* who earlier in his career was directing Steve McQueen in the film *The Reivers,* based on a William Faulkner novel. Rydell knew that McQueen was good for the first three takes and after that began to go stale. Clifton James, an actor with whom McQueen had to do an important scene, didn't start to really cook until around the tenth take. So Rydell rehearsed with James and pretended that he was doing close-ups for ten takes to make sure James was warmed up. Then he brought McQueen in for three more takes and got the performances he wanted from both actors.

Some directors, like Rydell, understand and support the actor's process. There are other directors who know nothing about acting but think they do. They really do think that you're puppets and they don't understand why you can't do anything they want you to do. You will meet them, for they are out there, and they will try to blame you for their inadequacy. There are other directors who are really into the mechanics of filmmaking—they're technical wizards at creating gorgeous shots and making you look fabulous. But if you don't know what you're doing in the scene, indeed you'll look fabulous but you'll be lousy. Some of these directors know they don't know how to help actors and sometimes even admit it. They hope they've cast the film right because they're counting on you. That's why it's important to know how to be your own director, if necessary.

Whatever kind of director you encounter, *don't be a victim!*

The good news is that the more prepared you are, the less chance you have of falling into the victim role. If you're not prepared, if you don't have some choices from your homework that excite you and you expect the director to give you juicy and creative ideas and they don't have them, you're in big trouble. A director is not an acting teacher or a coach, and beginning actors need to know this right away. In the theater, their job is to put the production on its feet, and in film or television to get it in the can under certain time and budgetary restraints. In hiring you, they're hiring your preparation, even if they don't know it. It's your job to apply the techniques for script analysis and interpretation that I've given you in this book. And only you can discover your personal reason to play the part—your emotional connection to the role. It's not the director's job to give this to you.

You may have a small role in the script but you're still there for a reason. Most small roles exist either to impart information that advances the plot or to bring out certain aspects of a major character. If you're imparting information, don't be busy and fussy in your choices, be simple, direct, and economical so that the information is delivered. Remember that sending that information is your main job and be truthful as a human being while you do it. If you are there to bring out an aspect of a major character by interacting with them, know precisely what you're bringing out—and actively go after it.

In theater, it's important to have friends who can support you and give you constructive feedback by coming to late rehearsals or early previews. This is delicate, because as actors we are very vulnerable to criticism, especially when we're about to open in a show, and incorrect or destructive feedback can really harm your confidence. So make sure the people you invite are really on your side. And make sure they're smart about theater and are aware of your acting problems as well as questions you may have about the way you've been directed. If you have mannerisms—certain physical gestures that you tend to use again and again, vocal ruts, or if you overly adrenalize your performance or court the audience's approval, for example—it's helpful to have people who will gently call you on falling into your old patterns and wake you up to being pure in your specific characterization. If you don't feel comfortable physically in the way you've been staged, you need someone out there to tell you if it's your problem or the director's.

An actor I know won a Tony Award for a truly memorable performance in a Broadway play. During rehearsals he felt he wasn't getting the kind of direction he needed to soar in the part, so every night he rehearsed with a trusted friend for three or four hours after the eight hours of regular rehearsal. When I saw the play he was brilliant, though he said it wasn't because the director was able to give him what he needed but because he went outside the production and worked hard on his own. That's called self-preservation, but it's also honoring the play and being excited to play it.

As a director I shuddered when I heard about this outside rehearsal process, because if the actor had gotten bad advice, it could have destroyed his performance. Luckily, in this instance, it helped him and the play. Ironically, the director, who never knew about the night rehearsals, got credit for it. My belief is that there are few people who are objective, clear-sighted, and knowledgeable enough to give you a critique that will improve your performance, so choose wisely—even if it's just one or two people that you trust—before inviting anyone to late rehearsals or early previews. Again, make sure to choose people who are on your side and are not competitive with you.

Be intelligent and know when you're directed well. Learn to accept direction—take input. If you find you're always fighting authority or that you are interpreting direction as criticism and feel wounded by it or constantly disagree with it, go to a good therapist, and go fast! There are people who like to argue in rehearsals and that's part of their process; they want to make sure that what they're asked to do really works for them in the part. This doesn't have to be a destructive behavior as long as it's for creative reasons and not for personal pathology. If it's for creative reasons, there will be no need for you to be overly confrontational or hostile; you'll just ask pertinent questions that will make the rehearsal process exciting. Or you can be that proverbial pain in the ass who likes to cause trouble, to challenge people just to have adversity around you; you feel that gets your blood boiling and it makes you creative. Well, all I can say to you is good luck. If you're a star, that will work because people will put up with it. If you're not and you create a lot of problems, directors will talk about you to other directors in a negative way and you will start to lose jobs. If this sounds like you, be honest about it and change it.

When the director isn't helpful, go back to the text, go back to your technique, and go back to the trusted friends who can help you.

Be a colleague to the director, your other actors, and the production staff. If you have problems, find ways of talking about your problems so that you are being constructive. What you want is help and clarity, not points for being right. Everything should be about bettering the performance.

If the director is too general in his criticism or direction, you're going to have to translate what he says so that you understand how to fix the problem—if you agree with him. Suppose a director tells you you're playing your part "too angry." Maybe that means you're playing it too angry too much of the time. Maybe the director is trying to bring from you other emotions and their intensities that build up to the anger or cool down from it. Listen to that. However, if a director is afraid of your anger because he is personally uncomfortable with anger, you have to be smart enough to understand that's his problem, not the problem of the script or of your performance. How do you decide this? You go back to the script! If you feel the script supports your way of playing anger, go over the text with the director—again, not confrontationally but as a colleague. The director may be able to show you points you've missed, or the director may come to agree with you. The point is that you should always go back to the text.

In an interview Paul Newman told a story about translating what a director tells you into technical acting terms. Newman said that when he gets a note from a director that his performance is too slow, he immediately understands that he has not justified the emotional need of his character strongly enough. In one particular film, after being told this, he went back and did more homework, the scene was reshot, and the director told him how improved his performance was. Newman then asked the script supervisor how long the take was. The surprising answer: it was three seconds longer than "the slow take." Newman understood that the first take seemed slow because not enough was at stake for him emotionally to take up the screen time; during the second take, his work was more intensely justified, more was happening within him internally, and that made him more interesting to the camera.

Of course, sometimes you really do just have to speed up. Certain material doesn't support long pauses even if you're very real in the pause. This is especially true for light comedies, which are very verbally oriented and where pauses can kill the humor and destroy the pace necessary for success. But even in a drama it can be important for the director to get a take in which the cues are picked up quickly. This is important because when editing your performance, the director creates the rhythms and the tempos of all the performances and finds the structure of the film and how it gains momentum as the story builds to its conclusion. When you study films, you'll see that they are successful or not because the director understands how to keep the audience's attention by changing rhythms and tempos. Long pauses are particularly destructive when they are about the actors getting more film time instead of about serving the scene. This is the verbal equivalent of the empty close-up. Even if the director doesn't ask you, make sure there's a take where you, *without rushing,* simply pick up your cues. If you do that, you'll give the director more options to find a variety of rhythms, which will help your performance and the film.

It's just as detrimental to work too hard on a part that doesn't require it as it is to underprepare when you know you have a creative mountain to climb. There is a story about Gregory Peck that drives this point home. It seems that after a day's shooting, a crew member found Peck's script left behind on a chair, and that Peck had annotated every page with one of two things: NAR or AR. The next day when he returned the script to Peck, he asked him what the initials stood for. Peck replied, "NAR means 'no acting required' and AR means 'acting required.' " Peck knew when playing a simple reality was enough because he was personally connected to the scene; he also knew when he wasn't and had to work at it. This goes back to Stella Adler's great remark, "It's not enough to have talent. You have to have a talent for your talent."

When Tobey Maguire was preparing to play the part of the jockey Red Pollard in *Seabiscuit,* there was an aspect of Red's personality that he felt didn't come easily to him and that he'd never had to play before. This trait was Red's extravagant and gregarious ability to tell elaborate stories to the other jockeys. Tobey knew he had this trait within him but he wanted exercises and work to help him bring it out. If you've seen Tobey's work, you know there is a wonderful simple truth and a quiet and intense intelligence that filters through every part he's played. Tobey wanted to add the dimension of storytelling as well as a harder edge of defenses to accompany Red's tough life.

The first thing I asked Tobey to do was to tell me jokes—which he didn't want to do but he forced himself to, and they were pretty hilarious. He was a lot better at it than he'd thought. He was challenged and delighted when I then asked him to work on one of Chance Wayne's monologues from Williams's *Sweet Bird of Youth*. It's a complicated monologue full of Chance's personal history. It also has high emotional stakes because in a sense, Chance is auditioning for Princess, who has the power in their relationship since she's a famous film star. He wants her to help him with his hoped-for Hollywood career. This paralleled Red's desire to impress and be liked and accepted by his colleagues.

I asked Tobey to do the monologue in several different ways. One day I asked him to do Chance's monologue across a room and to reach me with vocal volume and physical expressiveness. When he committed himself to those tasks, what we found was a terrific potential, as young as he is, to find the truth in the part of Chance, who is several years older. We also found that having to reach across the room and express himself loudly and vigorously with the monologue cracked open the part of him that he needed to tell Red's stories in that somewhat flamboyant way.

Since there's little or no rehearsal in television dramas and most films, getting a coach to assist in your preparation can be a good way to feel confident when you show up on the set. Top-flight actors use coaches more than you might think. In what's often referred to as the golden age of Hollywood—from the 1940s to the 1960s—acting teachers and coaches were part of the studio system. Today actors have to hire them for themselves. Often I get calls from directors, too, asking me to prepare actors for a role.

For film work, remember that you have to be ready to shoot out of sequence. Regardless of the director, almost no film ever shoots in chronological order, even if the director would like to because he knows it would help your characterization. The reason for this, of course, is money: it saves money to shoot all the scenes at each location at one time instead of going back and forth. I just worked with a star who arrived at a distant location for her film and was greeted with the news that her first day of shooting would be the last scene in the script. I think this story illustrates quite simply, and terrifyingly, the virtue of being prepared. She had done all her homework, and nervous as she was at the announcement, it was doable. She had worked through the entire role scene by scene, made choices, and defined relationships so she knew where she was emotionally in the last scene and what her relationship to her leading man was. This, by the way, was complex and required a nuanced performance because her character, even at the end of the film, was still hiding many secrets.

Very early on in my teaching career I coached Madeline Kahn for her role in Peter Bogdanovich's film *Paper Moon*. Madeline was playing a kind of sexy grifter during the Depression, who uses her female pulchritude to win over men who'll give her money and keep her in the style she wishes to become accustomed to. The pivotal scene for her character is when she pleads with a young child, played by Tatum O'Neal, to sit in the backseat of the car they are driving in, so that she can sit up front and be close to the child's father—because, as she explains it, she doesn't have a lot of years left to be attractive. This emotional scene was done in full close-up and, if you see the film—which I recommend you do—you'll see why Madeline prepared so thoroughly for it. Madeline called me at different intervals from the location and each time she called she'd say it was the day she was going to shoot the scene. And every time, the scene was canceled, usually because of weather.

One day Madeline got a call from the production office telling her that they were not going to use her and that she had the day off. A few hours later, as Madeline was lolling around her apartment, the phone rang and a desperate voice at the other end said, "We're shooting your big scene in an hour!" Madeline was hustled off into costumes, hair, and makeup and was in front of the camera an hour later. Madeline was an incredibly sensitive and serious performer and these kinds of delays and pressures played havoc with her nervous system, but because of her preparation and her keen ability to concentrate, she did her close-up in one take, and that is what you see in the film.

Depending on the production, you may or may not have input into your costume, hair, and makeup. Some directors and producers are more open to input than others. Obviously, if you're a star you'll have a lot of input. If you are allowed input, the worst mistake you can make is to get stuck in your ego about appearing attractive in a certain way that is not true for your character.

The second-worst mistake you can make is to go against your instincts and to agree to a physical image for the character that you feel is completely wrong. I recently worked with an actress who got into a major tug-of-war with the director of a film she was starring in. She thought he wanted to dress her in a way that was inappropriate for how her character would want to appear in the world. In explaining her reasons to the director and costume designer, she ultimately convinced them that she was right because they came to understand that she was purely involved with the psychological truth of the character, not her own vanity.

Whatever costume you have on, you have to endow it as your own. And you must wear the costume, it must not wear you: you must move in the clothes according to the style of the period in which the play or film takes place and you must make yourself comfortable in those clothes. The sooner you can work in the costume, including the shoes, the better. This is something some directors don't think about but you *must*.

Since television is so fast, when you're doing television, ask for another take but, as I've said, try not to be too upset if you don't get it, if the director says "We're moving on." This can happen to established actors as well as beginners, even in major films. Nobody ever gets everything they want. You may feel you were terrible and be surprised when you see the finished product that you're as good as you are. You may be disappointed and feel that you were right, that you could have done it better if you'd been given another take. But the more prepared you are, the better you will have done it in whatever number of takes you were given. And that's the point.

Be aware that some directors will hardly say anything to you at all. That can mean you're doing just fine or that they don't know what to tell you, so don't make yourself crazy because you're not hearing anything. Just do the best you can. Again, *don't look for other people's approval*.

Jason Alexander told me this story about a film he was in: after the first take the director said, "Jason, that was absolutely fabulous! Fantastic! Let's do it again." And after the second take, the director said, "Brilliant. Absolutely brilliant. Let's do it again." This happened five or six more times—great praise, but let's do it again. Finally, after the seventh take, Jason said to the director, "Is there something you want that I'm not giving you?" He was greeted with the news that he was "totally superb and why don't we do it again?" Twenty takes later there had been no adjustments given or comments made about how he could improve his performance. Nothing was ever said except, after the last take, "Well, we've got that. Let's move on."

Remember, each job is a chance to improve on an acting problem you may have had. Likewise, it's a chance to work on your social skills as an actor, which is part of every job you'll ever have. If you're shy in situations with new people, as I am, reach out to people even if it's difficult for you and engage in conversations. Ask people about themselves but at the same time, if you're working on a scene where you need to be alone and separate for your preparation, that is your right and you must give that to yourself. I've heard that the great Albert Finney says to the assistant director on the day when he has to do an intensely emotional scene, "Please advise people on the set that I won't be particularly social today, I need to be in my own private thoughts."

When you learn people's names on the set and are friendly and easy to work with and then do an excellent job, you are building your career. Don't ever be disrespectful or unkind to anyone you work with. And don't gossip about anyone, ever. Treat people as you wish to be treated. People do talk about people on sets, and you want your reputation to be a positive one.

One final piece of advice: don't be a brat. It's not just all about you. It's about a group of people trying their best to make a good piece of art, and if you're a narcissistic child going, "Oh, it's me, it's me, it's me, it's me!" you're not an actor, you're just a self-important little pain in the ass who is saying, "I want to have my way." The reason it's necessary for me to say this is that I've seen the problems that are created when people act this way and how it hurts them, and, most importantly, the project.

23

THE POWER OF YES

The most important word in acting is *yes*. Why do I say that? Because if you are negative about what you attempt in acting, you'll never be good at it. You'll never follow through in exploring your acting choices, and you'll never push past your fear. The antidote to self-criticism and fear is yes.

A friend of mine was directing a movie and I was an observer on the set. An actress in a key role was having trouble with a phone call. The phone call was pivotal to the film. It had to be funny, it had to be sad, it had to convey a lot of very important information, and they were doing take after take after take but the phone call refused to come alive. My friend, the director, gave the actress acting adjustments for each take, none of which she was able to make work. Finally, he gave her another new way of approaching the phone call and I saw her face light up at the new suggestion. He called "Action!" and she started to do the scene. It was breathtaking. You couldn't want it done any better. And in the middle of the phone call she suddenly stopped, and said, "This is not working."

Instead of following through with the scene and staying confident in exploring the new choice, she allowed the self-critical voice inside her to stop her from finishing. Sadly, she never came near repeating that performance.

It's interesting to note that this actress who started out with a very big career in films has had diminishing success and I think it's because of this internalized negative judgment that she hasn't solved and may not be aware of.

Being nervous, high-strung, or desperate to succeed is a part of almost every actor's experience at some time in their lives. But you can learn to use your nervousness in a positive way. Nerves are about desire. Being nervous is about needing something or feeling you're lacking something. That's emotion. So you say yes to that feeling of nervousness because it's energy. You focus that energy into your active intention and into the story.

Everything you feel in this yes experience is positive. Everything. Hatred, envy, joy, humor, fear of humiliation, fear of death, attraction. You see someone you're attracted to and you say, "I don't want to be attracted to them" or "I shouldn't be attracted to them" or "I shouldn't have that fantasy about them." Well, you had it, why are you scared of it? It can't hurt you. And anyway, what you feel or think is not an action; an action is what you *do*. As an actor you have to say yes to everything you smell, see, taste, touch, or hear, yes to every bizarre fantasy you have, every dream you have. Just when you think, *That's too horrible, I can't go there,* you are standing in front of a door that opens to a very usable part of your creativity. It's all yes.

I was in my forties when I read *Introduction to the Work of Melanie Klein* and was introduced to the concept of the *negative introject*. I realized my negative introject was an enormous part of my inner world, and I'd lived with it so long that I believed it was the truth. Everything I'd accomplished until then had been despite my negative introject, and nothing I'd accomplished had lessened it, because my point of view about myself was distorted. I'm a very simple person in certain ways, and so I thought, *Okay, I'm going to make my negative introject a cowboy with a black hat and a black horse and I'm going to make my positive introject a cowboy hero with a white hat and a white horse.*

Once I created these childlike visual images for myself, boy did they go to town! These two guys would argue in my head vehemently every day. My negative introject would say, "You know, you're not that good at what you do. You're not teaching well. You look lousy. Your apartment's a mess." I could get negative about anything; I had a real talent for it. Every time my negative introject would say something like that about me, I would have the guy on the white horse confront him and fight for me: "You're a wonderful teacher. You're a wonderful person. You look great. You have a fabulous personality." And every day their argument would make me want to throw up.

And then I did what I felt was a really disgusting thing: I actually got in front of my bathroom mirror every morning and said, "I love you, Larry." I had to force myself to do this. But then a kind of miracle happened. I went to the mirror, looked at myself, and said, "I love you, Larry," and I actually felt that I did. This struggle took about a year, and it changed my life. And that was a yes!

Before that yes, I had a great therapist in New York, Dr. De La Vega, who asked me at one of my 8:00 A.M. daily sessions, "Why do you think more people are negative than positive?" I said through my tears, "I have no clue." He said in his very concerned and direct way, and with a thick Cuban accent, "Because, Larry, it takes more courage to be positive." That was an absolute revelation to me. Suddenly I understood the truth of what he said. If you are negative, you can never be disappointed if something doesn't work out. If you're positive, you may not always get what you want: you risk disappointment. That's why being positive takes courage.

There's more: if you love someone, if you build a great career that you're proud of, if you have great friendships, one day it's all going to end. We're all going to die, everyone we love will die, our world will end. So a lot of people stay negative to remain safe, so they're not disappointed when something doesn't work out or when it's all taken away. But that means you never live fully.

It takes courage to be a good actor—and a good human. The only way to keep growing in your work is to love your choices, your intentions, your back story, to say to yourself, *I believe in me, I believe in this character and in the story, and though I may not be feeling what I want to at this moment in a scene, I'm going to say yes to whatever feeling I have and use that energy to help me send the ideas to the other actor.* You can absolutely ruin your career and your life by saying no to yourself. You can change your career and your life by finding the yes.

Suppose you're playing in a comedy and suddenly in the middle of a scene you start to feel angry at the woman you love. She's insecure and feels unworthy of your love, and suddenly you want to yell at her. Your negative introject jumps up, and says, "You can't be angry at this point in the scene, you're telling this poor, insecure woman you love her. Be tender. And besides, you're in a comedy." But something in you knows better, and so you say yes to that anger when you say "I love you!" You start yelling it at her and it gets a huge laugh you never even knew was there. Your intuition was trying to help you and knew there was a funnier, better choice, so when you say, "Oh no, that's not appropriate to be angry on this line," you are stopping the creative process with no.

Wait a minute, you say. What about the young actor playing Treplyev who started smacking Nina around because he had an impulse not to be a victim? Or the other young actor who destroyed the kitchen table in *A Hatful of Rain*? Weren't they saying yes? The difference is that these actors hadn't done their homework and they didn't fully understand the plays they were in. Their impulses came from ignorance and self-inflation rather than from creative inspiration grounded in truthful character interpretation and living in the given circumstances of that play.

But the actor who had the impulse to yell "I love you!" stayed with his objective: *to get the woman to understand that she was lovable to him*. What changed was his response to her obstacle, her feeling of unworthiness that stood in the way of his happiness. His impulse changed his intention to *angrily demand that she understand that he loved her*. This was a valid intention, a valid emotional response.

So when I tell you to say yes to your creative impulses, how do you know the difference? Sometimes you don't, but you will learn. Trial and error, my friends, trial and error. (So, in a way, the young actors I critiqued were right to say yes, too. They were in class, the right place to make honest mistakes and learn.) If you've done all the homework you can, and you're fully invested in the given circumstances and in your objectives, and you're truly acting moment to moment with the other actors, your impulses at each moment are going to be truthful and useful. That's what I'm asking you to say yes to.

I recall sitting in the theater watching the original production of Neil Simon's *Lost in Yonkers*. There's a scene between the rigid German matriarch of the family and her grown son, who is a two-bit gangster. The suffocating and judgmental mother berates her son for being a failure and a complete disappointment for not living up to her expectations. She tells him how ashamed she is of him. After this diatribe of disgust, Kevin Spacey, who played the son, turns to his mother, who was played by Irene

Worth, and says, "Nah. You can't get me down, Ma. I'm too tough. You taught me good. And whatever I've accomplished in this life, just remember you're my partner, you made me." Then Spacey blew his mother a kiss and the scene ended. I sat in the audience and felt my heart break with the truth of that moment. In one simple human gesture Spacey said, "I kiss you off, I hate you, I love you, it's your fault, and I wish you were dead."

When I went to see the play again after a new actor had taken over the role of the son, this gesture was not repeated. I realized then that it was Spacey's own. Now, however, it is in the published version of the play. There must have been a moment in rehearsal when Spacey spontaneously blew his mother that kiss from an impulse, because he trusted that impulse and said yes to it. His creativity, his total immersion in the text, put a button on the scene that enriched an already great line and made the break between child and parent gut-wrenchingly alive.

24

WHEN RACE, RACIAL STEREOTYPES, CLASS, ETHNICITY, AND SEXUALITY BECOME ISSUES

The Owl and the Pussycat by Bill Manhoff is a modern version of the Pygmalion story. It is about Felix, a sexually repressed writer and would-be intellectual, and Doris, a working-class hooker who calls herself a model and an actress. Diana Sands, a black actress, originated the role of Doris on Broadway, although it can be played by an actress of any race or ethnicity. I assigned the role to an African-American actress in one of my classes. She was upper-middle-class, very elegant, and so committed to being safe in her choices that she never disturbed her elegance with real emotion of any kind. In particular, she did not own her anger or her sensuality and since she was young and attractive, her refusal to express these sides of herself was a recipe for disaster. Why was she so committed to keeping herself so limited? Because she identified anger and earthiness as lower-class and negative black stereotypes.

Obviously, anger and earthiness are part of our humanity. When actors disown crucial aspects of themselves, I believe it's a teacher's responsibility to give them material that allows them to crash into the problem.

This actress robbed herself of a kind of sexiness and power, which is why I picked *The Owl and the Pussycat,* a play about people that demanded her to be sexual and powerful. Also, it's a play about people who hide from themselves and others—until falling in love forces them into the open. Beneath Doris's predatory sexuality is a profusion of insecurities about her lack of education and her value as a person; behind his mask of intellectual superiority, Felix is hiding his feelings of failure, isolation, and an inability to accept his own animal passion. Again, the play is not about race, and in fact the part of Doris has often been played by white actresses. But there is no way to play Doris without playing her as working-class, uneducated, brash, and tempestuous as well as insecure and vulnerable.

The actress, whom I will call Nina, began working on the part. When she brought her scene into class, she played Doris as the same elegant, upper-middle-class, untarnished, unemotional person she always played and felt comfortable with. In my critique, I asked her, "Can you own your own earthiness? Can you own playing a street hooker without being insulted by it and realize that it is a character just as it would be for anyone playing a blue-collar hooker of any color?" I reminded her that she didn't have to play Doris as any kind of racist cliché, but that she couldn't ignore the text. Since Doris was working-class and since Nina was black, Doris was therefore black and working-class, and the script demanded that she show a lack of education and polish as well as a mercurial rather than a placid personality.

Nina continued working on the part, trying to break through her inhibitions. As part of her homework and in front of the class, she did exercises that called for bumps and grinds and roars. Alone in her apartment, she danced naked to wild music because I told her to. She was appalled by all the exercises I gave her, but she had a fantastic desire to grow, and so she did them. But still when she brought the scene into class, her hips were locked, her emotions were small, careful, and neat, and there was a stinginess and a lack of commitment to her work that would stifle her career. Nina is a kind, gentle, and deeply sensitive woman and I could tell that she had been seriously emotionally wounded in her life. She had an apologetic, trembly quality every time she bravely ventured onto the stage but that didn't stop me from pushing her because I knew how much she wanted to change.

When she brought in the scene for a third time still without any sensuality or temperament in her portrayal of Doris, I stood up and yelled at her, "You are not a black woman, you are a repressed white woman!" I knew this would come over as a racist remark and I wanted it to. I wanted to shock her. Sometimes political correctness isn't helpful. Nina looked at me in horror with her mouth open wide. Her body started shaking, her eyes were blazing, she stood ramrod straight and screamed at the top of her lungs. No words came out, just animal screams. To her great credit, she did not run off the stage. I am sure she wanted to absolutely annihilate me and I understood why. I pushed the race button again and again because it was the center of her acting problem. As long as she felt that all human behavior except well-mannered gentility was unacceptable, she was trapped in a prison she had created for herself.

Ultimately Nina realized that I was coming from support, not from criticism or racism. I said to her, "Please own all of yourself and don't say no to any part of your feelings, whether you approve of them or not. It will stop your life and your career." What we are afraid to reveal about ourselves to the audience is sometimes our greatest breakthrough when we do reveal it because it unclogs a torrent of powerful feelings and gives us freedom.

The next class after my explosion, Nina walked onto the stage to do the scene in the highest heels that any human could walk on, a skintight dress that accentuated her breasts and hips to the maximum, and became a human tornado of sexual intimidation. She had a look in her eye that suggested that if this poor schnook Felix didn't give her what she wanted, she would devour him and all the furniture in his room. She gave a performance that raised the roof. The class roared with laughter and then, at the end, celebrated her triumph. It is the only time in my career as a teacher that I got down on my hands and knees and crawled over to a student and did salaams. Nina had faced one of the greatest fears in her life and she grabbed it in both her hands and hurled it behind her. Doing this gave her the freedom she so deserved and longed for. After that night, Nina got her first professional job in the wonderful play *Wit,* and she has worked continually since.

I know what it is to be treated negatively because of something you have no choice about being. My birth name is Moskovitz, but in post–World War II Los Angeles, my father took pains not to identify our family as Jewish. When we went to a restaurant and had to wait for a table, the loudspeaker would announce, "Table ready for Moss." It always gave me a queasy feeling in my stomach. I asked my father why he changed our name, and he would answer, "Oh, they never pronounce it properly." But something in my gut knew that wasn't the reason.

One day I was playing hide-and-seek with my friends Jimmy and Janet, who lived down the street. The game suddenly stopped and Jimmy turned to me and said, "Larry, you have to go home now." And I said, "Why?" He said, "We can't play with you anymore, you're a Jew." I ran home ashamed and crying and asked my mother what was wrong with me. She tried to reassure me. Some people are ignorant, she said, and I should just forget about it. But of course I never did, and because I was one of the few Jews in a basically gentile neighborhood, more and more I began to feel the pain of being a minority and that there was indeed something wrong with me. Like most children I wanted to fit in and be popular but my Jewishness stood in the way and I began to hate it. Sometimes growing up I even said I wasn't Jewish. Technically this was true because while my mother's father was Jewish, her mother was not, and although I was raised culturally Jewish, there was always a feeling at home that we were never committed to a sense of religious faith.

So what does all this mean? It means that I have this rich, multifaceted heritage to draw on—blood memory from so many different sources—*if* and *only if*—I allow myself to own it. As an actor, the moment I let shame cut me off from any part of who I am, I am literally disabling myself. I discovered this as a young man during a Passover seder given by some friends. During the seder, each person at the table reads from the Haggadah, which tells the story of Passover and includes prayers. When it became my turn to read, I got only about four words out before my body convulsed and I burst into tears. At the time I was very embarrassed, but something within me recognized and knew how connected I was to the Jewish part of myself and therefore to who I am. I felt more whole and solid after that experience.

As a young actor I embarked on my career during a transitional moment in the entertainment business when a greater number of Jewish actors and performers were beginning to keep their ethnic names and becoming stars—among them Dustin Hoffman, Elliott Gould, George Segal, Barbra Streisand, Paul Simon, and Art Garfunkel. I had a decision to make: Was I Larry Moskovitz or Larry Moss? By that time I had already embraced my Jewishness to the point where I was married by a rabbi under a *chuppah*. But because I didn't want to identify myself with the family I grew up with, not because of their Jewishness but because of their ideas, I decided I would be Jewish *and* Larry Moss.

As an actor, identifying with my Jewishness helped me in getting and playing parts. But as importantly, accepting *all* of myself, including my

Jewishness, helps me every time I act whether I'm playing a Jewish character or not, because it's a true part of me and trying to deny it robs me
of my authentic self, a disaster for any kind of good acting. Any part of
you—your socio-economic background, your nationality, your race, your
color, your sexual identity—that you dissociate yourself from is destructive to your artistic freedom. Any emotion or behavior that you disown
because you identify it with part of yourself that *you* judge, because you
feel that others judge it, will be difficult for you to express and you will
have to work through it as Nina did.

No actor should ever play a racial stereotype. The word *stereotype* implies generality and a lack of human specificity, and as I've said, acting is
all about specificity. Even if a character as written seems stereotypical or
clichéd, it's your job to make sure they're not. You do this by giving them
a specific personality and unique emotional life. The great actor Zero
Mostel indelibly created the role of Tevye in the original Broadway production of *Fiddler on the Roof*. Tevye is a Jewish father in a small Russian
village, who along with his wife, Golde, worried about the marriages of
his daughters and the survival of their family and friends because of the
Russian persecution of Jews. Mostel's genius was to make Tevye such a
specific human being—voraciously alive, full of humor, fear, anger, and
love for his family—that not for one moment did you think of him as having any quality that was a cliché of being a Jewish father and husband.

Zero Mostel was what we call a naughty actor. If you saw him on the
wrong night, he could be overbearing, he could overact, chew the scenery,
and literally make up the script. But when he was reined in, his performance had a dignity, a simplicity, and a heart that brought out the emotional
texture of the play and what it meant to be Jewish in those terrifying circumstances. Through the specificity of the character he created, his Tevye
became a person anyone could relate to and identify with, and thus he became universal; he became all people who suffer persecution.

Issues of identity come up for actors in all sorts of ways. Straight actors may be uncomfortable about portraying gay characters, even though
the public's ignorance and fear around sexuality is beginning to diminish.
This has been helped enormously because of such openly gay actors as Ian
McKellen, Harvey Fierstein, and Ellen DeGeneres, to name a few.
Straight actors' problems with playing gay characters may have to do with
what they fear about public perception or with their own difficulty expressing feelings they consider taboo. Yet Tom Hanks had no such problem when he played the gay protagonist in *Philadelphia*. If you're a straight

actor looking at a gay part and you find yourself uncomfortable with it, you have to a decision to make: How good is the part? How much do you want it? Are you willing to work through your discomfort and your fear of other people's judgments and find out what it's like to have increased emotional access as an actor?

Michael C. Hall, a straight actor, was interviewed about playing the gay character of David in *Six Feet Under,* who had been closeted for a very long time. Hall talked about growing up heterosexual in a homophobic culture, and how he rethought what he was told about homosexuality in order to understand David's self-hate. "I had to reexamine, through the prism of David, the world that I grew up in and the messages that I got about being gay," he said. "At NYU, we were trained to ask this magical 'what if.' I look at my life and think of the messages sent to me about being gay—and filter those through the sense of 'What if I were a closeted homosexual when I heard those things? What would that have meant to me?' " Hall realized that these messages would have fallen very differently on David's ears than they did on his, and, because he wanted to play this great part, he made it his business to understand this emotionally as well as intellectually.

Gay actors may be uncomfortable about portraying gay parts because they want the industry and the public to perceive them as straight. Despite the advances, there's never been an example of a Hollywood sex symbol, male or female, who has been openly gay. So again, the question comes down to how good is the part? If you're an actor who can play many different kinds of parts, why be threatened? I understand why people are threatened by this, but I don't think they should be. Being a bisexual man myself I know the fear on a very personal level. Hollywood stardom is a double-edged sword. The tragedies of Montgomery Clift and Rock Hudson, who had to closet themselves because they had to be perceived as red-blooded ideals of masculinity, show the lack of education and imagination of the culture in which they lived and in which we still live. I say imagination because we should be able to imagine actors in roles that they fully inhabit regardless of their sexuality. And it's toward achieving this that I say, why be threatened? When actors are courageous enough to take any kind of part that is well written, progress is made and fear subsides.

Of course there may be times when you turn down a role because the writing is so inferior or caricatured or because the director insists on your playing a role in a one-note, stereotypical way, because he wants it to be seen as ridiculous or negative. In those cases it is absolutely your right to turn it down.

As a teacher, I've always talked about the necessity of giving yourself a vocal range and a choice of accents that you can use for different roles. But, as I've discovered, this, too, can challenge a person's ethnic identity. Such was the case with a beautiful and talented Hispanic actress in one of my classes. I kept urging her to learn to Americanize her speech, because I knew that if she didn't, it would limit her career. When I say to you that she resented it deeply, I am understating it. I respected her fierceness in protecting her own identity, but I told her that if she insisted on speaking *only* with a thick Mexican accent she would be limited to playing characters who spoke with thick Mexican accents. The good news is that she did the work. Now she is a regular on a television series in which she's using her more Americanized accent.

If any of the above issues have struck a chord in you and you think it may be important to confront yourself, do so as quickly as you can. We all want to avoid pain, but short-term pain is a lot less difficult to handle than a lifetime filled with it. Avoidance of issues that stop the flow of your creative and personal life makes your work and your life so much less enjoyable. And to add another provocative thought: a lot of people stay in long-term pain because it's comfortable and it becomes habitual. But once you face your own inner obstacles and do the work you need to do to transcend them, you will be expressing your intention to live with more richness and fullness.

I've only talked here about African-American, Hispanic, and Jewish actors, and about issues of sexual identity, but I'm intensely aware how frustrating it is for actors from any ethnic group or nationality that isn't considered "commercial" to have to Americanize themselves in order to work in this country. When I taught in Paris in 2003, I met actors from all over the world who are grappling with this and struggling to have their voices heard. I want to say to anyone who is reading this book anywhere in the world that your cultural identity and stories are needed, whether they seem on the surface to be commercially viable or not. Like the Hispanic actress in my class, if you want to work in American media you must Americanize your English enough to be readily understood. In the next chapter, I'm going to give you a technique for creating a performance piece that will show your talents as an actor and also tell your story, preserving your identity and illuminating it for others.

We are already seeing more and more collaborations among writers, actors, and directors from different countries. I personally feel the need to explore cultures outside my own, and I see, as I work with these international artists, that they do, too. To me, the interchange of talent and experience from different cultures inside and outside America is exciting and invigorating, and it is desperately needed to keep the art of acting healthy and growing.

25

THE STORY EXERCISE:
BECOMING THE WRITER AND STAR
OF YOUR OWN PLAY

The Story exercise was created after I went to my longtime New York astrologer, Maria Napoli. I had been directing in-house productions at my studio, but I had intense feelings of wanting to build a piece from scratch. Maria said, as she read my astrological chart, that it showed why I was feeling frustrated by working with material that had already been written. "You must create theater with a writer and work with them to develop material that you sculpt together." Since I trusted her so much and what she said intrigued me, I thought about it all the way home on the plane to Los Angeles. This led me to come up with the Story exercise, which then led to the development of *The Syringa Tree,* a one-person play that has now played all over the world.

Maria told me to work with a writer. Reflecting on her words, I began to realize that I had been thinking about actors as writers for a long time but had never put it into practice. My belief was that all actors—like all people—have a story to tell, although they are not always aware of it. In fact, when an actor has a tremendous success in a given piece of material, sometimes it parallels their own story in an emotional, psycho-logical way. For example, Jason Robards Jr. had an affinity for interpret-ing Eugene O'Neill's alcoholic antiheroes like James Tyrone Jr. in *Long Day's Journey into Night,* Jamie, a hack Broadway actor in *Moon for the Misbegotten,* and Hickey, the tragic "life of the party" with a deep dark secret in *The Iceman Cometh.* To play these characters Robards found and used an aspect of his personal life; he battled alcoholism for many years of his career, and he brought his experiences to O'Neill's work in a beautiful and haunting way.

Again, I'm not suggesting that you groom your problems or feed your suffering so that you can use it in your acting. The truth of it is that the suffering has already happened to all of us, nobody escapes suffering, and suffering can be healed or lessened when you use it for your craft as an actor. Every play, novel, and screenplay has themes, and every human being's life has particular themes. Your theme can be surviving parental abuse and finding a way to live life fully and positively; it can be about the struggle to resolve the loss of a loved one or the loss of a beloved place; it can be about surviving racial or sexual prejudice or a personal spiritual crisis; it can be about overcoming poverty or an oppressive government; it can be about overcoming too great a sense of entitlement or your own shame or guilt. Addiction and substance abuse can be a symptom of any of these themes.

On the airplane home after my appointment with Maria, I was think-ing about all of this in—I'm happy to say—a very self-serving way. How could I find a wonderful actor/writer in my class to create a piece of the-ater that would be important to me and to the actor/writer and maybe even to an audience? When I went back to teach that Monday, I began the class by announcing that I was going to do an exercise with them that I had never done before. I had a terrific group of hardworking, creative ac-tors who were hungry and ready to be challenged.

I gave them the Story exercise.

I said, "Let's begin, as we always do, with the Relaxation exercise. I want you to sit in your chair and breathe and go through your body, re-laxing muscles that you find are tense. Breathe into the tension and ask the muscle to let go on the exhale." After fifteen minutes of this work, I said, "I want you to allow an event to come forward into your awareness. It could have happened yesterday at the bank or twenty years ago, it doesn't matter. Don't consciously pick it. Let it pick you. Just ask yourself, gently, for a memory, and see what comes up. Don't judge the first memory and don't edit it. Use the first event that finds you."

Once I gave them time to allow an event to join them, I asked them to remember every conceivable sensory reality they could in connection with the memory, everything they saw, smelled, tasted, touched, and heard. I was using an aspect of the Physical Sensation exercise, but I was taking it in a particular direction.

Within five minutes, the thirty-five people in the class were in different states of intense emotional response. I was surprised by the avalanche of feeling that was flooding forth. I don't mean just tears, I mean fear, embarrassed giggling, laughter, awe, and shock. This is when my instinct told me to repeat to them that they should make sure they did not change the first memory that came to them.

I gave the class a good period of time to remember the experience and fill it in with sensory detail so that it became very real and present to them in the NOW.

For the next part of the exercise, I divided the class into partners and asked them, one at a time, to tell each other their memories, and then to have their acting partner repeat their memory back to them. I instructed them to tell the memory with as much sensory richness as they could, describing in detail again what they saw, smelled, tasted, touched, and heard, and to let these sense memories affect them as they recounted their story. When the partner repeated the story, the partner would then repeat this sensory detail, too.

Watching and listening to this was riveting because I was experiencing thirty-five memories coming alive through the actors' bodies and voices in an absolutely authentic way. People's eyes were blazing, they were roaring with laughter, weeping with grief, holding on to each other and sharing their experiences. As I observed the incredible aliveness of each actor's face and body, I knew I had hit gold. I could not hear the individual memories since everyone was talking at the same time, but I could certainly hear in the tonality of their voices a deep emotional connection to what they were saying. I saw and, in that tonality, heard the power of personal memory with no text but that which the actors provided for themselves in their telling of it.

We all have unresolved emotional experiences or moments of great emotional meaning in our past, many of which are kept in our unconscious mind but are ready to be tapped if we have the right tools and are brave enough. After each partner took their turn, the next step in the exercise was one that terrified each and every actor in the room. I said, beaming and jubilant, "You must now bring this memory onto the stage, playing every character in your memory vocally and physically. If you are playing people who are speaking to each other, you have to morph second-by-second back into the voice and physical manner of both people you are portraying." I asked the actors to begin working on this at home and then to bring in the memory in a theatrical style that appealed to them. I wanted to give them the freedom of different styles—abstract, literal, farce, satire, or stream of consciousness—and to costume it and light it in any way their imagination compelled them to tell their story.

I don't think this is an original idea. I'm sure it has been done many times in different ways. This is the way that I discovered it and taught it. One theatrical experience I had that made me realize this was possible was seeing Meryl Streep in a musical production of *Alice in Wonderland,* written by Elizabeth Swados, at The Public Theater. In a two-minute scene, Streep played the White Queen yelling and sobbing at Alice, then turned around and, in a completely different voice and manner of sobbing, and with a different physicalization, played Alice yelling and sobbing at the Queen. The two minutes stunned me and I went back twice to observe the show just to watch those two minutes. The next time I saw and was excited by seeing one actor playing multiple roles was watching Patrick Stewart on Broadway in Charles Dickens's *A Christmas Carol.* Stewart played everybody in the story and brought it to complete and vivid life as if a full cast of actors were in front of you playing the rich and varied idiosyncratic Dickensian characters.

A month after I first gave the Story exercise to my class, Pamela Gien, a white South African actress with a fine gift for acting, hesitantly took the stage to perform her story. At that moment, I realized I had to have reverence for the life experience that she and every actor and actress in the class was going to reveal because it took such courage. *The Syringa Tree* was born from the memory that Pamela didn't want to have and tried to forget until she heard me say not to edit the memory, no matter how painful. What Pamela remembered was the murder of her grandfather on his South African farm when she was a child. Her Grandpa George was stabbed twenty-two times in the back by a Rhodesian freedom fighter. In her exercise, Pamela played herself as a six-year-old child and also her mother and father, her grandparents and her black nanny, Salamina.

I am going to describe to you the process through which *The Syringa*

Tree was created because it will give you insight and techniques to begin your own use of the Story exercise.

On the stage, from the props I had in class and others she brought from home, Pamela created her stage picture of the outside of her childhood house, the kitchen, and her bedroom. She did this with a tree stump, which was her symbol of the syringa tree in her yard; an ironing board and an iron, which represented Salamina's kitchen domain; a pair of old brown lace-ups that were the symbol of Salamina's friend Zephyr, the black African gardener who lived next door; a wedding veil hung on the back wall that the child could play with when she talked about her dreams of marriage; and bedsheets hung over a door so that when she stood up in front of them, it looked like she was lying down in her bedroom. Pamela's costume was her grandmother's floor-length wedding dress and, tied on her back, a satchel that played as Salamina's newborn baby.

When Pamela was finished, she was embarrassed and extremely fearful that no one would understand her or have compassion for her story. Who wanted to see a white woman talk about the terror of apartheid? If you were white, you were guilty. The truth was her family had tried with everything in them, as some other white families did, too, to stop the carnage and the madness. Specifically, Pamela's father, who was a doctor, saw black patients in the same room as he did white patients when there were emergencies, and this caused tension and mistrust in his community. Eventually, Pamela, unable to bear the reality of apartheid, gave up her homeland before the system ended and fled to America, exiling herself from a country she loved because of the inequities she could not bear.

What I was startled by in Pamela's exercise was the idea of violence being witnessed through the innocence of a child's eyes. I was moved by the way the child kept trying to find fantasies and beauty in her imagination while the reality that surrounded her was so vicious, and I was moved by the child's immense struggle to understand the society whose extreme prejudices and ignorance did not make sense to her or to the family she was raised in. It dawned on me slowly as Pamela worked that this gifted actress had the potential for full and deep characterizations, that she could switch back and forth between them in a scintilla of a second, and that I had found the writer and the story that I wanted to tell as a director.

As Pamela finished working, her body was shaking and she was unable to look out at the class or at me. I was aware that the entire class had stood up and were in different states of emotion in response to Pamela's work. I said to her, "Look out and see your colleagues' reaction to your memory and to the extraordinary and creative commitment that you made." The Story exercise that Pamela accomplished set the bar high and began a profound change in the entire class's perspective on their own potential.

Since that night I have been fortunate to witness actors' courage in surpassing my own expectations of the Story exercise work. I have witnessed actors giving birth to themselves as actors and writers by empowering themselves not to wait for someone to give them something but rather to see themselves as having a gift to give. The actor's dilemma can be, "I must wait for someone to give me material so that I can excel." This infuriates me. I will not tolerate actors being victims because it is completely unnecessary and destructive. That's why I have been so insistent in blaming actors for their passivity, self-indulgence, and entitlement while they wait for someone to pick them up and carry them on their shoulders to exultation. *No! No! No! No!* If you're young, learn this now; if you're middle-aged, learn it now; and if you're old, and only have a few more days left, learn it now!

An actor is only as great as the parts they get to play. The Story exercise gives you a way of creating your own great parts. One of the truly educational and eye-opening aspects of the exercise is that you must play characters that are different from yourself and—maybe for the first time in your life—play young and old, male and female, different races and different psychologies. You must also learn to tell a story that is clear, and doing this makes you understand and respect a writer's words because, in this case, you are the writer. I believe that respect for a writer's text is enormously helped by being in the writer's shoes, at least one time in your life, and building a story from the ground up.

The night Pamela brought her memory to life for the class, she no longer had to wonder whether or not anyone understood or was moved by her story. After talking about the excellence of her work, I demanded that she write a full screenplay because I saw it as a film, but I was also aware of the possibility of doing it as a play. Pamela walked out of that class like a startled deer. Six weeks later she handed me a screenplay of *The Syringa Tree*. I read it immediately and realized afterward that I had to do it as a play, and told her, "Now go and write the play." Thank God she listened to me.

After I read the first draft of the play, I knew there was no turning back. I asked Pamela if she would agree to work on the play as a performance piece with me directing her. She agreed. The first day of rehearsal, she asked me where all the other actors were. She had written the script as if the parts would be played by different actors and she had anticipated playing her mother and, perhaps, herself as a child. When I made it clear to Pamela that there would be no other actors appearing in this room ever, she looked horrified as only Pamela can. She then blurted out, "You're insane!" I responded that she was probably quite correct and that she should just be quiet and say the first line.

Pamela and I met three to four times a week for a few hours and began to dissect the story scene by scene, character by character. I love the process of working with people to create plays and films, and my dear astrologer knew better than I where I should put my energy. But once I knew, I did what Stella Adler taught me: find out what you do well, and do it like Hercules.

We did four workshop productions of *The Syringa Tree*. I learned that one must always invite the most intelligent and compassionate people to workshops, for their comments can be profoundly helpful. Don't think that just because you have an interesting story to tell that you will necessarily be able to come up with a moving and successful telling of it the first, second, third, or even fourth time. You have to love what you're working on and keep at it until it pleases you *and* an audience. I think it's incredibly important to listen to comments from your audience.

One comment that helped me as a director was, "Make sure to keep the show primitive"; I knew then and there I had to cut every prop that was on the stage except for a real swing that hung from the imaginary tree (we hung the swing from a beam above the stage). I cut the props slowly, starting with the ironing board and moved through everything else that was on the stage, leaving Pamela and the swing. Pamela felt concerned about being so alone on the stage, stating that now she would look like a bad mime since she was going to have to mime everything she was doing in the play, as well as playing all twenty-six characters. Pamela finally bravely agreed to eliminate all props but the swing and continued working on each character's physical life and intentions. We eventually brought in an extraordinary Alexander teacher, Jean-Louis Rodrigue, who worked with Pam on accessing the natural reserve of energy in the body through breath, specifically by lowering the center of her breath from the upper chest to the pelvis and the back of the ribs. Pam used this method of breathing both before and during her performance—as a calming mechanism, but also to gain energy in extreme moments. Pam said, "It opened my body in a split second, and particularly toward the end of the year, after doing seven performances a week in New York, this was a saving grace." Jean-Louis also helped the morphing from character to character—not waiting to complete lines or gestures, but blending them into the next character to make the transitions split-second and seamless.

Throughout the process I never doubted, and this is rare for me, that *The Syringa Tree* was involving theater. I just wanted to make sure that Pamela and I didn't get in the way of delivering it as purely and power-fully as its potential allowed. We did Q & A after most performances dur-ing the two years we workshopped the play, I took people to lunch and picked their brains, and Pamela and I worked for hundreds of hours re-hearsing. Pamela's immersion and concentration were indefatigable.

Neither Pamela nor I asked for or received any money whatsoever until the fourth year of our work. So money was never the issue. And since neither of us knew what the comercial viability of the project would be, it never dawned on us that it would take our careers anywhere other than where they had been. We were fortunate to find a producer who be-lieved in the project, a smart and thoughtful man named Matt Salinger, who protected and shepherded the play for three years before bringing it to New York. As a producer, Matt was consistently creative and passion-ate, and without him *The Syringa Tree* could not have succeeded at the level it did.

The Syringa Tree opened Off-Broadway in 2001 and, to our astonish-ment, won the Obie for the Best Off-Broadway Play. Pamela also won the Drama Desk Award and the Outer Critics Circle Award for Best Solo Performance of the Year. Besides playing in New York, London, and in cities throughout the United States, the play has also toured Canada and Pamela performed it in full production for the arts cable network Trio. Her performance was captured live, and I was fortunate to be able to di-rect it for Trio and find a cinematic equivalent to her stirring stage per-formance. As I write this, Pamela is writing a novel for Random House based on her play. And there are plans afoot for a motion picture.

As an actor, it's vital for you to know that technically one of the com-mitments Pamela made when she did seven performances of *The Syringa Tree* every week for a year was to do two half-hour warm-up sessions for her voice every day. This was an absolute necessity for her vocal health, for she had to speak from the very top of her falsetto to create a childlike voice and dig deep down to her bass notes to play the men in the story. The warm-up exercise strengthened her vocal range, gave her full control of making choices to play twenty-six different voices, and kept her voice healthy and fresh for the entire run.

Pamela received hundreds of letters about *The Syringa Tree*. When you get an outpouring of the depth of feeling that these letters express, you feel grateful that you were able to be part of something that talked about man's inhumanity to man and the terrible price of this inhumanity and, more importantly, that love between people, no matter what anybody says, is stronger.

The Story exercise gives you a way of exploring your own life through specific memory and seeing what you can give to others and, perhaps, discover other abilities that lie dormant within you as you develop a memory into a performance piece. Your Story exercise may not evolve into a one-person show but could eventually turn out to be a play with many characters, or a film, a short story, or a novel. Or it may lead you in another creative direction. When one young woman in my class was asked to do the Story exercise and began witnessing the power and rawness of the other actors' work, she left class and didn't come back for two years. When she returned, the first work she signed up to do in class was her Story exercise, a memory of the crippling sexual abuse she had experienced as a child and her subsequent life filled with terror and mistrust. During her two-year absence, she began to paint in oil images that her imagination brought forward from this trauma, and she has turned out to be a first-rate painter who now has a career as a professional artist as well as an actress. She performed her Story exercise with dance, mime, and sounds in front of a series of her paintings. It was breathtaking.

One last Story exercise among many that were moving was performed by an actor whose father had committed suicide with a handgun in the front seat of his truck. The actor, a teenager at the time, was playing basketball with the neighbors. When he played basketball he always tried to emulate his older brother's technique, because he had the perfect shot. The way he moved into position, focused on the basket, and hurled the ball was coordinated with the words, "Bend, cock, shoot." When he came home, he passed the truck, and as he saw his father slumped in the front seat, the handgun in his lap, his head bleeding and blood on the seat behind it, he said to himself, "Bend, cock, shoot." The way the actor portrayed this was painful and shocking, yes, but also theatrical, creative, and brave. This was a young man who carried tremendous grief and rage that he turned into art. He is now in New York, performing in his first Broadway play. Courage pays off.

These Story exercises were three personal tragedies for the actors; what followed was freedom and joy. If you're not in a class where this kind of work is done and you're interested in doing it, form your own group or just get a partner you trust, or if you're one of those brave souls who can work alone, you can do it on your own. Start with the Release exercise, allow a memory or a string of memories to come forward, and fill them in with specific sensory detail. If you're working with a partner, you and your partner will tell your stories to each other, with all their sensory details, and then repeat the other's story back to them. If you're working alone, tell the story into a tape recorder and then play it back. However you're working, the next step is to get it on its feet, trying out different characters vocally and physically. It is also helpful to videotape or audiotape your work, and then, as many of my students have done, have the story transcribed so that you have a script to work from.

Take the Story exercise and see what doors it opens for you. It can become a great gift if you commit to it with the full force of your ability.

26

CONFIDENCE VERSUS ARROGANCE
AND THE WORK ETHIC

There was a very wealthy man who wanted desperately to be a professional actor. After years of studying and auditioning and never getting a part, he became so frustrated that he decided to use his money to produce and star in *Hamlet* on Broadway, hiring a first-rate director and surrounding himself with an all-star cast. He even went so far as to put his name above the title—not "Seymour David in *Hamlet*" but "Seymour David *Is Hamlet*." He took out full-page ads in the *New York Times* and created so much publicity that all the gliteratti and Shakespeare aficionados came to opening night.

The audience was respectfully quiet as Mr. David began his first soliloquy, "O that this too too solid flesh would melt, thaw and resolve itself into a dew." But when it became clear that Mr. David had no clue what he was talking about and that he was swaying back and forth for no apparent reason as he spoke, the audience became restless. Soon Mr. David could not help but hear a kind of buzz sweeping through the theater. He began to shout the poetry. Then the catcalls erupted: "Boo! Boo! Get off the stage!" Finally his solid flesh did begin to melt. He became so enraged that he stopped speaking, walked downstage center, and yelled at the audience, "Listen! I didn't write this shit!"

You may have guessed by now that this is not a true story, although I know it's been close to the truth. I call Mr. David's attitude unhealthy arrogance. It's unhealthy arrogance because it has no awareness of limitations.

You have to know what your strengths are as an actor but you also have to know your weaknesses. That's self-knowledge. Confidence comes from self-knowledge combined with the ability to stand behind your choices as an actor when you believe in them, fight creatively for choices that you know illuminate the play or film, even if the director disagrees with you. Believe in yourself even in tough times when your career isn't on an upswing. This doesn't refute my belief that it is important to be cooperative and collegial with your director and fellow actors, but sometimes you do have to stand alone to fight for what you know is right and go as far as you can without turning people into enemies. You may or may not get exactly what you want but if you don't get it, your clarity and passion may influence the director's interpretation in a way that benefits all parties and, of course, the text that you're playing.

A marvelous example of confidence, perhaps one might even say of healthy arrogance, is when during his cubist period Pablo Picasso painted Gertrude Stein. When the painting was revealed to a group of friends, including Ms. Stein, the reaction was utter silence. Finally someone had the courage to express an opinion. "But Pablo," he said, "it doesn't look like Gertrude." And there was another pause. Finally Picasso said calmly, "It will." That's true confidence!

At the end of Elia Kazan's wonderful autobiography, *A Life,* he wrote: "Effort is all." On one level, in terms of acting technique, this means committing yourself diligently to your study and to the choices you make in a part. But Kazan took it further: "Effort is all" in terms of living itself. This means committing ourselves diligently to the work of knowing ourselves, warts and all, facing our terrors, our anger, our biases, our lack of education in certain areas, because if we do we become more honest people and, therefore, better artists.

Real growing artists are excited by and open to new ideas. For example, I've been lucky enough to work with the gifted French actress Juliette Binoche. We worked together in a class in Verbier, Switzerland, and explored a danced and spoken version of August Strindberg's great one-act play *Miss Julie*. Juliette created a particular kind of movement that was seductive, violent, repressed, and shameless. We also worked on songs, because Juliette loves to sing. As we worked, I kept having a vision in my mind's eye of Juliette on a stage, facing a live audience with her arms spread wide open, singing her heart out. When I told her this, she said, "I would love to do that, but first I must study and improve." And this was after she had already won an Oscar for her work in *The English Patient*. Shortly after our workshop, she called me from Paris to tell me that she had been called about starring in a film about the great legendary French singer Edith Piaf. A good actor never stops growing.

My greatest strength as a young actor was my ability and my desire to have someone help me, teachers and therapists. And that's self-knowledge: to admit to yourself, "I have too much fear or too much anger" or "I'm too sensitive to criticism" or "I have passivity problems—I don't propel myself forward in ways I know I need to" or "I'm passive-aggressive" (meaning I control people not by being assertive but by playing victim) or "I blame other people for things I'm actually responsible for." Sometimes a teacher or a friend or a director will tell you a truth and you've got to know it's the truth, you've got to admit it, even if it's painful.

The reason self-knowledge is so vital is that once you admit the truth about your weaknesses, you can change them. Through forty years as an actor, teacher, and director I've seen countless people deny their weaknesses and be hurt by that denial. I've heard all the excuses: "It's not me, it's the business. I just didn't get the luck." But when I look at my classes and my colleagues, I realize that the people who are fulfilling their creative goals are the people who have worked at it. They may have had speech impediments or problems with being emotionally open or being physically graceful, so they found help to overcome these problems, which made all the difference in their careers. It wasn't easy for them to do it but they did it anyway.

In the class that I taught today, a young actor said in angst and frustration, "Why didn't I understand the real objective of the scene when I've been working on it for two weeks?" He also said to me, "I will admit to you that this is the hardest I've ever worked on any material in my life, and last night as I fell asleep I suddenly understood the play." So I said to the actor, "How can you expect yourself to be good at analyzing and then understanding a text when you do it so rarely and so rarely commit to all the tools at your disposal?" The actor started to weep. He wept because he was relieved that his work on this scene was so good, and he wept because he was ashamed of his own laziness.

In the same class, a young woman from Eastern Europe also told me that this was the first time she'd ever worked with such commitment. She also began to weep, because, as she explained, at that moment she understood that in her life up to then, to her work was something she only did to avoid a beating from her father. She related how in all of her acting, she never did more than learn the lines and have a general point of view about the emotional circumstances. Sometimes, she said, that was enough, but that the rich experience she had in her scene work today made her realize that her lack of a work ethic had to do with defying her father.

I told her one of the most important ideas in pursuing an acting career is being able to work for your own excellence because *you* want to. And when she saw that she was stopping herself from being as successful as her talent would allow her to be, she realized that she had been trapped in a belief system, responding to traumas from her past as if they were happening in the present. She had spent too many years in her life being reactive to a difficult childhood and maintaining the same defiance toward her father as if she still lived with him. In defying her father, she won as a child, but as she painfully realized, she was losing as an adult. Survival skills that were effective in childhood can become prisons in adulthood if you don't work to separate internally from the negative past.

There was a young actress in my class who was in love with the part of Juliet in *Romeo and Juliet*. Whenever she wasn't working professionally, she was in my class doing every monologue and scene Juliet has in the play. She went to a costume company and created Juliet's wardrobe, brought her own music, directed the actors who played opposite her, and grew in the part to such a degree that when she finally got an audition for a production of it, not only did she get the part but the casting director said she blew every other actress off the stage. No wonder—doing her daily homework and class work she came into the audition with a reading so alive it was almost performance level.

Self-knowledge is important for every human being. But as an actor, it has a peculiar relationship to your professional life because *you are your instrument*. What you can play is limited by your personal limitations and your willingness or your unwillingness to work in areas that are uncomfortable but necessary for taking the next step in your career. Again, I'm talking about technical and personal limitations. As an actor, you're always out there in the marketplace—forever. How you behave day to day can influence your career as much as what you can deliver on the stage, movie screen, or television screen. If you can play a certain kind of part very well and one movie or television series becomes a huge hit, you can become a star without any self-knowledge. Now, that's what I call frightening. It's frightening because if you have personal problems but no motivation to solve them because you can hide behind your success, then your personal problems can ruin your career and devour your life.

I come from the point of view that your life is more than your career. I'm passionate about that idea, because actors particularly are compared, judged, overpraised, underpraised, and those things in themselves can make your life unstable. But if you have self-knowledge, you have what I call inner structure as a human being: you know, "I always have human value regardless of how my talent is judged." For fifteen years Edward Albee was out of fashion in the Broadway theater. After he won the 2001 Tony Award for Best Play for *The Goat,* he was asked, "How did it feel to be out of fashion?" Albee replied, "I didn't stop writing because you didn't like it." In fact, Albee wrote nonstop during all those years because his craft fascinated him and *he was motivated by something inside himself.*

John Huston gave his daughter, Anjelica Huston, the leading part in his film *A Walk with Love and Death* when she was eighteen years old, and she and the film got the worst reviews that you can possibly imagine. They actually said that her performance gave nepotism a bad name. She didn't work professionally for seven years. She studied intensively with the late Peggy Feury, then began acting in films again. She found the novel *Prizzi's Honor,* got Jack Nicholson to star and John Huston to direct, and put them together so that she could play Maerose Prizzi, the manipulative, ruthless daughter of a mobster. Her performance was so vivid that it propelled her to an Oscar and to the top of her profession. Her performance in *The Grifters* is sensational and riveting, a searing portrait of sociopathology that is just startling. Anjelica Huston comes from cinematic royalty and she also came from unbelievable failure and humiliation of the most public kind. But Ms. Huston embodies self-knowledge and the work ethic. She has proved herself a true artist; she was able to garner the strength to persevere and to give the gift of her talent to all of us.

I tell my students that they must accept the reality of being a professional actor, the reality that "I will be criticized both negatively and positively, and I can't let either of those stop me from what I perceive to be my potential." And I tell them that art, like life, is about ascension. If you can't tolerate looking at your own weaknesses as well as your strengths, you will not reach your potential or even have an idea of what your potential can be. And if you overreact to criticism, you are putting your career completely in the hands of others. This must not happen. I myself have gone through tremendous ups and downs in my career but finally I truly understand that each of us has a voice that wants to be heard and that we ourselves have to listen to. Part of listening to it in a way that really propels you forward is being scrupulously honest about where you are in your ascension as an actor. I truly believe that actors never have to stop growing and augmenting their talent. Artists must try to die in ascension.

As you gain experience, if you are honest with yourself, you will be able to gauge your own progress in reaching your goals in each performance and in each year that you live. You will come to understand in a profound way what Stella Adler meant when she said, "Actors must have the soul of a rose and the hide of a rhinoceros." You must continue to let the rose become more sensitive; you must also increase the thickness of the hide. Translate criticism for yourself; see if it's apt. If it is, don't deny it, learn from it. If it's not, move on.

27

ON BEING COOL: A RANT

As I near the end of this book, I'd like to take two pages to do a very personal rant.

We live in a world where a lot of people—and particularly young actors and actresses—like to be seen as "cool." I hate that word. I can't imagine anything more profoundly stupid than wanting to be seen as cool. The very meaning of the word suggests to me a lack of vibrancy, a sense of being cut off. *Cool* denies the frailties of living life and the inevitable loss of everything that is dear to us; it leaches the passion from life.

The virus of coolness that I observe in some young actors and actresses makes them appear shallow, adolescent, and self-centered, both in real life and in performance. For these people it becomes all about externals, that is, how I look, how I come off to other people, and a confusion that indifference somehow shows strength.

Yes, I know someone reading this is going to say, "But James Dean was cool," "Marlon Brando was cool," "Audrey Hepburn was cool," and

"Johnny Depp is cool!" But they simply were and are *not*! The great icons of the past were passionate, sophisticated, deeply wounded, brave, and idiosyncratic, and they blasted their way into the audience consciousness. And Johnny Depp, despite his playfulness and ease, is one of the most serious, dedicated, and imaginative actors working today.

River Phoenix, God rest his soul, in Rob Reiner's beautiful film *Stand by Me* revealed the anguish of childhood so movingly and memorably that we held our breath as we watched him. That little boy was not cool, he was almost unbearably human, and the sad fact that he got involved in the wrong lifestyle, ran from his inner feelings that were obviously so intense and painful to him, that he ended his life on a sidewalk, his body filled with drugs, is his testament to the tragedy of trying to be cool.

For fuck's sake, be hot! Be mad! Be witty! Be loving! Be heartfelt! Be sunny! Be fiercely cold! But, Jesus, don't be cool!

28

Breaking In and Breaking Out:
How I Learned Not to Be
a Demented Puppy

I arrived in New York at eighteen years old, a demented puppy, eager for approval, dreaming of Broadway stardom, and terrified of everything.

I had reason to be terrified. The summer before I had taken a musical-theater class at UCLA and had been told by the teacher that I had the worst singing voice he had ever heard. My fear of negative judgment translated into muscular tension, which only compounded the problem. I also had a fear of revealing who I was emotionally. But even those things didn't stop my hungry ambition. I enrolled at AMDA (American Musical and Dramatic Theater of America) and studied eight hours a day, five days a week. I worked so diligently on improving my singing voice that I got the first professional job I auditioned for, to be a member of a summer stock company.

I was in ten plays that summer, singing in the chorus and playing small roles. After three months of performing I was so on fire to act professionally that I quit AMDA and didn't go back for the second year of the program. Instead, I wrangled myself a meeting with a very good agent,

Brett Adams. The meeting lasted all of five minutes. "You don't have enough experience," he said. "Get some, and when you do, come back and see me." I marched right out to the secretary and told her that he wanted to hear me sing, and she, poor soul, set up the appointment. The following week I showed up with my accompanist and Brett was standing at the doorway with folded arms and an attitude. He said, "I hear I want to hear you sing," and I said in my best nineteen-year-old Mickey Rooney impression, "Gee, Brett, give me a chance. If you don't like the first song, I'll walk right out of your office." He smiled in a paternal way that said, "You've got guts, kid, but this is probably hopeless," then he told me to go into his office. I did two songs for him with wild enthusiasm and that desperate need you'll understand if you have to be in the theater or die. When I finished, Brett smiled, and said, "You're lucky you're talented," and set me up for an audition.

I got a job in a production of *South Pacific,* directed by Joe Layton. I think because I looked a little bit like Joe and because my commitment was so passionate, he liked me, and one year after I did *South Pacific* for him and *West Side Story* for Jerome Robbins, Joe cast me in the Broadway musical *Drat! The Cat!* starring Elliott Gould and Lesley Ann Warren. I was in the chorus and I was Elliott Gould's understudy. Even though I was offered a bigger part in the Broadway comedy *The Impossible Years,* there was nothing that could stop me from accepting the job from Joe, because musical theater was my dream.

Joe and the producer, Jerry Adler, asked me to help raise money for *Drat!* by doing backers' auditions, which meant that two other actors and I sang the entire score for a lot of rich people at the Plaza Hotel. I was working as a telephone operator for an answering service called Actor Phone. I'm sure when actors called to find out whether or not they got a message about an audition, they were surprised to hear me rehearsing the lyrics to "She Touched Me," a beautiful song that Elliott Gould sang in the show and that Barbra Streisand, Elliott's wife at the time, made famous.

When you've dreamed your whole life about appearing in a Broadway musical, to actually be in rehearsal for one with a top-flight director and a superb cast of new young performers and old-timers feels like a kind of heaven. Learning a new musical score and dance steps created for you alongside people who were as excited to be there as I was made me feel completely immersed in the world that I had admired from afar for so long. When I ran up to Elliott like the overgrown demented puppy I was to say how thrilled I was to be his understudy, he gently smashed me into reality by saying, "Don't be so thrilled, kid. I saw the backers' audition. You're good and I hope you never go on." It was a compliment but it was also a wake-up call to stop being so naïve. I was naïve in another sense, too: *Drat! The Cat!* closed in two weeks, while the comedy *The Impossible Years* ran for two years—so much for my good business sense—but I wouldn't have made a different choice, even though at the time I wished I had had the income.

After *Drat! The Cat!* closed, I went back to working at Actor Phone, studying my craft and auditioning. Occasionally, to work out material in front of an audience, I sang at Bud Freedman's The Improvisation, the famous comedy club where Richard Pryor, Robert Klein, Lily Tomlin, Bette Midler, Rodney Dangerfield, and a host of others honed their skills nightly. None of us got paid.

One particular night I was given the 11:00 P.M. spot. The club was sold out, packed to the walls. I was now twenty-one years old, a terrified, shitting, pissing, demented puppy, waiting to go on to sing my four songs in front of that most dangerous Improv audience, who could turn you into dog meat in one second.

My first song was from a musical with a score by Bob Merrill based on Eugene O'Neill's play *Ah, Wilderness.* It was called *Take Me Along* and it had starred the amazing Jackie Gleason and Robert Morse (another idol of mine who later became my acting partner in *So Long, 174th Street,* another of my Broadway musical-theater dreams, a bomb but I loved it). The song I sang that night at the Improv, "My Little Green Snake," was about a young man having alcoholic hallucinations during his first hangover. You know, sometimes there's a thing called divine intervention, and it occurred to me during the tense moments before I went onstage that the character in the song was *looking* for his little green snake. It must have been blind terror that after they introduced me I walked through the audience at the Improv and, to my own surprise, began looking for my snake under all the tables, something I had never done or thought about doing in rehearsing the song.

I asked people in the audience to get up and look under their seats, I moved chairs, all the while George Taros, my accompanist, playing my entrance music as I improvised this drunken search. Finally I walked up to the microphone and with all ten-billion watts of energy pouring out of every cell of my body, I asked the audience quite earnestly and needfully, "Did you see my green snake?" Well, the house came down; I mean the kind of roar you only dream about. The song was alive! "Last night I tasted that giggly water, oh Mama, Mama, I shouldn't have oughta," and on and on through that bluesy, jazzy desperate search for my imaginary friend. I did what I had longed to do my entire short life: I knocked them out, I slayed them, I stopped the show. I don't think I ever have or ever will experience that kind of electricity through my body again.

After the applause died down, I went on to my second song, a ballad called "Once in a Lifetime" by Anthony Newley and Leslie Bricusse, and the audience went bananas. Why were they responding like this? I wondered. What did I do? A hush fell over the room and a very surprised performer began his third number, "Will She Like Me?" The song asks the question again and again, and at the end of the song, I extended the last word, which was *me*. As I held the note for a long time, George the Greek began the vamp underneath the note for the next song in the medley, which was a snappy uptune, "She Loves Me." I guess after hearing this poor kid begging for someone to love him, for me to turn on a dime and sing with complete confidence "She loves me" was highly comic, and once again the audience's bell went off and they were roaring, clapping, and laughing. I got to the end of the song, which was very intense—"I'd like to scrawl on every wall I see—she loves me!"—and I began to literally write in the air on an imaginary wall "She loves me" ending with a big physical exclamation point! I had learned the idea of physicalizing the song in Charles Nelson Reilly's wonderful class at HB Studios, the home of Uta Hagen and Herbert Berghof. I don't want to overstate this but the response at the end of the performance was atomic.

The real truth of that experience was that I shared everything I was feeling in my life in those songs. In a sense, I wrote them; they were that personal to me. I was always a hard worker even though sometimes, because of emotional problems and laziness and wanting to be the victim my parents had raised, I would shoot myself in the foot by giving up. But music always called me, language always called me, and movement always called me back to life.

I had a terrible problem as a performer: being a demented puppy, I wanted the audience to love me but when they did I always felt scared I couldn't do it again. I was connected to my creativity but I was also connected to self-destructive patterns that I had learned in childhood. If I succeeded in my career I had to pay myself back by failing because failing was my way of having a family. In other words, if I was successful I would look strong, independent, and solid; I didn't want to look that way consistently because, irrationally, I felt I needed someone to take care of me and I didn't believe people took care of you if you were strong.

I remember the most attention I got as a child was when I was in either extreme physical or deep emotional pain. I had to outdo my parents and brother in suffering in order to get my parents to realize I was there. The only other time they knew I was there was when they saw me as an object of desire, and although I don't think my parents were conscious of this, there were control issues, statements, and sexual innuendoes that were frightening and, eventually, for a long time, crippling. I emerged from my parents' household feeling a tremendous sense of shame about my body. The ignited performance at the Improv was the shucking off of that shame—for that night—which is why I believe it was so explosive.

A few months later, walking in the theater district, I ran into Jerry Adler, who had produced *Drat! The Cat!* Jerry liked me and my work, and said, "You've got to come over and audition for Mike's [meaning Mike Nichols's] new musical." It was *The Apple Tree,* with a book by Jules Feiffer and a score by Jerry Bock and Sheldon Harnick, who had also written the scores for *Fiddler on the Roof* and *She Loves Me. The Apple Tree* was going to star the great Barbara Harris, Alan Alda, and Larry Blyden. Well, once again I became like a demented puppy dog, ran to my accompanist, George. George looked exactly like Omar Sharif and bit his fingernails down to the quick, but boy could he play piano, and when he accompanied me did I soar!

The problem was that on the day of the audition I realized that Jerry had not told me what theater the auditions were being held in. George and I literally went to every Broadway theater except, of course, the one in which Mike Nichols was waiting for me. It was 100 degrees, I had on a suit with a vest and tie, I was sweating profusely, and I was late. As George and I approached the Mark Hellinger Theater (now a church, God help us!), George revealed to me that because it was so late he had to leave for therapy. When you arrive at an audition without your pianist and your pianist has all the arrangements in his head (*big mistake*), you have to settle for the pianist that the production has provided. I could not do any of the special material I'd planned on doing with George and decided instead to sing "On a Clear Day You Can See Forever" (not on this particular day, however).

The Mark Hellinger was a huge theater and I raced in, sweat pouring down my face, apologizing that I was late and that my accompanist had to see his analyst. Mike Nichols, the composers, and all the producers stared at me impatiently while I rummaged through piles of sheet music to make my disastrous musical choice. I walked shakily to the edge of the stage, peered down into the pit, and gave the pianist the sheet music and asked him to give me an arpeggio as an introduction. I walked to the center of the stage pretending to be confident, nodded my head to give the signal for the pianist to begin, which he did. I was extremely anxious because I was late and they were waiting. I didn't have my regular accompanist who could help me out if I had any musical complications. I was so nervous that I became completely deaf and couldn't decipher the note on which I was supposed to start the song. So I tried to "fake it" (*wrong*). I started "On a Clear Day" eight times, by which time Mike Nichols and the crew were laughing hysterically and Mike Nichols said, "Thanks so much for coming in today, Larry. You're not really right for *The Apple Tree* but you've certainly made an impression." That was followed by a solid month of self-hate and depression on my part.

I remained that demented puppy and literally got a kind of phobia about auditioning because I idealized the Broadway theater and the people in it I admired. I got a paying job that lasted for two years appearing at a very sophisticated cabaret, Upstairs at the Downstairs, singing and doing political satire alongside Lily Tomlin and Madeline Kahn. Every now and then I did an audition for a Broadway show but, despite my honing my comic timing and my singing skills at the Upstairs at the Downstairs and occasional jobs in regional theater, and going to therapy, I continued to feel intimidated and I sabotaged myself at these auditions.

On my twenty-ninth birthday, my brother sent me a birthday card wishing me a happy twenty-ninth, which completely freaked me out because I thought, *I have been alive twenty-nine years and have not been on Broadway since I was twenty-one! Why am I holding myself back?* A friend of mine had won a Tony Award that year and I felt jealous and worthless, so I made a pact with myself that I would be back on Broadway that year no matter what. I got an audition for Michael Bennett and Neil Simon for *God's Favorite,* Simon's comic telling of the story of Job. This may not sound like the greatest idea for a comedy but Charles Nelson Reilly and Vincent Gardenia were hilarious playing Job and God's messenger.

The morning of my audition for Neil Simon and Michael Bennett for *God's Favorite,* I also had an audition as a French cook for Dustin Hoffman and Murray Schisgal for Schisgal's play *All Over Town.* Schisgal was the brilliant writer of one of my favorite comedies, *Luv,* about three highly neurotic New Yorkers who connive and betray each other to epic degrees, and the whole gut-busting comedy takes place on the Brooklyn Bridge. If you haven't read it and you're neurotic, go out and buy the script immediately, you will have the best time of your life reading it. When I went to my dialect coach at 8:00 A.M. to prepare my French accent for *All Over Town,* my coach said, "You better have a drink and calm down because my entire apartment is vibrating." She gave me a glass of brandy.

I was having money problems at the time and it made me feel like a pauper. To get over that feeling, I did all my private script analysis for my audition for *God's Favorite* sitting in the foyer of the elegant Plaza Hotel. Sitting there made me feel upper-crust, good enough to be on Broadway. I walked into the Eugene O'Neill Theater for my audition at 11:00 A.M. still vibrating but with one brandy under my belt. I placed the two casting directors exactly where I wanted them on the stage and gave a focused and terrific audition for the role of Ben, a twenty-year-old hysteric who constantly seemed like he wanted to do nasty things to his twin sister while at the same time being Job's greatest son. At the end of the audition, much to my surprise, I saw both Neil Simon and Michael Bennett smiling widely and walking toward me with their hands extended, congratulating me on my audition. I ran out of the theater and down Broadway yelling at the top of my lungs, "They loved me, they loved me, they loved me, they loved me!" Talk about a desperate demented puppy.

I went directly to Dustin Hoffman's offices and said in my lousy French accent, " 'Allo, Dusteen, ow r u?" Dustin's reply was, "Your French accent sucks," and I said, continuing in my lousy French accent, "Zat duz not mattur, Dusteen, bicauz I am goi-ing to be in Nieel Simon's nu play, so it duz not mattur ow dis audition goes." Dustin laughed and Murray Schisgal asked me where I got my shoes.

When the company managers called to offer me the job in *God's Favorite* they said to my agent, "Don't even try to negotiate. There are no negotiations. Nobody turns down a Neil Simon play." Of course they were right. I was paid poorly but still being a desperate child, I couldn't have cared less—and, anyway, they told me I could have my dressing room painted in whatever color I liked. *My dressing room on Broadway painted whatever color I liked! Yellow, like the sun that brought me my greatest dreams!* Opening night as I stood looking out of the third-story window of my yellow dressing room, contemplating suicide, I thought to myself, *They can't make me go on if I'm dead.*

When you are an adult child, people's judgments weigh heavily. Added to that, the opening night of *God's Favorite* had a guest list that included Robert Redford, Shirley MacLaine, Lena Horne, and too many celebrities to remember, plus two hundred critics. I walked down the stairs to the stage in my fire-engine red fright wig to meet Laura Esterman, who played my twin sister and who was dressed to look exactly like me, wig and all. We did our preparation, which I think was holding hands and jumping up and down, and the curtain went up and I ran onstage to announce to my father that the fire alarm had gone off in another part of our Long Island mansion.

The most astounding part of that opening performance was that when I walked out onto that stage, my heart rate actually slowed down. This was because I was in the imaginary circumstances of *God's Favorite*, living in a mansion on Long Island to help my father and to be there whenever he needed me. One of my choices in playing the part of Ben was to stay glued to my father so that whenever he looked my way he could see that I was ready to do his bidding. The only time I looked away from my father was to catch a glimpse of my sister's breasts or ass. I knew who I was, where I was, who my father was to me, and I knew what I wanted. Technique works.

That night, after the performance, we were invited to a dinner party by Mike Nichols at Katja, a very ritzy restaurant at Sixtieth and Third Avenue. When I walked through the door, Mike Nichols was standing there. He extended his hand, and said very warmly, "You were wonderful tonight. Very truthful." *No, no, no, oh man, my God, Mike Nichols! "You were wonderful tonight. Very truthful." I did have parents! Not the twisted, suburban parents I was born with but the dazzling, golden Broadway theater parents I had so longed for!*

Down, puppy!

In my performing life I think I have done some very good work; I certainly know I have done some bad work, when I didn't commit, when I wasn't present, when I didn't make it personal to myself by investigating the material and making it mine, but that night at the Improv and in *God's Favorite,* I did all my work to a fare-thee-well. I tell you this not to brag or show off but rather to tell you once again that making specific choices that excite you, trusting yourself in the moment of performance, and making a supreme effort to not let your fear stop you is the key to being successful and to finally becoming generous in your work.

I have been privileged to work several times with the great choreographer Twyla Tharp. I was privy to a moment in an empty rehearsal studio when Twyla brought her boom box into the middle of the room, put on some rock-and-roll music and improvised for an hour, letting her feet follow impulses from the music and from her own personal choreographic muse. Her intense concentration was amazing to watch. I could see the music pouring into her body and producing choreographic patterns that had her unique stamp on them. It was a great example of artistic trust—trust of herself—no judgment, no obstacle, just music and physical impulses wild and free. I know that many young choreographers in the last few decades have gotten a multitude of ideas about movement from Twyla because she believed that the body could do almost anything and actually demanded it. I think Twyla drew her inspiration from many sources—Hollywood film musicals, George Balanchine, Martha Graham, and Jerome Robbins as well as a number of great composers both classical and contemporary. She never stops looking for new ways to respond to music and to express feelings and ideas through the human body.

The need to create art comes from something deep inside a person and is related to the desire to be close to God. We write, we compose, we paint, we act, we sing, we create beautiful buildings; we discover life-saving miracle drugs because we want to celebrate the miracle of being alive. We create to live, and don't think for one second I am being an elitist about only the creative arts; I know that parents who raise their children well are deeply creative, that the hundreds of hours given freely to stimulate love, safety, and a sense of a child's own identity have contributed something that moves on into the world and gives strength to the fabric of life. I also know that people can be creative in all professions and everyone who celebrates and supports the miracle of being alive is creative.

I had one more disastrous audition for Mike Nichols for a musical he did out of town with Tommy Tune that folded and never came to Broadway. I was asked to audition for this show based on the work I was doing at the time in *The Robber Bridegroom*. By that time, I had overcome my intimidation of Broadway and the people who inhabited it. But again, not on the day of that audition. I was doing eight shows a week, I was exhausted, and I was going through an emotional crisis and I let all of it distract me in my audition instead of doing my work. And so the saga of succeeding and failing in front of Mike Nichols continued my whole acting life, culminating ironically in Nichols and his wife, Diane Sawyer, becoming the patron saints for my directorial debut in New York with *The Syringa Tree*. Nichols, who saw the play after it opened, gave us a great quote for publicity and Diane Sawyer wrote in all her Christmas cards, "If you see one play this year, make it *The Syringa Tree.*"

Mike Nichols was a symbol of success for me and my desire for his approval epitomized the need I had for validation outside of myself. This desire stood in the way of my independent creative process during the first twenty years of my career. Sometimes I succeeded anyway, as I did when I performed in *West Side Story* and *Drat! The Cat!* at twenty-one and in *God's Favorite* at twenty-nine and that night at the Improv when my desire to create was stronger than my intense need for outside validation and I was, therefore, able to honor the material and focus my fear into my objective—to find that little green snake. I didn't understand what made it work that night. I didn't know why sometimes it was like magic and sometimes it just wasn't there. I had no idea that my deep need for external validation was robbing me of my integrity and of building genuine self-respect. I've said several times in this book that none of this stopped my hunger to be good at what I do and to succeed in the real world. So throughout all of this, I kept studying, I continued in therapy with good therapists, and I committed myself to learning. And of course I am still learning, even as I write this book. In fulfilling my duties as a teacher and in directing *The Syringa Tree,* I finally became an adult with the knowledge that I have something artistic to give back to the world, and in learning that, I ceased to be a desperate, dependent, demented puppy and recognized that I was an actual independent adult and mature artistic citizen. The beautiful irony is that when I had stopped looking for Mike Nichols's approval, and wasn't even expecting it, I got it.

The last idea I want to leave you with is that it is an honor to be an actor. It is also joyous, educational, challenging, and something that can be your life's work. If you feel a deep calling, don't let anything or anyone, including yourself, stop you from giving the gift. Flee forward, actors!

Essential Questions for Working on a Part

1. What does the scene tell me about who my character is: their age, physical condition, or any other defining details, including socio-economic class, that is vital for the scene to work?
2. What literally happens to my character in the scene?
3. Why is my character in this particular scene? What information or events would be missing if I weren't in it?
4. What does my character actually do in the scene?
5. At the beginning of the scene, what's my character's point of view? Hostile? Loving? Friendly? Competitive? Supportive? Humorous?
6. How and why does it change?
7. What do I want (what's my objective)?
8. How high are the stakes?
9. What's standing between me and what I want (what's my obstacle)?
10. What does my character do to try to overcome it (what are my intentions)?

11. What inner imagery do I have to create?

12. What emotional triggers do I need?

13. What are my specific emotional relationships to all persons, places, objects, and events in the script?

14. How do my relationships change emotionally to the other characters within scenes and from scene to scene?

15. What personalizations or "as ifs" do I need to create for these persons, places, objects, and events? (Remember: sometimes the specifics of the script stir you emotionally every time you work on the material so that you don't need personalizations and "as ifs.")

16. What physical choices do I need to make? Does the character have any specific impediments? A specific walk or carriage? A habitual gesture or a gesture at a specific moment? What physical business can I create to illuminate the character and the text?

17. What is my character's back story? (Remember: be specific and detailed, and if you create a back story, make sure it triggers you emotionally, not just intellectually.)

18. Can I do an animal exercise to help me with my interpretation of the character?

19. What piece of music would you pick to symbolize the character? (Listening to the music can be used as part of your preparation. It can be especially helpful as you explore movement for the character.)

20. How does the location where the scene takes place influence my character's behavior?

21. What are the sensory realities of the scene and what preparations can I do to bring them to life?

22. What is the moment before each scene?

23. What accent and vocal choices do I need?

24. What size should my performance be for the medium that I'm working in?

A Case Study: *Lobby Hero*

PART I: THE SCENE

The following case study will show you how two actors applied the tools and techniques I've given you to prepare a scene for my class.

The first section is the full text of a scene from Kenneth Lonergan's play *Lobby Hero*. The play takes place entirely in the spacious lobby of an apartment building in New York City. The protagonists are Dawn, a young policewoman, and Jeff, a security guard in his late twenties. It's a funny and touching play about personal ethics and the price you pay to stand up for your own ideals when everything is going against you.

In the second section, two excellent actors from my Tuesday night class (Aaron MacPherson and Amy Pietz) and I analyze the work they did on this scene. In order to understand our discussion, of course, you have to read the scene first. And if you want to get the absolute most out of my interview with Aaron and Amy, read the entire play and work out your own acting choices before you read the interview. How do their choices differ from yours? See if their process stimulates you to go further in making choices that ignite you to more interesting behavior.

LOBBY HERO Act I, Scene 2

JEFF: How you doin'?
DAWN: Good.
JEFF: Busy night?
DAWN: Not so busy.
JEFF: Things have really been hoppin' around here, I gotta tell you.
DAWN: Oh yeah?
JEFF: Oh my God, I haven't had a minute to sit down. People coming *in* the lobby, people goin' *out* of the lobby. Elevator goin' up, elevator goin' down. *Thoughts* flyin' in and out of my head: It's been crazy.
DAWN: Maybe you better just slow it down.
JEFF: (*Gesturing to the busy lobby around him*) How can I?
DAWN: I don't know.
JEFF: Hey, can I ask you something, Officer?
DAWN: Yeah?
JEFF: Do you know why the New York City cops changed from the light blue shirts to the dark blue shirts recently? Like a couple of years ago?
DAWN: No, why?
JEFF: No—I'm not sayin' like, "Do you know," and then like I tell you the *answer*. I'm really asking, 'cause I thought you might know.
DAWN: Oh. No. I don't.
JEFF: But remember how a long time ago, like when we were kids, the police uniforms used to be all dark blue? And then around the 1980s I guess, they switched to the dark blue pants and a light blue shirt? And then recently they switched 'em back to the dark blue pants and a dark blue shirt again? What *I* always wondered was, did they throw out all the old dark blue pants when they did that? Or did they just throw out the light blue shirts and then get dark blue shirts that matched the old dark blue pants, so they wouldn't

have to buy all new pants? Because that would be quite a
savings.

DAWN: I have no idea.

JEFF: If you think about it, you could be wearing pants right now
that were being worn by some lady cop in 1975, if you think
about it. Except I guess the women police officers didn't
wear pants back in 1975. I don't mean they didn't wear
pants, like they were walkin' around in their underwear. I
just mean I think they were still wearin' skirts back then,
weren't they? I know I'm blathering, I'm just completely in
love with you—can I just say that?

DAWN: OK, take it easy.

JEFF: No, I am, man: I seen you go by a lot over the last few
weeks and I just think you are *it,* man; I'd do anything if you
would just give me the time of *day.*

DAWN: OK—

JEFF: And it's not just because I'm intrigued by the feminine
mystique of the female cop—

DAWN: All right—

JEFF: And I don't mean any disrespect—

DAWN: Oh of course not.

JEFF: Your generation of lady cops are like *pioneers* as far as I'm
concerned. I think you guys are *great.* But I also happen to
find most of you extremely sexy, OK?

DAWN: Get outta here.

JEFF: How long have you been a cop?

DAWN: I don't know. How long you been a doorman?

(*Pause*)

JEFF: No, I'm not a doorman. I'm a security officer.

DAWN: Congratulations. Now how about givin' me a break.

JEFF: Sure. Fine. (*Pause*) Givin' the cop a break. (*Pause*) I guess it's
just the gun, and the handcuffs . . . the big stick.

DAWN: All right already.

JEFF: Hey, look: You're wearin' a uniform and I'm wearin' a
uniform.

DAWN: So?

JEFF: So wc both got uniforms. Let's get together.

DAWN: You meet a lot of girls this way?

JEFF: No, hardly any. (*Pause*) What do you work, ten to six?

DAWN: So?

JEFF: Just askin'. I'm on twelve to eight. But I don't mind it. It's quiet. Plus, like, that's the other thing: Not a lot of people come in after one or two A.M., so I always have a newspaper, see, so what I do is after two I lock the door, and I take the newspaper, and I sit like this . . . (*Putting the newspaper in front of his face*) . . . so it looks like I'm reading the paper, and I can just sleep that way. And if somebody's at the door they knock, and if somebody comes downstairs the elevator dings, and I just swing around and here I am. (*He demonstrates*) See?

DAWN: Oh yeah, if I lived here that'd make me feel real safe.

JEFF: They feel safe. They don't know I'm sleeping. But I actually—See, this is just temporary for me. I've only been doin' this nine months. And it's a good job, but I couldn't be a security guard my whole life. You know? I'm way too restless. Plus I lived all over the world when I was a kid, 'cause my dad was in the Navy, and then I was in the Navy, so I know there's a bigger world out there. I really actually want to get into advertising, is what my dream is.

DAWN: Oh yeah . . . ?

JEFF: I don't mean that to sound too pathetic, like "How's *this* guy ever gonna get into advertising?" But I often thought that that could be a field that I might be kind of good at. Thinkin' up funny slogans for things . . .

DAWN: Uh-huh . . . ?

JEFF: . . . Thinkin' up different ways to advertise things. Well, I know it's probably a pretty hard field to get into, obviously, so at this point it's pretty much in fantasy land, but . . . (*Pause*) Must be interesting being a cop.

DAWN: It's interesting.

JEFF: You're a rookie, right? Come on, I can tell you're a rookie.

DAWN: Oh yeah?

JEFF: Boy, you must have a lot of guts. That's all I can say. I mean I know it takes guts just to be a cop in the first place, but to be a woman cop? That takes guts. Hats off to you. I'm not kidding.

DAWN: Yeah, well, I wouldn't know about that.

JEFF: Are there a lot of cops in your family or something?

DAWN: I'm the first.

JEFF: Good for you, man. That's awesome. I'm the first security guard in my family.

DAWN: Oh yeah?

JEFF: Yeah. It's kind of a point of pride with me.

DAWN: Yeah, I could see that.

JEFF: Hey, is it true that a female cop—(*As she starts to bristle*) Now wait a minute, this is not bullshit, I'm really curious.

DAWN: Yeah . . . ?

JEFF: Is it true that a female cop is likelier to shoot her gun or use her weapon or whatever than a male cop because she can't—you know, because she can't overpower you in any other way?

DAWN: No. That's a myth. They teach you a lot more than shooting, believe me.

JEFF: Really? Like what? (*Stepping back*) I'm not asking for a demonstration, I'm just asking like what do they teach you. Have you been involved in—

DAWN: (*On "been"*) They teach you a lot of things; you just try to control the situation.

JEFF: DAWN:

So like how do you—   Like tonight we had to break up

JEFF: this brawl—

Oh yeah? Sorry—

DAWN: That is all right. So we get there and these two guys are goin' at it outside this restaurant, right? So Bill—that's my partner—

JEFF: (*Overlapping*) Uh-huh? Yeah, I know—

DAWN: —he pulls this one guy away, and I go, "OK, let's break it up." So then this big fat guy whips around, he says, "Why? What are *you* gonna do about it, bitch?" Then he starts *chargin'* me.

JEFF: Really? This is a fantastic story!

DAWN: Oh yeah. But what you do is you just pivot back, like you pivot back and then you bring your nightstick up—you know, not to take their head off, but just to bring 'em down. Except I guess I got a little enthusiastic and I really whacked this guy, and that was it. Boom.

JEFF: What do you mean, boom? What happened to him?

DAWN: Nothin'. He had to go to the hospital.

JEFF: Really? You put him in the hospital?

DAWN: Oh yeah. You shoulda seen him. There was fuckin' blood *every*where. It was superficial of course. But your head can really bleed a lot.

JEFF: So . . . don't take this the wrong way, but would that qualify as police brutality at all?

DAWN: No. No way! He was totally comin' at me. And this guy was huge. But then, naturally of course two seconds later his wife comes outta the restaurant and she's screamin' "I'm an attorney, I'm calling the CCRB, I'm gonna sue you . . ."

JEFF: Calling the who?

DAWN:	JEFF:
The CCRB? The Civilian Complaint Review Board?	Oh, yeah, OK, yeah.

Which—you know—is definitely their right to do that. But that could be kinda serious for me, 'cause I'm still on my Probation? Like your first six months you're not like a full cop. You're what they call a Probationary Officer. And if you can't handle it or you just screw up, you're just out. You're off the Force. But Bill saw the whole thing and he says it's no problem. So I gotta go through a little song and dance. Big deal.

JEFF: And you didn't have to use your gun.

DAWN: Oh no. Definitely not. He was just some stupid drunk.

JEFF: But are you a pretty good shot?

DAWN: Yeah. I'm OK.

JEFF: That's excellent. (*Pause*) So what's he doin' up there anyway? Investigatin' a crime or somethin'?

DAWN: No, he's just saying hello to a friend.

JEFF: He's a friend of Mrs. Heinvald?

(*Pause*)

DAWN: Who?

JEFF: Mrs. Heinvald. The lady in 22-J.

DAWN: (*Confused*) No. Yeah. (*Pause*) 22-J—Yeah. I guess so. (*Pause*) *I* don't know her. *I* don't know who lives there.

JEFF: Well, I don't wanna say nothin', but he's liable to be up there a long time.

DAWN: What's it to you?

JEFF: I didn't say anything. I just don't see why you should have to cool your heels in the lobby eating your heart out while he's upstairs gettin' laid.

(*Pause*)

DAWN: He's not gettin' laid.

JEFF: Oh, come on.

DAWN: Hey, look: First of all—we're in the middle of our shift.

JEFF: Oh my God, excuse me, you're right, it's impossible.

(*Pause*)

DAWN: Who did you say lives in that apartment?

JEFF: Mrs. Heinvald. Amy Heinvald. She's an actress or a model or something. She's divorced. She's . . .

DAWN: Have you seen him here a lot?

JEFF: Sure, I seen him a few times. How long you been working together?

(*Pause*)

DAWN: What makes you think he's . . . you know.

JEFF: Because the lady he's visiting has a very active social schedule, if you see what I mean.

DAWN: No. I don't.

JEFF: I just mean she—

DAWN: What do you mean?

JEFF: I mean she's got a lot of boyfriends. That's all. (*Dawn's heart slowly breaks*) Hey, don't listen to me. I don't know what I'm talking about. Maybe I'm wrong. Maybe your partner is like, her favorite uncle or something.

DAWN: Yeah.

(*She moves away from him*)

JEFF: Hey . . . how come male cops are so big and fat and female cops are so young and beautiful?

DAWN: Yeah, how come doormen never know when to shut up?

JEFF: I don't know. That's an interesting point. Only I wouldn't be able to comment on it because I'm not a doorman. I'm a security guard.

DAWN: I don't fucking believe this.

JEFF: Hey, the guy is only human. You gotta *see* this lady—

DAWN: Hey, look: I'm not talking about him. I don't even—Look, you wanna know something? I don't even know why I'm *talking* to you. And if my partner wants to take time off his shift to go get laid with Mrs. Whatever-She-Is, you know what? More power to him, that's what I say—

JEFF: I agree!

DAWN: Because I seen him do more good for more people than anybody I ever met in my *life*. And if he wants to see that *model* in 22-J, that is his business, not mine—

JEFF: Sure!

DAWN: —and not yours. And I don't need to get *hit* on by the night *doorman* while he's upstairs gettin' his rocks off with some fuckin' whore.

JEFF:
Hey lady, I am not a doorman, I'm a security guard. I told you three fuckin' times already—In fact, I'm a security *specialist*! So—

DAWN:
I don't give a shit what you are, just keep your mouth shut! Good! Just keep your mouth shut! You talk to me, you keep your mouth shut, you understand?

JEFF: What?

DAWN: What?

(*Pause*)

JEFF:
How can I talk to you and keep my mouth shut at the same time?

DAWN:
Forget it. For*get* about it. For*get* about it.

(*Pause*)

JEFF: I'm not trying to make trouble.

DAWN: Just stop trying to pick me up.

JEFF: I'm not trying to pick you up—

DAWN: Why don't you try speaking to me like I'm an officer of the law? Just like, as an experiment.

JEFF: I'm sorry. I'm not usually this attracted to police officers.

DAWN: Well, you're lucky.

(*She moves away from him*)

JEFF: What's your name?

DAWN: Officer Wilson.

JEFF: Oh come on. What's your name? (*Pause*) Are you a sports fan? Come on. That's a harmless question. What do you like, basketball? A lot of girls like basketball. It's graceful. Well, a lot of sports are very graceful though, actually. What's your feeling about the impending garbage strike? My name's Jeff. Twenty-seven, never been married, never been in debt. Well, I have been in a little bit of debt actually but that's pretty much all cleared up now. I'm a different person now. Really. I've turned over a whole new leaf—

DAWN: Would you shut *up*?

JEFF: Sure, I'd be glad to. Why don't *you* say something for a few seconds and then I'll say something back and we'll go on like that. I'm a Goddamn security guard for Christ's sake. I'm lonely as shit. There's three other guys in this building and I never see them except on the video screen. I'll shut up. I'd love to hear somebody else talk.

DAWN: I just don't feel like it right this minute.

JEFF: I understand. I'm not trying to make trouble. And don't listen to me. I don't know what he's doin' up there. I don't know anything about it.

DAWN: Hey, what do I care? The fucking guy is married anyway.

(*Jeff goes back to his station and picks up his book. Long silence.*)

DAWN: Can you believe this shit?

JEFF: (*Puts down his book*) Yeah . . . They probably don't warn you about this kind of thing in the Police Academy.

DAWN: (*A bitter joke*) Sure they do. I took a seminar.

JEFF: What happens if there's a major outbreak of crime on your beat under these circumstances?

DAWN: Oh, then I'm supposed to buzz him.

JEFF: Are there a lot of romances between cops?

DAWN: I don't know . . . Some of them get married.

JEFF: No, but, I mean like illicit, kind of behind-the-scenes in the back of the squad car type romances.

DAWN: *You're* gonna end up in the back of the squad car in a minute.

JEFF: But seriously, is that a pretty widespread problem?

DAWN: I'm sure it's no different than any other kinds of jobs.

JEFF: Well, in other kinds of jobs people have affairs all the time.

DAWN: Well.

(*Pause*)

JEFF: Are you in love with that guy?

DAWN: Who.

JEFF: You know. Your partner. (*Pause*) Because if you are, I would say that you were in love with the wrong guy.

DAWN: I'm not in love with anybody. I just admired him, that's all. OK? He made life a little easier for me in the Department. OK? I mean, you look up to somebody, you take them seriously—and then—That's all. OK?

JEFF: OK. (*Pause*) I think it's great what you're doing. (*Pause*) Your family must be proud of you.

DAWN: Oh, they think I'm nuts. (*Pause*) Well, not exactly, I mean, my mother thinks I'm a little bit nuts, but I happen to think that she's nuts too, so there's no harm done there, right?

JEFF: You have a lot of brothers? I bet you have a lot of—

DAWN: (*On "bet"*) But I guess generally they're proud . . . I was near the top of my class at the Academy . . . I just . . . I just fucked up with *this* prick, that's all. And now I'm *screwed*. Because I obviously really misjudged him, you know? And for all I know he's been shootin' his mouth off all over the department. And it wouldn't have been so hard to avoid the whole thing in the first place. But these guys . . . I mean, they seen so much horrible shit, it's like they don't give a damn about anything. So you gotta walk around like you don't give a damn about anything either. But they know you still do. And they wanna like, stamp it out of you or something. And like, test you, all the time. And it's always like: "Hey—you're not men, you're not women: You're cops. Act like cops and you'll be treated like cops." Only then it turns out they got a pool going as to who's gonna fuck you first, OK? And that's fine. I can handle it. You *make* them respect you. But then somebody decent comes along, and goes out of his way to make life easier for you—and I didn't even *ask* him, because I didn't expect anything different—I didn't *want* anything different. And then, Oh my God, it's true love—except when he comes down in that elevator, just watch: because *I'm* gonna be the one who's gonna be supposed to act like I'm a cop! I mean . . . (*Pause*) And then I got *you*.

JEFF: So far I'm like the nicest guy in the whole story.

DAWN: Yeah . . . !

JEFF: So why don't you tell me your name?

DAWN: Because maybe I don't feel like it, Jeff.

JEFF: OK. You don't have to tell me your name. But, uh, do you want to, uh, do you want to go to a basketball game with me tomorrow afternoon? I got tickets to the Knicks game.

DAWN: I don't like basketball.

JEFF: OK. Well, um, after I'm finished watchin' the basketball game with my *mother,* would you like to go dancing with me? I don't want to get you on the rebound or anything, but I don't know if I'm ever gonna see you again . . . I know I'll see your *partner* again . . . Sorry. I'm sorry.

DAWN: I don't care.

JEFF: . . . We'll put on our dress uniforms, we'll go dancin', get bombed and come to work.

(*Dawn starts crying and turns away*)

DAWN: God damn it . . . !

JEFF: What's the matter?

DAWN: I can't be cryin' on duty . . . !

JEFF: Come on . . . You'll drive around, you'll shoot some perpetrator, you'll feel better.

DAWN: He is a son of a bitch . . . !

JEFF: You know what? You're damn right. And I'll tell you something else—

(*Offstage the elevator pings. They both look sharp as Bill enters [NOTE: He is hatless now]*)

PART II: THE PROCESS

Here is my interview with Aaron and Amy. We talk about how they developed their characters, did their script analysis, found the structure of the scene, and found a truthful way into it.

LARRY: I'm going to start off by asking what the overall experience was like.

AMY: Enjoyable is the first word. It was fun. I felt comfortable with the character I was playing, with my scene partner and with the script, and I was excited to show our scene. It was titillating—it was like we had little secrets that we were going to share with the audience.

LARRY: Talk about the little secrets.

AMY: I felt like maybe these people weren't so far away from who we really are. I felt particular permission to say that I had a lot of things in common with this woman.

LARRY: What do you mean?

AMY: There were a lot of internal things . . . a desire for what's right in the world, a passion about her career, feeling as though you have to protect yourself under certain circumstances. . . .

LARRY: You mean as a woman or just as a human being or as a policeman?

AMY: As a woman and as a woman policeman.

LARRY: Good, that's very specific. A woman policeman in a boy's club?

AMY: Yes, a woman in a boy's club and a woman whose job is protection and defense. So being an actress, I don't know why I felt that I had a lot in common with her—probably it stemmed from my childhood, and just being a woman in the world and having to deal with men professionally.

LARRY: That's right, it doesn't matter whether you're on the police force—

AMY: Right—

LARRY: That a woman is a second-class citizen in some men's points of view.

AMY: And having it in the police force only heightens and expands that reality. . . .

LARRY: So you could find a way into that character through your own understanding—

AMY: Yes. As a woman, you have to strategize your every move in order to get paid the same, in order to be seen with the same amount of respect you actually have to perform better, or at least you feel you have to perform better. It affects you vocally, it affects you physically.

LARRY: In what way vocally?

AMY: For me personally, I had vocal cord surgery six months ago and prior to that I had developed or aggravated some nodes because of how I was speaking, and I know how I was speaking had a lot to do with how I wanted to be perceived.

LARRY: Perceived by men, you mean, as what?

AMY: Perceived as a comrade, a fellow, a player, someone who isn't very soft, someone who couldn't be pushed over, someone who would meet things head-on, someone who was direct with them so that they would believe what I'm saying. I felt men didn't really believe what I was saying.

LARRY: You felt that men didn't respect you as an equal?

AMY: Right—

LARRY: That they might listen to a man before they listen to you?

AMY: Right. My perception was that they wouldn't believe me.

LARRY: And the vocal production that gave you the nodules on your vocal cords was about talking from a throaty place that made men feel you were more dominant?

AMY: I thought I was creating a sound that would be listened to more readily than the other softer sounds. I didn't necessarily do this consciously. But I did it.

LARRY: Did that influence your vocal production of the character in *Lobby Hero*?

AMY: Yes. And one of the notes you gave me the first and second times we did it was that there was a stridency to my voice. I don't know if you said strident or if you said it needed more vocal variation. . . .

LARRY: I'm sure I said you needed more vocal variation.

AMY: That's exactly what my speech pathologist said had been my speaking pattern in my life. And when we worked on finding variation and raising my pitch a little bit, it gave me a lot more variation. But I didn't feel that this woman spoke that way, I did feel that she spoke in a flat kind of voice.

LARRY: So as a choice you edited out some of the melodic aspects of her speech.

AMY: But I didn't want to do it to such a degree that her voice was completely unvaried. I wanted her to be powerful to listen to, I wanted certain things to pop, I wanted to have a vocal technique that could underline certain phrases.

LARRY: It seems to me that what you're on your way to accomplishing in the role, and maybe in your acting in general, is you're saying, "I want to have this flat voice when I'm trying to be dominant but when I'm vulnerable, like with my boyfriend upstairs who is betraying me in the scene, the female melody begins to play in my vocal performance." I hear from you that you want to convey certain aspects of your character vocally, based on whether you're in a vulnerable place or a defensive place.

AMY: Right. I played around a little bit with saying the word "Bill"—the cop upstairs, who was my lover—a little softer, but it's such a short word that you couldn't really hear that I had softened the word Bill.

LARRY: You said you identified the character with yourself when you started to play her—

AMY: Yes. And it feels very raw to do so. It feels very vulnerable, you feel like you're not acting.

LARRY: Exactly. That you're living in what we call the imaginary circumstances but in fact there's not such a difference in walking though the stage door and walking on the stage, because basically there's an authentic self, which is being expressed all the time. That's the best acting, when, as the saying goes, you don't get caught.

AMY: And what you said in class Friday about vocal production when you're acting really struck me. You had said to an actor doing *After the Fall,* when you are speaking, you are so uncommitted to the ideas you are supposed to be sending that you are communicating nothing other than "I am not worthy of being heard, I am not even a person." People don't want to watch that, people want to see human beings who are worthy of telling their story.

LARRY: Human beings who say, "I should be on a stage, I've prepared, I have trained, and I am an artist and I am interpreting a text and you're right to sit there and I'm right to be up here."

AMY: You can trust me.

LARRY: Yes. When an actor walks on the stage they say by their performance, "You can trust me, you're in good hands," which is what I felt when I was watching you both times and most particularly the second time, only because there was very little that wasn't living. In other words, it was very good work the first time but the second time it was not acting.

AMY: Yeah.

LARRY: There was just literal human behavior on the stage. It was very powerful. Aaron, what about for you in terms of when you first began interpreting the script?

AARON: There was a real excitement to start to work. I knew I had a good partner, I knew that the things we had found I was excited to share with the audience, and little secrets I had made for my character about how my character felt about the other people in the play. I fantasized about what their lives were like.

LARRY: So as you read the script and began to analyze it you began to create for this man your interpretation of his relationships to other people in the play.

AARON: As my character, I thought I had a relationship with the policewoman before I even had one just from the fact that she walked in and out of my lobby. Everything she did meant so much to me because I got to sit there for four to five hours and ponder it after she left. And when someone reacted differently than I had imagined, it was interesting—you know what I mean—if she became more vulnerable than I expected, because she was supposed to be a cop. . . .

LARRY: So that made your character curious—

AARON: It made me curious, right. Working more specifically after the first critique, I made a commitment to start from a very simple, real place and to accept my preparation and not judge how much emotion came up. I didn't try to amp my prep—I didn't try to get somewhere I couldn't be at the moment. I tried to walk onto the stage as a person and tried to find something very simple and real to do.

LARRY: Give me an example of what that was.

AARON: Like starting a crossword puzzle. I sat down in my guard chair and really did the crossword puzzle. I was, like, "Here I am as a person doing a crossword puzzle." It's not that I was about to go "Lights up, acting!" Instead I had a task that I could commit to.

LARRY: And the thing is, as in life, if she had never entered into the lobby you would have finished the crossword puzzle—

AARON: Yeah—

LARRY: Which is another key to good acting, that when you have a task as a moment before, you must have a relationship with that task that you commit to, so that when the scene starts and something interrupts that task, it's a surprise.

AARON: Just like a physical destination. Finishing the crossword puzzle was my destination and she altered my destination. That was what was so exciting for me, especially the second time we did the scene. I also found character things I loved. Anything I could find that was a parallel in his life to mine, I said yes to it, and I endowed it more.

LARRY: Give me an example.

AARON: Like his father died before he could make his father proud, and so I said okay. I'll say yes to that.

LARRY: Because you know that personally.

AARON: Yes, deeply. And it's not something I often use, personal stuff like that, but in this case it fit.

LARRY: You're saying, "That parallel between me and the character, I said yes to, because I can believe it, it's happened to me, I understand it on an emotional level." But then you said something else. You said you don't often use personal things like that. So my question to you is, what do you usually do?

AARON: I imagine things. I find something in the text that I develop with details in my imagination. For example, in *Lobby Hero* there's another scene where my boss says I'm witty. And I ran with that description of my character and brought it into this scene. I said, "Okay, I'm witty. That's one of my good qualities." And that was one of the qualities I know I can use to get this lady cop to respond to me.

LARRY: So that was something that somebody in the play said about your character and you took that and said yes to it and began to explore your idea of his wit and applied it to how he began to approach her.

AARON: And in the text, he tries to turn phrases wittily and I got to play with it. I also found out the Marx Brothers were from Astoria and that's where he was from.

LARRY: Now tell me about that.

AARON: Well, this is not specified in the text but I decided okay, if as my character I saw Marx Brothers movies on television and I knew they grew up in my hometown, I could be like them. So I'm going to be like a Marx Brother and put on a show for this lady cop—you know, being kind of Marx Brothery.

LARRY: What was the time frame when you started working on this text and found out the Marx Brothers were from Astoria?

AARON: I didn't find out till the second time we did the scene. I knew I was from New York, I knew I was working in Manhattan, but which borough? I went to the text, which told me I'm meeting with my brother in Astoria, and I interpreted that I was meeting him in the old

family house. I created this in my back story   that he got the family
house 'cause he has kids.

LARRY: So the script says you live in Astoria?

AARON: Yes.

LARRY: Then you built on that.

AARON: Yes. I researched Astoria and I have pictures of different hotel lobbies and public schools there. I looked at that and how the Marx
Brothers used to hang out at a certain hotel. And that's what it was, just
something simple like that. I said, "Oh, this will be great. I can use some
of the behavior of the Marx Brothers."

LARRY: That was the subtle Marx Brothers stuff you added to your
characterization the second time?

AARON: Right. I also decided I was really strung out on coffee and
that maybe I was a little bit ADD [attention deficit disorder] and I put it
all into my right foot. That really carbonated my energy.

LARRY: You said he's a nighttime clerk so he drinks a lot of caffeine.
What made you come to the idea that he had ADD?

AARON: 'Cause he can't decide on a career, he can't hold down one
job, he's always jumping from one thing to another—he's going to go
into the advertising, no maybe he might write. . . . He can't focus. . . .
What other characters say about me in the script is a great way to create
truth because I have to justify what they say about me to myself so I believe it's part of my life.

LARRY: The way you justified for yourself his inability to make decisions was to give yourself a case of ADD. That's interpretation, Aaron,
and it brought you to a funny and volatile life. And because the ADD was
physicalized, it made the scene very urgent.

AARON: I also felt that one of the fears I had was that as a character I
wasn't seen by other people, 'cause I wanted to be seen by my father in
the script, and people in the lobby definitely didn't give me the time of
day and I wasn't seen.

LARRY: Is that what you did? Because you had a wonderful quality of
needing feedback, needing to be mirrored back. I felt that very much in
your performance, which was very irritating to Amy's character but finally won her over because you were so needful and vulnerable and desperate to engage.

AMY: That's what that was.

AARON: Any time I could try to catch her eye, I did. I needed for her to see me, my father didn't see me, my family didn't see me, I wasn't seen in the navy, and not being seen by her was so painful to me that another choice I made was to create the sound of my own voice as soothing to me.

LARRY: That's also a very interesting choice, that when people are very lonely they find ways to soothe themselves.

AARON: Yes, my character is very lonely and very verbal in the script. I'm always begging my boss to talk, "You do some of the talking 'cause I'd be happy to stop doing some of the talking but I just need to hear something because I'm alone at work." I say that I'm alone at work, I'm alone at home, I'm alone.

LARRY: This is why you hear some people who live alone say, "I need to have the radio or the TV on just to feel some life in the house."

AMY: It's a good choice to choose your own voice as being soothing, especially if you want to add another dimension to your verbal life that fits with your character.

LARRY: What I'm taken by in both of you is how interested and capable you are in script analysis. And once you analyzed it, you found parallels to your own lives that you can believe so that you don't have to act. Aaron, you also found things in your imagination, based on clues in the script, and made them real to you so that you don't have to act. So what I'm understanding from you about your process is that you read a script till you understand it, and then personalize it and use your imagination to fill in the rest, and that you can't do the second two steps without the first.

AMY: No, you can't. I mean the first thing I did, the first thing I always do, is make a list of everything the script tells me about the character, everything I do and where I'm physically at in a scene. Just get the facts, man. You do your investigative work and then it is like a puzzle. It's wonderful. At first it feels very cerebral and it feels very intellectual to dissect things but it infects you emotionally. As your mind is being used, your intuition is being used as well.

AARON: You've got to fill in all the blanks, you've got the facts but then you've got to make the bridges between the facts.

LARRY: What does it mean to fill in the blanks?

AMY: Some of the blanks are environmental, object based, they are physical things. We put this scene on its feet early because we knew that as characters we're stuck in a room together, a very basic lobby, and we had to find ways of communicating about ourselves through the objects and the environment—the inside of the lobby and what we were seeing outside the lobby through a window. Also my character believes that my boyfriend is visiting a friend upstairs from the lobby, and when the guard informs her that the friend is a hotsy-totsy who sees a lot of men and is wildly promiscuous, it sends the scene into a whole other orbit and brings the two characters together. All of this takes place in the lobby but the characters' relationships to outside and upstairs became alive for us and really helped shape our behavior.

LARRY: Right, but you were already smart actors, so basically you asked yourself in relationship to your environment, "What is my physical behavior?" A cop on her beat, a security guard in his chair and moving toward the lady cop for possible romance. Then as the cop you fill that up with your relationship to the nightstick you carry, to the belt and gun you wear, and your choices for observing what's outside the window on the fourth wall.

AMY: I like to start physically with the time, the weather, what's in the room, what the floor looks like, and the temperature.

AARON: We actually talked about what the tile looked like on the floor of the lobby.

AMY: It was gray-and-white marble.

LARRY: And what did that do?

AARON: It gave it a certain level of class.

AMY: A formality.

LARRY: Okay, so you were in an upper-class—

AMY: Upper-middle-class—

LARRY: Upper-middle-class building and that made you feel what?

AMY: Upper-middle-class.

LARRY: And was her character upper middle class?

AMY: No, but I definitely felt a little taller and little more important because I was serving and protecting folks who were important.

LARRY: So you considered the socioeconomic circumstances of your characters and how they feel and behave in different social environments?

AMY: Status would be everything, I guess.

LARRY: Right. Because both characters are longing for something more than what they have. Aaron, would you say the marble floor did the same for you?

AARON: Yes, it made me feel I had some status because of where my job was. It also made me feel I was being watched a little more because my employers expected more from me. A great example of us filling in the blanks the second time was the bum outside.

LARRY: Talk about that, because I thought that choice made us believe more in the place that you were operating in.

AMY: That was fun because we really did a dance in rehearsal. We came up with the bum idea together, don't you think?

AARON: Yeah, yeah.

AMY: And it was through your urging of course to make more of that outer environment come inside.

AARON: You know you said to her, I remember, "Maybe there's a prostitute at the gas station across the street trying to turn a trick," and then I don't know if she said or I said, "What if there was a bum right outside the lobby?" I said, "Well, it's the same guy who's always there and he's always giving me a bad time and I'm going to try to get him to move." And then Amy came up with a great idea that showed status and relationship. The lady cop goes to the window and motions to the bum to try to get him to move but he won't, so I come up behind her and, because the bum is afraid of me because I go after him every night, he moves, but the lady cop doesn't see this and she feels she's won over the bum.

AMY: At first we thought of creating somebody to enter the lobby but then we realized we couldn't do that. He had to truly be on the fourth wall, technically speaking, because if he entered the lobby, the audience would have to see him just as they saw us, but what we saw outside the window we could imagine and choose as long as we made it very specific and it enlivened our relationship with each other and the lobby we were in.

LARRY: So you created a life around the lobby that you believed. Aaron, because you worked there every night, you knew this bum, you had a certain relationship with him, which allowed you a kind of superiority, which is obviously extremely important to your character, who needs some kind of power because he feels so unimportant.

AMY: This is just one little piece of my beat. This isn't my whole life, this lobby, like it is for him. It's just one more lobby, one more guy, one more doorman—which he is always correcting me about, telling me he's a security guard.

LARRY: What do you think your character feels nightly when you don the uniform, put on the nightstick and fasten the handcuffs to your belt, what kind of a point of view does it give you?

AMY: It's very different than when she's not in the uniform. In uniform, I think she sees herself as a menace, as a real threat. That's how I felt. But it was hard to believe it from my experience personally as me,

Amy, outside the scene. Because when I would look at myself in the mirror in the police uniform, or my real-life husband would see me in it or Aaron would react to me when I first put the uniform on, they would react to me in a kind of jokey way. And I got a real feeling of "I am not powerful. . . . I mean, if this is how men are viewing me, they laugh at me in this uniform, this is horrifying, I better try even harder to be like [she shouts], 'You're not going to fuck with me, man!'" And I couldn't be big enough or tough enough or strong enough.

LARRY: Which gave you something very active to try to accomplish—

AMY: Exactly

LARRY: Which you could work on whether you were speaking or not, so that's another blank you filled in. You had an attitude about what you had to project to be a policewoman.

AMY: I felt very inadequate—

LARRY: Which made you have to be more dominant, which affected your tonality of voice, your rhythms and tempos and your relationship toward everyone you encountered when you were in that officer's uniform. But when you were out of that uniform, you didn't feel that?

AMY: No.

LARRY: So basically that uniform gives you power.

AMY: Part of imagining her everyday life is imagining a very plain woman, who desperately wants to make a difference in the world, and she feels like this is her calling. She definitely feels like that but when she's not in the uniform it's a different story. She's dominated by her mother and she doesn't like her family and although she's going out with Bill, she doesn't have a committed relationship because he's married to someone else and he's being unfaithful to his wife and to me all at the same time.

LARRY: Did each of you build a biography once you read the text?

AMY: The text gave us a lot of information about their families.

LARRY: I'd like you to discuss, when you write a biography, a) how you do it?, and b) once you've done it, what does it do for you in a performance?

AARON: I always learn from the biography very quickly because it gives me a sense of self, it relaxes me. I know that there are certain things in the biography I write that I play off of.

LARRY: Give me an example.

AARON: There's a point in the scene when she puts down her cap. I wanted to be a police officer but I couldn't 'cause I have a discharge from the navy, and I created in my biography how my father acted the day I came home in my uniform, how disappointed he was that I was discharged. I didn't know when that piece of biography I created was going to hit me in the scene or how it was going to hit me, but when she put down her hat that second time and I picked it up and said to her, "Your family must be proud of you," it sank so deeply into me that I got choked up, and I realized that it's all from biography. I didn't have to work, I didn't have to do anything.

LARRY: Because you knew what your family felt about your failures.

AARON: Yes, my failures and that I couldn't achieve something like she did, I couldn't physically have this badge. The way that happened was cool. Biography's great because it creates memory for the characters and makes you fly, 'cause you don't have to work, you have memories.

LARRY: You're coming from a real life that you created. When you're writing biography for a character, do either of you ever add real events from your own life or is it really from the character's life as the author describes it in the script?

AMY: Sometimes I add events from my own life or make the mother like my mother if it fits.

LARRY: Since you did very good work the first time you did the scene in class but we all felt there was more to accomplish, what did you take from my critique that you felt you could run with, and what did that do to fill in more life?

AMY: Well, the bum was created just to make the life outside the building more real. It was real for me in my brain the first time, but I didn't use my imagination enough and realize, "Hey, there's a possibility of finding behavior in the lobby based on what we could see outside the building," and how could that be facilitated. Then there were things to make more specific about my relationship to Bill. So your assessment after the first session was that I, as an actor and as a person, have so much further to go with my imagination, it's an unutilized tool, and there's a whole other way to create things for myself onstage instead of trying to adhere only to the clues that are written down by someone else or trying to give a performance that I think people want to see. The habit of doing that has to do with auditioning quickly and trying to figure out what people want.

LARRY: So the epiphany for you, Amy, was when I asked you to develop Bill—this man that you were in love with and that you thought was going to change your life—very specifically, so that it had emotional resonance for you, even though he doesn't appear in the scene. Talk about how you built him.

AMY: Originally I kept trying to find someone from my life, which is how I worked in the past and it had always worked before to some degree but it also was a huge amount of effort for me. It was too effortful, I think. It was like you can't lie to yourself and as I tried to match one of them to substitute and personalize for Bill I would constantly keep trying to justify my choice, which kept putting me in my head because my relationships with these men had changed for the better and it was hard for me to think about them in the old way. Maybe for someone else they could separate the past person from the present, but I couldn't. It just didn't work for me.

But when I started fresh, with a fresh piece of clay, it worked a lot better and it was more exciting and much more fun. I was much more excited about the Bill I created than any Bill I ever really knew. And so I started by writing. I thought maybe writing a biography for my relationship to Bill was the way to bring it alive for me but that didn't work for me. So I put down the pen and paper and I sat in a recliner and I sort of meditated on it, and lo and behold, certain parts of different people I knew came into formation and almost a complete man was formed. But the first thing that formed was his jaw. He had a little bit of an overbite and a little bit of a lisp, and I remember I fixated on his jaw and I fantasized about certain things we had done together while we were walking our beat.

One of the things I imagined that he entrusted me with was that he had to go get laser surgery on his lunch hour, and he said, "Come with me." It was kind of our first moment of closeness, to go with him to have laser surgery. So we went to the doctor's office and the surgery's performed and they gave him a little teddy bear to hug and I thought that was so sweet, that he needed to hug a teddy bear during his surgery, and after the surgery he asked them if he could give me the teddy bear and they wouldn't let him do that and so he ended up giving me a teddy bear necklace the next day. Because he was grateful that I stuck with him during the surgery. And that's when I fell in love with him. I think that necklace idea came because I had just been upstairs in my house before I meditated on Bill and I had just seen a necklace, it wasn't a teddy bear, it was a heart, but I knew I wanted to somehow give my character something private underneath her uniform that was just about her private life and had nothing to do with the uniform.

LARRY: And it was connected to Bill.

AMY: Yes, I wanted to have a personal object on my body that connected me to him, and seeing that necklace in my own house sparked the idea during my meditation.

LARRY: So my note to you was to create a deeper and more specific emotional connection to Bill, and from imagining a jaw, you built an entire imaginary man that was your Bill that you could believe in. And the incident of the laser surgery came to you without your even looking for it.

AMY: Yes, and the whole thing took about five minutes.

LARRY: I think that's important. The whole thing was not agony, it was playful, it was creative, impulsive. The reason it was fun was that you had read the play very carefully, you had done the scene once, you had made choices that worked well in key parts of some of the scene, so you were ready to find the Bill that you really needed, that was going to really activate you emotionally in the scene. The memories of going to the laser surgery and of him giving you this teddy bear necklace made him personal to you and intimate. Those memories really established human truth with him, that he was tender with you.

AMY: And he wasn't the Bill that everybody else in the play knew 'cause he was the biggest asshole to everybody else who knew him. This was a horrible person, this Bill, but not to her.

LARRY: And tell me about the laser surgery on his cornea that you witnessed in your imagination.

AMY: I could see the doctor cut his cornea open, and I could see into his eye, his soul basically, and I just thought it was so intimate that I was watching this.

LARRY: And this all happened in five minutes reclining on a recliner.

AMY: Yes, the morning before we did the scene the second time. I was glad I was patient with myself because I knew that the first time we went up I didn't have a strong enough Bill, but I didn't want to yell at myself, I didn't want to say, "Well, you didn't do this and that." I tried but it wasn't there and we did the best we could. But it was so important to me that in doing this scene I would allow myself to enjoy my own process. And because I allowed myself to enjoy it, my imagination was freer to open.

AARON: There were times when we got frustrated but we each pulled each other up and said, "We're going to have fun, don't make it agony." We'd get a little amped or we'd get frustrated with something or she'd say something to me or I'd say something to her and we'd be, like, "Let's just keep playing, it's okay."

AMY: Because I find that I am more inspired when I'm lighter.

LARRY: Yes, because you are also more available emotionally in the scene to the darker feelings because you were playful—

AMY: It's true—

LARRY: Your imagination took flight because you were in the circumstances of these characters in this lobby. And it seems to me that what I hear you both saying is that you connected dots, that it was a process, that you were patient with it, that you were playful with it, that you didn't beat yourself up, that you kept helping your partner to stay playful and allow yourselves to try different choices.

AARON: That's right—

LARRY: It was fun, and when it was difficult, you didn't go to the frustration, you went to something creative, different, and new.

AMY: And when we would reach a trouble spot when one of or both of us seemed vague about the meaning of what we were saying, we would work it out together. It was very collaborative.

LARRY: What I also get is that you trusted each other enough to try stuff and recommend stuff to each other without being defensive, because it was all about what was best for the scene.

AARON: Yes. I know her, she knows me, and we had developed that trust and we kept it about the scene. So there wasn't a problem with us helping each other. Sometimes it was the characters' ideas that we talked about and sometimes it was a physicalization.

AMY: We did animals. Aaron's really good at animals and I felt I needed to work in that area with my imagination a little bit. He helped me out because he's technically proficient with those tools.

AARON: Sometimes we started from a silly place, too, not necessarily that we were going to use it. We really overdid the animals. We'd laugh at each other, but then some good things would come out of it, like the way Amy would look around and she felt like this hawk.

AMY: Originally I wanted to be a tiger but it wasn't working and then he suggested a hawk and that was perfect.

LARRY: And what did the hawk do?

AMY: It gave me extraordinary vision and affected the way that my character sat. I don't have as good vision but when I played her with this hawklike laser-beam vision, it gave me a different sense of my neck. It made me proud—with a wide wingspan. It made me want to take up more space. And the sense of a wide wingspan gave me a sense of expansion. And then Aaron worked on a prairie dog 'cause hawks hunt prairie dogs.

LARRY: And did you come up with that together? You gave her the hawk, Aaron, because you knew about hawks preying on prairie dogs?

AARON: Yeah.

LARRY: So you brought that to the scene. Talk about your prairie dog.

AARON: Prairie dogs are often—I feel silly talking about this—but they're often out on a field all by themselves, peeking out of a hole, looking to see what's going on, and if you see them their little hearts are like thump, thump, thump, thump. They have long spines and they sit on their haunches, which is how I found the way I sat on my stool. Their little hearts pound but they're very inquisitive. Their bodies are still but they're fast with their little hands, they're curious about everything. I mean a blade of grass goes by in the wind and they go check that out.

AMY: And one time you put a pillow in your shirt.

AARON: They have these little paunches, these little stomachs, and one time we got some pillows and I walked around a bit with a pillow and it gave me a kind of rounded shoulders and a little bit of a paunch thing. I was trying that out to see how that made me feel.

AMY: It made you feel like a loser.

AARON: More of a loser, more of an oaf, more of a slacker.

LARRY: And what did you keep of the prairie dog in your performance?

AARON: I kept the alertness, the sitting up erect on my stool, some of the prairie dog movement—how I looked around the lobby with my head.

LARRY: So the swivel of the head was from the prairie dog—

AARON: Yeah—

LARRY: And what about the fast hands?

AARON: That also played right into my ADD, the coffee, and always having to touch things, and I always gave myself paperwork at my desk to do. But the thing that you just brought up is that the pillow did make me feel like a slacker and that affected what I thought of myself and, emotionally, how I wasn't enough. It's funny listening to Amy talk about it now, 'cause we didn't talk about it.

LARRY: You just did that work on your own.

AARON: Yeah, that was the other great thing. We worked to a certain place in rehearsal about physicality and stuff, staging, then we'd just go off in our corners and brainstorm on our own.

LARRY: Would you take a break in rehearsal, go and think for a while and come back and do the scene or did you just go home and work on your own before the next rehearsal?

AMY: Went home.

LARRY: Did you always leave rehearsal with the sense that you had made a little bit of a step that led you to ask more questions to come to the next rehearsal with?

AMY: There was one rehearsal that at the time didn't feel productive. Do you remember that one?

AARON: The second one?

AMY: Yeah, the second one. But stuff soaked in anyway, we just didn't know.

AARON: We weren't really aware of how fast we worked either.

AMY: We did work really quickly. I think we had a total of four or five rehearsals.

LARRY: One thing I see with both of you is that you've gotten to that place technically and also psychologically and humanly to say, "I want my acting to be pleasurable," but I want to make the point that perhaps you couldn't be as playful if you weren't as technically proficient.

AMY: And you're always honing that every time you rehearse, every time you work. Techniques are little toys you bring to the playground—I have this cool truck, you want to try it?—and that's the animal exercise and then there's biography. I'm starting to believe that you can't divorce the joy from the process ever, even if it's painful, even if what you're exploring is pain and despair, there has to be a desire to explore that despair, an intense desire to feel that pain for the love of bringing the characters to life.

LARRY: Yes, because it's playful in the sense that you've got to have Bill mean something to you and Aaron, you have to have Amy's character mean something to you, you have to need her, and that has a longing and a loneliness in it, just as having Bill betray you, Amy, is painful. But it's that wonderful pain, that wonderful, joyful vulnerability which comes with the imaginary circumstances, which says, "I don't have to pay the human price for this as my actual life but I can visit the experience fully and vulnerably and still know somewhere in the back of my mind I am safe to be absolutely vulnerable and raw because in my real life I don't have to deal with the consequences." Part of an actor's music is their raw emotionality. It's part of your instrument as an actor that you have to open up in order to be human in your work. It makes you have the capability of playing Medea or Mary Tyrone or Oedipus Rex or Willy Loman, even at their most painful moments, and still to experience the joy of creation.

AMY: Absolutely. Expressing humanity.

LARRY: You were both very vulnerable in the scene the second time you performed it. Your eyes filled up with tears many times, but you always sculpted the emotion because you were on your way to your next accomplishing, your next action, your next doing; you were always in the process of trying to accomplish something rather than hanging on to any emotion. What would you say the difference was in terms of living more fully the second time you did the scene? Certainly for you, Amy, it was Bill and the fourth wall. You examined the fourth wall and created off the fourth wall more, you created a real, powerful, imaginary Bill. What else?

AARON: You gave me the note about being more specific in my relationships to the props I had in my job. Everything had to mean something to me. The advertisements in the paper I was reading. I really had to think about what my physical life was as a guard in this lobby, 'cause I lean on the physicality as an actor. I know this about myself—I love physicality.

AMY: We drew a floor plan and we specified every possible object that could be in the lobby.

LARRY: You put everything in that could possibly be there. And then you went about seeing which objects attracted you in a behavioral way.

AARON: Right. Then we endowed those objects more. I sat down, and thought, *Well, my boss said I was witty and I'm looking through these advertisements in magazines all the time, this is something possibly I can do, I can be an advertisement man and I could live in Manhattan in my own high-rise, in my own apartment.* And I got really excited about it so when I went to do the line to her, I got really excited, and I said, I really actually want to get into advertising, is what my dream is, I got really excited about my potential life, about the possibility of being an advertising man and having a better job.

LARRY: Right, and the prop was?

AARON: The prop was the magazine. The ads.

LARRY: The real estate ads?

AARON: Right.

LARRY: Where did that come from? You just thought that would be there in the lobby?

AARON: Yeah, newspapers and magazines in the lobby. I also had playing cards with me. You know, I'm in debt to my brother—the script tells me that but it doesn't say how I got in debt—so I made up a gambling addiction to justify it for myself. I borrowed money from my brother to pay off gambling debts. And that's why the cards have life for me.

LARRY: So what you did is you took the information the writer gave you and you fleshed it out by saying, "If I'm in debt, how am I in debt? And if I'm in debt to my brother, how and why?" You built the back story of why you were in debt and how you were in debt and how it is connected to your brother. The actor's job is to say the writer has given me these truths and I have to imagine them in detail and fill them up with specifics and emotion. An actor who isn't really technically proficient would say, "Well, I'm in debt, I'll just believe that." This is why I always say that it's only bad actors who are general, life never is. It's always specific. You always know how much you owe and how you feel about the person you owe it to. Someone who really wants to live onstage says, "I have to know why I'm in debt, I have to know how much I am in debt, how much of it I've paid back and how it affects my relationship with my brother" so then I don't have to act anything—I've created it, I've made it real.

AMY: The work we did on this scene helped me get my next professional job. I auditioned two days after we completed our work on the scene, and you had given me the note on filling in the blanks more with my imagination. They gave me the audition scene in advance for the job I was up for so I decided to fill in the blanks for that, too. I always thought in the past I didn't have the time to do this work, but it doesn't take that long, you just have to do it. There were lines in the audition script about my character being in with some bad cops, so I had to create who the cops were, what they looked like, what my relationships with them were. Had they been over to my house for dinner? Do they have any kids? Do I know their wives? Who are these assholes that I only mention briefly in relation to me? If I don't answer these questions, then I'm acting.

LARRY: That's right. How long did it take you, ten minutes?

AMY: Yeah.

LARRY: To make it specific to you.

AMY: And you have to carry that through all the different callbacks, 'cause when you're under the pressure of going to audition for the network for the final audition, and you feel that you're the low man on the totem pole, your heart is racing and you need something solid to hold on to. When you've filled in all the blanks and have made everything specific, that's what you're carrying in with you—the life you created for your character. If you've lived it, it's never going to leave you.

LARRY: Both of you are first-rate actors, so you can bring your confidence to an audition, which you obviously did, Amy, and it was there even though your heart may be racing. The confidence came from the fact that you did an amount of homework that was usable for you, you didn't overwork it, but you created a life so you can live as the character in that audition. It doesn't matter if it's in front of twenty people for a final callback for the network or if it's a first reading with a casting director or projecting forward onto the first day of shooting. Acting is acting. Certainly if you get a script overnight you can't do as much biography work as you could if you have longer, but you can certainly take ten or twenty minutes or an hour and fill in the persons, places, objects, and events so you don't have to act.

Acting work is very concrete, and it's the concreteness of it that makes you able to tolerate the fear of being judged or rejected. It's the concreteness that always keeps you creative and empowered in an audition or a stage performance or a film shoot. You're always empowered because you're there to show your interpretation, and if you've truly worked on your interpretation, what is there to be scared of? The worst thing they can say, which actors have to get used to, is "No," but it's sometimes just as scary to hear "Yes." Right?

AMY: Yeah.

LARRY: So in other words judgment is something we bring to our craft that we could get rid of if we could just say "I don't have to waste my time being involved in other people's judgment." There is only my work, whether I am auditioning, performing, or doing my twenty-third take on a movie because a plane flew by during the twenty-second take, I can do this work, I can do this work anywhere.

AMY: And the more technique you have the more confidence you get from it because really you feel you know what you're doing, even if you don't get the job or get the moment at that audition, you know how to fix it.

LARRY: Which is exactly what you did the second time you did the scene from *Lobby Hero,* you fixed the problems. And you did it with technique. I could not see you acting. I felt you were living, it's just that that living was based on techniques. I mean you did biography, you did an animal exercise, you did a relationship to place, you did endow objects, and you understood the action of the scene.

Now can you tell me a little about how you worked with objectives and intentions?

AARON: My overall objective was to end my loneliness and isolation, to find a way not to be alone, to find a way to connect with her. And that led me to what my intentions can possibly be to achieve my objective. I go through and map the scene intention by intention to see if *she's* going to do *this,* what am *I* going to do to overcome her series of obstacles and achieve my objective?

Some of my intentions to achieve my objective were *to joke with her, to warm her up*—and that led me to physicalize it and offer her a cup of coffee from my thermos, which I endowed as my father's thermos—*to catch her eye, to allure her by showing her how alike we are*—"You're wearing a uniform, I'm wearing a uniform," like two kids in the playground saying, "I wear Nikes, you have Nikes"—*to wow her, to dote on her, to recruit her, to pry, to deflect, to admonish, to flatter, to clarify to captivate her with more stories, to bomb her boyfriend, to cheer her up, to tickle, to clown, to tempt, to bring the attention back to myself.*

LARRY: What I hear in the intentions you picked, Aaron, is a commitment to active verbs that connect her to you and keep you physically and emotionally active and engage you in the pursuit of your objective. Let me ask you another question, was this particular night in the lobby special for you?

AARON: Yes, it was because I had fantastized that tonight was the night I had to ask her out.

LARRY: Why did you make that choice?

AARON: Because it excited me and raised the stakes.

LARRY: Did it increase your anxiety as a character?

AARON: Absolutely. Because I had built and justified that he was racing inside, his heart pounding, drank too much coffee, yet outwardly I had to act calm. But I allowed myself one physical expression of it, and that was my right leg bouncing.

LARRY: Yes, your right leg always seemed to be on the verge of almost flying off your body in different directions. It gave you a counterpoint in the scene, which as an audience I found fascinating—that your body was expressing one feeling that was unexpressed in your verbal life and the way you wanted to come across to her, which was cool, calm, collected, and in charge.

AARON: It was like a frozen river but underneath it was like rapids going on and the rapids manifested in my right leg.

LARRY: How did you work with these intentions?

AARON: I would use specific intentions on different lines and put them in my script next to the line. That creates my map. Then when I was actually performing the scene, it was like playing with a great tennis player. If she hit a shot different from the one I thought I was going to get, in response I would either modify or change my intention.

LARRY: See, that's why I say tennis is such a fabulous game to watch in terms of understanding the formula for juicy improvisational acting that has focus. When you watch good tennis, you know that the tennis players on both sides have specific shots in their technique bag to return the ball, but they never know precisely what they're going to get from the other player, and that makes them have to make a snap decision in the second they receive the ball. That's what's exciting about watching that game.

AARON: The shot has to fit inside the court just like the intention has to fit with the text and the objective and what your partner is giving you. I felt secure playing moment to moment because I'd made justified choices about the character.

LARRY: What if you were working with another actor with whom you didn't feel as *sympathique* as you did with Amy? How would you apply this craft? What if you didn't get as interesting responses to carbonate you?

AARON: That's a tough question because that's my problem sometimes. I go off on my own and sometimes if the other person isn't provocative to me I withdraw into myself and won't engage with them, which hurts my work and the scene. For the audience it could be like watching two different scenes going on and the tension in the scene is lost. So what I'm learning is if I'm not getting something that excites me or that I like from the other person, I either have to use what they are giving and find a way to stay in the scene with that person or one way I've tried to overcome it is to imagine that they are giving me what I want and to invest that with reality.

LARRY: The point of what you're saying is that you have to find a way of using what's in front of you or else you lose the tennis game that fascinates the audience and makes them want to watch.

AARON: You play to the other actor's strengths instead of complaining about or focusing on their weaknesses.

LARRY: Amy, what were your objectives in the scene?

AMY: This character is different from almost anything else I've played and she's particularly different in this scene. Because the scene for her is so much about what happened before the scene and what she hopes will happen after the scene.

There were two highly charged events that happened. One is that she bashed a man over the head—which she talks about in the scene—and she's frightened that the police hierarchy will condemn her and turn against her, and she's hoping that Bill, her partner and her lover, will protect her. The other event that's important is that Bill has asked her out for coffee after their shift, and she's so excited because she's hoping the coffee will lead to another sexual encounter, which she's hoping will turn into a relationship.

The character's fantasy life is very rich in terms of her potential future with Bill. She sees him as a great warrior and herself as a warrior goddess, specifically the god and goddess Shiva and Shakti, who were not only superpowers but had supersex. Her want in the scene is to keep control of her emotions and keep control of her environment. In terms of the security guard, she wants to keep him off her case romantically and intimidate him into leaving her alone while she waits for Bill.

LARRY: How do things change for your character during the scene?

AMY: My dreams are smashed and my greatest fear is revealed, which is that I have no control and that Bill is not even near the god I thought he was and that I start to need the security guard as a kind of therapist and friend. So what was exciting for me in the acting was to build my prior circumstances really fully and my dreams for the future really fully, so that when the security guard tells me my so-called god upstairs is screwing a model, my dreams of a great sexual experience that night and my dreams of our future together are completely destroyed. And I don't want the guard to see this right away—and, most of all, I don't want to see this right away myself.

LARRY: I think this proves a point, Amy. That working specifically on prior circumstances in your imagination—in this case prior circumstances that are actually mentioned in the play—became key to playing the scene successfully because it gave her so far to fall.

Let me end this interview by thanking you both for your time and commitment, and for helping me to bring readers into a work process that came from actors, and to show the ideas I've talked about in action. Lastly, what I felt in interviewing you was how joyful and passionate an experience you had in bringing Kenneth Lonergan's *Lobby Hero* to life.

As this book goes to press, Amy and Aaron are going into rehearsal for *Lobby Hero* at the Odyssey Theater in Los Angeles. They optioned the play, brought in the scene they did in class for Ron Sossi, the artistic director of the theater, to show what they could do with the material and excited him with their work so much, he committed to producing the premiere of the play in Los Angeles.

The Monologue
Workout Program

In her excellent book *The Creative Habit,* Twyla Tharp says that we should discipline ourselves to be addicted to goals that make us better artists. For some people this discipline comes naturally, for others, it takes work. Wherever you are now in your career, if you apply yourself to a daily ritual of the exercises I'm about to give you, the results will start to show immediately and give you a way of life that constantly supports your chosen profession.

The beginning of this daily ritual is to learn four monologues from four different plays: two contemporary monologues (one comedy, one drama from any play written after 1920 that is not in verse or set prior to 1920) and two classical monologues (one comedy, one drama from plays by writers including Shakespeare, Molière, Ibsen, Strindberg, Shaw, any of the Greek comedies or dramas). It would be educational and I think exhilarating for you to learn four new monologues every three months. Yes, my friends, it's a lot of work, but the greater the variety of the texts that you read, analyze, and commit to working with on your own, the more your technical abilities grow between professional jobs and the readier you are to take on any new job that comes your way.

These monologues are your workout program for working on given circumstances, superobjective and objectives, obstacles and intentions, stakes, emotional justification, rhythms and tempo, physical choices, and other aspects of interpretation.

When you've got your monologues prepared, you are ready for the exercises. You can do them on your own or you can take them into a class where the teacher is receptive or you can put together a group of actors and do the exercises together and give each other feedback. The only problem with having a group without a teacher is that it can be a field day for uneducated criticism, which can be destructive, so make sure you have positive, constructive people in your group who give you feedback that supports good work and excites you to work on new ideas and choices. Don't ever allow anyone to say destructive or competitive things to you, and by the same token, don't take criticism so personally that it ever stops your creative process.

MOVING THE FEELINGS

This exercise reminds me of how the art of dance began. You can see it in tribal dances from all cultures and you can see it in rap artists and, most poignantly, in small children. Children talk nonverbally all the time because they don't have the verbal sophistication to express certain emotions. They move around a lot in their chair, they wiggle their legs, they pound rhythmically on a table. Movement is an important way for children to relieve stress, and that energy segues into sports, dance, and other physical activities. As we get older, as actors we can forget how important it is to continue the process of expressing things nonverbally. So what I suggest you do at some point every day of your life is to go into a room by yourself and move in a way that expresses what you're feeling. In particular, I want you to do an improvisatory exploration of antisocial movement. What I mean by antisocial movement is that you may get up one day feeling a lot of aggression, and you may have impulses to punch and kick and, along with that, there may be impulses to grunt, yell, and scream along with the movements. Don't stop the sounds; concentrate on expressing the feelings through the way you move your body.

The harder this exercise is for you, the more you need to do it. I've watched students who've studied for years in acting classes, and who may even have successful careers, but they never achieve a kind of physical fluidity that allows them to play a wide range of characters and also to express silliness, sexuality, gracefulness, and perhaps even brutal power. I strongly believe that this exercise would be good for every person in the world to do every day, but I think it's an enormously helpful exercise for the actor to do because it gets you out of your head and into your body while also reaching your emotions.

Once you've explored moving the feeling for at least five minutes—take as long as you need or want in order to feel physically released and alive—begin to add one of the monologues and just let the words accompany your movement. *The monologue doesn't have to be related to the feeling.* It just has to be one that you know so well you don't have to think about it at all.

Now, as you say the monologue, let the movement affect how you speak. Don't try to interpret the monologue. Just allow your body and emotions to move through the text any way that the words come out. One of the most interesting aspects of this exercise is that as you're allowing yourself *not* to interpret the monologue, an emotion moving through you will suddenly match up with the text in a provocative way, and suddenly you will see the material with new eyes.

Because you have four different texts to work with, you'll find new parts of yourself that you may not think you have in your acting palette. All at once, to your shock and amazement, a new and possibly thrilling emotional reaction can come to the surface. You need to be brave and follow those impulses with physical and emotional commitment. If it's an emotion you're not familiar with, don't stop the flow of it, even if you feel scared or embarrassed. March on and be courageous. As a teacher I'm trying to inspire you to do things that you don't want to do because you may be frightened or inexperienced or lazy. There's nothing wrong with being lazy *as long as you don't give in to it!* As I've said to my classes many times, left to my own slothlike nature, I would spend many more hours eating Häagen-Dazs and watching bad TV, but thankfully I learned earlier in my life that that was a recipe for failure, so I only give in to it after a really hard day of work.

THE STATUE EXERCISE

This is a variation on Moving the Feelings. Stand with your feet about twelve to fourteen inches apart and take a few minutes to be aware of and release any tension you find in your body at that moment. Once your feet feel connected to the floor and you're breathing easily and naturally, feel the emotion that is inside of you, and let your body move into a freeze frame that would express that particular emotion. If you're sad, you may fall to the floor and curl up, and that's the freeze frame, the statue. On another day you may feel angry and your fists may punch out at the world and that's the statue. Another day you may be filled with a kind of joy and well-being and you may expand your chest, feeling that your heart is like the sun, and open your arms wide, and that would be the statue.

When you've become the statue, stay there long enough to feel how your stance affects you emotionally. Be aware of the feelings that come up within you in that still statue and hold it. Then ask yourself, where does my body want to go next? As you get an impulse to move, imagine in your mind's eye your body going to the next physical statue, but *don't* allow yourself to; just *want* to. Feel the muscles you would have to use to go there, feel the impulse to move, but stay frozen.

One of the things this teaches you is how frustrating it is to want to do something and to hold yourself back. It shows you the power of your creative impulses and that you, in fact, have them, even if you don't think you do. It teaches you how destructive it is to want to do something and to inhibit yourself for reasons you may not even be aware of. And it teaches you to notice how many times in a play or film a character wants to kiss someone, hit someone, hold someone, and even kill someone, and has to hold it back. You will feel how *alive* the moment of repression is. You will also feel what a gesture can mean for a character when the character's feeling is unexpressed verbally but shown physically either subtly or on a grand scale as in the example I gave earlier of Susan Sarandon's living statue when she played Sister Helen Prejean, reaching her arm to Sean Penn's Matthew Poncelet in a final gesture of compassion and love when he was being executed.

When you can't bear stopping the impulse any longer, allow yourself to blast into the next statue. Once you're there, again, feel your emotional responses to this second statue and explore the impulse that is pushing you toward your next statue. Once again, don't let yourself move but feel the desire and the exact muscles you would use to go there. When the desire to move becomes overwhelming, allow yourself to move into a third statue.

When you've completed four statues, finish the exercise by letting yourself move through space from one statue pose to another, starting with the first, then the second, third, and fourth, finding a completely honest, intuitive expression of your inner emotional world as you move from one pose to the next.

I always ask my students to name in their own heads what each statue would be called if it were in a museum. Is it compassion, loneliness, terror, joy, frustration, the love of God? See what comes up for you.

One of the interesting uses of this exercise is that when you're creating a character, you can find a pose for the character at the beginning of the journey of the play or film, a pose that suggests the psychological starting point of that character. Then choose a statue for the end of the script. You will see the arc of your character's journey through physical expression as they move from the initial position to the final one.

THE THESAURUS EXERCISE

Take one of the four monologues that you're working on at the present time and choose as your intention an active verb for the monologue or for a portion of it and do the monologue with that specific intention. It doesn't matter whether the active verb seems to go with the monologue or not, it's just an exploration of an intention with text.

For example, let's say you pick the active verb *to celebrate,* and let's say you use it to do the opening monologue from *Richard III.* When you begin to explore the text, "Now is the winter of our discontent," the verb *to celebrate* doesn't seem to go with the tone or the idea that Richard is stating, but one of the fascinating and stimulating results of this exercise is that by choosing an opposite or seemingly inappropriate intention, you can find original, stimulating choices that are not clichéd and you may find meanings in the text that more obvious choices don't illuminate.

Once you've explored the text with your first active verb—*to celebrate,* in this case—take your thesaurus and look for synonyms. In my thesaurus, I find, among others: *to make merry, revel, roister, make whoopee, let oneself go, blow* or *let off steam; cut loose, let loose, let go, whoop it up, kick up one's heels, raise hell,* or *blow off the lid.* As you read through these synonyms, some of them will particularly provoke you to a physical and emotional impulse. When you feel this combination of impulses, you know you've found an active intention that works for you. For some actors, *to celebrate* will leave them uncreative or bored, while *to make merry* or *to raise hell* will excite them to move and speak in such a way that they are deeply connected to their creative impulse. Again, this is what you want in choosing an intention. When you're deeply connected to your creative impulse, the material comes alive. Explore the text with each synonym that carbonates you.

Whenever I use the thesaurus, I'm in awe at the number of changing colors that different verbs meaning roughly the same thing can bring to the interpretation of a role and I'm excited to see verbs that I had forgotten I knew and that can be used effectively. I'm always astonished that as actors explore scenes and monologues with five or six different synonyms for one verb, their physical behavior and emotional responses change completely with each synonym. Even though the words have similar meanings, they bring out different behaviors and readings in the performances of every actor I've coached.

DEDICATION TO ACCENTS

A lot of actors wait for their agent to call them and ask, "Do you have a Danish, cockney, German, Arkansas, Bronx, or Lithuanian accent?" Because if they do, the agent says, they can go tomorrow morning and read for the new Steven Spielberg film—but only if the accent is really good and believable. The actor then lies through his teeth and says, with great confidence, "Oh yes, I can do that particular accent extremely well." Then he hangs up the phone and breaks out in a cold sweat as he begins to rummage frantically through any books or accent tapes that he has packed away for a rainy day. When the actor finds he has no tape for the Lithuanian dialect, he makes hysterical calls to his actor friends to see if they will stay up with him all night, because his friend's grandparents came from Lithuania. I'm not saying that this may not work on a very, very lucky day when you have a feel for the accent, for the rhythm and the melody, and a good ear that picks up the vowels and an instinct for how to use your tongue, lips, and jaw to be believable as a Lithuanian aristocrat.

What of course is being overlooked is that in this twelve- or fourteen-hour period, you also have to work on the script. To introduce a totally new physiological experience (the accent) *and* do the script analysis that you need for a successful audition is a kind of madness and creates a lot of unnecessary stress. You don't have to go through this nightmare. The accent exercise will prepare you for when you get the agent's call, because when you work through the exercise, you will have five to six or more accents at your immediate disposal.

I've mentioned the term *blood memory,* which Stella Adler used to describe the sense of the land, the history, and the language that each of us inherits from our ancestors—and that each character we play also carries within him. Start this exercise with an accent that is *your particular blood memory* and learn one of the four monologues in that accent. If you know the accent because you grew up with it you're more than halfway there. If you need a refresher, and you have family members or friends who speak with that accent, get them to tape-record the monologue for you and watch them while they speak, specifically the way their mouth works and the way their body responds as they talk. Not only will you get the accent this way, you may even pick up some interesting behavior. If this isn't available to you, and if you can afford it, go to a private dialect coach and have the coach read the monologue and work with you on it and, again, make sure you tape-record it.

Once you have worked on all the accents that are from your personal blood memory, then pick other accents that intrigue you and that you would like to be successful at playing. Get tape recordings of those accents, too, and keep an organized file. Do your monologues with each of these accents until you feel completely at ease with each accent both verbally and physically. Don't get caught up in the false idea of not wanting to do this work until you get a part that needs that accent. When you get that call from your agent, you will be so happy you did this work that you will send me a money order.

THE MUSEUM EXERCISE

In this exercise, you create your own monologue. It can become an intense exploration of your talent for interpretation. The exercise is simply this: you go to a museum or get a book that has excellent reproductions of great painters' portraits or paintings containing people or animals. When you come upon a painting that rivets you and calls to you, study the painting meticulously and, if it has more than one person or animal in it, find the one that inspires the most feeling in you. The objective of this exercise is to play that character and create a story for them. Study the expression on the character's face until your imagination begins to travel to ideas about why that expression is there.

People have talked for centuries about Leonardo da Vinci's Mona Lisa. Why is she smiling in that secretive, Gioconda way? One of the most interesting theories I've heard is that she could have been pregnant. We don't know when we look at the Mona Lisa exactly why she's smiling, but it's fun to conjecture. That's what this exercise requires you to do with the person in the painting you've chosen.

Your task is to write a monologue from that particular character's point of view. They can be speaking to another person in the painting, or to someone you've imagined outside the frame, or to someone you decide they're thinking of. If you're in a class, bring a reproduction of the picture to your class so that your colleagues can see it. Bring everything you need to create for yourself the physical appearance of that painting.

This exercise is particularly effective when done in front of people who give you feedback. So, once again, if you're not in a class, or if the class doesn't do these kinds of exercises, create a group of your own that meets once or twice a month and supports you to do the Museum exercise—but remember to choose the group members for their intelligent supportiveness.

Begin the monologue in exactly the same physical position as the character in the painting, with the same facial expression, and as close as possible to the same clothing. Doing this will birth in you the character's emotional point of view. Finding the shirt, blouse, belt buckle, shoes, creating the specific hairstyle, and even using makeup to look like the character will strengthen your entire technical base. Also, you must speak the monologue in English with the accent of the character in the painting.

One actress in my class chose a painting by Degas. Two peasant women are slaving over washtubs, one of them with a wine bottle in her hand looking dejected and enraged and the other looking at her with a questioning face. The story the actress built was of the washerwoman with the wine bottle. When she came to life out of the pose of the painting, the first thing she said right after she took a great guzzle of wine was, "I'll tell you why I am so angry and why I am going to get drunk." She went on to tell her companion that the cobblestone street that they were working beside was the same kind of street that her three year-old daughter was killed on when she ran out into the street and was hit by a carriage and her skull was crushed. She went on to bitterly curse God and her life. At the end of the exercise, she went back into the freeze frame of the painting, but this time when we looked at her, the life in the painting became explosively human, and we could hear in our imagination the sound of the carriage on the cobblestone street, the terrible crunch of her child's skull, the mother's screams, and we could feel the unbearable grief that comes from loss, poverty, and the inability to heal a wound. The actress also found a specific lower-class French accent with which to play her part.

I don't want to make this sound like the solution to all your acting problems, but I will tell you that after committing to this exercise, the actress got a job that kept her working for three years.

Another actor chose a contemporary painting of a preadolescent boy pulling a red wagon with a bunch of sticks in it. When the actor came to life as this young boy, he told us it was the Fourth of July and he was taking all the sticks to build a bonfire to celebrate the holiday. That's what his dad and he did on every July Fourth. Except his father had just died, and this was the first time he ever had to do it alone. As he shared with us his feelings about his father before he died and his feelings about the loss, he went from exuberance to intense anger to the memory of love he had for his dad, and finally to bravery as he took the handle of the red wagon and started to go off to build his fire. This exercise broke open the actor's inhibitions, which had included a physical stiffness in his body, an inability to be playful, and a terror of raw emotion that he finally could allow because he was a child.

You don't have to pick a dark subject for this exercise. One of the funniest ones ever done in my class was based on Picasso's *Lobster and Cat*. Someone has dropped a live lobster on the floor as a cat was walking by. It's a hilarious painting because all of the fur on the cat's back is standing on end and his face is in absolute horror while the lobster just lies there. The actor chose to play the cat and used a wonderfully over-the-top Spanish accent with a hint of French, because Picasso was Spanish but lived in France. He began the exercise with a bloodcurdling yelping meow as he scampered away from the lobster, cursing not only at the half-dead crustacean but at the stupid human who had dropped it in his path. Then he slowly and stealthily moved toward the lobster, touched it with his paw, and, screaming, ran one more time into the corner. So you can see that your choices for this exercise can be wide and as brave as you're willing to be.

THE ANIMAL EXERCISE

I mentioned using an animal exercise as part of my interpretation of the role of Little Harp in *The Robber Bridegroom*. I chose a baby rattlesnake for Little Harp because as a person he was dangerous, quick to strike when confronted with danger, and stayed close to the ground. For a role I did in the Noël Coward vaudeville sketch, *Red Peppers,* I worked on a cockatoo to give George Pepper his particular imperiousness. It helped me so much to fluff the feathers on the back of my neck every time I was trying to challenge or intimidate my wife and to use my head and neck in that specific way that a cockatoo does as I looked down on her, detached and almost mechanical.

What animal does the character in each of your monologues remind you of? You must do the animal exercise separately from the monologue first. Read about the animal. See documentaries and go to the zoo and watch the animal's body. Discover where the most powerful muscles are because those are the muscles the animal uses to stalk its prey or run away from its predators. What are the animal's physical habits? How does it move, eat, play, stalk, and mate? As you explore these realities, you will begin to pick certain aspects of the animal to add to the physical behavior of your character.

Some humans have a desperate, panting quality to their energy, like a dog who craves constant affection. Others seem to live sideways, like the snake called a sidewinder. They look at you out of the corner of their eye and move toward objects and people on an angle, in a shifty, almost slithery way.

The animal exercise is done indelibly in Marlon Brando's last reel in *The Godfather,* right before he dies, as he's playing with his grandson. You can see that Brando's use of his hands and arms is very simian and primitive; it says more nonverbally about the nature of the man than anything he ever says. Brando has said that he used a gorilla exercise in creating the aged Don Corleone. Working with the animal exercise as part of your daily routine makes you discover for yourself how you might use an animal in a role that you create for performance.

These exercises were created to get you used to exploring physical and emotional freedom and to give you greater access to it. I promise you that practicing them every day will strengthen you to the point that even when you're working at 4:00 A.M. on a movie set and you feel blocked and tired, you can use these exercises to help your instrument stay open and give you the physical and emotional richness you want for your character.

ACKNOWLEDGMENTS

I want to thank my editor, Toni Burbank, who was extraordinarily patient, supportive, and insightful. My agent, Ellen Geiger, was loving and committed, and when I lost my way she introduced me to Mark Rosin who interviewed me on tape for the chapters in this book, who stayed with me for many hours keeping my ideas focused, and who was relentlessly committed to helping me bring this book to life. I owe each of these people a great debt of gratitude.

And a great thank you to Cynthia Hoppenfeld, who read every chapter and gave me clear, insightful, no-nonsense advice. Deep gratitude to my brilliant assistant Catie LeOrisa, who helps me every day to sort out my complicated life and does so with humor, patience, and elegance. I also want to thank and celebrate all the fantastic students who worked so hard and brought me so much joy and learning. Michelle Danner, for her passionate commitment to creating the beautiful Edgemar Center for the Arts.

Every person mentioned here has enriched my life in some extraordinary way, and I thank them from the bottom of my heart:

Jason Alexander, Morgan Ames, Nancy Banks, Juliette Binoche, Patricia Bosworth, David Allen Brooks, James L. Brooks, Karl Bury, Kate Capshaw, Jim Carrey, Sharon Chatten, John Cirigliano, Winship Cooke, Lisa Lee Cooper, Frank Darabont, Sherry Darling, Leonardo DiCaprio, Brian Drillinger, David Duchovny, Michael Clarke Duncan, Bo and Dawn Eason, Kurt Elling, Rohen Elliott, Ronnie Farer, Sally Field, Lorraine Garay, Anna Garduno, Brad Garrett, Jason Gedrick, Pamela Gien, Boris Van Gils, Michaël Goldberg, Ian Gregory, Melanie and Joel Gretsch, Stephanie and David Grillo, Alexandra Guarnieri, Karen Gustafson, Patricia Heaton, Clint Holmes, Jack Holmes, David Hunt, Helen Hunt, Denise Huth, Adam Isaacs, Kristof Konrad, Swoosie Kurtz, Deborah LaVine, Sharon Lawrence, Téa Leoni, Vicki Light, Chad Lowe, Tobey Maguire, Andrea Martin, Jeff McCracken, Gates McFadden, Carolyn Mignini, Allan Montaine, Vincent Mosso, Patrick Muldoon, Donna Murphy, Ariadne Myers, Maria Napoli, Kathleen and Ron Orbach, Fred Orner, Thomas J. Quinn, Michael Rainer, Lisa Robertson, Patsy Rodenburg, Gary Ross, Jean-Louis Rodrigue, Rich Ronat, Matt Salinger, Garry Shandling, Pamela Shaw, Charles Shyer, Christian Slater, Susan Slavin, Steven Spielberg, Christopher Stone, Marni St. Regis, Stephan Streker, Hilary Swank, Twyla Tharp, Diane Venora, Steve Vinovich, Daisy White, Noah Wyle, Kevin Quinn, Miguel Esteban, Martin Engstroem, Minh Tam-Tam, and the entire Verbier staff.

Index of Names
and Performances